RETHINKING THE GAY AND LESBIAN MOVEMENT

Rethinking the Gay and Lesbian Movement provides a short, accessible overview of an important and transformational struggle for social change, highlighting key individuals and events, influential groups and networks, strong alliances and coalitions, difficult challenges and obstacles, major successes and failures, and the movement's lasting effects on the country.

From the homophile activism of the 1950s and 1960s, through the rise of gay liberation and lesbian feminism in the 1970s, to the multicultural and AIDS activist movements of the 1980s, *Rethinking the Gay and Lesbian Movement* will be valued by everyone interested in gay and lesbian history, the history of social movements, and the history of the United States, and provides a strong foundation for understanding gay, lesbian, bisexual, transgender, and queer politics today.

Marc Stein is Professor of History and Gender, Sexuality, and Women's Studies at York University in Toronto, Ontario, Canada.

American Social and Political Movements of the Twentieth Century

Series Editor: Heather Ann Thompson

RETHINKING THE GAY AND LESBIAN MOVEMENT

Marc Stein

Routledge
Taylor & Francis Group

NEW YORK AND LONDON

First published 2012
by Routledge
711 Third Avenue, New York, NY 10017

Simultaneously published in the UK
by Routledge
2 Park Square, Milton Park, Abingdon, Oxon OX14 4RN

Routledge is an imprint of the Taylor & Francis Group, an informa business

© 2012 Taylor & Francis

Library of Congress Cataloging-in-Publication Data
Stein, Marc.
Rethinking the gay and lesbian movement / by Marc Stein.
p. cm. - - (American social and political movements) 1. Gay liberation movement- -United States- -History. 2. Gay rights- -United States- -History. I. Title.
HQ76.8.U5S75 2012
323.3′2640973- -dc23
2011048599

ISBN: 978-0-415-87409-0 (hbk)
ISBN: 978-0-415-87410-6 (pbk)
ISBN: 978-0-203-12221-1 (ebk)

Typeset in Bembo
by T&F Books

CONTENTS

EDITOR'S SERIES INTRODUCTION

Welcome to the *American Social and Political Movements of the Twentieth Century* series at Routledge. This collection of works by top historians from around the nation and world introduces students to the myriad movements that came together in the United States during the 20th century to expand democracy, to reshape the political economy, and to increase social justice.

Each book in this series explores a particular movement's origins, its central goals, its leading as well as grassroots figures, its actions as well as ideas, and its most important accomplishments as well as serious missteps.

With this series of concise yet synthetic overviews and reassessments, students not only will gain a richer understanding of the many human rights and civil liberties that they take for granted today, but they will also newly appreciate how recent, how deeply contested, and thus how inherently fragile, are these same elements of American citizenship.

Heather Ann Thompson
Temple University

ACKNOWLEDGMENTS

This book would not have been possible to write without the extraordinary work of the scholars whose publications are referenced in the Suggestions for Further Reading at the end of this volume. I am very grateful to all of them.

I thank Routledge editor Kimberly Guinta, production editor Meesha Nehru, and series editor Heather Thompson for their enthusiastic encouragement and expert guidance.

Four exceptionally generous and accomplished scholars read all or parts of the manuscript and offered excellent comments and suggestions, many of which I used in the revision process. Susan Stryker provided assistance with the introduction; Steven Maynard did so with the introduction and first two chapters; Leila Rupp reviewed all but the final chapter; and Jorge Olivares read the entire draft (twice!). I hope they all know how deeply appreciative I am.

Jorge deserves special thanks, for everything.

ABBREVIATIONS

ACLU	American Civil Liberties Union
AFL-CIO	American Federation of Labor and Congress of Industrial Organizations
AIGL	American Indian Gays and Lesbians
APA	American Psychiatric Association
ASOs	AIDS service organizations
CDC	Centers for Disease Control
CSC	Civil Service Commission (U.S.)
DOB	Daughters of Bilitis
GAA	Gay Activists Alliance
GAI	Gay American Indians
GLAAD	Gay and Lesbian Alliance Against Defamation
GLF	Gay Liberation Front
LCE	League for Civil Education
LGBT	Lesbian, gay, bisexual, and transgender
INS	Immigration and Naturalization Service
MCC	Metropolitan Community Church
NGLTF/NGTF	National Gay and Lesbian Task Force
NGRA	National Gay Rights Advocates
NOW	National Organization for Women
PHS	Public Health Service (U.S.)
PRIDE	Personal Rights in Defense and Education
PWA	People With AIDS
SIR	Society for Individual Rights
SLA	State Liquor Authority (New York)
STAR	Street Transvestite Action Revolutionaries
YMCA	Young Men's Christian Association

INTRODUCTION

Over the course of the last seven decades, the gay and lesbian movement has changed the United States. The movement has influenced popular conceptions and lived experiences of sex, gender, sexuality, love, marriage, and family, while also helping to revise law, reorient politics, and redefine citizenship. Gay and lesbian activists have fought successfully for reform and revolution in medical science, corporate capitalism, organized religion, and popular culture. The wide-ranging results of their efforts are evident in diverse geographic sites, multifaceted social contexts, and multiple aspects of daily life. U.S. Americans may disagree about whether all of this change has been positive and how much more they would like to see, but it is difficult to deny the far-reaching nature of sexual change and the important roles played by the gay and lesbian movement in prompting social, cultural, and political transformation.

All of this is true, and yet the movement also has failed to change the United States. Many people continue to regard homosexuality as a sin, crime, and disease; many view it as deviant, degenerate, pathetic, and pathological. Antihomosexual discrimination remains legal in most U.S. jurisdictions and in policies affecting education, employment, health, housing, immigration, marriage, military service, parenthood, prisons, taxation, and welfare. In many contexts, homosexuality is tolerated but not treated as equal to heterosexuality. Those perceived to be gay or lesbian experience substantial abuse, bullying, harassment, and violence. Gays and lesbians who challenge dominant norms of masculinity and femininity and others who are thought to be gay or lesbian because they violate gender norms remain distinctly vulnerable to hate and hostility. This is also the case for gays and lesbians who are young, old, people of color, people with disabilities, immigrants, non-Christians, and nonnative English speakers. If anything, the treatment of homosexuality and heterosexuality as mutually exclusive orientations has become more common. Given all of this, it is difficult to deny that the nature of sexual change has been limited and many of the movement's goals have not been achieved.

In the context of decades of change and continuity, rethinking the history of the U.S. gay and lesbian movement is a good idea for multiple reasons. Almost forty years have passed since Jonathan Ned Katz's *Gay American History* (1976) launched a new era in scholarly studies of the gay and lesbian movement. Approximately thirty have gone by since Toby Marotta and John D'Emilio published their ground-breaking monographs on gay and lesbian activism in the 1950s, 1960s, and 1970s. One of the great achievements of this work was its challenge to the myth that the movement began with the Stonewall riots of 1969, when thousands of New Yorkers fought back after a police raid of a gay bar. Katz, Marotta, and D'Emilio showed that the Mattachine Society, the Daughters of Bilitis, and a network of other groups that referred to themselves as the homophile movement constituted an important early chapter in the history of gay and lesbian activism and laid the foundation for much of what followed.[1]

New scholarship has sustained, modified, and challenged Katz's, Marotta's, and D'Emilio's conclusions about the movement's early years and today we have access to significant research on gay and lesbian activism in more recent decades. Yet amazingly enough, we do not have an up-to-date account of the movement that is national in scope, comprehensive in chronology, and synthetic in ambition. We have books that briefly mention the early decades of gay and lesbian activism before focusing on more recent developments. There are collections of primary documents and oral histories that address gay and lesbian resistance in the past. We have studies that examine specific local communities or particular components of the movement. There are broad surveys of the U.S. gay and lesbian past that do not focus primarily on political activism; three of the best are by Michael Bronski, Vicki Eaklor, and Leila Rupp. There are works on the transnational gay and lesbian movement, including an excellent book by Barry Adam. We have many studies that rely on Katz's, Marotta's, and D'Emilio's work without taking more recent scholarship into consideration. One reason to rethink the history of the U.S. gay and lesbian movement is that we have learned much about that history and it is time to syn-thesize what we know, reflect on what we do not know, and think about what we might want to know in the future.

A second reason to rethink the history of the gay and lesbian movement is that doing so might help us address the widespread lack of knowledge about that history. Pick up many of the best-selling college and university textbooks on U.S. history and you may find passing references to the gay and lesbian past, but little in-depth discussion. Influenced by conservative campaigns to control and censor what can be taught in public schools, the coverage of gay and lesbian history is even weaker in primary and secondary school textbooks. When college and university history departments refuse to hire faculty whose work focuses on the sexual past, when government officials veto funding for meritorious research projects on gay and lesbian history, and when specialists in sexuality studies fail to take note of new historical scholarship on the movement, it is no wonder that the subject is ignored in mainstream culture or is presented in ways that sustain popular fictions and fantasies. Rethinking the movement's history might convince more people of its relevance and significance.[2]

A third reason to rethink the history of the gay and lesbian movement is that doing so may have special importance for today's gender and sexual dissidents and for those who care about family members, friends, neighbors, coworkers, and others who identify with the movement's agendas and aspirations. Understood in this way, gay and lesbian history potentially is important for all of us. Because most people do not grow up in families that consider themselves gay or lesbian, they do not typically learn about gay and lesbian history through family stories. Nor are they likely to learn much about that history in religious or educational institutions. Exploring the sexual past can help people with same-sex sexual interests address prejudices and stereotypes and create meaningful relationships and communities. Studying the movement's history can help everyone reflect more intelligently on the progress that has been made, the losses that have been sustained, the initiatives that have succeeded and failed, and the challenges and possibilities that confront us today. Inspired and troubled by the stories we encounter, we can become agents of change. Ultimately, thinking more creatively about the history of gay and lesbian activism can help us understand how our world has come to exist, what alternative worlds are imaginable for the future, and how we might get from here to there.

Gay and lesbian movement history is also worth rethinking because it has much to teach us about other important subjects, including some of the major political and philosophical questions that have absorbed the United States for centuries. What have U.S. Americans meant when they have referred to freedom, liberty, equality, and democracy? How have they put these principles to work in practice? What is the relationship between freedom and equality? What is the right balance between unity and diversity? Who should be included in and excluded from the community, polity, and country? What is private and what is public? What is the proper role of the state in society? What values do U.S. Americans share with the people of other countries and what values are distinctly American? Is the United States moving away from or toward its ideals?

The history of the gay and lesbian movement has even more direct relevance for those who are interested in the history of social movements and the history of sexuality. Studying the history of the movement can help us reflect on why some people become activists and others do not, why movements develop when and where they do, why they adopt particular strategies and goals, and why they rise and fall. Doing this work can encourage us to think about relationships between reform and revolution, between political and cultural activism, between issue- and identity-based movements, between conservatism and liberalism, and between liberalism and the left. Gay and lesbian activism offers case studies for exploring how political coalitions come together and break apart, how movements relate to one another, how they police boundaries between insiders and outsiders, how they respond to various forms of diversity, how individuals with multiple agendas and identities engage with different movements, and how struggles against oppression often become oppressive themselves. It also can help us address how activists interact with their imagined communities, why movements represent some constituencies better than others, and when activists succeed and fail in changing the United States.

As for the relevance of gay and lesbian activism for the history of sexuality, the history of the movement underscores the historicity and variability of sex, gender, and sexuality. This notion—that sex, gender, and sexuality change over time and are influenced by social, cultural, and political factors—has been the most significant contribution of scholarship on the history of sexuality. In studying gay and lesbian activism, we can examine how the movement has changed the regulation of sex and how the regulation of sex has changed the movement. We can reflect on how the movement has influenced and been influenced by sexual desires, acts, identities, and communities. We can explore how activists have understood same-sex, cross-sex, and other forms of sex and whether the movement has viewed same-sex sexuality as a fixed orientation of a minority, a universal potential in everyone, or both. We can ask whether the movement has been concerned primarily with sexual freedom for everyone or the interests of gays and lesbians specifically. We can study relationships between the gay and lesbian movement and movements that address other issues related to sex, including abortion, birth control, interracial sex, polygamy, pornography, prostitution, rape, and sexually transmitted disease. We can compare gay and lesbian political organizing to parallel and intersecting efforts to organize adulterers, cohabitants, cross-dressers, fornicators, masturbators, polyamorists, polygamists, pornographers, prostitutes, sadomasochists, sodomites, transgenders, and transsexuals. In short, the history of the U.S. gay and lesbian movement can provide us with illuminating perspectives on U.S. history, the history of social movements, and the history of sexuality.

There is one final reason to rethink the history of the gay and lesbian movement: doing so can support those who are working to promote equality, freedom, and justice in the twenty-first century. Learning about the oppression faced by gays and lesbians in the past can motivate us to address sexual and gender injustice today. Reading about movement successes and failures can inspire us to redouble and reorient our efforts in the future. Thinking about why the movement acted as it did in the past, and what the results of those actions were, can encourage us to reflect more critically on the choices we face today. The lessons of the past are rarely clear. We each may reach different conclusions about the relevance of the past. But in spite of or as a result of these differences, exploring the history of the U.S. gay and lesbian movement can help us move forward in our struggles for equality, freedom, and justice in the present and the future.

Key Terms and Parameters

Before proceeding, it will be helpful to address some of the book's key terms and parameters. Doing so will simultaneously introduce several concepts that are useful to consider when exploring the history of the gay and lesbian movement. First, why does the book's title refer to the gay and lesbian movement, as opposed to the homosexual, homophile, LGBT (lesbian, gay, bisexual, and transgender), or queer movement? The activists discussed in this book did not have a consistent way of referring to themselves, so there are no easy choices to make about nomenclature. Each of the available terms has different meanings and connotations; each has implications for inclusions and exclusions; each has advantages and disadvantages. Ultimately, in a book that focuses on the years from 1950 to 1990, it makes good sense to refer to the gay and lesbian movement. This is what the movement most commonly came to call itself in this period. Referring to the "LGBT" movement may feel more inclusive given recent coalition-building developments, but it risks falsely and ahistorically pretending that the movement of 1950–90 was broader than it was. Calling the movement "queer" may be fashionable in the early twenty-first century, but it makes less sense to call the pre-1990 movement "queer."

Some readers may wonder why historians do not generally refer to the "homosexual" movement. For many activists discussed in this book, the word "homosexuality" was derived from medical science, which adopted the term in the late nineteenth and early twentieth centuries in the context of its pathologizing work of classification, diagnosis, and treatment. Historical research has now shown that the term was initially coined and promoted by European supporters of "homosexuals," but this has not changed its association with the treatment of same-sex sexuality as an illness or disease. Moreover, many activists have argued that the term was favored more by community outsiders than insiders, more by the middle class than the working class, more by men than women, and more by whites than people of color.

Today, historians commonly refer to the "homophile" movement of the 1950s and 1960s, primarily because this was a term used in the period, when many activists wanted to emphasize love (*philia* in ancient Greek) rather than sex. For some, this was an accurate characterization of the movement; for others, it was a strategy to disarm movement enemies. This was opposed by more sexually radical activists in the 1950s and 1960s. Use of "homophile" then declined in the 1970s, making it less desirable as a term for a chronologically expansive study. This book uses "homophile" for activism in the 1950s and 1960s, but not for the movement as a whole.

Of the many community-based terms widely used for people who engaged in same-sex sex in the late nineteenth and early twentieth centuries (including butch, dyke, fairy, faggot, fem, invert, pansy, punk, queer, sodomite, and stud), "gay" became the most popular in the mid-twentieth century. "Gay" had been used by earlier gender and sexual dissidents because of its associations with happiness, pleasure, flamboyance, and transgression and because it functioned as an effective code word. In the early twentieth century, "gay" had complex class and gender connotations that varied across time and place. By the time the movement was organized in the 1950s and 1960s, it was becoming the term most commonly used by people who regarded their same-sex sexual preferences as important aspects of their lives. Community-based terminology varied by age, class, gender, generation, region, race, and sex, but "gay" was used across these social categories. That said, "gay" was more widely used by middle-class white men than by others, so when more activists began to call their movement "gay" in the late 1960s and early 1970s, they were choosing a word that theoretically could apply to everyone but in practice privileged middle-class white men. Calling the movement "gay" thus can highlight the movement's inclusive aspirations and its less-than-inclusive realities.

In the period from 1950 to 1990, the greatest resistance to the use of "gay" as an inclusive movement term came from lesbians. The word "lesbian" derives from the Mediterranean island of Lesbos, home of the ancient Greek writer Sappho, who wrote romantically and erotically charged poems to other women. References to "lesbians" can be found across several centuries of European and North American history, but the term competed with others for dominance and for a long time was by no means preeminent. Beginning in the 1950s and continuing in the 1960s, lesbian activists began privileging the term, arguing that a word other than "gay" was needed to capture the distinct characteristics and interests of women. In adopting this position, these activists were challenging not only their putative gay male allies, but also community-based "gay" women. While there were probably more women who called themselves "gay" in the 1950s and 1960s, there were probably more women in the homophile movement who called themselves "lesbian." In the 1970s, lesbian feminists promoted use of the term "lesbian," which became the preferred designation among activists and nonactivists. By the 1980s, the movement commonly referred to itself as "gay and lesbian."

Why not refer to the movement as "bisexual" as well? This term has its own complex history, emerging initially in the context of the same pathologizing discourse that produced "homosexuality" and "heterosexuality." The term is also problematic because in many historical contexts it has not referred to people interested sexually in both males and females but rather to the integration and combination of masculinity and femininity. In addition, many people who might be classified as bisexual do not favor the term because they do not see themselves as having "two" orientations; they see themselves as "sexual" individuals who respond to people as people. All of that said, bisexuals asserted their distinct agendas and interests in the homophile era and have continued to do so, so the term deserves respect. And bisexual activists have raised compelling criticisms of the gay and lesbian movement for treating their sexual desires, practices, and identities as artificial, illegitimate, and untrustworthy.

The main reason that this book does not use "bisexual" in the title is that the movement rarely referred to itself in this way in the period from 1950 to 1990. Calling the movement "gay and lesbian" can underscore the partially inclusive and partially exclusive nature of the forms of activism discussed in this book. In many respects, activists in this period did not constitute themselves as a "gay, lesbian, and bisexual" movement. In addition, using the term "bisexual" alongside "gay and lesbian" can constrain the meanings of the latter. In many components of the movement, the terms "gay" and "lesbian" have been seen as inclusively incorporating everyone who is sexually attracted to people of the same sex, regardless of whether they also have cross-sex attractions. Because this book highlights moments in the movement's history when the words "gay" and "lesbian" have been defined expansively, the term "bisexual" is reserved for moments when bisexuality became a subject of debate and discussion.

In the 1990s and early 2000s, it has become increasingly common to refer to the LGBT movement, which raises the question of whether this is a useful way to refer to the movement before 1990. The recent vintage of "LGBT" raises distinct problems for historians, who try to be careful about assuming that today's ways of thinking are appropriate to use in describing and analyzing the past. Was the gay and lesbian movement aligned with the transgender movement in the pre-1990 era? Definitions of the terms "transgender," "transsexual," and "trans" are complex and changing. Historian Susan Stryker uses "transgender" to refer to "people who move away from the gender they were assigned at birth, people who cross over (*trans-*) the boundaries constructed by their culture to define and contain that gender." Historian Joanne Meyerowitz defines transsexuality as "the quest to transform the bodily characteristics of sex via hormones and surgery." Many people now use "trans" and "genderqueer" to refer to a broad range of people and practices that challenge conventional norms of sex and gender, whereas "gay" and "lesbian" typically refer to same-sex sexualities, which may or may not be genderqueer.[3]

Many people who today might be called trans have thought of themselves and have been classified by others in the past as gay or lesbian, sometimes because of links between gender-transgression and homosexuality, sometimes because they have lived as gay or lesbian before or after transitioning, sometimes because transitioning has not been possible, and sometimes because the terms "gay" and "lesbian" have been defined expansively to include diverse forms of gender and sexual variance. Other people who might be called trans today have not referred to themselves as gay or lesbian and many gays and lesbians have denied that gender-transgression is necessarily associated with homosexuality. There are similar and related complications when thinking about intersex identities, which have been claimed by people not easily classifiable as anatomically and biologically male or female, such as people who have atypical sex chromosomes or atypical responsiveness to sex hormones.

Trans activism and trans studies emphasize that relationships between sex, gender, and sexuality should not be assumed. Depending on how the terms are defined, gay, lesbian, bisexual, trans, intersex, and other forms of gender and sexual activism have overlapped to a greater or lesser extent and this has changed over time. In many historical contexts, we can identify profound differences and conflicts between these forms of activism, some of which relates to the privileging of sexual orientation or gender expression, the mutual hostility these groups have displayed toward one another, or the divergent relationships they have had with social, cultural, political, and scientific authorities. At times over the last seven decades the trans movement has intersected with the gay and lesbian movement, but at other times it has not. Trans activism developed inside and outside the gay and lesbian movement. Gay and lesbian activists have been among the strongest supporters and strongest critics of the trans movement. Trans activists have played central roles in the gay and lesbian movement, but also have been excluded from that movement. In the early twenty-first century, strong coalitions have been formed between the gay/lesbian and trans movements, but this has not always been the case. In the future, the coalitional acronym "LGBT" will likely become outdated as new and old genders and sexualities form, reform, aggregate and disaggregate.

For all of these reasons, this book refers to and concentrates on the "gay and lesbian" movement. The trans and intersex movements deserve in-depth historical studies of their own. That said, this volume explores trans issues when they have been addressed in gay and lesbian activism. The book thus highlights the history of trans inclusion and exclusion within the gay and lesbian movement, examines moments of cooperation and conflict between the gay/lesbian and trans movements, and explores the history of trans activists who thought of themselves as gay or lesbian and gay and lesbian activists who thought of themselves as trans.

This leaves the question of why this book is not titled "Rethinking the Queer Movement." The word "queer" has been used for centuries to refer to non-normative genders and sexualities. Often deployed as a term of derision, it also was embraced by people who referred to themselves as queer. As was the case with "gay," the term had distinct meanings related to class, gender, race, and sex and those meanings varied across time and space. In the 1960s, some homophile activists referred to radical gay and lesbian resistance as queer; gay liberationists and lesbian feminists did likewise in the 1970s. Recent usage derives more directly from the formation of the group Queer Nation in the early 1990s and the development of queer theory as a field of scholarly inquiry around the same time. Over the last twenty years, the term "queer" has continued to be used as a negative epithet, but it also has been reclaimed. For some, the term is useful shorthand for LGBT, intersex, and other alternative genders and sexualities. For others, it refers to gender and sexual radicalism, subversion, and transgression, which implies that conservative homosexuals are nonqueer and that queer heterosexualities are imaginable. "Queer" can refer to conceptions of sex, gender, and sexuality that reject biological essentialism, identity politics, and minority models. In this sense, queer activism challenges binary classification systems that treat male and female, masculine and feminine, and heterosexual and homosexual as fixed, innate, and mutually exclusive categories. "Queer" has also been favored by some activists because it seems less white, middle-class, and gender-normative than "gay and lesbian."

Calling this book "Rethinking the Queer Movement" would be problematic because most gay and lesbian activists from 1950 to 1990 would have rejected "queer" as the appropriate term for their movement. In addition, if the term "queer" is used to convey a sense of radicalism and transgression, it does not work very well for the components of the gay and lesbian movement that were not particularly radical or transgressive. Since the term "queer" is often used to challenge the limitations of mainstream gay and lesbian activism, it does not seem useful to call the whole movement "queer." One can refer to a particular set of critical perspectives on the gay and lesbian movement as queer and one can locate important antecedents of recent queer activism in the gay and lesbian movement, but that does not mean that the movement of 1950–90 is best described as queer. A history of the queer movement would be very interesting, but it would be different from a history of the gay and lesbian movement.

By now it should be clear that one important thing that merits rethinking is what to call the movement. It also would be useful to rethink what we mean by the term "movement." As defined in this book, the gay and lesbian movement has been a small but influential component of a much larger gay and lesbian world, which in turn has been a small but influential component of a much larger universe of people who engage in same-sex sex. Most people who engage in same-sex sex do not think of themselves as gay or lesbian and most gay and lesbian people are not activists. This has always been the case. The working definition of a movement that is used in this book has four elements: a movement is an (1) organized, (2) collective, and (3) sustained (4) effort to produce, prevent, or reverse social change. The level of organization can vary from highly structured and formalized to more casual and informal, but a random act of gay and lesbian resistance is not a movement. Nor does an individual or isolated action meet the criteria. A movement can be small or large, but it is not a movement if it does not involve a significant number of people and if it does not last for a significant amount of time (with the definition of "significant" intentionally left open). There were individuals who resisted anti-homosexual oppression before the 1950s and there were short-lived organizations as well, but if we use the definition offered above, the gay and lesbian movement did not begin until the 1950s. As for the fourth element, this is useful for distinguishing movement activism from other forms of cultural and social action that are not linked to a vision or program of social change.

In this book, a "movement," which is roughly equivalent to "activism," is different from "agency" and "resistance," which might consist of individual or one-time acts and which might be aimed at advancing personal or collective interests rather than making social change. "Agency" and "resistance" are necessary components of a movement, but nor all forms of "agency" and "resistance" are connected to a movement. What, then, do we do with the history of everyday acts of resistance, such as coming out to one's family, expressing same-sex affection in public, or participating in gay and lesbian culture? After D'Emilio's monograph on the homophile movement was published in 1983, several of the next major books on pre-Stonewall U.S. gay and lesbian history did not focus on political activism. For example, George Chauncey's study of New York, Elizabeth Kennedy and

Madeline Davis's examination of Buffalo, and Esther Newton's monograph on Cherry Grove, Fire Island, all published in the early 1990s, argue that the history of gay and lesbian resistance has to be understood as encompassing more than movement activism. In this respect, gay and lesbian resistance, which they trace back to the late nineteenth and early twentieth centuries, began much earlier than the organized gay and lesbian movement, which began in the United States in the 1950s. Their works suggest that participating in gay bar culture, for example, or presenting one's self as a gender or sexual "deviant" in public should be considered part of the history of gay and lesbian resistance.[4]

This is a useful and valuable point, but it is also important to distinguish between everyday acts of resistance and organized political activism. Everyday acts can be conceptualized as forms of agency and resistance. They can even be regarded as precursors to and sustainers of movement activism. But it is less clear that they can be characterized as forms of movement activism in and of themselves. In the last few decades, there has been a curious reversal in the fortunes of everyday resisters and movement activists in sexuality studies. While it used to be the case that political activists were central figures in many scholarly works on gay and lesbian topics, in more recent studies it has increasingly seemed like they were not worthy of much attention, while other types of resisters have been presented as positive paragons of performative virtue. For example, Judith Butler's influential book *Gender Trouble*, which has much to say about subversive performances by individuals, has little to say about movement activism. Nor does this type of work provide much help for thinking about the relationship between political activism and cultural activism, with the latter encompassing the work of artists, dancers, filmmakers, novelists, musicians, performers, photographers, poets, screenwriters, and others. Cultural activism has played important roles in making social change, but it does not always conform to conventional ways of thinking about political activism. This book makes efforts to link political and cultural activism, but has less to say about everyday forms of resistance that are not connected to movement activism.[5]

One additional point about the focus on activism: in placing the movement at the center of this study, the book does not offer a celebratory account or a narrative of linear progress. Gay and lesbian activism has played important roles in making social change. This does not mean that all of the changes made by the movement have been positive, or that the movement has succeeded in representing the diverse interests of gay men and lesbians, or that the movement has always made the best possible choices. This book underscores the importance of the movement, but the perspective is critical rather than celebratory. And to avoid any misunderstanding, "critical" does not mean "antigay" or "antilesbian." It means, for example, addressing the fact that the movement has often been liberal and reformist, without missing moments when it has been leftist and radical. It means recognizing that the movement has often been dominated by gender-normative middle-class white men, but not erasing the contributions of others. It means foregrounding the movement's politics of respectability, but not forgetting about its more transgressive tendencies. It means acknowledging that the movement has often promoted the notion that gays and lesbians are a minority group made up of people "born this way," but not ignoring activists who have championed the liberation of everyone's gender and sexual desires. One of the book's main goals is to highlight the many ways in which the movement, for better and for worse, has made the world in which we live.

Finally, why does this book adopt a national framework? Social movements can be organized in local, national, or international ways; the gay and lesbian movement has operated on all three levels. One reason to produce a national study is that we now have many local studies of gay and lesbian history, but we do not have an up-to-date synthetic overview of the movement at the national level. That said, at a time when scholars are increasingly interested in global and transnational history, why restrict this study to the United States? U.S. Americans often think of their country as exceptional, but U.S. movements have been influenced by transnational developments and it can help to adopt a comparative perspective to understand what is taken for granted inside a particular nation-state. U.S. movements have also influenced developments in other countries; if we ignore this fact, we miss some of the larger significance of U.S. history.

We know, for example, that the U.S. homophile movement paid attention to European and Canadian sex reform in the 1950s and 1960s, but we have not wrestled much with the significance of this. The U.S. homophile press published accounts of same-sex sexuality in Asia, Africa, Latin America, and Native America, but we have not seen much work addressing the movement's relationship to colonialism and postcolonialism. When radical activists created Gay Liberation Fronts in many U.S. locations after the Stonewall riots, they were modeling themselves on National Liberation Fronts in Algeria, Vietnam, and elsewhere, but few of us have considered the many ways in which the U.S. movement was implicated in transnational dynamics. More recently, when U.S. activists contributed to and then criticized the homosexualization of AIDS, they created opportunities and challenges for struggles against AIDS in other countries. Similar dynamics have been at play when activists in other parts of the world have appropriated or rejected what they regard as U.S. models of gay and lesbian activism. When the U.S. Supreme Court struck down state sodomy laws in 2003, the justices relied on European and Canadian examples to challenge the claim that Western civilization has always and everywhere criminalized same-sex sex. The legalization of same-sex marriage in other countries will likely have similar results, providing evidence for U.S. activists who want to challenge conservative predictions about how same-sex marriage will lead to the end of civilization.

Notwithstanding these reasons for thinking transnationally, nation-states remain terribly powerful in today's world, especially in the ways they deal with legal rights, social benefits, human migration, and political citizenship; it would be naïve to ignore the significance of national borders. In addition, many powerful gay and lesbian movement organizations and campaigns have organized themselves nationally rather than transnationally. In the end, there are good reasons to adopt a national framework for this study, though there are also good reasons to locate the national movement in relation to its local and transnational counterparts. Critical readers will notice that this book is not as national as it might be. In many respects, this reflects the fact that it is a work of synthesis and thus relies heavily on the scholarship of others. For example, historians have published in-depth studies of homophile activism, gay liberation, and lesbian feminism in Los Angeles, New York, Philadelphia, San Francisco, Seattle, and Washington, D.C., but we know much less about the early history of gay and lesbian activism in many other large cities, not to mention most smaller cities and towns. Much of the scholarship on the early years of AIDS activism focuses on Chicago, Los Angeles, New York, and San Francisco; other locations have received less attention. Scholars have studied gay and lesbian activism in many cities that have been important in the movement's history, but new research on other sites will likely challenge this book's arguments and conclusions. This is often the way that historical scholarship develops over time.

This book, then, concentrates on the U.S. gay and lesbian movement from 1950 to 1990. The first chapter provides a broad overview of the history of same-sex sexuality in the United States before the movement began. The second begins in the 1940s and then focuses on three distinct periods of homophile activism (1950–53, 1953–61, and 1961–69). Chapter 3 begins with the Stonewall riots of 1969 and then examines gay liberation, lesbian feminism, and gay and lesbian liberalism, which are presented as distinct political tendencies in the 1969–73 era. The fourth chapter addresses gay and lesbian activism in the years between the American Psychiatric Association's declassification of homosexuality as a mental disorder in 1973 and the beginning of the AIDS epidemic in 1981. Chapter 5 concentrates on AIDS activism and the gay and lesbian movement in the 1980s. A concluding chapter presents a broad overview of post-1990 developments, including the emergence of the LGBT and queer movements.

Readers should know that while most of the activists highlighted in this book identified as gay or lesbian, the movement also featured significant contributions by straight people, so in this way the book defines the movement broadly. In other respects, the book defines the movement narrowly; this is a not a broad survey of gay and lesbian history but a focused study of political activism. As indicated above, most people who have engaged in same-sex sex have not become gay and lesbian activists. To understand how some U.S. Americans came to identify as gay or lesbian, participate in movement activism, and join together with allies who supported their efforts, we first need to consider the earlier developments that made it possible to organize a gay and lesbian movement in the United States in the 1950s.

1

BEFORE THE MOVEMENT, 1500–1940

If a movement is defined as an organized, collective, and sustained effort to produce, prevent, or reverse social change, the U.S. gay and lesbian movement began in the 1950s. Earlier developments, however, influenced the movement's emergence and character. Same-sex sex was commonly practiced in North America before and after Europeans invaded the continent, but political and religious leaders in the European colonies generally regarded it as a crime and a sin, as did early U.S. authorities. There was no sense that some people were homosexual and others heterosexual; same-sex sex was conceptualized as an act rather than an identity. In the nineteenth century, many scientists argued that same-sex sex was a sign of disease and a symptom of gender inversion. Toward the end of the century, it continued to be viewed as an act and it continued to be conceptualized as a sin, a crime, and a disease, but a significant number of people who engaged in same-sex sex began to think of themselves as having distinct gender and sexual identities; some experts began referring to them as "inverts" and "homosexuals." By the beginning of the twentieth century, there were sexual communities in many locations that featured diverse groups of people interested in same-sex sex, including some who saw their sexual preferences as core components of their identities and some who believed that everyone could enjoy same-sex sex. Early resistance to sexual oppression took many shapes and forms, but it included people who defended homosexuals as a persecuted group in society and people who believed in sexual and homosexual liberation for all. The history of same-sex sexual desires, acts, identities, and communities, which interacted with the history of sexual oppression and resistance, created the necessary conditions for the emergence of the U.S. gay and lesbian movement in the mid-twentieth century.

Native and Colonial America before the American Revolution

For centuries before Europeans began invading and conquering the territories later claimed by the United States, Native Americans and the peoples of Alaska, the Pacific Islands, and the Caribbean treated same-sex sex in diverse and complex ways. Most of the historical scholarship on gender and sexual variance in these cultures has focused on "third sex" and "fourth sex" traditions, which featured distinct roles for biological males who lived beyond the parameters of conventional manhood and biological females who lived beyond the parameters of conventional womanhood. The terms used for these people varied, but after the European invasions they came to be known as "berdaches," which is derived from a Persian term for young male sexual slaves. Today, in recognition of their masculine and feminine qualities, they are typically called "two spirits." Some indigenous cultures treated male and female two spirits in similar or parallel ways; others treated them differently. In many indigenous cultures, the artistic, economic, diplomatic, military, sexual, and spiritual contributions of two spirits were respected. Other indigenous cultures did not feature institutionalized roles for two-spirits or treated them with disrespect, hostility, and violence.

For our purposes, the history of two-spirit traditions immediately raises questions about the relationship between trans history and gay/lesbian history. From one perspective, biologically male two spirits who had sex with men and biologically female two spirits who had sex with women were having same-sex sex and therefore can be considered part of gay/lesbian history (broadly defined). From another perspective, they were not having same-sex sex because their sexes were not the same; they are better thought of as part of trans history (broadly defined). Nor is it easy to decide how to view the sexualities of men and women who partnered with two spirits. They may have recognized many of the same body parts in their partners, without concluding that they were of the same sex. This is just one example of many where the history of gender variance is intertwined with the history of sexual variance.

There has been limited historical research on same-sex sex in indigenous North American and Pacific Islander cultures outside the context of two-spirit traditions, though there are reasons to believe that it was common and not regarded as mutually exclusive with cross-sex sex. In general, these cultures treated sex as natural and pleasurable; this attitude may have extended to same-sex intimacy. Diverse gender systems that structured the lives, loves, and labors of males and females likely influenced same-sex erotic practices. The lack of evidence about same-sex sex beyond the context of two-spirit traditions could reflect the fact that it was uncommon, but it could have been so ubiquitous that it was not deemed worthy of note. The significance of two-spirit traditions also may have displaced attention away from other forms of same-sex sex.

When Europeans invaded the Americas and Pacific Islands in the fifteenth, sixteenth, seventeenth, and eighteenth centuries, Native American, Native Alaskan,

Pacific Islander, and Caribbean peoples probably found their sexual practices to be familiar and unfamiliar. They also probably ascribed erotic meanings to European gender practices that differed from their own. We do not know much about how they responded to the all-male or predominantly male character of the first Europeans they encountered, but they may have wondered about whether Europeans behaved sexually as they themselves did in single-sex contexts. They also may have been struck by the diversity of European attitudes and practices. In some contexts, they likely viewed the invaders as having relaxed and casual attitudes toward sex; the average European sailor, soldier, trader, settler, and servant probably seemed to enjoy different forms of sex. In other contexts, especially when they encountered political and religious leaders influenced by strict forms of Christianity, they likely viewed Europeans as hostile to nonmarital and same-sex sex, though colonial words often conflicted with colonial deeds. They also may have come to understand that Europeans used same-sex sexual violence as a tool of power. In multiple contexts, indigenous North Americans and Pacific Islanders likely experienced same-sex sexual attraction, disinterest, and repulsion when they encountered Europeans.

We know more about how Europeans viewed the sexual practices of the people living on the lands they invaded. But even here we have to be careful, because most of what we know comes from religious, political, intellectual, and scientific leaders; other Europeans may have responded differently. The available evidence suggests that Europeans viewed indigenous sexual practices with a mix of desire, fear, and hostility. They also ascribed erotic meanings to gender practices that differed from their own. When Europeans and Euro-Americans looked at the bodies of the peoples they encountered, they sometimes responded with homoerotic curiosity, interest, and lust, but they also viewed indigenous sexual characteristics and traditions as proof of their inferiority. These beliefs helped rationalize the violence they committed. "Heathen" sexual practices became one of the justifications Europeans used for invading, conquering, and "civilizing" the Americas and the Pacific. As war and disease devastated Native American, Native Alaskan, Pacific Islander, and Caribbean cultures and as Europeans tried to impose their gender and sexual values, indigenous peoples responded with resistance and accommodation.

We do not have evidence of an organized movement to defend same-sex sexual practices or two-spirit traditions before or during the era of the European invasions. But we can surmise from the limited evidence available that indigenous peoples maintained and modified their distinct gender and sexual cultures by passing down their traditions to new generations, fighting back against opponents within their communities, and doing what was necessary to survive and thrive. They also kept their traditions hidden from hostile outsiders, migrated beyond the reach of unfriendly authorities, reached out to Europeans perceived as sympathetic, developed hybrid cultural practices, and participated in struggles for indigenous autonomy and power. Successful forms of resistance depended on the strong bonds that indigenous peoples formed with one another; same-sex love and intimacy could strengthen those bonds or become sources of conflict. Meanwhile, same-sex sex with Europeans could be a tool of exploitation, hatred, violence, and war, though in limited and constrained circumstances it also could promote cross-cultural bonds of affection.

There were other residents of North America with complex and changing perspectives on same-sex sex in these centuries. Africans and their descendants were present in large numbers, with the vast majority living and dying as slaves and a smaller number existing as "free" people with limited rights. Africans who were forcibly transported to the Americas would have been familiar, if they were old enough, with the treatment of same-sex sex in their diverse cultures of origin, but the traumas of enslavement and migration did much to disrupt their beliefs and practices. What they witnessed in terms of same-sex sex in the process of enslavement and transport is mostly a matter of conjecture, but there is reason to believe that some would have seen European males having sex with one another, Europeans using same-sex sex as a tool of violence, and Africans engaging in same-sex sex. They may have witnessed Europeans and Euro-Americans gazing with homoerotic fear, loathing, and desire at the bodies of Africans. How they returned those gazes—and whether they experienced same-sex sexual attraction, disinterest, or repulsion—is mostly a matter of speculation.

African American slaves lived in social contexts that ranged from large-scale plantations with thousands of residents to small households with limited opportunities for human contact. Some were worked to death and not presumed to have sex; others were expected to maximize the wealth of their "owners" by engaging in reproductive sex to the maximum extent possible. In the work they performed, the clothes they wore, and the deference they were expected to display, slaves were masculinized and feminized; they and their "owners" likely ascribed erotic meanings to these and other gender practices. In diverse contexts, slaves experienced same-sex sex in a variety of ways—as a violent imposition by whites; as a situational phenomenon shaped by single-sex environments and other institutional arrangements; and as a source of relief, comfort, and pleasure in a hostile world. Same-sex love and intimacy could strengthen African American bonds and support resistance to slavery, but also could lead to conflicts within their communities. Same-sex sexual contact between African Americans and Euro-Americans (and between African Americans and indigenous peoples) could help sustain the dehumanizing dynamics of life in the Americas, but in limited and constrained circumstances could challenge those dynamics.

In general, the European colonies established on the lands later claimed by the United States treated same-sex sex with a combination of condemnation, indifference, tolerance, and acceptance. Many Catholic and Protestant religious leaders condemned same-sex sex in the context of their hostility toward nonmarital, oral, and anal sex, which they viewed as terrible sins prohibited by their gods. Political systems of governance that drew on Christian values and traditions could be brutal when evidence of same-sex sex came to light. For most religious and political authorities, marriage and reproduction were important to the success of their colonies; nonmarital and nonreproductive sex were seen as threats. Same-sex

sex also was viewed as a challenge to the established gender order, which positioned men as superior and women as subordinate. Men who permitted other men to penetrate them were seen as relinquishing their manhood; women who initiated sex with other women were seen as usurping male prerogatives.

European colonial legal codes contained harsh penalties for same-sex sex. Some individuals found guilty of sodomy, buggery, crimes against nature, or other crimes related to same-sex sex were fined, jailed, whipped, expelled, or put to death. The legal system typically displayed greater hostility toward male than female same-sex sex, which partially reflected the belief that penetration with a penis was a necessary component of the most heinous sex crimes but also can be attributed to the fact that female sexuality was controlled in other ways. Occasionally, women also were charged, prosecuted, and convicted for same-sex sexual offenses. Some colonial legal codes contained more severe penalties for sex crimes committed by people of color. As for social condemnation, anyone believed to have engaged in same-sex sex could be subjected to exclusion, ostracism, ridicule, hatred, and violence. Men discovered to be biologically female, women discovered to be biologically male, and people whose sex and gender were ambiguous were especially vulnerable to legal and social sanctions for engaging in what the authorities might classify as same-sex sex or cross-dressing.

All of that said, many Euro-Americans treated same-sex sex with some degree of indifference, tolerance, or acceptance. In some contexts these attitudes applied to everyone; in others, they applied to dominant or subordinate groups. Some ministers and priests condemned sodomy from the pulpit, but then engaged in same-sex sex. Some European libertines brought their ideas about sex to the New World; some Euro-Americans adopted more permissive attitudes in frontier, colonial, and settler contexts. Popular beliefs about sex often diverged from the views of religious and political authorities; there is significant evidence of more casual attitudes among people who did not occupy positions of power. At the same time, the privileges of social elites often included greater tolerance for their sexual transgressions and more reluctance to challenge their behaviors. In some instances, it took decades of rumor and innuendo before community members acted against residents accused of engaging in same-sex sex. Imposed legal penalties were often fairly minimal. Colonial authorities enforced laws against same-sex sex primarily when they believed that force was used or minors were involved. Same-sex friendships, which often had erotic components, were tolerated, accepted, and even celebrated under certain circumstances. Same-sex sex also might be tolerated and accepted in domains with high male-to-female sex ratios—on ships, on the frontier, in the military, and in early settlements, for example—and it might be ignored when women were the protagonists. The fact that few colonials were charged with same-sex sexual crimes and few received harsh penalties, when we know that major police campaigns against same-sex sex occurred in various European cities, suggests that, beyond the reach of the authorities, same-sex sex was commonly treated as a minor indiscretion or a fact of life in the North American colonies.

Notwithstanding a certain level of tolerance for and acceptance of same-sex sex, we do not have evidence that there were colonial Americans who thought of themselves as having a fixed sexual orientation toward members of the same sex and believed that this was a core component of their identities. Scholars have debated and discussed whether such people (sometimes called sodomites or mollies) existed in Europe in the fifteenth through eighteenth centuries and there is evidence that some Americans knew about these European developments, but thus far no significant American counterparts have been identified. In Europe's North American colonies, same-sex sex was understood primarily as an act, sin, and crime that anyone might commit, but not as a reflection of an inner state of being or a chosen way of life that marked some people as sexually different from the rest. We come closer to these conceptions in a few cases. In seventeenth-century Connecticut, Nicholas Sension's long-standing sexual interest in young men, which was documented in a trial that found him guilty of attempted sodomy, was described in terms that referenced his predilection and proclivity for same-sex sex. In an eighteenth-century Connecticut case, the General Meeting of Baptist Churches temporarily suspended a minister, Stephen Gorton, for engaging in "unchaste behaviour" with men, which was said to reflect his "inward disposition." In general, however, we do not have significant evidence of proto-gay or lesbian identities.[1] Nor was there a movement that defended same-sex sex or promoted same-sex sexual reform. In the late seventeenth century, Pennsylvania was the first British colony in the Americas to eliminate capital punishment for sodomy, but this was not the result of a movement for sexual rights and the colony reinstated the death penalty in the early eighteenth century. Resistance to legal, religious, and social sanctions for same-sex sex more typically took the form of avoiding discovery, abandoning the jurisdiction, cross-dressing, denying that the sex occurred, promising redemption, and pleading for forgiveness.

From the American Revolution to the Civil War

The American Revolution, the establishment of the United States, and the ratification of the U.S. Constitution in the late eighteenth century had profound effects on many aspects of life in North America, but the new country's rhetorical support for liberty, freedom, democracy, and equality did not lead to a revolution in the treatment of same-sex sex. From the 1770s through the Civil War of the 1860s, as the United States conquered more land in North America, Native and Mexican sexual traditions were challenged, threatened, and undermined. In this period, African American slavery was abolished in the northern states, but expanded in the South, intensifying many of the sexual dynamics that had existed in the colonial era. In the context of U.S. expansion, the growth of slavery, and the rise of capitalism, scholars have found evidence of same-sex sexual desires and acts in diverse circumstances: in urban and rural relationships involving African Americans, Mexican Americans, Native Americans, and Euro-Americans; in the intimacies of biological males who "passed" as women and biological females who "passed" as men; in assaults on slaves and servants; in the "wide open" spaces of the multicultural western frontier; in erotic and romantic friendships between men and between women; and in single-sex settings ranging from schools and prisons to mines and the military.

Three developments in this period are particularly noteworthy for thinking about the antecedents of the gay and lesbian movement. First, while the new nation celebrated and debated the meanings of liberty, freedom, democracy, and equality, the nation's states and territories adopted new legal codes that criminalized various forms of nonmarital sex, including same-sex sex. The contrast with the French Revolution, which led to the decriminalization of sodomy in several European countries, is striking. Most U.S. states eliminated capital punishment for sodomy, buggery, and crimes against nature and no state executed an individual for these crimes after the United States was established, but the states and territories continued to provide for a range of harsh penalties, including lengthy prison terms and large fines, for those convicted of these and related crimes. Sodomy was usually defined as anal sex with a penis, but other forms of same-sex sex could be punished under a variety of vaguely worded laws. Some jurisdictions also began to prohibit cross-dressing specifically, as opposed to dressing in disguise more generally, which had been restricted earlier. As had been the case in the colonial era, the vast majority of same-sex sex went unpunished and in practice these laws were used primarily to punish sexual assaults, sex with minors, and sex with nonhuman animals, but the criminalization of same-sex sex and the selective enforcement of sex laws left everyone vulnerable to legal penalties and social condemnation. The gap between the harsh legal penalties and the rare use of them meant that people who engaged in same-sex sex had strong incentives to avoid detection by hostile public authorities. At the same time, the renewed criminalization of same-sex sex, in the context of the new country's rhetorical embrace of liberty, freedom, democracy, and equality, set the stage for later debates and conflicts about national values and practices.

Second, changes in the social organization of everyday life—influenced by the growth of towns and cities, the decline of farming-based household economies, the reduction in average family size, the rise of wage labor, the expansion of slavery, the increase in migration and immigration, and the military mobilizations that occurred during the Revolutionary War, the War of 1812, the Mexican War, and the Civil War—created new possibilities for and constraints on same-sex sex. Most notably, as the size and complexity of U.S. cities grew and as more people lived, worked, and traveled beyond their families and communities of origin, opportunities to engage in same-sex sex increased, though so did the risks of nonfamilial discovery. Class, ethnicity, geography, race, region, religion, and sex influenced how these changes were experienced, but most people were affected. These transformations contributed to the emergence of new sexual identities and communities in the late nineteenth and early twentieth centuries, which influenced the development of the gay and lesbian movement several decades later.

Third, the growth of an ideology of separate but unequal spheres for women and men—and the practices associated with that ideology—created new opportunities for and constraints on same-sex love, intimacy, and sex. This was an ideology embraced most fully by middle-class whites, but others supported it or were judged according to its tenets. As women's roles and responsibilities came to be linked more to the private and domestic sphere of the home, men's came to be linked more to the public worlds of business and politics. New possibilities for same-sex eroticism emerged for both sexes in their respective spheres—in households and workplaces, leisure and entertainment venues, educational and religious institutions, reform groups and the women's movement, and countless other contexts. The worlds of men and women continued to intersect and many outside the middle class could not or did not live according to the ideology's dictates, but women and men increasingly came to see themselves as fundamentally different in nature, character, and ambition. Meanwhile, reversing centuries of beliefs about the passionate nature of female desire, women (if white and middle class) came to be seen as more spiritual whereas men were increasingly seen as forever engaged in struggles to control and channel their powerful sexual urges. Difference and distance could lead to intense cross-sex attractions, but many people who lived in increasingly separate spheres experienced strong same-sex desires. In various ways, the separate spheres ideology encouraged same-sex love, affection, and intimacy, which were not necessarily seen as transgressive or incompatible with cross-sex relationships.

For those who felt especially confined by the sex and sphere to which they had been assigned, one option was to switch. It was difficult for biological females to live as men and biological males to live as women, but some did. In some situations, the initial motivations may have had less to do with cross-gender identifications or same-sex desires and more to do with other types of economic, political, and social aspirations. This may have been the case for biological females who wanted to work in specific occupations, serve in the military, or travel around the world. In other situations, the initial motivations may have had more to do with cross-gender identifications, as was the case for people who did not identify with the sexes they were assigned at birth. In still other situations, the initial motivations may have had more to do with same-sex sexual desires; this was the case for those who cross-dressed strategically in order to facilitate same-sex relationships. In many situations, the initial motivations were multiple, they changed over time, and the practices changed over time. In addition, the meanings assigned by others diverged from the meanings assigned by those who switched.

In the context of all of these developments, some men may have begun to see themselves and be seen by others as having distinct sexual interests and inclinations. For example, in the 1840s two New York newspapers launched crusades against the city's "sodomites," who were identified as English, French, Portuguese, and Jewish immigrants bent on seducing good-looking young American men and boys. "Already do the beastly Sodomites of Gotham quake," one newspaper reported. "They feel their brute souls quiver with fear." One reason for fear was that the newspapers claimed to know "where these felons resort for the purpose of meeting and making appointments with their victims." The sodomites were characterized at one point as "genteel" and "feminine" foreigners who turned "men of respectability" into "victims of extortion," though other reports emphasized the feminization of the seduced. The "set of fiends" and "herd of beasts," who at one point were said to be "mostly of the Hebrew race," included a concert performer, a liquor merchant, and a wholesale importer who enticed his victims with offers of employment. A bar owner who "forced" a male employee to "lie with beasts in the shape of men" was said to be "the king of the Sodomites." Generally depicted in negative ways, sodomites also appeared in works of fiction published in this period.

Significantly, as "sodomites" began to be imagined as having a collective identity, new possibilities for collective resistance may have emerged. According to one of the newspapers that reported on the New York sodomites in the 1840s, "friends of these brutes threaten[ed] us with violence, if we persisted in our strictures." The friends insisted that the accused were "harmless young men," which implied that they were not guilty of the charges against them. We do not know whether the men attacked in these articles thought of themselves as sodomites, and, if they did, whether other U.S. men did as well. Nevertheless, it is possible that new sexual identities and communities were forming and that the friends were resisting the policing of same-sex sex.[2]

In the mid-nineteenth century, some U.S. Americans began to offer more affirmative defenses and celebrations of erotic same-sex relationships. Much of the evidence for this has been found in private writings—in journals, diaries, personal letters, etc.—but this suggests that something significant was happening in the ways in which people thought about same-sex sex. In public writings, including literary works by Emily Dickinson, Ralph Waldo Emerson, Herman Melville, and Henry David Thoreau, there were passages that extolled the virtues of same-sex friendships, though the sexual character of these relationships was typically ambiguous. Walt Whitman, whose private writings reveal that he enjoyed a lifetime of same-sex sex, love, and affection, was exceptional in offering more public, more explicit, and more explicitly political comments. In the first editions of *Leaves of Grass*, published in the 1850s and 1860s, Whitman wrote of speaking up for "forbidden voices, voices of sexes and lusts … , voices indecent by me clarified and transfigured." More specifically, he wrote about sex, love, and affection between male comrades, which he called "manly love" and "adhesive" love, and he did so in extraordinarily affirmative and erotic ways.[3] As he did so, he denounced the reluctance of other writers to address sex openly and he criticized sexual censorship. He also depicted the passionate bonds of American men as the foundation of U.S. democracy and the basis for national reconciliation after the Civil War. Significantly, Whitman celebrated homoerotic relationships, but did not present them as mutually exclusive with the erotic relationships of men and women, which he also celebrated. After the Civil War, Whitman's work became an important resource, nationally and internationally, for those interested in defending and celebrating same-sex sex, though Whitman was reluctant to endorse these interpretations of his work.

From the Civil War to World War One

In the last decades of the nineteenth century and the first years of the twentieth, a significant number of U.S. Americans began to view their same-sex sexual desires as important aspects of their identities—some even thought of themselves as having distinct sexual identities—and began to form social and cultural communities based on shared interests in same-sex sex, love, and affection. Some came to think of themselves as members of a sexual minority group; some believed that everyone had the potential to enjoy same-sex sex; some did not see any conflict between these two ways of thinking. Most people who engaged in same-sex sex did not think of themselves as members of a distinct minority (a fact that remains true today), but more and more people did. These two conceptions—one minoritizing and the other universalizing—later helped shape the dual character of the gay and lesbian movement, which from its earliest days was simultaneously dedicated to improving the status of a sexual minority and committed to the sexual transformation of society as a whole.

Those who came to see their same-sex desires as important aspects of their identities also developed two ways of thinking about the gendered aspects of those desires. Some believed that homoerotic desires were the products of gender inversion; in this view, the prototypical man who desired men was feminine and the prototypical woman who desired women was masculine. Others believed that homoerotic desires were the products of sexual orientation and were not necessarily linked to cross-gender identifications; in this view, the prototypical man who desired men was masculine and the prototypical woman who desired women was feminine. These two conceptions also later shaped the character of the gay and lesbian movement, which sometimes embraced and sometimes rejected linkages between gender and sexual dissidence.

Several major social, cultural, and political transformations influenced sexual developments in this period. Large-scale urbanization, industrialization, immigration, and migration made it more possible for people to lead lives in which same-sex sexual relationships could have greater significance. In part, this was because these changes disrupted traditional family economies and gender roles. Many urban residents, wage laborers, immigrants, and migrants spent less time with their families, more time in single-sex environments, and more money on leisure activities. The expanded world of commercialized amusements, which included bars, restaurants, and dance halls, encouraged the pursuit of pleasure. Same-sex domesticity and intimacy became distinctively important in racialized communities with high male-to-female sex ratios (such as Asian immigrant communities), in male-dominated occupational contexts (such as mining and the military), and in single-sex educational institutions, religious organizations, settlement houses, social clubs, and political groups.

As the pace of social change quickened, "new women," "new men," and other new cultural types encouraged U.S. Americans to envision new ways of organizing sex, gender, and sexuality in a modern world. Literary works by Natalie Barney, Willa Cather, Henry James, Sarah Orne Jewett, Gertrude Stein, Charles Warren Stoddard, and others were influential in offering new perspectives on same-sex desires, romances, and intimacies. Powerful movements of workers, women, and African Americans encouraged those who engaged in same-sex sex to conclude that they, too, were oppressed and they, too, could agitate for change. The women's movement not only facilitated close relationships between women, but also developed powerful critiques of gender and sexual subordination. Anarchists, socialists, and other radicals inspired visions of social transformation that would revolutionize the treatment of same-sex sex.

Some social reformers were not as favorable toward same-sex sex, but their efforts often had unintended consequences. Moral reformers initiated campaigns against various types of sexual vice, though this publicized, promoted, and popularized sexual deviance. Media reports about sex crimes and sins had similarly multiple effects, simultaneously discouraging and encouraging same-sex sex. Some medical doctors focused their work on describing, classifying, and treating sexual defects and disorders, but the publicity they provided and the terminology they invented encouraged the growth of alternative sexual communities. In some sectors of society, the medical discourse of homosexuality, which intersected in complex ways with ideas about class, race, and gender, was particularly influential, simultaneously pathologizing and empowering sexual dissidents. All of these changes help account for the existence and character of the first collective efforts to improve the treatment of same-sex sex in the United States.

Early sex reform campaigns were shaped by the structural features of the United States in this era. For Native Americans and the peoples of Alaska, the Pacific Islands, and the Caribbean, U.S. military actions, land seizures, territorial annexations, reservation policies, and white racism influenced all aspects of their lives. For African Americans, the end of slavery, its replacement by exploitative new systems of labor, the rise of racial segregation, the dynamics of legal and extralegal disenfranchisement, and the migration of millions from the agricultural South to the urban North had powerful effects. For European, Asian, and Latin American immigrants, segregation, ethnic violence, and racial prejudice were pervasive. Working-class life was transformed by the growth of industrial capitalism, the rise of new forms of labor exploitation, and battles between business and labor. Women confronted political disenfranchisement, second-class legal status, physical violence, economic discrimination, and sexism. Social hierarchies influenced early sex reform campaigns in multiple ways. They led middle- and upper-class white men to feel that they were being denied the special rights and privileges generally reserved for their class, race, and sex when they were persecuted for engaging in same-sex sex. Social divisions made it difficult for many immigrants, people of color, women, and working-class people to participate in some reform campaigns. At the same time, social inequality inspired critiques of U.S. power and politics, which influenced the rhetoric and reasoning of sex reform.

Most of the evidence of early campaigns to reform the treatment of same-sex sex suggests that white men led these efforts. The reasons for the predominance of men have been the subject of much debate. Did men have more opportunities to engage in same-sex sex, perhaps because of their greater economic wealth, geographic mobility, and public presence? Were women less likely to engage in same-sex sex or were they just less likely to be noticed and caught? Was invisibility a problem for women who engaged in same-sex sex or a sign of their success in avoiding hostile attention? Were men more persecuted or did the persecution of men and women take different forms, with men more likely to be arrested for sex crimes and women more likely to experience familial punishment and sexual violence? If women were disciplined more in the private sphere, did this make it less likely that they would respond publicly? If women were less persecuted, was this because female same-sex sex was not treated seriously or was regarded as erotically titillating by men? Did the greater involvement of men in sex reform reflect the privileging of men in general? Whatever the reasons, it is noteworthy that most of the evidence of early campaigns to reform the treatment of same-sex sex highlights the roles of men, though the most prominent advocate of revolution was anarchist Emma Goldman.

These campaigns developed in the context of the emergence of sizable urban communities of people who were interested in same-sex sex and who associated with others who shared their interests. In 1871, for example, a Philadelphia doctor reported that "every unnatural lust," including "the vice which called vengeance from heaven on Sodom," was practiced "deliberately and habitually in the great cities of our country." Moreover, there were "restaurants frequented by men in women's attire, yielding themselves to indescribable lewdness," and there was "literature so inconceivably devilish as to advocate and extoll this utter depravity." In 1889, a Chicago medical expert reported that "there is in every community of any size a colony of male sexual perverts; they are usually known to each other, and are likely to congregate together." Another doctor later recalled that in the 1880s and 1890s he learned that "perverts of both sexes maintained a sort of social set-up in New York," where they "had their places of meeting" and enjoyed the "advantage of the police protection for which they could pay." While this account mentioned female "perverts," an 1893 medical report referred to an "organization of colored erotopaths" in Washington, D.C. The organization's "annual convocation of negro men called the drag dance" was "an orgie of lascivious debauchery." The event featured men "lasciviously dressed in womanly attire" and sexual performances watched by "members of this lecherous gang of sexual perverts and phallic for-nicators." Five years later, a Massachusetts doctor observed that in "nearly every centre of importance" in the United States there was "a band of urnings, men of perverted tendencies, men known to each other as such, bound by ties of secrecy and fear and held together by mutual attraction." These comments and countless others in the early twentieth century highlight the emergence not only of new sexual and gender identities, but also new collective sensibilities, social solidarities, and cultural communities.[4]

Many of these accounts were produced by medical doctors who did not see themselves as members of the communities they were describing, but auto-biographical works by "Ralph Werther" referenced a social world that its narrator first joined in the 1890s. According to Werther, "nature" had made him an "androgyne" and he was "one of the rare humans who possess a strong claim, on anatomic grounds as well as psychic, to membership in both the recognized sexes." Having begun to have sex with male classmates when he was a child, he was later relieved to discover New York's "Paresis Hall," which attracted "androgynes," "bisexuals," "fairies," and "female-impersonators" of the "upper and middle classes." He also learned about "slum resorts" that were frequented by "the lowest class of bisexuals." In this case, "bisexual" referred to men who combined masculine and feminine features rather than men who enjoyed sex with both men and women. According to Werther, the "underworld" in many cities welcomed bisexuals and in several cities in the U.S. West "the sexual Underworld is more bold and wields more political power than anywhere else in the United States or Europe."[5]

There are fewer comparable accounts by women from this period, but in 1930 an autobiography by Mary Casal recalled the moment around the turn of the century when the author and her female lover realized that "there were other women who cared for each other," that "there existed a like propensity in men," and that there was a world of female sexual "inverts" in and beyond New York City: "At last … did I find that I was not a creature apart as I had always felt." Shortly thereafter Casal and her lover went "slumming" in the Bowery and saw "hundreds of male inverts … gathered together."[6]

The communities described in these and other sources were diverse and complex. Geographically, there were favoured city neighborhoods, streets, and parks, with the Bowery, Times Square, Harlem, and Greenwich Village in New York, Near North Side and South Side in Chicago, and the Barbary Coast, Tenderloin, and North Beach in San Francisco among the best known. For entertainment, there were popular bars, cafes, clubs, dance halls, drag balls, restaurants, and theaters. Some bathhouses, beaches, gymnasia, parks, and toilets were known to be frequented by people interested in same-sex erotic encounters. Male hustlers plied their trade in these and other venues, while drag queens and kings, female and male impersonators, sexual performers, and other transgressive artists attracted large audiences. Specific apartment buildings, boarding houses, and hotels served the community's needs, as did house parties, which could be intimate affairs for small circles of friends or large events with hundreds of guests. Beyond the country's large cities, there were distinct rhythms, rituals, and resources for people interested in same-sex sex in smaller cities and towns and in rural and suburban settings.

Along with the complexity of these worlds came a specialized vocabulary, often highly localized and rapidly changing, to refer to distinct subgroups, including bulldaggers, chickens, drag queens, fairies, gays, inverts, homosexuals, husbands, jockers, lesbians, pansies, punks, queers, studs, trade, and wolves. In some contexts, same-sex sexual partners were typically similar in age, class, race, and gender; in others, they were typically different (so that, for example, older men partnered with younger men, masculine women with feminine women, and whites with non-whites). Racism and sexism were common in these communities, as were social hierarchies based on ability, age, class, language, and religion. Many gay bars, for example, were all-white or all-male, though there were also bars that catered to all-black, all-female, or mixed groups of patrons. Social divisions and divisive dynamics shaped the character of the new sexual communities that formed in the late nineteenth and early twentieth centuries, just as they shaped the character of the gay and lesbian movement that developed later.

Participation in these communities often required brave acts of resistance. In many situations, silence about same-sex sex and the use of linguistic euphemisms made it difficult to locate supportive communities. Attempting to make a same-sex sexual connection could lead to abuse, humiliation, and violence. Engaging in same-sex sex in private or public space could result in discovery and disclosure, which might be followed by familial rejection, loss of employment, community ostracism, and legal punishment. Joining any of the social worlds described above could increase one's vulnerability to hostile publicity, police harassment, and popular hatred. Those most visible to outsiders, including masculine women, feminine men, and people of color, often suffered the most, meaning that they typically required the most courage to live as they wished. Those who participated in these communities developed complex strategies of resistance in order to communicate with others, claim public space, confront trouble, and live fulfilling lives. While they did not develop a collective, organized, and sustained gay and lesbian movement in this era, they made it possible for a movement to emerge in the decades to come.

Resistance to dominant social norms was particularly necessary in this period because federal, state, local, and military authorities increased their policing of same-sex sex. Over the long term, the growth of the state would have positive and negative implications for people who engaged in same-sex sex, but in this era the state was more of an enemy than an ally. The last states eliminated capital punishment for sodomy in the 1860s and 1870s, but the last states without sodomy laws adopted them in the 1880s and 1890s. Sodomy laws also were rewritten and reinterpreted so that increasingly they applied to women who engaged in same-sex sex and anyone who engaged in oral sex. It continued to be difficult for state and local authorities to obtain sodomy convictions, but most states and many local governments attempted to repress same-sex sex in the ways they passed, modified, interpreted, and enforced laws against carnal knowledge, cross-dressing, disorderly conduct, indecency, lewdness, loitering, solicitation, vagrancy, and other vaguely worded offenses. Federal, state, and local authorities targeted same-sex sex as they increased their policing of obscenity and prostitution, as the federal government authorized the exclusion and deportation of immigrants identified as sexual perverts, and as the U.S. military imprisoned and discharged more men found guilty of engaging in sodomy.

The overall results were major increases in arrests, prosecutions, and convictions, which directly affected thousands of people who engaged in same-sex sex or participated in alternative sexual communities. Far more were affected indirectly as they came to fear legal or extralegal repression. Penalties included not only prison terms and fines, but also sterilization, castration, and institutionalization. Working-class, poor, and nonwhite men were disproportionately represented among those charged with crimes related to same-sex sex, though women continued to be more vulnerable to other forms of punishment, including violent assaults, loss of financial support, and deprivation of parental rights. Beyond the increased policing of same-sex sex that occurred across the country, there were particularly intense episodes of repression in various locations, including the country's largest cities but also Long Beach, California (1914–15); Newport, Rhode Island (1919–21); and Portland, Oregon (1912–13). Most same-sex sex continued to go unpunished and there continued to be contexts—in general and in distinct class and race-based communities—in which same-sex sexuality was tolerated and accepted, but condemnation, hostility, and hatred were ever-present risks.

With repression came resistance. An organized gay and lesbian movement did not develop in the United States in this period, but some U.S. Americans began to challenge sexual oppression in ways not previously seen in this country. Representatives of the Scientific-Humanitarian Committee, a German-based homosexual emancipation organization, visited the United States in the early twentieth century and presented lectures to doctors, lawyers, ministers, and others. Before and after this occurred, there were U.S. doctors who supported reform in the treatment of homosexuality. As medical experts began to claim increased cultural, social, and political authority over sexual matters in this era, some began to argue that, from their vantage point as scientists, homosexuality was better conceptualized as a physical or mental illness rather than a religious sin or criminal offense. They were influenced by European psychoanalysts, psychiatrists, psychologists, and sexologists who had launched major projects to study, classify, diagnose, and treat a variety of illnesses related to gender and sexuality. They also were influenced by their patients.

Compared with their European counterparts, most U.S. medical experts responded to homosexuality in harsh ways, recommending and performing punitive "cures," but some were more sympathetic. For example, an anonymous female doctor wrote to a European sexologist in the 1890s about her work with eight female inverts, noting that they "acknowledge their feelings to be unusual, and perhaps morbid, but they unite in declaring them to be absolutely ineradicable." She concluded that "current views with regard to homosexuality are grossly erroneous and cruelly unjust." From her perspective, "homosexuality is not in itself a mark of mental deficiency or of moral degradation" and "to denounce such persons as degraded is the height of cruelty—a cruelty which must necessarily produce an acute sense of injustice." More commonly, medical doctors advocated that legal punishment be replaced by scientific treatment, which they presented as a progressive reform.[7]

A second type of reform effort, this one spearheaded by those more personally invested in same-sex sex, love, and romance, offered more sexually affirmative arguments for social change. In 1891, James Mills Peirce, a Harvard professor of literature, wrote an extraordinary statement published several years later by European sexologists. "It has long been my settled conviction," he declared, "that no breach of morality is involved in homosexual love; that, like every other passion, it tends, when duly understood and controlled by spiritual feeling, to the physical and moral health of the individual and the race." According to Peirce, "the subjects of this passion" are a "high-minded, upright, refined, and (I must add) pureminded class of men." Peirce was one of many turn-of-the-century advocates of the view that humans were born with the capacity to desire males and females both and that exclusive heterosexuality was as much of a perversion as was exclusive homosexuality. As he noted, "The abnormal form of love is that which has lost the power of excitability in either the one or the other of these directions. It is unisexual love … which is a perversion. The normal men love both." Peirce also rejected the notion that homosexuality was "inverted," presenting it as "a natural, pure and sound passion, as worthy of the reverence of all fine natures as the honourable devotion of husband and wife."[8]

Pierce was joined by others who called for sexual change. In 1901, a European sexologist reproduced a letter by a U.S. woman who declared,

> Inverts should have the courage and independence to be themselves, and to demand an investigation. If one strives to live honorably, and considers the greatest good to the greatest number, it is not a crime nor a disgrace to be an invert. I do not need the law to defend me, neither do I desire to have any concessions made for me, nor do I ask my friends to sacrifice their ideals for me. I too have ideals which I shall always hold. All that I desire—and I claim it as my right—is the freedom to exercise this divine gift of loving, which is not a menace to society nor a disgrace to me.

In 1915, Margaret Anderson, who co-edited the radical journal *The Little Review* with her lover Jane Heap, published an editorial criticizing a recent public lecture about sex for not offering a "vision of a future state when love in all its aspects is valued." The speaker "didn't mention homosexuality" and did not refer to "social efforts" on "behalf of the homosexualist." Nor did the lecturer respond to a prominent sexologist's claim that "intermediate sexual forms are 'normal, not pathological'" and that "'all organisms have both homosexuality and heterosexuality.'"[9]

Some reform advocates combined the pathologizing perspectives of doctors with the more sexually affirmative arguments of "homosexuals." In 1882, a U.S. immigrant wrote to a European sexologist about his early same-sex sexual experiences in Europe, which had allowed him to take "comfort" in "the satisfaction of association and the sense of no longer being alone." After a male partner "denounced" him to the police, however, he was arrested and charged with a sex crime, which led to his decision to emigrate. While the man referred to his "diseased and perverted instinct," he emphasized that he had "sinned against the common ideas of morality, but not against nature." More affirmatively, he wrote, "Our loves bear as fair and noble flowers, incite to as praiseworthy efforts as does the love of man for the woman of his affections. There are the same sacrifices, the same joy in abnegation even to the laying down of life, the same pain, the same joy, sorrow, happiness." At present, people like him were "persecuted," but science could "educate the people so that they shall rightly judge our unfortunate class."[10]

Much of what we know about these types of argument comes from the publications of medical doctors, but two notable works produced in the early twentieth century provide more direct access to the views of those who advocated reform on their own behalf. In 1908, Edward I. Prime-Stevenson (using the pseudonym Xavier Mayne) arranged for the publication of *The Intersexes*, which was his lengthy historical, scientific, and philosophical study of "the problem of homosexualism, similisexualism, urningism, inverted sexuality, uranianism, as it is variously termed." His text, published privately in Rome, challenged the notion that homosexuals were "pathological," that they suffered from "nervous disease," and that they were "morally vicious, degenerate, and criminal." In fact, he invoked Plato, Michelangelo, Shakespeare, Byron, Whitman, Wilde, and hundreds of others as examples of great artists, thinkers, and writers who were homosexual. Rhetorically asking, "Can we 'cure' Nature?" he criticized those who promised "a 'cure' of what is not a disease." He also attacked the "truculent severity" of laws against same-sex sex and denounced the "ignorant intolerance" and "social persecution" that made life difficult for Uranians. Prime-Stevenson was pessimistic about the prospects for reform in Great Britain and the United States, where he thought it likely that the homosexual would "remain a social and a legal victim for an indefinite time to come." At the same time, he was hopeful that "the world will progress slowly to wider sexual insights," he had positive things to say about the reforms supported by various European scientific experts, and he was optimistic about German movements that championed the "human and natural rights of the homosexual."[11]

Ralph Werther's works also offered affirmative defenses of gender inversion and homosexuality. According to Werther, as a teenager in the 1890s he had "arrived at the conviction that while the voice of the world would cry 'Shame!'" he was "acting according to the dictates of reason and conscience." Denouncing the "bitter persecution" of nature's "innocent stepchildren," who deserved "pity rather than scorn," he argued that "we androgynes who for two thousand years have been despised, hunted down, and crushed ... have no reason to be ashamed of our heritage." Even more affirmatively, he declared, "The emergence of androgynism is a sign of national health. ... The androgyne, being a combination of man and woman in a single individual, has a wider view of life than the full-fledged man or woman. ... Such duality is the reason artistic genius crops up far more frequently among androgynes."[12]

Werther's autobiography contains the earliest mention of a U.S. group organized to challenge the persecution of gender and sexual "deviants." So far, no evidence has come to light that would corroborate Werther's account, but such groups first formed in European countries in the late nineteenth century, so it is possible that something similar occurred in the United States. Even if the group did not exist in reality, Werther's narrative suggests that it had become possible to imagine something along these lines. According to Werther, in the 1890s an "androgyne" in New York's Paresis Hall told him that "a score of us have formed a little club, the Cercle Hermaphroditos," which was established "to unite for defense against the world's bitter persecution of bisexuals." Werther reported that the androgyne stated, "We care to admit only extreme types—such as like to doll themselves up in feminine finery. We sympathize with, but do not care to be intimate with, the mild types, some of whom you see here to-night even wearing a disgusting beard!" While the Cercle thus restricted which types of men could join, Werther's vision of the deviants oppressed by society included masculine women. Referring at one point to the female counterparts of androgynes, Werther noted that "gynanders, as well as androgynes, are doomed to suffer murder at the hands of hare-brained prudes." He also wrote, "A continuous string of both men-women and women-men are being struck down in New York for no other reason than loathing for those born bisexual." Werther claimed that the Cercle rented a room in Paresis Hall and that he participated in its conversations. One member reportedly declared, "Men-women are victims of birth and … their so-called 'depravity' brings not the least harm to any one." Another stated, "I can hardly bring myself to be ashamed of the handiwork of God. A bisexual has no more reason than a full-fledged man or woman to be ashamed of his God-given sexuality." Some participants used the examples of Socrates, Plato, and Michelangelo to challenge the notion that "bisexuals" were "depraved" and to argue against "bigotry and bias." If the Cercle existed, it stands as an important precursor of both gay/lesbian and trans activism.[13]

Perhaps the most far-reaching campaign to change the treatment of same-sex sex in the United States in the late nineteenth and early twentieth centuries was initiated by anarchists. This period's strong anarchist movement promoted the liberty of the individual, freedom from domination, and liberation from religion, capitalism, and the state. Some anarchists pursued these goals by challenging conventional gender and sexual values, campaigning against sexual censorship, and promoting access to birth control. They also criticized marriage, which they viewed as a coercive institution that oppressed women, repressed sex, and served the interests of property, religion, and the state. Instead, they advocated "free love," insisting that individuals should be free to express themselves sexually without the restrictions imposed by marriage. As they promoted their ideas, some anarchists initiated a sustained public discussion of homosexuality. Among the best known to do so were Benjamin Tucker, John William Lloyd, Ben Reitman, Alexander Berkman, and Emma Goldman. None of these figures called themselves homosexual, but most had close, intimate, and possibly erotic same-sex relationships that informed their arguments about sexual politics.

U.S. anarchists were inspired to speak out about homosexuality in the aftermath of the trials of writer Oscar Wilde in Great Britain in the 1890s. Wilde was convicted of committing gross indecencies with men and sentenced to a two-year prison term. Viewing him as a fellow libertarian with anarchist sympathies, as a martyr to the causes of free speech and sexual liberation, and as a victim of state repression, anarchists rallied to Wilde's defense. Goldman later recalled that, in public lectures and private conversations, she "pleaded his case against the miserable hypocrites who had sent him to his doom." She later wrote, "As an anarchist, my place has always been on the side of the persecuted. The entire persecution and sentencing of Wilde struck me as an act of cruel injustice and repulsive hypocrisy." As she further developed her thoughts about Wilde, she began to make more general and explicit comments about the politics of homosexuality. At a Chicago lecture in the late 1890s, she declared, "The sex organs ... are the property of the individual possessing them, and that individual and no other must be the sole authority and judge over his or her acts." At another Chicago lecture in 1901, she defended "any act entered into by two individuals voluntarily" and insisted that "what is usually hastily condemned as vice by thoughtless individuals, such as homosexuality, masturbation, etc., should be considered from a scientific standpoint, and not in a moralizing way."[14]

In denouncing the treatment of same-sex sex, anarchists often adopted a minoritarian perspective and in so doing criticized the persecution of "homosexuals." But anarchists also adopted a universalizing perspective in suggesting that all women and men should work against the repression of their same-sex desires. In 1902, for example, John William Lloyd wrote that "friendship between those of the same sex is a spontaneous and inborn passion—in every way equal in intensity and tragedy to that between the sexes—to a multitude of human beings." This hinted at a minoritarian formulation, but Lloyd also noted that "there is no reason why every kind of love that has ever been known to man should not be accepted, purified, understood, embraced, and wisely made to yield its joy and service to the life of every one of us." Along similar lines, he declared, "Our Hero must be that man or woman who can love the most men and women in the most beautiful, large, tender, and fearless way."[15]

Goldman probably did her most sustained public speaking about homosexuality during her lecture tours of 1915 and 1916, when she addressed "the problem most tabooed in polite society—homosexuality." She later recalled that some of her comrades "condemned" her because she "had taken up the cause of the Homo Sexuals and Lesbians as a persecuted faction in the human family." This only made her "more determined to plead for every victim, be it one of social wrong or of moral prejudice." Goldman also noted that many homosexuals spoke to her after her lectures and that their stories strengthened her conviction that "anarchism was not a mere theory for a distant future; it was a living influence to free us from inhibitions, internal no less than external, and from the destructive barriers that separate man from man." One woman who attended a lecture reported, "Every person who came to the lecture possessing contempt and disgust for homo-sexualists ... went away with a broad and sympathetic understanding of the question and a conviction that in matters of personal life, freedom should reign."[16]

Led by Goldman, anarchists spoke forcefully against the persecution of homosexuals and the mistreatment of same-sex sex, but they also criticized the communities they defended. In the 1920s, Goldman observed, "Any prejudice or antipathy toward homosexuals is totally foreign to me. On the contrary! Among my male and female friends, there are a few who are of either a completely Uranian or a bisexual disposition. I have found these individuals far above average in terms of intelligence, ability, sensitivity, and personal charm." At the same time, she criticized "the practice of claiming every possible prominent personality as one of their own," noting that "if one were to believe the assurances and claims of many homosexuals, one would be forced to the conclusion that no truly great person is or ever was to be found outside the circle of persons of a different sexual type." She also later wrote privately, "Really, the Lesbians are a crazy lot. Their antagonism to the male is almost a disease with them." Meanwhile, Alexander Berkman's 1912 memoir affirmed the value of the consensual homoerotic relationships he witnessed and formed while in prison, but also criticized the exploitative and hierarchical relationships he observed. For Berkman, abusive homosexual relationships could exemplify the oppression that was encouraged by repressive state institutions, but consensual ones had much to teach society about resistance to persecution and the capacity of human beings to form loving relationships.[17]

1920s and 1930s

By the 1920s and 1930s, many of the conditions that would later make it possible to create a U.S. gay and lesbian movement were in place. There were gay and lesbian communities in every large metropolis and in many smaller cities and towns. There were popular gay and lesbian vacation destinations such as Fire Island in New York and Provincetown in Massachusetts. More people who engaged in same-sex sex thought of themselves as members of a persecuted sexual minority; many believed that no one should be punished for engaging in activities that did not harm others. In the 1920s, there was a sexual revolution that loosened constraints on various forms of erotic expression. In the 1930s, there was a remarkable upsurge in political protest in the context of the Great Depression. Various European countries had gay and lesbian movements in this period. The United States, however, did not. Henry Gerber and the Chicago-based Society for Human Rights almost succeeded in establishing one in the 1920s; their failure helps reveal why it was so difficult to organize a U.S. gay and lesbian movement in this era. It is typically easier to account for why something happened in the past than to explain why it did not, but before turning to the emergence of the gay and lesbian movement after World War Two, it might be helpful to consider why a movement did not develop before the war.

Several cultural developments in the 1920s and 1930s could have inspired the creation of a gay and lesbian movement. In the context of the Roaring Twenties, the Jazz Age, and the Harlem Renaissance, a new generation of modernists challenged the authority of traditional values and institutions, with the results on display in music, theater, literature, film, visual arts, and other cultural fields. Widespread resistance to Prohibition, which banned the sale, manufacture, and transport of alcohol from 1920 to 1933, encouraged not only a large underground leisure economy but also more general disregard for the law. Many young people embraced the new and avant garde, rejecting the conservative moral and religious practices of their parents. During the sexual revolution, Victorian values were challenged, sex was celebrated as an icon of freedom, and women asserted themselves as sexual agents. The onset of the Great Depression in 1929 disrupted many of these developments, but during the New Deal era in the 1930s, there were new government initiatives to help the disadvantaged and new movements that challenged social inequities. If a gay and lesbian movement had developed in the United States in the 1920s and 1930s, we would likely point to these developments as contributing factors.

We would also point to developments that occurred in alternative sexual cultures. Local gay and lesbian communities formed, grew, and diversified across the United States. In bars, clubs, restaurants, bathhouses, and other sites, people who were interested in same-sex sex, love, and intimacy developed support networks, social bonds, and cultures of resistance. The entertainment world celebrated the performances of cross-dressers, fairies, impersonators, and pansies. Representations of same-sex sex, homoerotic relationships, and sexual dissidents appeared in a large number of novels, short stories, poems, plays, and films. Many presented same-sex sexualities in negative ways, but even these could promote collective sensibilities and politicized identities. Some, including literary works by Djuna Barnes, Charles Henri Ford and Parker Tyler, Blair Niles, and Gertrude Stein, presented more affirmative portrayals. In the Harlem Renaissance, African American artists such as Gladys Bentley, Countee Cullen, Langston Hughes, Nella Larsen, Claude McKay, Richard Bruce Nugent, and Wallace Thurman offered compelling depictions of homosexuality in literature, music, and the visual and performing arts. As impressive as these developments were, they were not inspired by an organized, collective, and sustained movement to reform the treatment of same-sex sex and they did not lead to the formation of one before or during World War Two.

One reason for this was the overall political context of the 1920s and 1930s. For all of its cultural ferment, the 1920s was a politically conservative decade. National elections led to conservative dominance in all three branches of the federal government through much of the decade; this was replicated in many states. Prohibition was the law of the land. The federal government adopted new immigration restrictions based on race, ethnicity, and nationality. A revived Ku Klux Klan was just one element of a new politics of racism. The women's movement struggled to define a new agenda after the achievement of women's suffrage. After World War

One, the United States reversed many of the progressive social and economic reforms that had been adopted before and during the war. Because many socialists and anarchists had opposed U.S. participation in World War One and because the Russian communist revolution was perceived as a major international threat, the U.S. government embarked on a Red Scare that crushed the U.S. left. While U.S. socialism and communism revived in the 1930s, they were less sexually radical than anarchism was, and anarchism did not re-emerge as a powerful movement in this period. To take just two examples, anarchists Emma Goldman and Alexander Berkman were imprisoned for advocating resistance to conscription during World War One and were deported from the United States in the 1920s, removing two of the country's most powerful defenders of homosexuality.

Along similar lines, for all the sexual ferment that occurred in this period, new waves of sexual repression advanced in the 1920s and 1930s. With notable exceptions in some locations and periods, the policing of same-sex sex increased, with escalating numbers arrested, convicted, and imprisoned for crimes against nature, cross-dressing, disorderly conduct, indecency, lewdness, loitering, sodomy, solicitation, vagrancy, and other sexual offenses. Based on what we know about several jurisdictions, thousands and perhaps tens of thousands were directly affected each year. In some contexts, increased repression reflected the strategic calculations of politicians who reaped electoral benefits from campaigning against sexual deviance. Harsh new laws targeted sexual degenerates and psychopaths; these were often used for people who engaged in consensual same-sex sex. Collaborative arrangements between legal and medical authorities meant that more gender and sexual "deviants" were punished or "treated" with involuntary sterilization, castration, lobotomy, or aversion therapy. Denunciations of same-sex sex by religious leaders and attacks in the popular press had powerful effects as well.

In the context of pervasive hostility to same-sex sex, the police felt empowered to harass, abuse, and deprive basic protections to gays, lesbians, and others who engaged in same-sex sex. Public officials also targeted social spaces where such people gathered, resulting in increased raids on and closures of bars, clubs, drag balls, and other venues. After Prohibition was repealed, liquor control policies and practices discriminated against businesses that served homosexuals. These establishments often were raided by police, had their liquor licenses revoked, and were forced to close. New Deal relief programs that targeted young men were terminated when allegations of sexual degeneracy surfaced. Civic organizations convinced local and state authorities to censor representations of gender and sexual deviance in popular culture. They also persuaded the entertainment industry to practice sexual self-censorship.

As if this were not enough, the gay and lesbian community was divided along lines of age, class, gender, race, region, religion, sex, and other factors, which made it more difficult to organize politically as a united group. Many younger, wealthier, and more urban gays and lesbians looked down on their older, poorer, and more rural counterparts. White racism made multiracial alliances less likely, while the tendency of people of color to prioritize race and class politics made it more difficult to mobilize on the basis of sexual oppression. Male sexism, sex differences, and the prominent role of lesbians in the women's movement meant that many gays and lesbians did not see themselves as members of a united community. Meanwhile, many were hostile to or embarrassed by feminine men and masculine women, while others were critical of those who embraced dominant gender values. For a strong gay and lesbian movement to develop, some of these divisions would have to be addressed.

None of this means that it would have been impossible for a U.S. gay and lesbian movement to form in the 1920s and 1930s, but it suggests the obstacles that stood in the way. When individuals could be arrested, convicted, and imprisoned for same-sex flirting, dating, dancing, or romancing or for expressing same-sex affection in public or private, it was difficult to mobilize a movement for same-sex sex reform. When homosexuality was commonly regarded as a mental illness and was diagnosed as symptomatic of neuroses or psychoses, there were risks in defending homosexuality in public. When people could be persecuted for speaking or writing about homosexuality or for possessing, selling, or distributing materials that addressed same-sex sex, the challenges for political organizing were substantial. When basic rights of assembly, expression, liberty, and equality did not apply for gender and sexual deviants, few were willing to defend homosexuality in public.

All of this makes the reform efforts undertaken in the 1920s and 1930s all the more impressive. One set of projects followed up on the work of the late nineteenth and early twentieth-century medical reformers. As was the case in the earlier period, U.S. medical science tended to pathologize homosexuality and recommend treatment, but in some instances doctors used the disease model to argue for compassion and against punishment. Perhaps the most notable effort along these lines was the work of the Committee for the Study of Sex Variants. Founded in 1935 by birth control advocate Robert Latou Dickinson and initially composed of nineteen prominent medical and scientific specialists, the Committee was created after gay and lesbian researchers "Jan Gay" and Thomas Painter contacted Dickinson in an effort to secure medical sponsorship for their work. The Committee's publications (principally a two-volume 1941 monograph titled *Sex Variants*) were attributed primarily to scientific experts such as psychiatrist George Henry who did not identify as homosexual, but they relied heavily on the work of "Gay," Painter, and another gay researcher, Alfred Gross. While the general perspective of the Committee's publications treated homosexuality as pathological, they promoted tolerance. "Gay," Painter, and Gross tried unsuccessfully to convince the Committee to adopt more homosexually affirmative positions, but the *Sex Variants* volumes reproduced the first-person accounts of a large and diverse group of individuals. Many presented narratives of loneliness and despair, but some defended their homosexual activities and interests.[18]

A second set of reform efforts emerged in the context of leftist, labor, and libertarian movements. In the 1920s and 1930s, some anarchists continued to defend homosexuals and homosexuality, but in the wake of strong state repression during and after World War One, anarchism struggled to regain the influence it had enjoyed before the war. Anarchism remained important as a source of ideas about homosexuality in the interwar period, but its efforts to mobilize a movement in support of sexual freedom waned. The pre-World War One labor movement did not have anarchism's record of support for sexual liberty and equality, but in the 1930s at least one union began to defend homosexuals and homosexuality. The Marine Cooks and Stewards Union, which represented waiters, cooks, laundry workers, and other service workers on Pacific Ocean ships, had a large percentage of gay members. The union, which became racially diverse and leftist in the 1930s, did not address homosexuality in its formal policies, but it defended men who experienced antigay harassment, likened antihomosexual bias to racism and anticommunism, and elected gay men to leadership positions.

Libertarians became more interested in the politics of sexuality in the 1920s and 1930s, especially when federal, state, and local authorities engaged in sexual censorship. After its founding in 1920, the American Civil Liberties Union (ACLU) emerged as a powerful defender of constitutional rights and freedoms; several decades later the ACLU became the gay and lesbian movement's most important ally. In the 1920s and 1930s, the ACLU did not play as prominent a role in defending sexual rights, but individuals affiliated with the ACLU challenged antihomosexual censorship in the courts. Perhaps the best example of this is the role played by ACLU co-founder Morris Ernst in defending the American publishers of *The Well of Loneliness*, a lesbian-themed novel by British author Radclyffe Hall. In 1928, after printing and selling an edition of *The Well*, publishers Pascal Covici and Donald Friede were charged with violating New York's obscenity law. For legal assistance, they turned to Ernst, who argued successfully that *The Well* did not meet the legal test of obscenity because it was not likely to corrupt its readers. While Ernst downplayed the sexual character of the book and emphasized that the main character was depicted as a tragic object of pity, he celebrated the novel for promoting "compassion" and "tolerance." This was an important legal victory and for the next several decades *The Well* was probably the most widely read novel about lesbianism in the United States. Meanwhile, in the 1930s, the ACLU helped establish the National Council on Freedom from Censorship, which challenged the suppression of works classified as obscene.[19]

A third set of reform activities, which overlapped with the first two, originated more directly in gay and lesbian subcultures. Commercial establishments that were frequented by large numbers of gay men and lesbians, including bars, clubs, restaurants, and theaters, had a long history of resisting repression, but they rarely did so in ways that publicly and openly affirmed their homosexual character or defended the rights of homosexuals to assemble. This began to change in the 1920s and 1930s, and a good example of the transition occurred in 1939–40, when Gloria's, a popular gay bar in New York, had its license revoked by the State Liquor Authority (SLA), which claimed that the bar permitted "homosexuals, degenerates and undesirable people to congregate on the premises." Challenging the SLA's actions in court, Gloria's integrated an older strategy of resistance, which consisted of denying that the authorities had proven that homosexuals were served at the bar, with a newer and bolder strategy, which asserted that as long as homosexuals were neither diseased nor disorderly, there was no legal basis for the actions of the authorities since "there is no rule or regulation ... which provides that a sex variant may not be served." The court ruled against Gloria's, but the types of argument made by the bar, some of which were based on the work of the Committee for the Study of Sex Variants, proved more persuasive in the post-World War Two era.[20]

The United States came close to developing a gay and lesbian movement in 1924–25, when postal worker Henry Gerber took the lead in forming the Society for Human Rights in Chicago. Born in Germany in the 1890s, Gerber had immigrated to the United States with his family in 1913 and was briefly institutionalized in a psychiatric hospital a few years later. In 1919–20, he enlisted in the U.S. military, and over the next few years, during the U.S. occupation of Germany, he learned about that country's gay movement. In two accounts published in homophile magazines in 1953 and 1962, Gerber explained that in the early 1920s he subscribed to German homophile magazines and visited Berlin, which had an active gay scene. He later recalled, "I had always bitterly felt the injustice with which my own American society accused the homosexual of 'immoral acts.' I hated this society which allowed the majority, frequently corrupt itself, to persecute those who deviated from the established norms in sexual matters." Inspired by the German gay movement, Gerber resolved to take action when he returned to the United States. Friends advised him against "doing anything so rash and futile," but Gerber had grandiose visions of "freeing the homosexual."[21]

According to the group's 1924 state charter, which named Reverend John Graves as its president, Gerber as its secretary, and five other men as officers and trustees, the Society aimed "to promote and to protect the interests of people who by reasons of mental and physical abnormalities are abused and hindered in the legal pursuit of happiness which is guaranteed them by the Declaration of Independence, and to combat the public prejudices against them by dissemination of facts according to modern science." Gerber later noted that the goal was "to ameliorate the plight of homosexuals" and that the organization's name was derived from a similarly named homophile group in Germany. Significantly, the charter used language suggesting that homosexuality was a type of mental and physical disability.[22]

Gerber's first challenge was to recruit members, which he claimed was difficult given that the "average homosexual" was "ignorant," "fearful," "depraved," or "blasé." Moreover, "many homosexuals" told him that "their search for forbidden fruit was the real spice of life," which led them to reject his group's aims. "Resistance from our own people" was a major obstacle, he later explained, though from another perspective it was Gerber who was resisting the popular conception of homosexuality as an act rather than an identity. Nevertheless, the Society developed a four-part plan, aiming to (1) recruit members, (2) sponsor a lecture series to highlight "the attitude of society," (3) create a publication titled *Friendship and Freedom* to "keep the homophile world in touch with the progress of our efforts," and (4) "win the confidence and assistance of legal authorities and legislators," who would be "educated on the futility and folly of long prison terms for those committing homosexual acts." In a sign of its cautious approach, the Society's plan emphasized that the group would discourage "the seduction of adolescents," refrain from "advocating sexual acts," and promote "self-discipline."[23]

According to Gerber, he wrote to many "prominent persons soliciting their support," but most seemed to misunderstand the purpose. He hoped to gain support from "noted medical authorities," but they "refused to endanger their reputations." Because the Society's other members were "illiterate and penniless," he wrote and funded the two issues of *Friendship and Freedom* that were published. As for the Society's other officers, Gerber indicated that Graves was an African American preacher who promoted "brotherly love to small groups of Negroes," another was a "laundry queen," and another was a railroad worker. Gerber later wrote that "movements always start small and only by organizing first and correcting mistakes later could we expect to go on at all." He also noted that the members agreed that the organization would be "purely homophile" and would "exclude the much larger circle of bisexuals for the time being," though they later learned that their vice president was "that type."[24]

In 1925, several months after the Society was created, Gerber was visited at the room he rented by a newspaper reporter and a police detective, who questioned him about his sexual activities. The policeman seized all of his materials related to the Society as well as his diaries. Gerber was jailed overnight. When he was taken to court the next day, he found out that the Society's other officers had also been detained. He soon learned that the police had taken them into custody after a Chicago newspaper published a front-page story headlined "Strange Sex Cult Exposed." The article claimed that the Society's vice president had performed "strange sex acts" with other men in front of his wife and children and that the wife had alerted a social worker, who contacted the police. When the police raided the vice president's home, they reportedly found a pamphlet that "urged men to leave their wives and children." In court, the detective "triumphantly produced a powder puff" that he claimed to have found in Gerber's room, though Gerber insisted that he never used "rouge or powder." Gerber also recalled that the social worker read a passage from his diary that suggested, out of context, that he loved another man. After the judge indicated that he believed the men had violated a federal law against sending obscene materials through the mails, presumably on the basis of their distribution of *Friendship and Freedom*, they were taken back to jail. There they managed to contact a "shyster" lawyer, who argued for their immediate release when they returned to court several days later. This time, postal inspectors were present, and they indicated that federal authorities were looking into "the obscenity angle." The judge reluctantly agreed to release the men on bail until the trial resumed the following week. Gerber soon learned that the Post Office had suspended him from his job.[25]

When the trial resumed, a new judge, believed by Gerber to be "queer," criticized the local authorities and said that it was an "outrage" to arrest people without a warrant. While the Society's vice president pleaded guilty to disorderly conduct and received a fine, the charges against the others were dismissed and the judge ordered the police to return Gerber's materials. Gerber later noted that while the police returned his typewriter, he never saw his diaries again. His legal fees had cost him $800. He later recounted, "We were up against a solid wall of ignorance, hypocrisy, meanness and corruption. The wall had won. The parting jibe of the detective had been, 'What was the idea of the Society for Human Rights anyway? Was it to give you birds the legal right to rape every boy on the street?'" A few weeks after the trial was over, Gerber was dismissed from his job for "conduct unbecoming a postal worker." He later explained, "That definitely meant the end of the Society for Human Rights."[26]

This episode did not mark the end of Gerber's efforts to defend homosexuality. After moving to New York City, he reenlisted in the U.S. Army, in which he served from 1925 to the 1940s. In the late 1920s and early 1930s, he contributed several articles to German gay periodicals. In 1932, the U.S. journal *Modern Thinker* published an essay about homosexuality by Gerber, this time using a pseudonym. Gerber praised a recent article that called for the decriminalization of homosexuality but criticized it for not addressing the persecution of homosexuals by psychoanalysts. Two years later, he began publishing a wide-ranging set of articles about homosexuality, sexual freedom, and sexual repression in *Chanticleer*, a literary periodical that he edited. His work on homosexuality also appeared in *American Mercury* and other periodicals. In the 1930s, he published a newsletter that promoted pen-pal relationships (straight and gay). In the final issue, published in 1939, Gerber described himself as a believer in "French sex morality," meaning that "it's not the state's business to interfere in the sexual enjoyment of adults so long as rights of others are not violated."[27]

In the early 1940s, when a friend suggested that there was a need to create an organization to challenge antihomosexual persecution, Gerber warned that most homosexuals were too fearful to get involved and many were interested only in sex. He also indicated that for a movement like this to succeed it would need substantial amounts of money, as well as "medical authorities of note and lawyers to defend us." Several years later, Gerber wrote to his friend with detailed plans for an organization to challenge "sex superstition" and "fascism in sex," though his main purpose was to "protect homosexuals against persecution." Having noted that "homosexuals already have the most successful underground movement," which effectively nullified laws against sodomy, Gerber now proposed the creation of a public movement whose philosophy would emphasize that "it is nobody's business what two adults (at the age of 16) decide to do to enjoy themselves sexually, as long as they act in mutual agreement, without violating the rights of others." Gerber's plans called for alliances with others who valued "sex liberty," regardless of whether they were homosexual. While nothing came of these plans, in the 1950s and 1960s Gerber contributed to homophile periodicals and supported the gay and lesbian movement financially. Harry Hay, who is credited with founding the homophile movement in the 1950s, learned about the Society for Human Rights in the 1920s; the earlier group may have served as one of his inspirations.[28]

A recent biographical sketch describes Gerber as "dour" and "misogynist" and his writings contain anti-Semitic references. Having been disappointed by his early efforts, Gerber also became an elitist who advocated a "top down" movement in which the "better sort of homosexuals" would convince the authorities to support reform. None of this makes him an attractive figure for those who envision the gay and lesbian movement as democratic, egalitarian, and inclusive. Nevertheless, Gerber was an important visionary and his creation of the Society for Human Rights was a notable achievement that prefigured the emergence of the gay and lesbian movement after World War Two. As Gerber wrote in an anonymous letter he sent to *Time* magazine in 1944, he was a "prophet of things to come," and perhaps this is true in positive and negative ways. As he also noted in a private letter in 1946, "I think the best thing is to let the coming generations fight for the things we could not accomplish."[29]

2

HOMOPHILE ACTIVISM, 1940–69

Influenced by major historical developments in the 1940s, the U.S. homophile movement began in 1950–51. For the next two decades, it championed gay and lesbian rights in an era of dramatic social, cultural, and political change. Most people who engaged in same-sex sex in this period did not think of themselves as gay or lesbian and most gays and lesbians did not become activists, but thousands participated in homophile political projects. Inspired by other national and transnational struggles, including the civil rights and women's movements, gay and lesbian activists used multiple tactics and strategies to achieve their goals. Movement participants had a wide range of political orientations; there were Marxist leftists and conservative libertarians, feminists and misogynists, proponents and opponents of gender transgression, and supporters and critics of sexual radicalism. Most were gay, lesbian, or bisexual, but some were straight. The movement also changed over time, with distinguishable periods of activism in 1950–53, when the dominant orientation was leftist, 1953–61, when it was predominantly liberal, and 1961–69, when gay and lesbian activism began to diversify and radicalize. While the movement remained small in comparison to other major movements and did not achieve the mass mobilization that occurred after the Stonewall riots of 1969, homophile activism in the 1950s and 1960s had significant achievements and laid the foundation for the movement's future successes and failures.

World War Two and the 1940s

The founding of the U.S. gay and lesbian movement in the 1950s was preceded by a decade of major developments. The U.S. decision to enter World War Two after the 1941 Japanese attack on Hawaii led to unprecedented national mobilization. From 1941 through 1945, millions of U.S. Americans left their homes, families, friends, and communities for military service overseas, employment opportunities on the home front, or involuntary incarceration in internment camps. This disrupted the structures of society, placed many people in single-sex and alternative sexual contexts, and exposed them to diverse social patterns and cultural values. U.S. Americans also were affected by patriotic wartime rhetoric that presented their country as the world's leading defender of democracy and freedom, despite persistent evidence of inequality. For many, the Holocaust and the treatment of ethnic, national, racial, and religious minorities by the country's wartime enemies prompted questions about the treatment of minorities, the status of women, and the denial of human rights in the United States. Among the people whose lives were transformed were many who came out as gay or lesbian before, during, or after the war and many who had same-sex sex but never thought of themselves as gay or lesbian. Some of these people became homophile activists in the post-World War Two era.

The politicization of people who engaged in same-sex sex occurred in part because of the unjust policies and practices they experienced and witnessed in the context and aftermath of the war. The U.S. military had long punished soldiers and sailors for having same-sex sex, but during World War Two the armed forces classified some people as homosexuals and excluded or discharged them on that basis. The new women's branches, anxious to protect their reputations, had distinct concerns when evidence of homosexuality came to light. The military's new anti-homosexual psychiatric screening methods were largely ineffective (they led to approximately 5000 rejections), but they left thousands who wanted to serve in the armed forces unable to do so and deprived such people of a major way in which U.S. Americans affirmed their social value. In the military, homosexuality was grounds for imprisonment and discharge, though when staffing needs were great some same-sex sex was defined as situational and some repressive policies were relaxed. The roughly 9000 people discharged based on homosexuality faced not only the dishonor associated with sexual transgression, gender deviance, and failure to provide military service, but also lost eligibility for the educational, employment, financial, health, housing, and other benefits otherwise available to veterans. The vast majority of people who engaged in same-sex sex escaped detection, but many came to believe that there was something fundamentally wrong with the way the United States handled sexual diversity.

After the war ended in 1945, those who cared about the mistreatment of homosexuality acquired new reasons for concern. As the United States transitioned from fighting a hot war against Germany and Japan to struggling against the Soviet Union and China in the Cold War, the country mobilized against perceived threats to domestic unity and strength. The dynamics of decolonization around the world also challenged the United States, which had interests and investments in promoting U.S. global supremacy. In these contexts, a "red scare" targeted real and imagined communists, while a "lavender scare" focused on real and imagined homosexuals. Beginning in 1947, the State Department's employee security system targeted homosexuals, who were regarded as risks because of their "weak" characters and their vulnerability to blackmail. From 1947 through 1950, more than 1700 federal government job applicants were denied employment based on allegations related to homosexuality. By the end of 1950, more than 400 federal employees had resigned or been dismissed based on similar claims. In the same period, the U.S. military discharged approximately 1000 people per year based on allegations about homosexuality; military women in particular confronted increased surveillance and repression.

Many of these developments went unnoticed by the public, but in February 1950, a State Department official testified before Congress that ninety-one department employees under investigation for homosexuality and sexual perversion had been forced to resign. This led to months of conservative attacks on the administration of President Harry Truman, which was accused of not taking seriously the threat posed by sexual subversion. In June, the Senate authorized an investigation into the federal government's employment of homosexuals. Even before the results were released in December, federal government monthly dismissals based on homosexuality increased from approximately five to sixty. Government policies encouraged the hostility to homosexuality that had long existed in the United States, with ramifications that included but extended beyond the workplace. Over the course of the 1950s, the repressive campaigns escalated, but as gay men and lesbians experienced and learned about these developments, some began to think that political repression demanded political responses.

Changes in sexual consciousness were also stimulated by developments in popular culture and social science. New works of fiction by John Horne Burns, Truman Capote, Charles Jackson, Carson McCullers, Thomas Hal Phillips, Jo Sinclair, Tereska Torres, Gore Vidal, and others questioned social hostility to same-sex sexuality; some even presented it as attractive and desirable. Physique photography magazines and physical culture businesses, including Bob Mizer's Athletic Model Guild, promoted homoerotic visual culture. In 1944, poet Robert Duncan, who had received an undesirable military discharge, published "The Homosexual in Society" in the journal *Politics*. Duncan asked why, in contrast to "Negroes" and Jews, there were no homosexuals willing to challenge their persecution as part of a larger struggle for human freedom. In 1947, *Newsweek*'s "Homosexuals in Uniform" brought greater attention to the military's policies. Two years later, *Cosmopolitan* ran a feature titled "The Unmentionable Minority," the *Saturday Review of Literature* printed a series of letters under the headline "Homosexual Minority," and African American writer James Baldwin criticized the mistreatment of homosexuals in the Moroccan journal *Zero*.

The decade's most influential text addressing same-sex sex was Alfred Kinsey's *Sexual Behavior in the Human Male* (1948), which was followed by *Sexual Behavior in the Human Female* (1953). As the titles suggested, Kinsey emphasized behaviors rather than identities, and he stated repeatedly that homosexuality was best conceptualized in these terms, thus rejecting the idea that homosexuals constituted a minority group. For Kinsey, the notion that homosexuality and heterosexuality were mutually exclusive orientations was at odds with the behavioral realities revealed in the thousands of interviews that he and his associates conducted. In the years to come, Kinsey's work would be misinterpreted as indicating that 10 percent of the population was homosexual; his volumes actually proposed a seven-point scale ranging from exclusive heterosexuality to exclusive homosexuality, with most people's behaviors falling between the extremes. According to Kinsey, 10 percent of white males were predominantly homosexual for at least three years between the ages of sixteen and fifty-five, but a smaller percentage were exclusively homosexual and a larger percentage had significant homosexual experiences. Kinsey used the evidence he found of extensive participation in same-sex sexual activities (37 percent of white men and 13 percent of white women) to argue that homosexuality should not be treated as pathological or criminal. Some used these findings to insist on the need to prevent and contain homosexuality, but for others, the results suggested that there was nothing wrong with engaging in same-sex sex and that sexual discrimination was a matter of prejudice.

Whether they believed that they were members of a sexual minority, that homosexuality was a common behavior, or that both things were true, many people interested in same-sex sex, love, and intimacy migrated to towns and cities with sizable gay and lesbian communities during and after World War Two. Urban neighborhoods with large numbers of gay and lesbian residents increased in number, size, and complexity, as did gay and lesbian rural enclaves and vacation destinations. Examples include Boystown in Chicago, Capitol Hill in Seattle, the Castro in San Francisco, Center City in Philadelphia, Dupont Circle in Washington, D.C., Greenwich Village in New York, Montrose in Houston, the South End in Boston, and West Hollywood in Los Angeles. These developments were linked to the growth of gay and lesbian bars, clubs, restaurants, and bathhouses, which were vulnerable to police raids but were also places where sexual communities formed. These businesses often catered to specific class-, race-, and gender-defined groups. Many reproduced the class, race, and gender segregation that was characteristic of other aspects of U.S. society, though others were more integrated. House parties were popular alternatives, especially for women and people of color. In private and public sites across the country, people who enjoyed same-sex sex, love, and intimacy learned to reject the hostile judgments of society, resist their mistreatment, and defend their interests.

They also began to organize. In 1945, a group of New Yorkers founded the Veterans Benevolent Association, which functioned primarily as a support group and social organization for several hundred gay men. In 1946, George Hyde and John Kazantks founded the Eucharistic Catholic Church, which ministered to gays and lesbians in Atlanta and later in other southern locations. Also in 1946, Alfred Gross, one of the gay researchers who had begun collaborating with psychiatrist George Henry in the 1930s, became the executive secretary of the Civil Readjustment Committee of the Quaker Emergency Service, which worked with men arrested for homosexual offenses in New York. Two years later, Gross became the executive secretary of the George W. Henry Foundation, which provided advocacy and counselling services for men who had sex with men. In the late 1940s, Merton Bird and Dorr Legg formed Knights of the Clock, which promoted interracial homosexual fellowship in Los Angeles. In 1947, Edythe Eyde (later known as "Lisa Ben," an anagram of "lesbian") began producing *Vice Versa: America's Gayest Magazine*. The limited-run periodical, published in Los Angeles for about a year, focused primarily on lesbians. One essay by Eyde declared, "Whether the unsympathetic majority approves or not, it looks as though the third sex is here to stay. ... Today, a woman may live independently from man if she so chooses. ... Never before have circumstances and conditions been so suitable for those of lesbian tendencies."[1]

In the late 1940s, some U.S. Americans initiated political campaigns to defend the rights of homosexuals. The U.S. military was a major target. In opposition to the harsh policies that governed the treatment of veterans who received undesirable discharges, which included thousands expelled based on homosexuality, a diverse coalition advocated for change. Among the leading proponents of reform were the *Pittsburgh Courier* (an influential African American newspaper concerned about the large number of African Americans given undesirable discharges), the National Association for the Advancement of Colored People, the Congress of Industrial Organizations (a massive labor federation), the ACLU, the George W. Henry Foundation, several members of the U.S. Congress, and various veterans' organizations. With the assistance of gay and lesbian veterans, the reformers won the support of a House special committee appointed to study the issue. Individual veterans also challenged the deprivation of their rights before discharge review boards; from 1945 to 1947 many were successful. Opposition was fierce, however, and in 1947 the military adopted new policies stipulating that homosexuals were to be discharged and deprived of standard veteran benefits.

A more general plan to mobilize homosexuals emerged in the context of left politics. The plan was developed by Harry Hay, who had emigrated from England to California as a child. By the late 1940s, Hay was a long-time member of the Communist Party, a Marxist arts educator with special expertise in folk music, and a married man with two children. He also was a gay man with extensive same-sex sexual experiences, knowledge of gay subcultures, familiarity with scientific sexology, and personal knowledge (through a lover's lover) of Henry Gerber's ill-fated Society for Human Rights. The Communist Party was critical of homosexuality, regarding it as a form of bourgeois decadence, a distraction from the class struggle, and a justification for dismissal from the party. Hay, however, viewed homosexuality through the prism of the Party's conceptual frameworks for dealing with "national minorities" such as African Americans. He came to believe that homosexuals were a cultural minority with distinct traditions, histories, values, and psychologies. He also concluded that to challenge their oppression, they would have to organize politically. In 1948, Hay proposed to several friends that they form "Bachelors for Wallace," which would mobilize support for Progressive Party presidential candidate Henry Wallace in exchange for a sexual privacy plank in Wallace's platform. Hay did not succeed in recruiting others to support his efforts in 1948, but he continued to develop his ideas. In the 1950s, his plans to organize a new movement came to fruition.

Homophile Politics, 1950–53

In November 1950, Harry Hay began to have success in turning his one-man crusade into a collective and organized movement. At a meeting with four other gay men in his Los Angeles home, Hay presented a proposal to pursue "the heroic objective of liberating one of our largest minorities from the solitary confinement of social persecution and civil insecurity."[2] Within months, they and two other men had founded the Mattachine Society, whose name was based on Hay's ruminations about masked medieval European performers called "mattachines." Of the seven original members, all were white men, two were immigrants, two were veterans, one was Jewish, and most were interested in the arts. Having worked on various labor, antifascist, and civil rights campaigns, they also were experienced activists.

Mattachine's first mission statement, adopted in 1951, emphasized three goals. First, the group aimed to "unify" homosexuals by addressing the isolation that many experienced and promoting a "feeling of 'belonging'" among "our people." This formulation did not assume that homosexuals were already unified, but it was based on a type of identity politics that distinguished between the homosexual minority and the heterosexual majority. Second, Mattachine would strive "to educate." This would be pursued in relation to "interested homosexuals" as well as "the public at large." To challenge the "woefully meager" information about homosexuality that was available, Mattachine would conduct research. Once "ignorance and prejudice" were resisted, it would be possible to promote an "ethical homosexual culture" in which individuals would lead "well-adjusted, wholesome, and socially productive lives." This would "parallel" the "emerging cultures of our fellow-minorities—the Negro, Mexican, and Jewish Peoples." The new ethic would be "disciplined, moral, and socially responsible."

The implied criticism of the existing homosexual culture was elaborated in the description of the third goal, which was "to lead." According to the statement, "It is necessary that the more far-seeing and socially conscious homosexuals provide leadership to the whole mass of social deviants." After promoting unity and education, Mattachine would "push forward into the realm of political action to erase from our law books the discriminatory and oppressive legislation presently directed against the homosexual minority." The "enlightened leadership" would provide "an example for homosexuals to follow" and a "dignified standard upon which the rest of society can base a more intelligent and accurate picture of the nature of homosexuality." Appropriating a diverse set of conceptual tools and political strategies that had been used in various class- and race-based movements in the United States,

Mattachine oriented itself in two directions: toward a hostile society and toward homosexuals themselves.[3]

Mattachine's ideas were influenced by the political backgrounds of its founders. Most of the original members were communists or fellow travellers, which in some respects is surprising given the sexual politics of the U.S. Communist Party. Led by Hay, however, the founders made use of four elements of communist theory and practice. First, they appropriated Marxist concepts to define homosexuals as an oppressed cultural minority. One founder later explained that they used the term "minority" in "the sociological sense" and based this usage on the "language, feelings, thinking, and experiences" that homosexuals "share in common."[4] This was not necessarily a form of biological essentialism, but it assumed that people who engaged in same-sex sex had more in common than they did. It did not envision a movement to liberate everyone's same-sex desires. Second, the founders adapted Marxist ideas about the false consciousness of the working class to challenge what they viewed as the false consciousness of homosexuals. In part, they were targeting those who had internalized antihomosexual attitudes, but they also were criticizing those who did not think of themselves as homosexuals or did not think that homosexuals were a persecuted minority group. Third, they emphasized the need for homosexuals to take pride in their sexual character, celebrate their achievements, and organize on their own behalf. Fourth, they borrowed communist organizing tactics to develop a mobilization plan based on small and secretive cells that would take direction from a centralized leadership. The founders believed that secrecy and anonymity were necessary given the legitimate fears of exposure felt by many potential recruits.

The founders of Mattachine were not the only U.S. leftists thinking about the politics of homosexuality in this period. In 1952, *Young Socialist*, a Socialist Party youth group periodical, published an essay by H. L. Small titled "Socialism and Sex." Small argued that "the freedom of the legally of-age adult of both sexes to have sexual relations with whomever he or she wishes of the same or opposite sex" was "an important libertarian principle" and should be adopted by the Socialist Party. This would be a positive step for "the individual 'deviant'" and show potential party recruits "the type of freedom that can be maintained in a free American socialist society."[5] Significantly, Small's essay considered homosexuality within a larger politics of sexual freedom and not within a minority rights framework. Around this time, the party's youth organization instructed Vern Davidson, its homosexually active national chair, to propose a sexual rights plank at the party's 1952 convention. Although the platform committee offered to consider the idea if the youth group developed the proposal, no formal submission was made.

There were other important influences on the early U.S. homophile movement beyond Marxism, communism, and socialism. Transnational struggles against fascism, international human rights campaigns, and anticolonial movements around the world provided useful frameworks, as did the work of sex reformers in other countries, including the members of the International Congress for Sexual Equality, founded in Europe in 1951. At the same time, the U.S. movement was distinctly American and homophile activists frequently deployed U.S. discourses of freedom, liberty, democracy, and equality. From movements of African Americans, Asian Americans, Latinos, Native Americans, and Jews, homophile activists learned about strategies and tactics, alliances and coalitions, and discourses of minority and civil rights. Influenced by anarchism and libertarianism, the movement emphasized privacy rights and civil liberties. Scientific sexology also shaped homophile activism. In particular, Kinsey's work provided the basis for the movement's claim to represent 10 percent of the population, even as some activists used his work to argue that homosexuality was more commonly practiced. From anthropological, historical, and sociological studies of alternative gender and sexual traditions around the world, homophiles learned about the variability of sexual values and practices, the static and changing nature of sexual arrangements, and the conceptual frameworks that sustained and challenged sexual hierarchies.

Mattachine's organizing efforts were supported by the publication in 1951 of Donald Webster Cory's *The Homosexual in America*. Cory was the pseudonym of sociologist Edward Sagarin, who later became involved in the homophile movement, and his book described homosexuals as a persecuted minority group: "Our minority status is similar, in a variety of respects, to that of national, religious and other ethnic groups: in the denial of civil liberties; in the legal, extra-legal, and quasi-legal discrimination; in the assignment of an inferior social position; in the exclusion from the mainstreams of life and culture; in the development of a special language and literature and a set of moral tenets within our group." According to Cory, "Until we are willing to speak out openly and frankly in defense of our activities, and to identify ourselves with the millions pursuing these activities, we are unlikely to find the attitudes of the world undergoing any significant change." Cory's book endorsed the notion that homosexuals were a minority group, but also embraced a more general vision of sexual freedom, which he described as "the right of adults to enter into any voluntary sexual arrangement with each other without fear of reprisal by society." For Cory, homosexuals had "historic missions to perform" in promoting freedom of expression, sexual liberalization, and democratic rights for all, and he encouraged his readers—homosexual and heterosexual—to support sex reform.[6]

Mattachine activists were also inspired by successful forms of resistance that originated elsewhere in U.S. gay and lesbian culture. For example, in 1951, Sol Stoumen, the owner of San Francisco's Black Cat bar, won a state supreme court ruling holding that the state could not revoke the bar's license simply because the bar had homosexual clientele; evidence of illegal or immoral conduct was required. In 1952, the D.C. Circuit Court overturned the conviction of Edward Kelly because the evidence that he had solicited sex from an undercover police officer was uncorroborated. These and other developments helped convince homophile activists that legal reform was possible and that court-based strategies had great promise.

Mattachine's organizing efforts were aided and constrained by the escalation of the Lavender Scare in the early 1950s. In this period, military discharges based on homosexuality doubled to 2000 per year. Federal government dismissals also increased; by the end of 1953, the State Department's loyalty security system had resulted in the dismissal or resignation of more than 400 people based on allegations concerning homosexuality. State and local governments and private businesses developed their own initiatives to exclude homosexuals from public and private sector jobs. Many local police forces increased their arrests and harassment of "deviants." The best estimate is that from 1946 to 1965 there were approximately 1000–4000 annual sodomy arrests based on consensual adult same-sex sex in the United States and more than ten times as many arrests for related offenses. In 1952, the U.S. Immigration and Nationality Act authorized the exclusion and deportation of aliens "afflicted with psychopathic personality," which the U.S. government interpreted to apply to homosexuals. In the same year, the American Psychiatric Association's first *Diagnostic and Statistical Manual* classified homosexuality as a "sociopathic personality disturbance." Government policy and scientific expertise aided and abetted the antihomosexual prejudice, harassment, and violence that many people experienced in their families, workplaces, and communities.

Despite the fears unleashed by the antihomosexual campaigns, Mattachine succeeded in attracting members by organizing, largely through personal networks, a set of discussion groups. By the fall of 1951, more than ten were meeting in southern California. The discussions served many purposes, but perhaps the most important were the opportunities to challenge society's negative judgments and cultivate a sense of collective identity. Over the next few months, Mattachine's leaders began to think about moving from talk to action. Their opportunity to do so came in February 1952, when Dale Jennings, one of Mattachine's founders, was arrested for allegedly engaging in lewd behavior with an undercover policeman. Taking advantage of the chance to expose police entrapment practices and mobilize political support, Mattachine's leaders decided to fight the charges in court. As the public face of their efforts, they created the Citizens' Committee to Outlaw Entrapment. The committee publicized the case, raised funds for legal expenses, and promoted Mattachine. The Committee also emphasized that entrapment practices victimized racial minorities as well and tried to develop a cooperative relationship with the local Civil Rights Congress. In court, Jennings admitted that he was homosexual but denied that he was guilty of the charges against him. After the jury deadlocked, the charges were dropped and Mattachine had its first legal victory.

As word spread about what had happened, Mattachine grew significantly; by May 1953, thousands were participating in the organization's fifty to a hundred discussion groups in California. As had been the case earlier, white men predominated, though some groups had significant numbers of women and people of color. Mattachine likely was primarily white and male because the social networks of most of the early participants were primarily white and male; the locations where the discussion groups met were more accessible to white men; some participants acted in racist and sexist ways; and the movement's agendas and strategies tended to privilege whites and men. Police entrapment, for example, affected gay men more than lesbians. In addition, the political priorities of many women and people of color focused more on gender, race, and class.

In the summer of 1952, Mattachine's leaders began the process of incorporating the Mattachine Foundation as a nonprofit educational organization. Around this time, Mattachine began working with psychologist Evelyn Hooker, whose personal contacts with homophile activists helped inspire her influential research challenging the notion that gay men were mentally ill. Also in 1952, several Mattachine men decided to launch an independent gay and lesbian magazine, which they named *ONE* (based on nineteenth-century Scottish writer Thomas Carlyle's declaration that "a mystic bond of brotherhood makes all men one.") ONE, Incorporated, the magazine's sponsor, initially had a multiracial board of trustees and several women were actively involved with the magazine. First published in 1953, *ONE* soon was selling more than 2000 copies a month and reaching an audience that extended beyond California.

From the earliest days of Mattachine and ONE, the homophile movement included participants with diverse views on gender, sexuality, and politics. Many early homophile activists were leftists, but others were anti-left liberals and some were conservative. For example, while Mattachine was led by communists, Dorr Legg, who became the dominant figure at ONE, was a lifelong Republican, as were several other ONE leaders. Some homophiles found appealing the left's commitment to political equality and social transformation; some were drawn to liberalism's emphasis on individual rights and social reform; some thought homophile interests would best be served by anti-government libertarian conservatism.

The early homophile movement also featured diverse perspectives on sex, gender, and sexuality. While the movement tended to present homosexuals as a sexual minority, there were contexts in which activists depicted homosexuality as a universal human potential. The movement thus encouraged all individuals to acknowledge their same-sex desires while simultaneously urging those who did to constitute themselves as a distinct sexual minority. Meanwhile, some homophiles viewed the movement as offering a respectable alternative to gay and lesbian bars, public sex, and sexual cruising. Others, however, enjoyed these aspects of gay and lesbian life and saw the bars as promising sites for movement recruitment and mobilization. Some hoped the movement would promote homosexual monogamy and marriage; others wanted to celebrate sexual freedom and expression. Some had in mind an identity-based movement that would act in the collective interests of gays and lesbians; others envisioned an issue-based movement that would address a range of subjects related to sex, including abortion, birth control, interracial sex, nonmarital sex, pornography, and prostitution. Some participants were misogynist; others were feminist. Some supported the inclusion of bisexuals in the movement; others accused bisexuals of having divided loyalties, enjoying heterosexual privilege, and denying the primacy of their same-sex desires. There were also differences of opinion about whether homosexuality was appropriately viewed as a defect, disability, handicap, or illness.

For the future of the movement, some of the most significant discussions concerned gender transgression. Led by Virginia Prince, some transvestites began to organize separately in the 1950s, but these efforts focused mostly on straight men who cross-dressed, not homosexuals, transsexuals, or biological women who cross-dressed. Transsexual social networks also formed, providing assistance to many individuals but not forging strong connections to the homophile movement. Many homophiles expressed concerns about male effeminacy, female masculinity, and the damage both could do to the movement, but butch lesbians, male queens, and others who admired the strength and sympathized with the struggles of gender dissidents insisted that the movement affirm their presence and recognize their contributions. Homophiles had diverse perspectives on transsexualism, especially after Christine Jorgensen's well-publicized sex reassignment surgery in 1952. Some viewed transsexuals as fellow victims of gender and sexual persecution; some thought they were homosexuals who failed to accept themselves as such; some rejected them in ways that echoed the rejection of transsexuals in U.S. society more generally. Transsexuals had similarly diverse perspectives on homosexuals and some identified as homosexual before or after they transitioned. The terms used for the population served by the homophile movement varied; each had the potential for inclusions and exclusions. Some of Harry Hay's early proposals, for example, referred to the movement as representing bachelors, which excluded women, or androgynes, which was less appealing to masculine men and feminine women. The term that came to be favored—homosexuals—left bisexuals, transvestites, and transsexuals unclear about their place in the movement. In the context of these debates, there was general agreement on two basic premises: there was something fundamentally wrong with the treatment of homosexuality in the United States and there was a need for an organized movement to challenge that treatment.

The first stage of Mattachine organizing came to an end in 1953, when internal and external dynamics converged to produce new political orientations, priorities, and tactics. The immediate catalyst of change was Mattachine's decision to ask Los Angeles city council, school board, and state legislative candidates to identify their positions on police harassment of homosexuals and sex education in the public schools. When a local newspaper columnist learned about this, he investigated and reported on Mattachine. His articles discussed the "tremendous political power" that homosexuals could wield and raised questions about the communist ties and secretive nature of Mattachine's leaders.[7] The Federal Bureau of Investigation soon launched an investigation of the homophile movement; over the next few decades, the FBI conducted secret surveillance of gay and lesbian political meetings, recruited informants, and shared information with various government, military, police, and postal officials. In the context of the Red Scare, the timing of the media publicity could not have been worse.

By this time, Mattachine's membership extended well beyond the leftists who had founded the organization. Some discussion group participants demanded that the leaders identify themselves publicly, that members be required to affirm their loyalty to the United States, and that Mattachine affirm its opposition to communism. In response, Mattachine's founders organized a convention in Los Angeles where the membership could restructure the organization, elect new leaders, and discuss goals and strategies. At convention sessions in April and May 1953, several founders strongly defended their politics and principles. Others denounced political radicalism and communist subversion. There were also debates about whether the minority group concept conflicted with the goals of social integration and whether it was based on the false notion that there were fundamental differences between homosexuals and heterosexuals. In the end, the convention rejected the more contentious proposals of the dissidents, but the founders, who publicly identified themselves as such, decided that it would be best if they declined to run for election in the newly restructured Mattachine. The convention then elected the dissidents as the organization's new leaders. They soon charted a new direction for the homophile movement.

Homophile Politics, 1953–61

The period from 1953 through 1961 was one of growth and change for the homophile movement. Just as the politics of anticommunism devastated the left and shifted the terms of political debate in the United States, the politics of anti-communism devastated the gay and lesbian left and shifted the terms of debate in the homophile movement. At the same time, this was an era of resurgent movement activism, as civil rights supporters recorded victories in the *Brown v. Board of Education* desegregation case (1954) and the Montgomery bus boycott (1955–56). Influenced by these and other developments, homophile activists continued their discussions about strategies and goals, but the balance of power shifted. Although the movement continued to feature diverse political orientations, the new leadership was more liberal than leftist. The homophile leftists of the earlier period had viewed their work as consistent with U.S. radical traditions and international revolutionary politics, but the ascendant liberals worked within the frameworks of patriotic Cold War nationalism. The founders had emphasized popular mobilization, public education, and political action; the new leadership focused on public education and social service. The earlier movement had believed in the importance of working with experts and elites to change public opinion, but the new one made this a higher priority and was less interested in alliances with other movements. The earlier leadership had tended to view homosexuals as a distinct cultural minority; the new one downplayed differences between homosexuals and heterosexuals. The earlier movement had promoted political integration but did not aspire to social or cultural assimilation; the new one was more fully assimilationist.

Notwithstanding these differences, the new and old movements had more in common than their leaders were willing to admit. The new leadership agreed with the old that there were fundamental problems in the ways in which society treated homosexuality and that activists could promote social change. The new movement adopted many of the strategies and goals favored by the old. Promoting public education, assisting individuals, working with experts, mobilizing support, and engaging in political action (the latter in cautious ways) remained the primary tactics. As was the case earlier, the movement had complex relationships with the community it claimed to represent. Like the old movement, the new one was predominantly white and middle class; at first it was also mostly male. Homophile activists continued to debate and often opposed gender transgression, public sex, and sexual promiscuity. At the same time, the movement continued to feature dissident voices that challenged gender and sexual conservatism. While more movement leaders criticized the notion that homosexuals were a distinct cultural minority, they often wrote and acted as though homosexuality was best conceptualized as a minority sexual orientation. Meanwhile, some homophiles continued to emphasize that homosexuality was a behavioral matter and a universal human potential.

Like the earlier movement, the new one operated in the context of severe political repression. In April 1953, U.S. President Dwight Eisenhower issued an executive order that listed "sexual perversion" as a basis for dismissing federal government employees. Over the next sixteen months, more than 600 federal workers lost their jobs based on allegations about homosexuality. Many more state and local public sector workers and private business employees were fired or forced to resign in similar circumstances. Annual military discharges based on homosexuality increased, rising from approximately 2000 in the early 1950s to 3000 by the early 1960s. Intense public campaigns against homosexuality—often spearheaded by politicians, journalists, and religious leaders—erupted in most large urban centers and many smaller cities and towns. Idaho and Florida witnessed particularly harsh and lengthy crackdowns. In Boise, the arrest of three men on sex charges in 1955 led to a two-year investigation of the "homosexual underground"; almost 1500 locals were questioned and fifteen received sentences ranging from probation to life in prison. In the late 1950s, the Florida Legislative Investigation Committee began targeting homosexual teachers, students, and staff in primary, secondary, and post-secondary schools; over the next several years, dozens of faculty and staff were dismissed, dozens lost their teaching certificates, and dozens of students were expelled. Among the prominent African Americans arrested on charges related to same-sex sex in this period were civil rights leader Bayard Rustin and Detroit minister Prophet Jones. Local police and liquor control authorities raided countless gay and lesbian bars. Police surveillance and entrapment practices were commonly used in these locations and in parks, theaters, and bathrooms. In this environment, the homophile movement faced major obstacles in recruiting participants and making social change.

Another changing context was the evolving character of U.S. urban, suburban, and rural communities. In the 1940s, 1950s, and 1960s, many white families abandoned the cities for the suburbs, in part because of declining urban economies, government and business policies that favored suburban development, and opposition to racial desegregation in city schools and neighborhoods. In the same period, many white gays and lesbians migrated to cities, which strengthened the gay and lesbian communities that had taken shape there but displaced other residents, including people of color and poor people who could not afford the rising housing costs that accompanied urban gentrification. All of this contributed to the primarily urban character of the homophile movement, the challenges of gay and lesbian organizing in rural and suburban contexts, and the complex race and class politics of homophile activism.

Homophile mobilization was constrained by pervasive cultural messages that presented homosexuality not only as sin, crime, and disease, but also as inferior, immoral, and undesirable. At the same time, there were cracks in the cultural consensus. Scientific and social scientific scholarship by Kinsey, Hooker, Frank Beach, Cleland Ford, and Thomas Szasz challenged the notion that homosexuality was pathological and diseased. Social critic Paul Goodman and popular writers Ann Aldrich and John Gerassi offered complex portrayals of gay and lesbian life. Novels by Aldrich, James Baldwin, Ann Bannon, James Barr, Patricia Highsmith, Christopher Isherwood, Valerie Taylor, Marguerite Yourcenar, and others presented new perspectives on same-sex sex, love, and intimacy. Some African American periodicals, especially in the early 1950s, reported regularly and positively on cross-dressing, drag balls, female impersonation, and homosexuality. In 1959, the *Village Voice* published a groundbreaking article titled "The Revolt of the Homosexual." Beat poet Allen Ginsberg and other countercultural writers produced homoerotic works that inspired homophile activists. Gay and lesbian consumer culture, which included pulp novels, bar guides, physique magazines, and sexual photography and film, helped build the bonds that sustained homophile activism. Some gay and lesbian business entrepreneurs supported the movement financially and referred their customers to movement groups.

As was the case earlier, the movement was encouraged and challenged by resistance practices that originated in other parts of the gay and lesbian world. In 1955, Bob Mizer's *Physique Pictorial* began to publish editorials denouncing censorship; Mizer also successfully appealed a conviction for selling indecent literature. In 1957, San Francisco bookstore owner Lawrence Ferlinghetti was victorious in an obscenity case concerning Ginsberg's *Howl and Other Poems*, which featured passages that were far more homoerotically explicit than anything published by homophile groups. In 1959, a Los Angeles movie theater operator successfully challenged his conviction on gay-related obscenity charges. Meanwhile, homophiles cheered court victories in police entrapment cases in Washington, D.C., in 1956 and 1960. They also watched as community-based resistance practices increased in scale and intensity. African American gay and lesbian clubs in a dozen large cities defended their drag balls, dances, and parties. Gay and lesbian bars in several cities challenged the actions of police and liquor authorities in court. In 1959, a Philadelphia gay man filed an unsuccessful civil rights suit after the police raided his gay-friendly coffeehouse. In the same year, a police raid on Cooper's Doughnuts in Los Angeles turned into a riot when a multiracial group of patrons, including drag queens and male hustlers, fought back. Gay motorcycle clubs, lesbian softball teams, and gay and lesbian house party hosts defended their people and territories. Homophile groups did not participate in most of these activities, but their publications reported on them. Homophiles understood that they were acting in the context of a broad spectrum of resistance practices, but believed that an organized movement could be most effective in promoting social change.

Organizationally, this was a period of change in the movement. After 1953, many Mattachine groups in California collapsed, but new ones in Boston, Chicago, Denver, New York, Philadelphia, and Washington, D.C., joined the groups in Los Angeles and San Francisco. Some were formally organized chapters; others adopted the Mattachine name but maintained more loose affiliations with the national headquarters, which in 1957 moved to San Francisco. By the end of the decade, Mattachine had 200–300 members, though more participated in local activities. ONE continued to publish its magazine and in 1956 established the ONE Institute of Homophile Studies, which sponsored educational programs, organized public conferences, facilitated research projects, and published scholarly work. *ONE* magazine tended to be more assertive than Mattachine and sometimes criticized the movement's cautious conservatism. Small and short-lived homophile groups also formed in Louisiana, Mississippi, Texas, and Washington (state).

The movement's most significant organizational development in this period was the formation of the Daughters of Bilitis (DOB). Women had participated in Mattachine virtually from its inception, but their numbers were relatively small before and after 1953. Mattachine Philadelphia, established in 1960, was exceptional in having strong female leadership and membership. Several women played important roles in ONE and its magazine, but over time the involvement of women declined. In part, the reluctance of lesbians to participate in these organizations is attributable to gay sexism, but it also reflects the fact that the social worlds and political priorities of lesbians were different from those of gay men. Lesbians were oppressed as women and as homosexuals, and Mattachine and ONE were not committed to addressing the problems lesbians experienced as women. Moreover, while lesbians and gay men shared many concerns about state policies, police practices, and popular culture, they had distinct concerns related to employment, reproduction, parenthood, domestic violence, and sexual violence. Lesbians were also less likely to be motivated by campaigns that focused on pornography and public sex. In some respects, gay men's problems related to their negative visibility (when they were identified as degenerates, deviants, psychopaths, etc.) while lesbians confronted public invisibility. In addition, homophile groups served social and sexual functions; male-dominated groups did not serve those functions well for lesbians.

DOB was formed in San Francisco in 1955, when Rose Bamberger, a Filipina American, persuaded her partner and three other lesbian couples to establish a social club that would serve as a home-based alternative to gay and lesbian bars. The group's name was based on "Songs of Bilitis," a set of homoerotic poems by nineteenth-century French writer Pierre Louys. Shortly after the group formed, Del Martin and Phyllis Lyon, one of the founding couples, proposed that the group dedicate itself to the task of educating the public about lesbianism. This divided the group and the two working-class couples (including Bamberger) decided not to participate, but Martin and Lyon forged ahead. Having learned about Mattachine and ONE after DOB was founded, they adopted many of the strategies and goals developed by the older groups, but decided to remain independent and focus on women's issues.

DOB's statement of purpose described the group as a women's organization that relied on four strategies for fostering "the integration of the homosexual into society." First, DOB promoted the "education of the variant" to help her make the necessary "adjustment to society." To accomplish this goal, DOB planned to maintain a library, sponsor public presentations by professional experts, and encourage lesbians to adopt "a mode of behavior and dress acceptable to society." Second, the group supported public education to challenge "erroneous taboos and prejudices." Third, DOB advocated "participation in research projects" to "further knowledge of the homosexual." Fourth, the group promoted legal reforms to "provide for the equitable handling of cases involving this minority group." Within a few years, DOB was publishing its own magazine, *The Ladder*, and DOB chapters in Chicago, Los Angeles, New York, and Rhode Island had joined the original group in San Francisco. By the end of the decade, DOB had more than 100 members and additional women participated in chapter activities. DOB cooperated with Mattachine and ONE, but criticized the other two groups when they treated lesbians as "second class homosexuals." In this respect and others, DOB adopted a form of liberal feminism that challenged the gender conservatism of the 1950s.[8]

While DOB ensured that women's voices were represented in the movement, the leadership and membership of Mattachine, ONE, and DOB were predominantly white, middle class, and Christian. In terms of race, the movement learned many lessons about strategies and goals from the African American-led civil rights movement, but proved more adept at making analogies between racial and sexual oppression than in attracting large numbers of people who experienced both. There were notable exceptions. ONE's leadership included several African Americans, Asian Americans, and Latinos. One of the founders and leaders of Mattachine New York was Cuban American Tony Segura. DOB's original eight members included a Filipina and a Chicana. An African American woman, Pat Walker, became the president of DOB San Francisco in 1960 and African American writer Lorraine Hansberry was an early contributor to *The Ladder*. Notwithstanding these and other exceptions, people of color were not well-represented in most homophile groups.

The class status of homophile activists is more difficult to assess. Most evidence points to middle-class over-representation, but working-class people participated in significant ways. Some of the movement's critical comments about gender and sexual transgression in gay and lesbian cultural contexts, including bars, may have discouraged working-class participation, but this should not be overstated since many working-class gays and lesbians shared those values, many middle-class gays and lesbians did not, and some homophiles had more radical gender and sexual politics. Moreover, a survey of women affiliated with DOB in 1958 indicated that 38 percent regarded themselves as "predominantly masculine" in their relationships and many DOB leaders were masculine.[9] For the working-class women who founded DOB but then rejected it, the issue was less DOB's critical perspectives on bar culture and gender transgression and more its public and political orientations. In general, working-class people may have been less likely to participate in the homophile movement for reasons that paralleled and intersected with the reasons that women and people of color were less likely to participate. That said, many working-class people wrote letters to homophile periodicals, turned to homophile groups for assistance, participated in movement activities, and contributed to the movement's growth.

As for other kinds of diversity, the movement was overwhelmingly urban and relatively weak in the South, Midwest, Great Plains, and Mountain West. The movement was mostly Christian, though the percentage of Jews may have been greater in the movement and its leadership than it was in the country. In part this reflected the urban, liberal, and activist character of Jewish culture and the history of Jewish participation in sex reform. The movement was predominantly native-born and emphasized the rights of U.S. citizens, but European, Canadian, Asian, and Latin American immigrants participated, despite the risks for noncitizens, which included deportation. Many homophiles were veterans. Some were parents. Most were over the age of twenty-one; homophile groups typically restricted membership based on age because they feared playing into stereotypes of homosexuals as child molesters. At least five leading activists—Donald Webster Cory, James Kepner, Helen Sandoz, Valerie Taylor, and Pat Walker—had significant physical disabilities. Most homophile activists identified as gay or lesbian, but the movement recruited a significant number of straight allies, including doctors, lawyers, ministers, psychologists, and experts in politics, religion, and science.

In the period from 1953 to 1961, the movement engaged in four main activities. First, homophile groups organized meetings, discussions, and events at which participants could share their thoughts and feelings about topics related to sex, gender, and sexuality. They addressed the problems individuals experienced with partners, friends, families, coworkers, employers, and landlords, as well as the difficulties they encountered in business, leisure, and religion. For those who were coming out as gay or lesbian, struggling with their gender or sexual identities, or feeling isolated from sympathetic social networks, these discussions could be valuable in and of themselves and in the ways in which they were informative about gay and lesbian social geographies and cultural resources. For more experienced participants, movement meetings, discussions, and events helped develop strategies for dealing with prejudice and discrimination and promote new ways of thinking about sexuality. They also facilitated the development of friendships, partnerships, and relationships. In these contexts, some activists promoted dominant gender and sexual values (criticizing, for example, cross-dressing and sexual promiscuity); others defended gender diversity and sexual freedom. In general, the movement tried to help individuals while developing the social basis for political action.

The movement's second principal activity was to provide an array of services to individuals in need. Homophile groups received thousands of requests for assistance via telephone, correspondence, and office visits. One of the services provided was to refer individuals in need to sympathetic lawyers, doctors, psychologists, counsellors, and other professionals. To do this well, homophile groups had to find out who was willing and able to help, which could be challenging. In many contexts, activists themselves provided advice, counselling, and mentorship. As part of this work, homophile groups printed wallet-sized cards and published articles addressing "what to do in case of arrest." Individuals experiencing troubles with the law, conflicts with families, difficulties obtaining employment, problems accessing social assistance, and struggles related to depression, homelessness, illness, poverty, and violence turned to the movement for help. Assistance was provided to gay men, lesbians, cross-dressers, prostitutes, transsexuals, and others with questions and concerns. With limited resources, homophile groups provided substantial support.

The movement's third main activity focused on education and communication. In addition to the educational work that occurred in homophile meetings, Mattachine, ONE, and DOB organized public lectures, seminars, and conferences featuring experts on law and politics, science and medicine, psychology and psychiatry, anthropology and sociology, history and literature, and religion and spirituality. Some groups published and distributed books, magazines, and pamphlets on topics related to homosexuality. Some cultivated ties with and promoted the work of sympathetic experts, researchers, and professionals, including psychologist Evelyn Hooker, sexologist Alfred Kinsey, and lawyers affiliated with the ACLU. The educational process worked in two ways: gays and lesbians learned from outsiders and outsiders learned from gays and lesbians. Sometimes homophiles sponsored presentations by antihomosexual experts, in part to familiarize themselves with the arguments of their enemies, provide opportunities for debate, and strengthen the perception that the movement was open, reasonable, and scientific. More commonly, the movement favored those more sympathetic to their cause.

Toward the end of this period, the movement began to receive more respectful coverage in mainstream media. Sensational and critical stories remained the rule rather than the exception, but homophile activists began developing more productive relationships with journalists; sometimes this resulted in more affirmative or neutral coverage. One breakthrough occurred in 1958, when a two-hour radio program on homosexuality was broadcast by KPFA in Berkeley and other Pacifica network stations. The program featured interviews with Mattachine leaders and Mattachine-affiliated experts. Further breakthroughs occurred in 1958 and 1959 when WABD and WNTA in New York featured Mattachine representatives on television interview programs. In 1959, Mattachine began to have success in placing advertisements for homophile movement events in mainstream, black, and student newspapers in the Bay Area. Also in 1959, local newspapers provided respectful coverage of a national Mattachine convention in Denver.

The movement's efforts to promote education and communication were facilitated greatly by its magazines and newsletters. This was a period of growth and diversification in the homophile press. Joining *ONE* magazine was *Mattachine Review*, founded by the Mattachine Society in 1955, and *The Ladder*, founded by the DOB in 1956. Together, the three major homophile magazines of the 1950s probably had a peak monthly circulation of 10,000–20,000 and a readership several times larger than that. For the many gays and lesbians who lived in places that did not have a local homophile group, the magazines were particularly important sources of information and vehicles of communication. Local Mattachine and DOB chapters also began publishing their own newsletters. In 1958, ONE established the *ONE Institute Quarterly of Homophile Studies*, which was envisioned as a scholarly journal. More gays and lesbians learned about homosexuality from other sources—including mainstream popular culture, bar-based communities, novels with gay and lesbian themes, and homoerotic physique magazines—but homophile periodicals politicized homosexuality in distinct ways.

Homophile periodicals served many functions. They shared information about movement activities; reported on news from around the country and world; reviewed books, films, and plays; and published fiction, poetry, art, essays, and letters. They also reprinted mainstream media articles, published excerpts of speeches and books, and let readers know how they could obtain further information. Longer news articles and feature stories focused on a variety of topics, including homosexuality in other countries and cultures, police practices and political scandals, employment and military discrimination, censorship and obscenity, gay bars and sexual cruising, and marriage and parenthood. The biological, psychological, cultural, and historical aspects of homosexuality were discussed, as were public sex, sexual promiscuity, and gender transgression. The magazines were particularly effective in sharing information that was otherwise difficult to obtain, promoting a sense of community among their readers, and exposing the oppressive conditions of gay and lesbian life. They also were valuable vehicles of communication between the movement and the community it claimed to represent. Homophile leaders tended to favor a politics of respectability, but their periodicals published articles, stories, and letters that encompassed a broader spectrum of positions. Like the educational process that occurred between the movement and the experts invited to participate in homophile activities, the educational process involving homophiles and the readers of their periodicals was two-way.

The movement's fourth main activity consisted of direct political action to defend and promote gay and lesbian rights. Movement leaders in the 1950s and early 1960s sometimes publicly rejected calls for direct political action, but behind the scenes they acted otherwise and sometimes this came into public view. Homophile groups and their periodicals followed with great interest the progress of sex law reform in Europe and the United States. They were particularly interested in the proposals of the 1957 British Wolfenden Commission, which called for the decriminalization of private homosexual acts between consenting adults, and the similar initiatives of the American Law Institute. Homophiles developed close working relationships with ACLU lawyers, who were among the movement's most important allies. When the ACLU released a policy statement on homosexuality in 1957, gay and lesbian activists had mixed responses. On the one hand, the statement declared that "homosexuals, like members of other socially heretical or deviant groups, are more vulnerable than others to official persecution, denial of due process in prosecution, and entrapment." On the other hand, the statement indicated that the ACLU would not "evaluate the social validity of laws aimed at the suppression or elimination of homosexuals." Nor would it challenge the constitutionality of laws against "overt homosexual acts," "public acts of homosexuality," or "overt acts of solicitation for the purpose of committing a homosexual act."[10] Homophile activists lobbied the ACLU to change its positions and convinced many ACLU lawyers to help in ways that extended well beyond the limitations of the 1957 statement.

Homophile groups displayed strong interest in court cases related to gay and lesbian rights. Movement activists were often quite pessimistic about the chances of achieving reform through the executive or legislative branches of government; antihomosexual public opinion meant that elected officials were unlikely to support reform. Homophile groups urged their members to make their views known to their elected representatives and encouraged their supporters to vote, but they did not make this a high priority. The judicial branch of government seemed more promising. The movement watched with keen interest the successes of African Americans in court cases such as *Brown v. Board of Education*. Appointed judges were less beholden to popular majorities and some judges viewed the protection of minority rights and the defense of civil liberties as important responsibilities of the courts. Homophile groups did not get involved directly in much litigation in this period, but their periodicals provided extensive coverage of court cases.

In this period, homophile political action concentrated on government repression of gay and lesbian bars and publications, partly because rights of assembly and expression were seen as stepping stones toward freedom and equality. Some activists criticized bar culture and bemoaned the political apathy of bar owners and patrons, but homophile groups supported bar-based resistance practices. They did so, for example, by reporting on the hostile actions of public officials and the litigation that bar owners pursued. Behind the scenes, homophile activists published directories of gay and lesbian bars and bathhouses, provided financial support for bar-based litigation, referred bar owners and patrons to legal advocates, and worked with lawyers who participated in bar cases. For instance, after the 1951 victory in *Stoumen*, the California legislature authorized the state liquor authority to revoke the licenses of bars that served "sexual perverts." In 1959, with support from homophile activists, Mary's First and Last Chance Bar in Oakland won *Vallerga*, a state supreme court decision affirming the rights of homosexuals to congregate in bars. The victory was qualified since the court specified that the outcome would have been different if there had been evidence of illegal or harmful sexual activities on the premises, but homophiles hoped that the decision would lead to further positive developments.

The movement also targeted sexual censorship. In 1954, several Mattachine San Francisco leaders—including Hal Call and Don Lucas—established Pan-Graphic Press, which shared offices with Mattachine. Pan-Graphic printed *Mattachine Review*, *The Ladder*, and other homophile publications, which helped avoid problems with antihomosexual printers. In 1957, Mattachine San Francisco leaders established the Dorian Book Service, which purchased and distributed books and other materials about homosexuality. Around this time, Pan-Graphic began printing a periodical titled *Sex and Censorship*, which also was founded by Mattachine members. In 1960, Pan-Graphic began publishing the *Dorian Book Service Quarterly*, which provided information about books and magazines for sale along with reports on censorship and anticensorship activism. Many of these projects were kept institutionally separate in order to preserve Mattachine's respectable image and avoid legal troubles, but homophile activists were involved and provided financial and other kinds of support for anticensorship litigation.

The movement's greatest success in this period was *ONE* magazine's 1958 victory in a U.S. Supreme Court obscenity case. *ONE* had been concerned about postal censorship from its earliest years and took great care, with the advice of lawyers, to avoid publishing visual or other materials that would lead to trouble with government authorities. Like *Mattachine Review* and *The Ladder*, the magazine avoided overt depictions or descriptions of sexual acts, published no representations of nude bodies, and was more sexually respectable than many other publications aimed at straight and gay audiences. Nevertheless, the U.S. Post Office occasionally reviewed the magazine and delayed its distribution. In 1954, postal officials refused to distribute an issue based on allegations about obscene contents, which consisted of a short story featuring a lesbian kiss, a poem about a British sex scandal, and an advertisement for a Swiss gay magazine. *ONE* challenged the Post Office in court and lost the first two rounds. In 1958, however, the Supreme Court voted 5–4 to reverse the lower court decisions, ordering the Post Office to distribute the contested issue. The Court did not explain the basis for its decision, other than citing a previous obscenity ruling, but homophile activists justifiably claimed this as an important victory.

Unfortunately for the movement, this was also a period of significant challenges and setbacks. In 1959, Mattachine's annual convention was held in Denver. In many respects, it was a great success. There were featured presentations by the Colorado State Assembly majority leader and a representative of the state's ACLU affiliate. Local media stories were more respectful than was usually the case.

After the convention, however, local police raided the homes of Denver homophile activists, confiscated their mailing lists, and arrested one member on obscenity charges; he ended up serving sixty days in jail. Two local activists lost their jobs as a result of the publicity. Mattachine's Denver chapter never fully recovered.

Also in 1959, a San Francisco mayoral candidate blamed the incumbent for allowing the city to become "the national headquarters of the organized homosexuals in the United States" and exposing the city's children to homosexuality.[11] After the mainstream press criticized the candidate for making these allegations and Mattachine sued him for slander, he lost in a landslide. Nevertheless, the national publicity frightened activists elsewhere; soon Detroit's Mattachine chapter collapsed and plans to reactivate the Chicago one were cancelled. After the election in San Francisco, a political scandal erupted when the media exposed an extensive system of corruption whereby police and liquor control officials demanded payoffs by gay and lesbian bars in order to avoid raids and closures. Embarrassed by the critical attention, the mayor and police chief responded with a crackdown inside and outside the bars. San Francisco felony convictions based on homosexuality increased dramatically and misdemeanor charges in gay and lesbian bars increased as well. Toward the end of 1961, liquor control authorities announced license revocations for twelve of San Francisco's gay and lesbian bars and additional actions against another fifteen. The increased public visibility of the movement came with a heavy price.

Across the country, the homophile movement was reminded of the legal peril that could accompany gay and lesbian political organizing. In August 1960, Mattachine New York activists helped a group of Philadelphia-area residents organize a meeting to begin the process of forming a local homophile group. The plan was to show several gay-themed short films and discuss the homophile movement. A large group of people attended, but so did police and postal officials, who apparently were tipped off by publicity fliers that were distributed in the mail. Eighty-four people were arrested and jailed. By the next morning, most had been released without charge, but the owner of the home where the meeting had been held and a Mattachine New York activist were brought up on disorderly house charges. By early 1961, the charges had been dropped and Mattachine Philadelphia had been established, but the signs were not auspicious for the future of gay and lesbian political organizing.

Challenged by these developments and by conflicts with some of its local chapters, Mattachine's national board voted to restructure the organization in 1961. Henceforth the headquarters in San Francisco would retain control over *Mattachine Review* and other organizational resources, while the chapters would be dissolved. Some local groups continued to use the Mattachine name (without authorization by the national headquarters, so they are best not referred to as chapters) and some selected new names, but others collapsed. ONE and the DOB also experienced significant difficulties during this period, and conflicts within and between all three groups were reaching breaking point. As other social movements in the United States began to gather strength in the early 1960s, the future of homophile activism was uncertain.

Homophile Politics, 1961–69

While the homophile movement of the 1950s operated in a generally conservative political context that featured the Red and Lavender Scares, the movement of the 1960s developed in an era of polarization in which liberals were ascendant, leftists were mobilized, and conservatives were organizing to regain power. For many, the election of John F. Kennedy as U.S. president in 1960 signalled a transition in the country's politics. While moderates and liberals competed for influence with Kennedy and his successor, Lyndon Johnson, liberal and leftist movements succeeded in capturing public attention and pressing for social change.

The most powerful movement of the 1960s—and the one that had the most influence on homophile activism—was the African American-led civil rights movement. In 1960, a sit-in at a racially segregated Woolworth's lunch counter in Greensboro, North Carolina, sparked a wave of similar actions elsewhere. Over the next several years, the civil rights movement organized large-scale marches, demonstrations, boycotts, sit-ins, and other political actions aimed at ending racial segregation and race-based denials of voting rights. After the March on Washington in 1963, Congress passed the 1964 Civil Rights Act and the 1965 Voting Rights Act. Ongoing racism, however, led to ongoing protest, and in the mid-1960s many activists embraced the more radical goals and strategies of the Black Power movement and its counterparts in other racialized communities. In contrast to the respectable, nonviolent, and integrationist civil rights movement, the Black Power movement declared that "Black is Beautiful," advocated a more revolutionary transformation of U.S. society, and linked its struggles with radical anticolonial movements around the world.

A similar radicalization process occurred in other movements. The student movement revived in the early 1960s with the formation of Students for a Democratic Society and radicalized a few years later with the escalation of campus protests. The small antiwar movement of the early 1960s gathered strength over the next several years; by the end of the decade it had millions of supporters and was helping to bring an end to the war in Vietnam. The women's movement grew after the publication of Betty Friedan's *The Feminine Mystique* in 1963 and the formation of the National Organization for Women (NOW) in 1966; later in the decade radical women's liberationists challenged liberal feminists for movement leadership. Meanwhile, the counterculture grew from a relatively small group of beats, hipsters, and other cultural rebels into a mass phenomenon that was popularly associated with "sex, drugs, and rock 'n roll" but encompassed many other forms of cultural and political dissidence. All of these movements were homophobic and heterosexist, but they inspired and influenced gay and lesbian activism.

Homophile activism also was affected by the "sexual revolution," which challenged conventional ways of thinking about sex. Hugh Hefner's *Playboy* magazine had begun celebrating male heterosexuality in the 1950s and a series of court decisions in that decade loosened restrictions on many forms of pornography. In the early 1960s, Helen Gurley Brown's *Sex and the Single Girl* announced that more women were ready to join the revolution. Rates of nonmarital cohabitation, sex, and reproduction increased. New sexual lifestyles became more popular. Many aspects of the sexual revolution were relentlessly heterosexual, but others were more open to diverse forms of sexual expression. In the 1960s, for example, Hefner's "Playboy Philosophy" endorsed the notion that consenting adults should not face legal penalties for private sex acts, including homosexual ones. The sexual revolution encouraged homophile activists to reconsider the politics of pleasure, freedom, and equality.

Activists in this period worked in the context of significant changes in the representation of homosexuality in popular culture and substantial growth in gay and lesbian consumer culture. While homosexuality continued to be depicted as undesirable and unattractive in general, there were more exceptions. Novels by Richard Amory, James Baldwin, Ann Bannon, Christopher Isherwood, John Rechy, Alma Routsong, Jane Rule, Samuel Steward, Valerie Taylor, and Gore Vidal, for example, were critical of sexual prejudice; some offered strikingly explicit and appealing representations of same-sex sex, love, and intimacy. Nonfiction books by Ann Aldrich, R. E. L. Masters, and Jess Stearn introduced millions to gay and lesbian cultures. After the Supreme Court's 1962 *Manual* decision, which overturned the Post Office's designation of three physique magazines as obscene, gay pornography became increasingly popular, as did mail-order businesses that catered to the gay market. Beginning with *Philadelphia Magazine* and the *Village Voice* in 1962 and continuing in the next few years with the *Atlanta Journal and Constitution*, *Chicago Daily News*, *Denver Post*, *Harper's*, *Life*, *Look*, *New York Post*, *New York Times*, *Newsweek*, *Time*, and *Washington Post*, mainstream periodicals published major reports on homosexuality. Many were critical, but some included respectful coverage of gay and lesbian perspectives. Radio and television breakthroughs began with California, New York, and Pennsylvania-based shows that featured interviews with homophile activists in 1961–62, continued with other local programs later in the decade, and reached a national audience when *The David Susskind Show* featured a gay panel discussion in 1967. CBS broadcast a documentary on homosexuality in 1967; it mostly featured hostile condemnation, but informed millions of viewers about the existence of the homophile movement.

Social scientists helped weaken the antihomosexual consensus. Sociologist Donald Webster Cory published *The Homosexual and His Society* in 1963 and *The Lesbian in America* in 1964. Psychologist Evelyn Hooker, psychoanalysts Henry Ruitenbeek and Judd Marmor, psychiatrists Thomas Szasz and Martin Hoffman, sociologists Howard Becker, Erving Goffman, and Edwin Schur, and numerous others challenged the classification of homosexuality as a mental illness and pathological disease. Some legal studies scholars, influenced by changing perspectives on personal privacy, victimless crimes, civil liberties, and political equality, began calling for reform in the treatment of homosexuality.

They did so in the context of ongoing state repression, which continued to inspire and constrain homophile organizing. Antihomosexual government initiatives did not decline in the transition to the 1960s; in some respects, they escalated. Military exclusions and discharges increased. Government employment restrictions continued; the best estimate is that approximately 5000 federal government workers were dismissed during the 1950s and 1960s based on allegations about homosexuality. Many more were terminated or allowed to resign in ways that did not list homosexuality as the reason. This does not even begin to count the number dismissed from local and state government jobs, other public sector positions, and private business employment. Antihomosexual police practices continued to have devastating consequences; one of the most prominent people affected was presidential aide Walter Jenkins, a married man with six children who was forced to resign in 1964 after the police twice caught him having sex in a YMCA restroom. Immigration officials excluded and deported homosexuals as psychopathic personalities and immoral criminals; after new legislation in 1965, they were also excluded and deported as sexual deviates. In 1964, the U.S. Supreme Court overturned the deportation of a homosexual alien on a technicality, but in 1961 the Fifth Circuit upheld the deportation of a U.S. permanent resident from Mexico after she was classified by immigration authorities as a lesbian. In 1967, the Supreme Court ruled in *Boutilier* that the exclusion and deportation of homosexual aliens as psychopathic personalities was constitutional. U.S. Post Office, Customs, and state and local officials targeted homosexuality in their enforcement of obscenity laws. In *Womack* (1961), *Darnell* (1963), and *Mishkin* (1966), the Court affirmed obscenity convictions in cases involving descriptions or depictions of same-sex sex.

Homophile activists hoped that the Court's liberal rulings in cases concerning interracial cohabitation (1964), birth control (1965), and interracial marriage (1967) might have positive implications for gay and lesbian rights, but the language used in these decisions suggested that the Court's privacy, liberty, and equality doctrines did not apply to homosexuality. Illinois in 1961 and Connecticut in 1969 became the first states to repeal their sodomy laws, but in many jurisdictions the police continued to target homosexuality in their enforcement of laws against cross-dressing, disorderly conduct, indecency, lewdness, obscenity, sodomy, solicitation, and vagrancy. Liquor control officials and the police also continued to act in legal and extralegal ways against people and places associated with homosexuality.

Despite all of these challenges, the homophile movement strengthened in the 1960s as Mattachine, ONE, and DOB were joined by a diverse set of groups with different political orientations. After Mattachine's restructuring in 1961, Mattachine groups in New York and Washington, D.C., operated autonomously, as did later Mattachine groups in Chicago, Florida, and Philadelphia. The national office concentrated on the Bay Area and published *Mattachine Review*, though in 1964 the magazine began to appear on an irregular basis and the last issue was published in 1966. ONE continued to run its institute and magazine in Los Angeles, thanks in part to the financial contributions of transsexual Reid Erickson and his Louisiana-based Erickson Educational Foundation. ONE benefited from these contributions, but experienced divisive internal conflicts. In 1965, dissident factions began publishing two versions of *ONE* and suing each other in court; eventually the organization split and one version of *ONE* was renamed *Tangents*. Both magazines only lasted a few more years, though ONE continued to operate as a research and educational organization. DOB retained its centralized national structure through the 1960s, had chapters (some short-lived) in Boston, Chicago, Cleveland, Dallas, Los Angeles, New York, Philadelphia, Phoenix, and San Francisco, and continued to publish *The Ladder*. By the end of the decade, however, it, too, was fragmenting and weakening.

As the politics of the country and movement changed in the 1960s, new homophile groups were established. Influenced by the civil rights movement, Mattachine D.C. (led by Frank Kameny) and the Janus Society in Philadelphia (led by Clark Polak) called for more aggressive direct action tactics, more assertive defenses of homosexuality, and more forceful emphasis on civil rights. The militants were supported by several DOB allies, including Philadelphia's Barbara Gittings, who edited the *Ladder* from 1963 to 1966. Within a few years, militants also led Mattachine New York, PRIDE (Personal Rights in Defense and Education) in Los Angeles, the Homophile Action League in Philadelphia, and several groups in San Francisco. As of 1964, Janus's *Drum* magazine surpassed the older homophile periodicals in circulation, partly because it featured sexy photographs, risqué comics, and pro-sex politics. Three years later, PRIDE's newsletter became the independent newspaper *The Advocate*, which began referring to "gay power." By the end of the 1960s, there were other new homophile groups in California, Illinois, Kansas, New York, Ohio, Texas, Virginia, and Washington.

San Francisco had the most numerous set of homophile organizations. While Mattachine and DOB continued to operate in the city, the League for Civil Education, founded in 1961, mobilized gay and lesbian bar owners, staff, and patrons. Its newspaper, *LCE News* (later called *The News* and *The Citizens News*), was distributed for free in the bars, as was *Town Talk*, which was published by Pan-Graphic. The Tavern Guild was formed in 1962 to represent local gay and lesbian bar owners and staff. When the LCE dissolved in 1964, a group of gay men founded the Society for Individual Rights (SIR), which published *Vector* magazine and presented itself as a more radical, democratic, and community-based alternative to the older groups. In 1966, a group of San Francisco gay and trans youth (including hustlers, prostitutes, and runaways) formed Vanguard, which focused on "kids on the streets" and promoted "street power." Three years later, the Committee for Homosexual Freedom was formed by activists who found SIR too conservative. Several transsexual groups formed in San Francisco and New York in the late 1960s, but they did not generally see themselves as part of the homophile movement.[12]

As the movement grew, regional, national, and continental coalitions such as East Coast Homophile Organizations and the North American Conference of Homophile Organizations promoted cooperation and coordination. U.S. homophiles also communicated with gay and lesbian activists around the world. More specialized groups concentrated on religious, military, legal, student, and other issues. In 1964, the San Francisco-based Council on Religion and the Homosexual began to encourage dialogue between homophile activists and religious leaders. Similar groups were established elsewhere and homophiles participated in consultations with several religious denominations. In 1968, Troy Perry founded the Metropolitan Community Church, which initially ministered to gays and lesbians in Los Angeles and eventually became an international denomination. Also in 1968, Robert Clement founded the Church of the Beloved Disciple, an independent Catholic church for gays and lesbians in New York. Dignity, which served gay and lesbian Roman Catholics, began meeting in San Diego and Los Angeles in 1969. The Committee to Fight Exclusion of Homosexuals from the Armed Forces was founded in Los Angeles in 1966. Beginning in 1966 and 1967, the Philadelphia-based Homosexual Law Reform Society and the San Francisco-based National Legal Defense Fund initiated, funded, and supported litigation. In 1966, a Student Homophile League was established at Columbia University; similar groups soon followed at Cornell, University of Minnesota, New York University, and Stanford. Also in the late 1960s, Craig Rodwell, founder of the Oscar Wilde Memorial Bookshop in New York, established Homosexual Youth Movement in Neighborhoods. By the spring of 1969, there were approximately fifty homophile groups in the United States.

Some homophile groups remained small during the 1960s, but others grew large. In the mid-1960s, Mattachine New York had 500 members, the Society of Anubis in Los Angeles had 800, and SIR had 1000. Approximately 600 people attended a New Year's Eve dance held to raise funds for the Council on Religion and the Homosexual in San Francisco at the end of 1964. Homophile periodicals were read by tens of thousands. By 1963, *LCE News* was distributing 7000 copies of each issue. In 1968, the *Wall Street Journal* reported that *Drum*'s circulation was 15,000.

These numbers were impressive when compared with the movement's reach in the 1950s, but most people who engaged in same-sex sex were not involved. Around the country, several hundred people participated in homophile activism in substantial ways, but many more were too apathetic, fearful, or alienated by the movement's politics to do so. There were several reasons for this. Compared with the African American, labor, and women's movements, the homophile movement was quite new. Other than gay bars, the movement lacked the kinds of spaces (such as churches, factories, and schools) where other movements successfully recruited and mobilized. While some African Americans could pass as white and some women could pass as men, the ability of most gays and lesbians to pass as straight led many to avoid political visibility. Dominant cultural views of homosexuality as sinful, criminal, and diseased also hindered political mobilization. In addition, most people who engaged in same-sex sex did not think of themselves as gay or lesbian; the homophile movement's identity politics did not resonate for them. The movement accomplished a great deal during the 1960s, but its achievements were not the results of mass mobilization.

There is some evidence that the movement widened its demographic base in the 1960s, but it remained predominantly white, Christian, and middle class. Exceptions in the movement's leadership included several African Americans: Cleo Bonner was elected DOB president in 1963, Ernestine Eckstein was a DOB New York officer in the 1960s, and a male student served as the president of Mattachine Syracuse. Cuban American Ada Bello was one of the leaders of DOB Philadelphia and the Homophile Action League. Jose Sarria, who helped found the LCE, Tavern Guild, and SIR, was Latino. Japanese American Alfred Sawahata led the Mattachine New York membership committee in the mid-1960s and a straight Japanese American minister served as the public spokesperson for Seattle's Dorian Society. Immigration law reform in the 1960s had major long-term effects on the representation of Latinos and Asian Americans in the gay and lesbian movement, but these did not become evident until later.

At times, the movement tried to promote the visibility of people of color. *The Ladder*'s first cover photograph with a recognizable human subject featured an Indonesian woman in 1964 and the magazine featured Eckstein in a cover photograph and lengthy interview in 1966. *Drum* began to include erotic photographs of nonwhites in 1966. Published photographs of homophile demonstrations in the mid-1960s included several African American participants. These were significant steps, but some may have felt like token gestures, some may have seemed patronizing, and some may have been perceived as complicit with racism and colonialism. Even more problematic was the tendency of movement leaders to use rhetoric that compared racial and sexual struggles but did not acknowledge the distinct struggles of gays and lesbians of color and the ongoing problems of racism. In 1967, for example, one homophile demonstration sign declared, "Homosexual American citizens: Our last oppressed national minority."[13]

The homophile movement's relationships with other movements changed in the 1960s. The number of homophile activists with experiences in communist and socialist groups declined, though there were exceptions: the Chicago-based Mattachine Midwest group, for example, had a strong leftist contingent. The number of homophiles with experiences in antiwar, civil rights, countercultural, feminist, and student groups increased. Many gay and lesbian activists only participated in the homophile movement, but others were active in other struggles, either before, during, or after their period of involvement in the gay and lesbian movement.

Relations between the homophile and trans movements were complex. In many contexts, homophiles distanced themselves from trans struggles, but in others they were supportive. Some homophile groups criticized gender transgression, but some hosted and publicized drag events. In San Francisco, the Tavern Guild hosted an annual drag ball, Vanguard brought gay and trans street activists together, and homophile activist Jose Sarria established what eventually became the Imperial Court System, which was a network of charitable organizations that used drag events to raise funds for gay, lesbian, and other groups. Other groups, including Conversion Our Goal, California Advancement for Transsexuals Society, Labyrinth Foundation Counseling Service, and the National Gender-Sexual Identification Council (later renamed the National Transsexual Counseling Unit), focused on transsexuals or transvestites who did not necessarily identify as gay or lesbian. One potential division between homophiles and transsexuals opened up as the former increasingly rejected the medicalization of homosexuality while the latter increasingly demanded medical services, but there were efforts to build coalitions. Some activists envisioned a unified gay, lesbian, bisexual, and trans movement.

The ACLU continued to be the movement's strongest organizational ally, but gay and lesbian activists gained other valuable supporters during the 1960s. There were sympathetic journalists who provided respectful coverage of movement activities. There were liberal religious leaders who participated in locally organized Councils on Religion and the Homosexual. Dozens of scientists and social scientists supported movement initiatives. The Homosexual Law Reform Society, for example, successfully solicited more than thirty statements by scientists and social scientists for its legal briefs. ACLU lawyers assisted individuals with legal troubles, represented movement groups in legal proceedings, and defended gay and lesbian rights in court. In 1964, a national ACLU conference endorsed the decriminalization of private sexual behavior by consenting adults. Three years later, a new ACLU policy statement affirmed the group's opposition to the criminalization of private homosexual acts by consenting adults, condemned antihomosexual police and liquor control practices, and criticized government employment discrimination against homosexuals. Homophiles criticized the statement's language about the legitimacy of anti-solicitation laws and unspecified situations in which private sex acts might be a legitimate factor to consider in government employment decisions. Nevertheless, most knew that no nonhomophile group did more to defend gay and lesbian rights than the ACLU did.

The most significant change in homophile activism during the 1960s was the movement's political orientation. While it is difficult to generalize about movement politics during this period, there were six strong tendencies that competed for influence. The first represented a continuation and extension of the movement's dominant political orientation in the late 1950s. Activists who favored this approach focused on public education and social service, deferred to professional elites and allies, and were cautious about direct political action. They were far more active than their homophile critics assumed, but not as aggressive and militant as many of their rivals wanted them to be. Supported by several Mattachine chapters in the early 1960s, this tendency lost its dominant position over the course of the decade.

A second tendency was a feminist version of the first. During the 1960s, some DOB members grew increasingly alienated by the male-dominated homophile movement and increasingly attracted to the women's movement. In the mid-1960s, several DOB leaders more forcefully urged the homophile movement to increase its attention to lesbian issues and support women's rights. When the movement failed to do so, some DOB activists, including founders Del Martin and Phyllis Lyon, joined NOW and redirected their energies to the women's movement. In 1966, *The Ladder* began to pay more attention to feminist issues and in 1968 DOB elected feminist Rita Laporte as its president. While the DOB diverged from the first tendency in its feminist orientation, it joined the first in emphasizing public education, prioritizing social service, and expressing great caution about direct political action.

A third tendency, exemplified by Mattachine D.C., was more assertive and aggressive about gay and lesbian rights, though it continued to work within the frameworks of patriotic Cold War liberalism. This tendency diverged from the first two in several respects: it emphasized political action, it endorsed the use of direct action tactics, and it forcefully attacked sexual prejudice and discrimination. Over the course of the 1960s, more movement militants rejected the medical model of homosexuality, denied that homosexuality was an illness, and insisted that there was nothing pathological about same-sex sex. In 1965, Mattachine D.C. adopted a resolution, later endorsed by other groups, declaring that "homosexuality is not a sickness, disturbance, or other pathology in any sense, but is merely a preference, orientation, or propensity, on par with, and not different in kind from, hetero-sexuality."[14] While movement militants generally presented homosexuals as a minority group, they also used behavioral arguments that depicted homosexuality as a universal human potential. On these and other matters, they insisted that homosexuals should be recognized as the experts on homosexuality. Influenced by the Black Power slogan "Black is Beautiful," they began to declare that "Gay is Good," which was adopted as a slogan at a national movement conference in 1968. Over the course of the decade, homophile militants developed strong arguments in favor of sexual privacy, sexual equality, and civil rights.

A fourth tendency, best represented by SIR, PRIDE, and other California groups, shared the militant impulses of the third, but oriented itself more strongly to the gay and lesbian community. Activists who supported this tendency believed that bars and other places where gays and lesbians congregated should be defended and politicized by the movement. They also thought that in adopting this orientation, the movement could better serve community needs and promote mass mobilization. This was not always easy to accomplish. In 1962, for example, homophiles were pleased by the attention they received in a *Philadelphia Magazine* feature story, but were attacked by community members because the article mentioned the names and addresses of gay bars. In this instance, homophile strategies of visibility challenged the strategies of invisibility that many bar patrons favored. Other efforts along these lines were more successful. Beginning in 1964, SIR sponsored dances, parties, drag balls, fundraising events, classes, and other social activities in San Francisco. When Philadelphia police raided the city's most popular lesbian bar in

1968, local DOB activists assisted the women arrested and retained a lawyer who arranged for the charges to be dropped. Feeling constrained by the cautious politics of the national DOB, they soon voted to dissolve the chapter and form the Homophile Action League, which they hoped would be a better vehicle for community mobilization.

A fifth tendency, which was spearheaded by Philadelphia's Janus Society, joined the third in favoring political action and the fourth in orienting itself to the gay community, but differed in emphasizing sexual liberation. Janus's *Drum* magazine, which aspired to be "a gay *Playboy*," advertised itself as presenting "news for 'queers,'" "fiction for 'perverts,'" "photo essays for 'fairies,'" and "laughs for 'faggots.'" *Drum* combined the popular appeal of physique magazines with the political edge of homophile periodicals. While militant leader Frank Kameny insisted at a conference in 1966 that "this is the homophile movement—we are not fighting for sexual freedom," Janus leader and *Drum* editor Clark Polak attacked the movement's "anti-sexualism" and denounced laws against abortion, adultery, birth control, cohabitation, fornication, obscenity, prostitution, and sodomy.[15] Polak also used the profits from his pornography businesses to support the respectable activities of the Homosexual Law Reform Society. Meanwhile, in 1965 a Cleveland homophile activist opened the first of what eventually became a large network of gay bathhouses that generated major financial support for the movement. Toward the end of the 1960s, homophiles in Miami and San Francisco opened stores that specialized in gay porn. In 1968, two Mattachine D.C. activists began publishing a column called "The Homosexual Citizen" in *Screw*, a porn magazine that was oriented primarily to straights but advocated sexual liberation for all. While other factions denounced sexual radicalism, in part because they feared that it would tarnish their respectable reputations, many gay men found it more appealing than the movement's other political tendencies.

A sixth tendency arose in the late 1960s and gave expression to the more radical, countercultural, and antiwar sensibilities of a younger generation; Vanguard and the Committee for Homosexual Freedom in San Francisco and Fight Repression of Erotic Expression (FREE) in Minneapolis developed this political orientation. For example, while most homophile groups called for an end to policies that excluded homosexuals from the military, Vanguard denounced U.S. participation in the Vietnam War. In 1967, Vanguard began to participate in antiwar rallies and urged its supporters to "fuck for peace."[16] Two years later, the Committee for Homosexual Freedom began organizing gay and lesbian demonstrations, participating in antiwar and student protests, and announcing its support for revolutionary change. FREE was founded by the participants in a free university course on the "homosexual revolution." This political tendency has commonly been associated with the post-Stonewall era, but it began developing before the riots erupted in June 1969.

In the 1960s, the movement continued to engage in many of the activities it had favored in the 1950s—helping individuals in need, sponsoring discussion groups, hosting social events, organizing public lectures and conferences, publishing magazines and newsletters, engaging in educational outreach, and working with researchers and journalists. In this period, the periodicals produced by homophile groups reached more readers and the bar guides they published and publicized expanded in scale and distribution. In 1966, San Francisco activists opened what may have been the country's first gay and lesbian community center; they also helped secure government funding for an anti-poverty program that worked with gay, lesbian, trans, and other clients. In several cities, homophile groups supported the creation of education and treatment programs to address sexually transmitted diseases. As the Vietnam War escalated, they also began to offer draft counselling services. Around the country, homophile groups responded to hundreds of requests for speakers to address community-based organizations, college and university groups, and legal, political, and religious audiences. They also developed media response strategies when homosexuality was ignored or mistreated in mainstream popular culture—criticizing the coverage in their publications, sending letters to periodical editors, challenging radio and television broadcasters, requesting meetings to discuss problems, and demanding time and space to respond. By the end of the decade, the movement had assisted thousands, reached tens of thousands via its publications, and communicated with millions through public speaking and media activism.

Homophile militants appreciated the importance of these activities, but argued that the time had come to emphasize direct political action. At the federal level, they targeted discrimination by the Civil Service Commission, the military, the State Department, the Immigration and Naturalization Service (INS), and the Post Office. At the state and local levels, their primary targets were laws that criminalized private consensual sex between adults, antihomosexual police and liquor control practices, and sexual censorship. While direct action advocates also challenged private businesses and scientific experts, many of their efforts focused on government policies and practices. Most homophile political action was antistatist in the sense that it did not call upon public officials to take affirmative steps to serve gay and lesbian constituents; rather, the movement wanted the state to stop persecuting homosexuals.

Homophile direct action took many forms in the 1960s. In many situations, lobbying government officials seemed like the best approach. In 1962, Mattachine D.C. members wrote to the president and cabinet, senators and representatives, Supreme Court justices, and other government officials to request appointments to discuss antihomosexual discrimination. Most did not respond, but two U.S. House members agreed to have their staff meet with homophile activists, as did Pentagon and Selective Service officials. In 1963, when Congress considered legislation to revoke Mattachine D.C.'s license to raise funds as a charitable organization, gay activists testified before a House committee and helped defeat the bill; in the process they received extensive media attention. In 1965, the Civil Service Commission agreed to meet with Mattachine representatives to discuss employment discrimination. After the meeting, the Commission reaffirmed its rules against illegal and immoral conduct but emphasized that it did not discriminate against (or even recognize) homosexuals as a class. In 1965–66, homophile activists and their ACLU and *Playboy* allies exposed postal surveillance practices that targeted the recipients of allegedly obscene mail. They persuaded a Senate committee to investigate and eventually the Post Office promised to restrict the scope of its surveillance activities.

Homophile lobbying was more active at the state and local levels. In California, Delaware, Florida, New York, and Pennsylvania, the movement unsuccessfully lobbied state legislators to decriminalize sodomy. In 1961, however, activists helped convince the California legislature to revise the state's vagrancy law and its associated restrictions on disorderly conduct, solicitation, and lewd vagrancy. California police continued to target same-sex sex, but over the next few years arrest rates for lewd, indecent, and disorderly conduct declined in some locations. In 1965, a homophile activist met with Miami's mayor to discuss police practices. In 1966, Mattachine met with New York's mayor, who promised that police entrapment would end. In 1966, homophile agitation helped convince the New York City Civil Service Commission to abandon its policy against hiring homosexuals in most city government positions. Across the 1960s, homophile activists held discussions and filed complaints with police and liquor control officials. To exert added pressure, they helped journalists expose particularly heinous police practices. In Houston, New York, Philadelphia, San Francisco, and elsewhere, these efforts led to reductions in police entrapment practices, gay and lesbian bar raids, and antihomosexual harassment by public officials, though in some cases the improvements were only temporary.

Homophile activists also began to engage in new ways with electoral politics, especially in urban districts with large concentrations of gay and lesbian voters. They continued to report on the positions of candidates and encourage their members to vote, but now they organized voter registration drives and offered endorsements. Activists followed with great interest the 1961 candidacy of Jose Sarria for the San Francisco Board of Supervisors. Sarria, who was endorsed by the LCE, was a popular female impersonator at the Black Cat bar and well known for concluding his performances with collective renditions of "God Save Us Nelly Queens." Sarria was not elected, but his 5600 votes and his message of empowerment suggested to many activists that some of their goals might be achieved through electoral politics. In a sign that politicians were paying attention, San Francisco candidates began to purchase advertisements in homophile publications and attend homophile-sponsored candidate forums. Toward the end of the decade, homophiles began to take credit for influencing election outcomes. In May 1969, Los Angeles gay and lesbian activists successfully campaigned against the re-election of City Council member Paul Lamport. Homophile activists also claimed partial credit for the 1969 election of Dianne Feinstein as president of the San Francisco Board of Supervisors.

While homophile activists lobbied public officials and engaged in electoral politics, many favored court-based strategies, which they thought had the potential to
bypass unfavorable public attitudes and legislative dynamics. With the assistance of
ACLU lawyers, several homophile groups became more aggressive about instigating
and supporting litigation. One target was government employment discrimination.
In the late 1950s, Frank Kameny had gone to court after he was fired from
his federal government job because of an earlier lewd conduct arrest. After losing
several rounds of appeals, he revived Mattachine D.C., which supported multiple
challenges to government employment discrimination. One partial victory occurred
in 1965, when the D.C. Circuit Court ruled that the U.S. Civil Service Commission
could not fire an employee simply because he was a homosexual; the Commission
had to specify the conduct it found immoral and the relationship of that conduct to
occupational competence or fitness. Four years later, the D.C. Circuit Court ruled
that evidence of homosexual conduct alone was not a sufficient basis for dismissal
from federal government employment. There were also occasional employment
discrimination victories at the local level. In 1967–68, New York homophile
activists supported a successful suit by two men who had been denied employment
as city social workers based on allegations about homosexuality. Through these
types of effort, the movement began to reduce the scope of antihomosexual
employment discrimination in the public sector.

A second target of homophile litigation was repressive police and liquor control
practices. In 1961, after a raid on San Francisco's Tay-Bush Inn resulted in more
than 100 arrests, Mattachine activists found lawyers for the arrested and raised
money for their defense; the city eventually dropped the charges in all but two of
the cases. Over the next few years, Pan-Graphic, LCE, the Tavern Guild, and SIR
supported litigation in several California bar cases. In 1965, San Francisco homophile groups aided the successful defense of four people who were arrested when
the police raided a New Year's Day fundraising dance for the Council on Religion
and the Homosexual. A lawsuit by the Council helped convince local officials to
restrict the scope of antihomosexual police practices. In 1967, the Homosexual Law
Reform Society and DOB-NY supported successful appeals in several New Jersey
gay bar cases; the state's supreme court ruled that, without evidence of indecent
conduct, state officials could not deprive homosexuals of the right to assemble in
bars. Mattachine New York supported litigation that resulted in a 1967 state court
ruling making it more difficult for liquor control authorities to revoke bar licenses
based solely on allegations about homosexual patronage. Activists were not similarly
successful in 1968 when they asked the U.S. Supreme Court to overturn a Miami
ordinance that prohibited bars from employing or serving homosexuals, but by
the end of the decade, thanks in part to litigation supported by the movement,
antihomosexual police and liquor control practices in California, New Jersey,
New York, and Pennsylvania had declined.

Sexual censorship was a third target. Across the 1960s, homophile periodicals
reported on the legal struggles of physique magazines, some of which began to

publicly denounce antigay censorship. In 1962, Dorian Book Service successfully challenged a decision by U.S. Customs to restrict the importation of books with seminude male photographs. In 1967, Mattachine San Francisco's Hal Call testified in support of Directory Services in Minneapolis, one of the country's largest gay-oriented mail order businesses, in its successful appeal of an anti-obscenity ruling. In the late 1960s, Mattachine New York supported litigation against restrictions on the importation of magazines with nude male photographs. Also in the late 1960s, Mattachine San Francisco supported the successful appeal of a Los Angeles business that had been indicted on obscenity charges for mailing nude male photographs. Clark Polak, Janus, and the Homosexual Law Reform Society were particularly active in supporting anti-censorship litigation.

While the movement won several important victories in employment discrimination, gay bar, and sexual censorship cases, it was less successful when challenging the criminalization of same-sex sex. In 1962, the California Supreme Court overturned two same-sex sex convictions based on police surveillance of public bathrooms. In 1965, however, the Ninth Circuit Court upheld oral copulation convictions for two men caught having sex in a Yosemite National Park bathroom. In 1967, Mattachine New York failed in its effort to have the U.S. Supreme Court consider an appeal in a police entrapment case. Los Angeles activists were similarly unsuccessful in 1968 when they supported the appeal of two lewd conduct convictions (based on midnight kissing on New Year's Eve). Even in some of their employment discrimination and gay bar victories, homophile advocates won by distinguishing between homosexual character, which they challenged as a legitimate basis for discrimination, and homosexual conduct, which they implicitly or explicitly accepted as a basis for repressive state action.

The movement was also unsuccessful in using the courts to overturn anti-homosexual immigration and naturalization laws. Mattachine New York supported the unsuccessful litigation of a Danish lesbian whose petition for naturalization was denied by the INS. Perhaps the homophile movement's greatest courtroom defeat occurred in the 1967 *Boutilier* case, in which the Homosexual Law Reform Society failed to convince the U.S. Supreme Court to overturn the federal law authorizing the exclusion and deportation of homosexual aliens. The Society funded the litigation, worked on the case with immigration advocates and ACLU lawyers, and submitted a brief with statements by more than thirty experts who denied that homosexuality was psychopathological. The Supreme Court upheld the federal law and then did not accept another gay and lesbian rights case for full-fledged review until the 1980s.

While the movement increased its lobbying, electoral, and litigation activities in the 1960s, some of its most visible actions consisted of demonstrations and sit-ins. These were sometimes organized to produce concrete results, but more often were designed to educate the public, mobilize support, and highlight injustices. In 1964, Randy Wicker, who was a member of Mattachine New York and the New York League for Sexual Freedom, organized a small gay rights demonstration (without

Mattachine authorization) at a military draft center. Later that year, Wicker and a few allies picketed a forum entitled "Homosexuality: A Disease" at New York's Cooper Union, an art, architecture, and design school. In 1965, homophile groups began to sponsor demonstrations. Mattachine D.C. and New York organized pickets in front of the White House and the United Nations headquarters; their goal was to use recent publicity about the incarceration of homosexuals in Cuba to criticize antigay policies in Cuba and the United States. East Coast Homophile Organizations then organized demonstrations at the White House, Civil Service Commission, Pentagon, and State Department in D.C. and at Independence Hall in Philadelphia.

In the remainder of the decade, homophile demonstrations increased in scale. The Independence Hall protest, held on the July Fourth holiday, became an annual event and lasted until 1969. On Armed Forces Day in May 1966, nationally coordinated demonstrations in several cities protested the exclusion of homosexuals from the military. Later that year, Mattachine Midwest picketed the *Chicago Tribune* and *Chicago Sun-Times*. In 1967, Los Angeles homophiles organized a series of demonstrations—the largest with 200 participants at the Black Cat bar—to protest police abuse and harassment. In 1968, criticism of Los Angeles police practices continued at Griffith Park "gay-ins," which were inspired by countercultural "be-ins." Later in 1968, when police raided the Patch, a gay and lesbian bar in a Los Angeles suburb, the owner led an impromptu march to the police station where the arrested had been taken.

Some direct action tactics were used in combination with litigation. In 1966, three Mattachine New York members conducted a "sip-in" at several bars and restaurants. By declaring openly that they were homosexuals and asking to be served, they hoped to instigate a challenge to State Liquor Authority policies. After they were served without incident at two establishments and then were offered drinks at a third, the activists convinced the bar manager at the latter to refuse them service so the state policies could be challenged in court. In exchange, Mattachine promised to help the bar with a pending license suspension. After the activists were denied service, they announced that they would file a complaint against the SLA. Soon they had the support of the New York City Commission on Human Rights, which encouraged the activists to pursue a sex discrimination complaint. In the midst of the publicity about the sip-in, the SLA announced that bars could serve homosexuals. This was later confirmed in a state court ruling, though the SLA continued to apply its rules against disorderly conduct in ways that discriminated against same-sex touching, kissing, and dancing.

Most homophile demonstrations addressed government policies and practices, but there were other targets. In 1965, San Francisco activists demonstrated at an Episcopal church to protest the disciplinary actions taken against a minister for his work with the Council on Religion and the Homosexual. A few years later, homophiles picketed the offices of a Brooklyn newspaper and organized an advertising boycott to protest its antigay contents. In 1968, the Student Homophile League at

Columbia picketed a medical school forum featuring experts who believed that homosexuality was pathological. Also in 1968, homophile protesters distributed leaflets at the American Medical Association convention in San Francisco; they challenged antigay science and demanded that homophile experts and activists be represented in discussions about homosexuality. In April 1969, the Committee for Homosexual Freedom organized a series of demonstrations at a San Francisco steamship company that had fired an employee after he was identified as a gay revolutionary in a Berkeley newspaper and appeared shirtless in a *Vector* cover photograph. In May, the Committee demonstrated at a record store after activists were informed that the store had fired a clerk because he was gay.

Compared with many other demonstrations in the late 1960s, most homophile protests were small, and the self-imposed dress codes used in some of them (mandating jackets and ties for men and dresses and skirts for women) showed that many homophile militants were not as radicalized as were other activists in this era. This was also evident when homophiles challenged the exclusion of homosexuals from the armed forces at a time when antiwar protests were escalating. Nevertheless, the public protests signalled that the movement was becoming more aggressive and their visibility brought new attention to gay and lesbian concerns. Occasionally, movement protests abandoned the politics of respectability. In 1965, Janus leaders came to the aid of teenagers who were conducting a sit-in at Dewey's Restaurant in Philadelphia to protest the mistreatment of gay, lesbian, and trans patrons. Four participants were arrested, but homophile activists organized a five-day demonstration, won a promise of improved treatment, and publicized its support for "the masculine woman and the feminine man."[17] In 1966, Vanguard and other San Francisco activists picketed Compton's Cafeteria to protest its mistreatment of gay, lesbian, and trans patrons, including street queens, sex workers, and others who were struggling in the context of economic inequality, police harassment, and urban redevelopment. A short time later, when a police officer tried to arrest one of the queens, a group of patrons fought back, forced the police to leave the cafeteria, and rioted in the streets.

Homophile political action had significant effects during the 1960s, especially in some of the country's largest cities, but at the end of the decade trouble loomed again. Republican Richard Nixon's election as U.S. president in 1968 and his inauguration in 1969 brought eight years of liberal rule to an end, and Nixon's campaign coalition had included outspoken opponents of gay and lesbian rights. As New Right leaders developed their plans for taking over the Republican Party and winning government power, they increasingly viewed opposition to gay and lesbian rights as a critical component of their political agenda and a promising weapon in their efforts to win popular support. Some of the country's closest allies—including Canada, England, and West Germany—decriminalized private homosexual acts by consenting adults in the late 1960s. U.S. conservatives were determined to prevent the same thing from happening in the United States, even if this meant contradicting their own criticisms of "big government."

As the larger political context increasingly seemed unfavorable, the homophile movement experienced a set of major transitions. By the end of the decade, Mattachine in San Francisco and ONE in Los Angeles were no longer publishing their magazines or engaging in significant political activities. As the DOB increasingly oriented itself to the women's movement, it lost many of its connections to other homophile groups. In 1970, DOB dissolved its national structure and several women moved *The Ladder* to Nevada, where it lasted until 1972. In 1968, PRIDE fell apart in Los Angeles. In May 1969, SIR removed the editor of *Vector* from his position after he posed with a bare-chested friend for a photograph that was printed in the *Berkeley Barb*. The editor also had used *Vector* to denounce homophile conservatism, criticize movement racism and class bigotry, and announce his support for the "gay revolution."[18]

Meanwhile, in February 1969, Clark Polak, who had led Janus, *Drum*, and the Homosexual Law Reform Society for much of the decade, was arrested for selling obscene publications and showing obscene films at one of his Philadelphia bookstores. This was just one in a series of actions that local, state, and federal officials took in opposition to Polak's activities as a pornographic entrepreneur, sexual liberationist, and homophile militant. Obscenity charges were also used to disrupt the work of Miami's leading homophile activist in the late 1960s. In April 1969, Polak was found guilty and received a two-year prison sentence. Facing a lengthy and expensive appeals process, he announced in May that he was terminating *Drum*, which for five years had spearheaded homophile sexual radicalism. After additional obscenity charges were filed in 1969 and 1970, Polak accepted a plea bargain that required him to abandon his operations in Philadelphia. Janus, *Drum*, and the Homosexual Law Reform Society did not survive the campaign against the homophile movement's leading sexual liberationist and one of its most active proponents of homosexual law reform. If this was a sign of what to expect in Richard Nixon's America, the gay and lesbian movement was in trouble.

3

GAY LIBERATION, LESBIAN FEMINISM, AND GAY AND LESBIAN LIBERALISM, 1969–73

From the Stonewall riots of 1969 to the American Psychiatric Association's decision to declassify homosexuality as a mental disorder in 1973, the U.S. gay and lesbian movement achieved unprecedented mass mobilization and unparalleled social change. Building on two decades of homophile organizing and influenced by the radicalization of multiple movements, gay and lesbian activists pursued new political possibilities. Three distinct orientations—gay liberation, lesbian feminism, and gay and lesbian liberalism—were particularly influential in these years. Within the movement, radical gay liberation and radical lesbian feminism were initially ascendant, but reformist gay and lesbian liberalism was dominant by the end of this period. In a tumultuous period in U.S. history, which began with mass antiwar protests and concluded with the U.S. decision to withdraw from Vietnam, the gay and lesbian movement reinvented itself and reconstructed sexual activism for the post-1960s era.

Stonewall Riots

In the early morning hours of June 28, 1969, a police raid on the Stonewall Inn, a private club on Christopher Street in Greenwich Village, prompted several days of rioting by thousands of New Yorkers. As was the case with many gay and lesbian bars in this period, the Stonewall was owned and operated by men with links to organized crime who made payments to the police to avoid raids and closures. At the time of the raid, the Stonewall was one of the city's most popular gay bars, in part because of its reputation for dancing and drugs. Most of its patrons were working- and middle-class whites in their teens, twenties, and thirties, but there was a significant presence of African Americans and Latinos as well. Gay men, drag queens, street queens, transsexuals, sex workers, and others who transgressed gender and sexual norms frequented the bar, as did a small number of lesbians. On this night, the police lost control of the raid when patrons and passersby—gay, lesbian, trans, and straight—fought back with words, wits, and weapons in what soon became a gay power riot. Over the next few days, thousands of New Yorkers battled the police for control of the streets near the Stonewall. Over the next few years, thousands of activists battled one another over the meanings of the Stonewall rebellion.

In the aftermath of the uprising, many described the riots as the first acts of gay and lesbian resistance ever, which erased the long history of pre-Stonewall struggles. Others acknowledged the existence of the homophile movement, but minimized its significance with assertions about its small size, respectable strategies, conservative politics, and limited accomplishments. Simplistic portrayals of the homophile movement were useful for activists who wanted to highlight the mass mobilization, political radicalization, and substantive gains of the late 1960s and early 1970s, but this did not do justice to the diverse, changing, and complex nature of homophile activism in previous years. Dismissing the homophile movement encouraged post-Stonewall activists to concentrate on the present and future, but in the process they lost valuable opportunities to learn from the past.

Over the last several decades, historians have offered competing and complementary arguments about why the Stonewall riots occurred when and where they did. Few credit the popular notion that the riots were a spontaneous uprising with no antecedents. One argument emphasizes the influence of the homophile movement, which for two decades had promoted gay and lesbian mobilization, solidarity, and resistance. This argument works best when the movement's radicalization in the 1960s is recognized, when the tendencies that favored homophile militancy, sexual liberation, and community empowerment are acknowledged, and when homophile defenses of gay and lesbian bars are highlighted. The argument is strengthened when homophile activism receives credit for the rising gay and lesbian expectations that seemed threatened by the election of U.S. President Richard Nixon and the escalation of local, state, and national repression in the months leading up to the riots. Homophile activists were not present inside the Stonewall when the raid occurred and some denounced the riots, but other homophile activists participated in the street protests, many promoted the mass mobilization that followed, and the homophile movement helped create the conditions that made the rebellion possible.

A second argument turns away from the homophile movement and views the riots as the culmination of a long history of community-based resistance practices in gay, lesbian, and trans cultures. This argument emphasizes that the riots were not initiated or inspired by homophile activists; they began when bar patrons fought back using tactics that homophiles had not generally embraced. Historians who support this argument note that many of the people who played leading roles in the riots did not fit the profile of the typical homophile activist insofar as they were not white, middle class, gender normative, and over the age of twenty-one. According to this argument, for decades gay, lesbian, and trans patrons of bars, clubs, and restaurants had resisted persecution by police authorities and hostile straights. Their actions promoted the changes of consciousness that led to the riots. Some proponents of this perspective underscore the fact that the critical events began in a bar and thus the riots can be viewed as part of the same consumer protest tradition that led civil rights activists to target lunch counters and other sites of consumption. Others highlight the territorial sensibilities that accompanied the growth of urban gay and lesbian neighborhoods. Still others emphasize that a series of recent raids on New York bars contributed to the anger felt by many rioters. On some occasions in the past, including the sit-in at Dewey's in Philadelphia in 1965, the Compton's Cafeteria riot in San Francisco in 1966, and the Los Angeles gay bar demonstrations in 1967 and 1968, everyday resistance had escalated in extraordinary ways. The Stonewall riots were different in scale, but they can be understood in the context of long-standing resistance practices in gay, lesbian, and trans cultures.

A third argument highlights the influence of radicalization in other movements. While historians often discuss the 1960s as a unified whole, in many respects the decade's second half was remarkably different from the first half. The movement that most influenced homophiles in the early 1960s was the civil rights movement, but in the last few years of the decade, many riot participants were affected by the rise of women's liberation, the growth in student activism, and the radicalization of African Americans and other racialized minorities. They also joined many of their fellow Americans in rejecting the Vietnam War and criticizing the United States for not supporting anti-colonial struggles around the world. In addition, gender and sexual dissidents were influenced by the rise of the counterculture, which offered new ways of thinking about the liberation of mind and body and the limitations of liberalism. In 1968, after civil rights icon Martin Luther King, Jr., and U.S. presidential candidate Robert Kennedy were assassinated, many became further disillusioned by the failures of liberalism. The Stonewall rebels also knew about the riots that had broken out in various African American neighborhoods in recent summers and the Democratic Party convention riots in Chicago in 1968. Historians who highlight these factors argue that the Stonewall riots can be understood as a manifestation of the radicalization that affected many sectors of society in the late 1960s.

All three of these arguments and additional ones that focus on the distinctive history, geography, and politics of Greenwich Village and New York City have merit. All of them help us understand the Stonewall riots. But it is also important to note that the riots themselves did not lead to long-term mass mobilization and they did not, in and of themselves, change the direction of the gay and lesbian movement. What happened in the days, weeks, and months after the Stonewall rebellion was crucial for the future of gay and lesbian activism.

Gay Liberation

In the aftermath of the Stonewall riots, Mattachine New York organized community meetings and set up a political action committee. Soon, however, activists who viewed Mattachine as too conservative formed the Gay Liberation Front (GLF), which began meeting in New York in July 1969. All three elements of the new group's name were meaningful. In calling itself "gay," GLF signaled its opposition to the medical discourse of "homosexuality," its critique of "homophile" politics, and its proud and public orientation. There was also a presumption that "gay" was a capacious term that would appeal to all relevant constituencies. In embracing "liberation," GLF rejected a narrow liberal focus on legal rights and embraced a broader leftist agenda of freedom, justice, and equality. In calling itself a "front," the group presented itself as a radical coalition that would lead a revolutionary struggle. The group's name also reflected its affinities with the National Liberation Front in Vietnam, the politics of anticolonialism, and the antiwar movement. In the next few years, GLF-NY helped inspire the creation and growth of dozens of autonomous gay liberation groups in every U.S. region—many in towns and cities where homophile groups had not existed—and additional ones around the world.

Over the course of the 1970s and 1980s, gay and lesbian activists increasingly referred to their movement as "gay liberation" or "gay and lesbian liberation," even when their politics diverged from the radicalism of GLF and even after most GLFs disappeared. It thus becomes possible to refer to gay liberation in narrow or broad terms, but a good starting place for considering the historically specific radical politics of gay liberation is to concentrate on the influential GLFs in Los Angeles, New York, Philadelphia, and San Francisco, along with related and similarly named groups in these and other locations, in the period from 1969 through 1973.[1]

Demographically, gay liberation and homophile groups differed in several ways. With important exceptions, most gay liberationists were in their teens and twenties, whereas homophile groups had featured a more even distribution of people in their twenties, thirties, forties, and fifties. In part, this reflected the fact that there were many gay liberation student groups on college and university campuses, but most other gay liberationists were young as well. Interest was so great among young people that in 1970 GLF-NY established a Gay Youth caucus for people under the age of twenty-one. Led by Mark Segal, Gay Youth soon was functioning as an autonomous organization with affiliated groups elsewhere in the United States and Canada.

The gay liberation movement was predominantly white but more multiracial than the homophile movement had been. Gay liberation's greater appeal for people of color was partly the result of its radical politics, but developments in communities of color—including the effects of civil rights integrationism, the dynamics of homophobia and heterosexism in liberal and radical movements, and the influence of feminism, the counterculture, and the sexual revolution—also made it more likely that people of color would participate. Third World Gay Revolution, which initially was a caucus for people of color in GLF-NY, began meeting in 1970 and was influential in addressing the "triple oppression" of capitalism, racism, and sexism.[2] Street Transvestites for Gay Power, which became Street Transvestite Action Revolutionaries (STAR), was founded in New York in 1970 by Sylvia

Rivera, whose background was Puerto Rican and Venezuelan, and Marsha Johnson, who was African American. GLF-Chicago had a Black Caucus, which renamed itself Third World Gay Revolution, and its Women's Caucus was multiracial. Third World Gay People met in Berkeley. GLF-Philadelphia, led by Japanese American activist Kyoshi Kuromiya, was multiracial and predominantly nonwhite. GLF-LA's first president, Greg Byrd, was African American. Chinese American activist Jim Toy helped found and lead the Detroit Gay Liberation Movement and GLF-Ann Arbor. African American singer-songwriter Blackberri founded Gay Liberation Arizona Desert in Tucson. As for class, middle-class youth were well-represented in the movement, but gay liberation's anticapitalist, antiracist, and anti-establishment politics contributed to greater class diversity. STAR in New York and Breadbox in D.C. were exceptional as gay liberation groups made up primarily of poor people.

Most gay liberation groups were predominantly male, though many gay liberation men embraced feminism and linked their oppression to the oppression of women. In fact, gay liberationists tended to blame their troubles not on homophobia, a term first used in the late 1960s, but on sexism. Outnumbered by men, women still were active in gay liberation. Martha Shelley is credited by some with coming up with GLF's name; Shelley and Lois Hart were influential GLF-NY members; and lesbians played prominent roles in *Come Out*, a newspaper affiliated with GLF-NY. For a while, GLFs in Bloomington, Chicago, Los Angeles, New York, and elsewhere had women's caucuses, but over time fewer women participated in gay liberation groups. In part, this was because of the predominance of men, the emphasis on male-defined sexual liberation, the masculinism of gay liberation, and the sexism of gay men, which persisted even as gay activists declared their support for women's liberation. Many women in gay liberation groups became more interested in lesbian feminism in the early 1970s.

Gay liberation tended to be more welcoming to gender transgressors than the homophile movement had been. Many gay liberationist men desired and embodied the gay masculinities that became popular in the 1970s, but others embraced male femininities. In San Francisco, gay liberationists helped found the Cockettes and the Angels of Light, which were gender-fuck performance groups, and New York gay liberationists established the Effeminists. Many queens, transvestites, and transsexuals participated in gay liberation groups, even after they established separate trans ones. Sylvia Rivera and Marsha Johnson, who identified as queens and transvestites, were active in GLF-NY. Angela Douglas, who identified as transsexual, was a GLF-LA member. Some gay liberationists, however, criticized what they viewed as the antigay, artificial, sexist, and stereotypical aspects of trans genders. Others welcomed gay-identified transvestites but distanced themselves from straight-identified trans-sexuals. In part because gay liberation groups were not fully supportive of trans agendas, Lee Brewster founded Queens (later Queens Liberation Front) in New York in 1969. The following year, Rivera and Johnson created STAR to assist young street queens in New York, Judy Bowen founded Transsexuals and

Transvestites in New York, and Douglas established Transvestite-Transsexual Action Organization (later Transsexual Action Organization) in Los Angeles (and later in Miami). In 1971, Brewster began publishing *Drag Queen* magazine (later renamed *Drag*).

Gay liberation and homophile politics diverged in four important ways. First, gay liberationists emphasized "coming out" as gay—individually, collectively, privately, and publicly. On the personal level, gay liberation consciousness-raising discussions highlighted the transformative effects of revealing oneself as gay in all spheres of life; liberationists argued that this would help gay people overcome self-hate and help others transcend hostility. On the collective level, they believed that coming out in public would promote greater visibility for gays and lesbians, confront prejudice, and challenge the relegation of sexual matters to the private sphere. The popular GLF chant "Out of the Closets, Into the Streets" called on everyone who engaged in same-sex sex to move beyond the limited rights and freedoms that might be possible in the private sphere; gay liberationists wanted public recognition and political equality.

Gay liberationists also wanted *everyone* to come out. They joined homophiles in referring to gay people as a minority group, but simultaneously believed that all people could transcend the constraints that society placed on same-sex sexual expression. Some homophiles had made similar arguments, but gay liberationists embraced this notion more fully. Coming out did not require an exclusive commitment to same-sex sex; it rejected compulsory heterosexuality. As San Francisco's Carl Wittman declared in his influential 1969 manifesto, "Homosexuality is the capacity to love someone of the same sex. ... Bisexuality is good; it is the capacity to love people of either sex. ... Exclusive heterosexuality is fucked up." While Wittman wrote that he called himself "gay" because "bi" seemed like a "copout," the National Bisexual Liberation Group, founded in New York in 1972, embraced the term and concept.[3] More generally, gay liberationists hoped that everyone would come out as gay, but also wanted to transcend the categories of homosexuality and heterosexuality, which were seen as limiting human potential.

This relates to the second way in which gay liberationists diverged from their homophile predecessors. Some homophiles had supported sexual and gender liberation, but this was more central to gay liberation. In some contexts, this meant defending and celebrating anonymous sex, casual sex, group sex, intergenerational sex, public sex, sex work, pornography, promiscuity, sadomasochism, and sex for minors. In others, it meant challenging gender norms, sex roles, and sexual commodification, exploitation, and objectification. In some situations, trans liberation was central to gay liberation; in some, the goal was liberation from gender. Some gay liberationists were sexual libertarians; some promoted specific forms of sex; some wanted liberation *from* sex. These ways of thinking could and did come into conflict. Gay and lesbian radicals also debated the politics of marriage, reproduction, and the family. Many denounced marriage and the nuclear family, which they saw as conservative institutions that limited freedom. Others hoped to revolutionize marriage and the family. Notwithstanding these disagreements, gay liberationists generally agreed that sexual, gender, and gay liberation were inextricably intertwined.

The third way in which gay liberation diverged from homophile activism was its support for radical, leftist, and countercultural politics. Some groups were less radical than others, but gay liberation's general orientation was more leftist than liberal. When gay liberationists asked, "Do you think homosexuals are revolting?" they answered, "You bet your sweet ass we are!"[4] Gay liberation groups included radicalized homophiles, activists from other movements who became gay liberationists, and new activists whose politics were formed by gay liberation. Many gay and lesbian radicals were turned off by the sexual prejudices they encountered in other movements, but they viewed themselves as part of this era's "movement of movements" and wanted to link gay liberation to other struggles. Coalitions with other radical groups (especially the Black Panthers) led to conflicts with more mainstream gay and lesbian activists, some of whom were antiradical, did not want to alienate mainstream authorities and audiences, or did not think that gay and lesbian activists should form alliances with movements that did not support sexual equality. Gay liberation's rejection of established authorities, its way of doing politics by rejecting politics, and its countercultural ethos also led to conflicts, as did its "structureless structure," which typically involved no formal constitutions, minutes, officers, or rules for membership or decision-making. Gay liberationists, however, believed that their unique integration of radical, leftist, countercultural, feminist, and gay politics had great potential.

Gay liberation's fourth distinctive feature was the scope, scale, and style of its political activities. Compared with homophile demonstrations, for example, gay liberation protests were large, lively, and loud. GLF-NY's first public actions took place in July 1969, when the group joined a Black Panther demonstration and participated in a 400-person march organized by Mattachine and DOB to commemorate the one-month anniversary of the Stonewall riots. A short time later, Gay Liberation Theater in Berkeley performed "No Vietnamese Ever Called Me a Queer!" before 2000 university students during "disorientation" week. (The title was based on a line commonly attributed to boxing champion and political activist Mohammad Ali: "No Viet Cong ever called me nigger.")[5] In October, GLF-San Francisco, the Committee for Homosexual Freedom, and the Society for Individual Rights demonstrated at the *San Francisco Examiner* to criticize an offensive article about gay clubs. After a staff member dumped a bag of purple printer's ink on the protesters, the police arrived and began beating and arresting the activists. One day later, gay liberationists staged a sit-in at San Francisco City Hall to protest the police violence. In November, GLF-LA held a demonstration at the *Los Angeles Times* and announced a boycott of the paper and its advertisers because the *Times* refused to accept advertisements that used the word "homosexual"; the newspaper changed its policy several months later.

Public protests continued in 1970. In January, 100 gay liberationists demonstrated at a San Francisco radio/television station that had fired a gay activist. In March, after a series of New York bar raids, one of which led to the impalement of an Argentine immigrant on an iron fence after he jumped out of a window (in part because he feared deportation), GLF-NY helped organize a 500-person march to the police station. Later that year, during another period of increased police harassment, GLF-NY helped organize a protest march; after they were attacked by police, approximately 1000 people rioted. Gay liberationists also demonstrated and held a sit-in at New York University after administrators refused to allow Gay Student Liberation-NYU to sponsor a campus dance; the university eventually relented. Meanwhile, Los Angeles gay liberationists organized a ten-day fast and sit-in outside a federal office building to protest police abuses. In 1971, GLF activists demonstrated for several days at New Orleans City Hall and met with Atlanta's mayor to protest police harassment. Later that year, gay liberationists from various parts of New York State were among the thousands of gay and lesbian activists who demonstrated in Albany for the repeal of state laws against sodomy, solicitation, loitering, and impersonation. Californians similarly rallied in Sacramento in support of sex law reform. These actions, along with GLF marches in Atlanta, Chicago, Los Angeles, Philadelphia, and Seattle, mobilized the community and highlighted the ongoing nature of sexual persecution.

Gay liberationists also engaged in more creative protests. In 1969, GLF-NY began staging public confrontations with political candidates, asking what they planned to do to address antihomosexual oppression and whether they supported gay rights. Strategically planning their "zaps" (disruptive political actions, typically organised quickly and meant to surprise their targets) for maximum media exposure, gay liberationists asked these questions while shaking the hands of politicians (without letting go), during candidate forums, and at campaign fundraising events. In 1970, a GLF-NY-affiliated guerrilla theater group staged performances of a skit in which a drag queen gave five dollars to a bar owner, who gave it to the State Liquor Authority, who gave it to the Mafia, who gave it to a policeman, who beat the queen with his nightstick. Later in 1970, GLF-LA activists announced that they planned to take over California's rural Alpine County by encouraging mass gay and lesbian migration. Plans for "Stonewall Nation," as they called the project, were later abandoned, but many gay liberationists welcomed the media coverage that ensued. They received more attention in 1972 when Boston gay liberationist Charley Shively, wearing a dress, testified before the Democratic National Platform Committee about the need for a federal law prohibiting sexual orientation discrimination.

As some of these actions illustrate, while gay liberationists may have rejected conventional politics, they sometimes worked through conventional political channels. In 1969, the Committee for Homosexual Freedom began a petition and lobbying campaign to convince the San Francisco Board of Supervisors to prohibit antihomosexual employment discrimination by the city, its contractors, and its subcontractors. The board enacted the law in 1972, not long after Michigan activists convinced East Lansing to become the first U.S. municipality to prohibit various types of antihomosexual discrimination. This was a striking shift: homophile activists had generally struggled against state repression and now the movement envisioned the state as a potential ally. Meanwhile, when more mainstream New York gay and lesbian activists began lobbying for municipal legislation to prohibit antihomosexual discrimination in employment, housing, and public accommodations (not passed until 1986), STAR participated in public hearings and demanded that the legislation also prohibit antitrans discrimination.

Gay liberationists also filed legal appeals, complaints, and suits. In 1969, GLF-NY sued the *Village Voice* after it refused to run advertisements that used the word "gay." The lawsuit, demonstrations, and a meeting with the publisher convinced the *Voice* to change its policy. In 1970, GLF-Cornell filed a complaint with state liquor officials about an Ithaca bar that refused to serve gay and lesbian customers. The complaint, a sit-in, and a boycott led to victory. Also in 1970, GLF-LA arranged for a restraining order to curtail police harassment at its countercultural "gay-ins" and GLF-Chicago successfully challenged police practices that treated same-sex dancing as a form of public indecency. In 1970 and 1971, Minneapolis and Seattle gay liberationists tried unsuccessfully to obtain marriage licenses for same-sex couples and then filed appeals in state and federal courts, which denied their requests. These efforts received national publicity and Jack Baker, one of the litigants, was elected president of the University of Minnesota Student Association. In the early 1970s, GLFs at the Universities of Kansas, Kentucky, Tennessee, and Texas filed unsuccessful legal appeals when campus officials denied their requests for recognition as student groups, though similar efforts at Sacramento State and the Universities of Georgia and Missouri were successful. Around this time, Queens Liberation Front used litigation to overturn New York City's law against cross-dressing. Working through conventional legal channels was not the favored form of political action for radicals who rejected "the system," but gay liberationists lobbied and litigated.

Gay liberationists also targeted science, religion, and business. In 1970, Street Transvestites for Gay Power organized a rally at Bellevue Hospital to protest medical mistreatment. In the same year, gay liberationists organized protests at an American Psychiatric Association (APA) convention in San Francisco, an American Medical Association convention in Chicago, and a conference on behavior modification in Los Angeles. In 1971, homophile stalwart Frank Kameny worked with GLF-DC and other activists to declare war on psychiatry at the APA's annual convention in Washington, D.C. They appropriated microphones at convention sessions, denounced psychiatric efforts to "exterminate" homosexuals, threatened to tear down an exhibit on aversive conditioning (which the APA agreed to remove), and participated in a panel featuring five gay and lesbian speakers. Meanwhile, gay liberationists held protests at churches in Boston, Los Angeles, New York, Philadelphia, San Francisco, Seattle, and Washington, D.C. San Francisco activists zapped one airline for firing flight attendants based on allegations of lesbian sex and another for refusing to sell a ticket to a man with a gay power button. They also demonstrated against discrimination at local supermarkets and department stores.

Gay liberationists in the Twin Cities wrote to the region's twelve largest companies and threatened reprisals against those that did not renounce discrimination against gays and lesbians.

As suggested above, many gay liberation actions focused on mainstream media and popular culture. In 1969, they criticized various news outlets for ignoring the Stonewall riots or covering them in biased and offensive ways. To protest policies and practices that silenced their perspectives, censored their language, and depicted gay, lesbian, and trans people in negative ways, they staged demonstrations and disruptions at various newspapers, along with the offices and studios of ABC Television, *The Carol Burnett Show*, *Time*, and *The Tonight Show*. In several instances, they won apologies, concessions, and more favorable treatment. In 1969, Queens picketed a Broadway production of *A Patriot for Me*. Over the next few years, Transvestite-Transsexual Action Organization picketed a Los Angeles movie theater showing the film *Myra Breckinridge* and GLF activists around the country held protests at theaters showing the films *The Boys in the Band*, *The Gay Deceivers*, and *Some of My Best Friends Are …* . Gay liberationists also cultivated relationships with alternative newspapers, many of which provided more extensive and sympathetic coverage than was typical in the mainstream press.

While homophile activists generally had engaged in single-issue politics, gay liberationists formed coalitions with other radical groups. Thousands participated in antiwar demonstrations and did so with banners, chants, leaflets, signs, and slogans that identified themselves as gay. Gay liberation contingents joined protests organized by the Black Panthers, the Puerto Rican Young Lords, the United Farm Workers, and the National Welfare Rights Organization. In 1970, they travelled to Cuba as part of the Venceremos Brigade, which organized illegal trips for young U.S. leftists interested in working for and learning about Cuba's communist revolution. Later in 1970, after Panther leader Huey Newton called for an alliance between black radicals, women's liberationists, and gay liberationists, about sixty gay men attended the Panthers' Revolutionary People's Constitutional Convention in Philadelphia. Thousands of convention delegates applauded the Male Homosexual Workshop statement, which was based on a Third World Gay Revolution manifesto. In these and other activities, gay radicals expressed support for struggles against capitalism, imperialism, racism, and war, challenged straight allies to think differently about sexual politics, and criticized gays and lesbians who distanced themselves from other struggles. Gay liberationists also "let it all hang out" at countercultural "be-ins" and music festivals. Many straight radicals continued to reject homosexuality and many gays and lesbians continued to reject radicalism, but gay liberationists formed valuable, if sometimes temporary and tenuous, coalitions with other radical movements.

As part of their commitment to radicalism, gay liberationists critiqued oppressive dynamics within the gay and lesbian community. Consciousness-raising discussions challenged gay sexism, gay and lesbian racism, and in some contexts anti-trans prejudices. Gay liberationists also criticized gay and lesbian bars, clubs, and restaurants that charged exorbitant prices, had connections to organized crime, or were owned and operated by straights. Around the country, they organized protests at gay and lesbian bars that refused to permit the distribution of leaflets and newspapers, enforced rules against dancing, kissing, and touching, and excluded people of color, women, and gender transgressors. They challenged commercially oriented and straight-owned gay newspapers, including *Gay* and *Gay Power*. They regularly criticized homophile conservatism. In 1969, Bay Area gay liberationists disrupted a meeting of the Society for Individual Rights after it declined to participate in a major antiwar protest; they also picketed the Tavern Guild's annual drag ball for what they considered its conservative drag performances.

Gay liberationists critiqued but wanted to expand the terrain of the gay, lesbian, and trans community. Gay liberation was a product and producer of the growth in urban gay and lesbian neighborhoods that occurred in this period. At the same time, gay liberationists wanted to move beyond the "gay ghetto." In various cities, they staged actions at businesses that refused to serve gay, lesbian, and trans patrons and made their presence known in places where they were not typically visible. In 1970, GLF-LA organized demonstrations at Barney's Beanery, a West Hollywood restaurant with a "Fagots Stay Out" sign; after three months of protests, the sign came down. Also in 1970, gay liberationists staged a "kiss-in" at a New York bar that had ejected two men for kissing and zapped a D.C. bar that had ejected a multiracial group of four gay men. In 1971, GLF-Bloomington picketed a bar and restaurant that had posted a sign that read: "This is Not a Fruit Stand"; it was soon taken down. In 1972, after the managers of a suburban Seattle roller-skating rink had two GLF men arrested for holding hands, a group of gay supporters, some in drag, staged a protest by skating together in "mixed sex" couples. Gay liberationists regularly made a point of "looking" and "acting" gay in public, in part to challenge heteronormative privileges and presumptions. In these and other ways, gay liberationists tried to defend, liberate, and expand gay and lesbian territories.

Critical of capitalism, ambivalent about bars, and interested in mobilizing support, gay liberationists worked on developing social alternatives that would be consistent with the politics of gay liberation. The most successful way they did so was by sponsoring dances, which proved remarkably popular, attracting hundreds at a time in Boston, Chicago, Los Angeles, New York, Philadelphia, and San Francisco and hundreds more on college and university campuses. In various places, after women complained that the dances were dominated by men, all-female dances were held. In California, Massachusetts, and New York, gay liberationists organized large countercultural "gay-ins" in public parks. STAR established a shelter to provide social assistance and communal housing for trans youth. University of Michigan activists convinced campus officials to establish a gay and lesbian program office. Albany, Detroit, Los Angeles, Louisville, New York, and Seattle activists created gay and lesbian community centers, which were focal points for social and political activities. Much of the social and political work of gay liberation took place in affiliated consciousness-raising groups, coffeehouses, collectives, and communes.

As many of these activities suggest, gay liberationists were interested in building alternative cultures. Some endorsed gay and lesbian separatism, but this rarely was envisioned as complete separation from the alternative cultures that gay liberationists supported or the larger society they wanted to transform. More often than not, separatists wanted specific times and places reserved for people who identified as gay or lesbian. Liberationists also wanted the special character of urban gay and lesbian neighborhoods to be recognized and respected. One of the ways that activists discussed these ideas while putting them into practice was by publishing gay liberation newspapers and newsletters. Among the best known were *Come Out* in New York; *Fag Rag*, *Gay Community News*, and *Lavender Vision* in Boston; *Gay Liberator* in Detroit; *Gay Sunshine* in Berkeley; and *San Francisco Gay Free Press* in San Francisco. More mainstream periodicals, including the *Advocate* in Los Angeles, *Bay Area Reporter* in San Francisco, *Gay* and *Gay Power* in New York, and *Gay Blade* in D.C., boosted gay and lesbian periodical circulation beyond 100,000 by 1972, but the more radical gay liberation newspapers reached and radicalized tens of thousands. For a brief period, gay liberation, as it was defined by GLFs and similarly radical groups, was the most influential component of the gay and lesbian movement.

Gay liberation accomplished a great deal in a short period of time, but if conceptualized as a movement based organizationally in GLFs and groups with similarly radical politics, it collapsed in 1971 and 1972. In general, this was a difficult period for U.S. leftists, radicals and revolutionaries. As they succeeded in helping to bring an end to the Vietnam War, they lost the primary issue around which the movement of movements had coalesced. Many white-, male-, and straight-dominated groups failed to meet the challenges posed by the rise of black radicalism, women's liberation, gay liberation, and other movements, which damaged the prospects of coalition-building and contributed to fragmentation on the left. Some turned away from politics. As government repression increased and the country's politics shifted to the right, leftists, radicals, and revolutionaries increasingly found themselves on the defensive.

For GLFs and similar groups, political repression and personal burnout took their tolls, as did internal divisions within gay liberation, conflicts with non-radical gays and lesbians, and the disappointment and disillusionment that set in when straight activists continued to express antihomosexual sentiments. By 1972, many influential gay liberation groups had disbanded and their affiliated newspapers had ceased publication. In a sign of the changing times, most GLFs on college and university campuses renamed themselves; many continued to call themselves "gay," but fewer used the term "liberation" or described themselves as a "front." Gay liberation had attracted thousands to its demonstrations and dances, but the vast majority of gays and lesbians were not radicals. Gay liberation had convinced many people to come out, but most who did so came to think of themselves as members of a sexual minority group rather than radical critics of sexual categories. At the same time, most people who engaged in same-sex sex but did not think of themselves as gay or lesbian were not likely to join a "gay" liberation movement. In 1969 and 1970, gay liberation groups had competed successfully with homophile groups for support, but some homophile groups began to revive and newer groups with less radical politics began to mobilize larger numbers. Depending on one's perspective, they either rejected or redefined gay liberation. As for radical gay liberation, it continued to influence the movement long after the heyday of GLF activism.

Radical Lesbian Feminism

Like gay liberation, radical lesbian feminism can be conceptualized as a movement that was based initially in a set of groups that formed in the aftermath of a dramatic protest. In this case, the protest occurred in May 1970 at the NOW-sponsored Second Congress to Unite Women in New York. Also like gay liberation, radical lesbian feminism can be defined in narrow and historically specific terms, in which case it lasted for just a few years, or in broader terms, in which case it continued to exist but changed after the early 1970s.[6] Long before radical lesbian feminist groups formed, there were lesbians who were feminists and feminists who were lesbians. There were also women who integrated lesbian and feminist activism; in many respects, this was DOB's mission. Through most of the 1950s and 1960s, however, DOB's feminism was more liberal than radical. Just as radical gay liberationists distanced themselves from homophile liberals, radical lesbian feminists distanced themselves from homophile lesbians.

Radical lesbian feminism emerged when gay liberation women and radical feminists came together to create an autonomous movement that simultaneously maintained connections to gay liberation, women's liberation, and other radical movements. As discussed above, lesbians participated in gay liberation and influenced its ideas and practices. GLF women, some of whom were active in the women's movement, infused gay liberation with feminist values. Over time, however, many GLF lesbians became alienated by the male-dominated politics of gay liberation and more attracted to women's liberation. In New York, for example, lesbians initially participated in a full range of GLF activities, but many began to devote more attention to the GLF Women's Caucus. Appreciating the dynamics of all-female activities, the Caucus organized women's dances and other all-female projects. In 1970, several GLF-NY women began meeting with a group of women's liberationists who had not been involved with gay liberation; together, they formed Radicalesbians. Gay liberationist women similarly helped establish radical lesbian feminist groups in other locations.

Women's liberationists who had not been involved in gay liberation brought to Radicalesbians a different set of experiences and commitments. Established in the late 1960s by women who were active in antiwar, civil rights, countercultural, socialist, and student movements, the women's liberation movement viewed liberal feminism, which for them was typified by the politics of NOW, as insufficiently radical. In part, this was because many women's liberationists viewed themselves as part of, even as they criticized, the radical movement of movements. In addition, while liberal feminism concentrated on public policy and legal rights, women's liberationists emphasized the multiple meanings of the notion that "the personal is political." On the one hand, women's liberationists believed in the importance of exploring the political dimensions of personal life, which they did in consciousness-raising groups, communal households, arts projects, and feminist publications. On the other hand, they believed that matters typically classified as personal—including sex, gender, sexuality, marriage, family, and reproduction—were important subjects for political action. By 1970, some women's liberationists were troubled by manifestations of anti-lesbianism in the women's movement. In New York, several of these women joined together with GLF women to form Radicalesbians.

Radicalesbians was established in the aftermath of the 1970 Second Congress to Unite Women, which was attended by several hundred women in New York. In the weeks leading up to the Congress, approximately forty GLF and other women made plans to stage a disruption that would force the women's movement to address lesbianism in new ways. Just before the opening session of the conference was scheduled to begin, the protesters arranged for the lights to be turned off. When the lights were turned on several minutes later, twenty women with "Lavender Menace" shirts were standing. NOW founder Betty Friedan, in a recent warning to the women's movement, had referred to lesbians as a "lavender menace"; she also had helped remove lesbians from leadership positions in NOW. Calling themselves "Lavender Menace: Gay Liberation Front Women and Radical Lesbians," the protesters proudly adopted Friedan's derisive name for them. For two hours, they spoke to the conference participants about the difficulties lesbians experienced in a heterosexist world. The Congress later adopted a resolution proposed by the protesters, which defiantly declared that women's liberation is "a lesbian plot." Challenging the tendency of feminists to insist that they were not lesbians, the resolution called on women's liberationists to affirm lesbianism whenever the movement or individual women were attacked as lesbians.[7]

After the Congress, the Lavender Menaces began to call their New York-based group Radicalesbians. Among the more influential members were Rita Mae Brown, Lois Hart, and Martha Shelley. Radical Lesbians in Ann Arbor, Gay Women's Liberation in San Francisco and Los Angeles, and Gay Women's Alliance in Seattle also were established in 1970. New groups in 1971 included Gay Women's Liberation in Austin, Gay Women's Caucus in Chicago (renamed Chicago Lesbian Liberation in 1972), Lesbian Feminists in Los Angeles, Gay Women's Liberation Front in New York, Those Women (renamed the Furies in 1972) in D.C., and Radicalesbians in Buffalo, Chicago, Milwaukee, Philadelphia, San Francisco, and Yellow Springs. In 1972–73, the Atlanta Lesbian Feminist Alliance, Chicago Women's Liberation Union Gay Group, Gay Radical Organization for Women in Rochester, Radical Lesbians in Boston, and Lesbian Feminist Liberation in New York were established. Significantly, many of these names referred to "gay women" rather than "lesbians," though this became less common over time.

Most radical lesbian feminists in the early 1970s were in their late teens and twenties; many were students; most were white. The Furies, one of the more influential groups, was all-white. Ana Sanchez was exceptional as a woman of color in Radicalesbians-NY, as was Anita Cornwell (later the author of *Black Lesbian in White America*) in Radicalesbians-Philadelphia. Jeanne Cordova, whose background was Mexican and Irish, was the editor and publisher of *Lesbian Tide*, one of the more important lesbian feminist periodicals. Chicago's Gay Women's Caucus was multiracial at first, with several active African American members, but it became more white around the time that it became Chicago Lesbian Liberation. Radical lesbian feminist groups were predominantly middle class, but working-class women participated as well. The groups tended to include certain types of gender transgressors but exclude others. Many lesbian feminists rejected stereotypical femininity and celebrated countercultural styles, some of which were androgynous, but many butch lesbians and trans women felt unwelcome.

Radical lesbian feminism was greatly influenced by "The Woman-Identified Woman," a collectively authored manifesto produced by the Menaces for the Second Congress. The manifesto began by asking, "What is a lesbian?" The answer offered a new definition: "A lesbian is the rage of all women condensed to the point of explosion." On the one hand, the Menaces described lesbianism as "a category of behavior possible only in a sexist society characterized by rigid sex roles and dominated by male supremacy." Men, they argued, promoted heterosexuality and condemned homosexuality as a way of keeping women under control. This meant that "in a society in which men do not oppress women and sexual expression is allowed to follow feelings, the categories of homosexuality and heterosexuality would disappear." On the other hand, they redefined lesbianism to incorporate all "women-identified women" who were willing to declare their independence from men and make relationships with women their highest priority. As for sex, the manifesto ambiguously called on women to "see in each other the possibility of a primal commitment which includes sexual love." In essence, "The Woman-Identified Woman" challenged women to do what the Menaces asked the Second Congress to do: instead of recoiling in horror when they were accused of being lesbians, feminists should boldly and proudly declare that they *were* lesbians and they should make such declarations meaningful in the ways in which they related to other women. In some respects, these formulations paralleled gay liberation's call for everyone to come out as gay but also transcend the mutually exclusive categories of homosexuality and heterosexuality. In this case, however, the focus was on women.

As radical lesbian feminists worked out the meanings of these and related concepts, they developed a politics that converged with and diverged from gay liberation. Like gay liberationists, radical lesbian feminists emphasized the importance of coming out, but given the greater public invisibility of lesbianism and the presumption that women were dependent on men, coming out was distinctively important for women. At the same time, given the new ambiguities in the definition of lesbianism, coming out meant different things to different women. For some, coming out as a lesbian had a sexual meaning; for others (who came to be called "political lesbians"), it meant that one was a "woman-identified woman" and it did not necessarily imply that one had sex with women. In many contexts, lesbian feminists made productive use of these ambiguities. In 1970, for example, a San Francisco Gay Women's Liberation activist concluded her presentation at a Bay Area feminist conference by asking all women who thought they could be attracted to other women to stand up. Of the 300 women there, most stood up. "The Woman-Identified Woman" subsequently encouraged all women to come out as lesbians and a significant number did.

Radical lesbian feminism also joined gay liberation in emphasizing gender and sexual liberation, though it did so in distinct ways. Many radical lesbians hoped to liberate women sexually, celebrate female eroticism, and "smash monogamy." Anne Koedt's 1970 essay "The Myth of the Vaginal Orgasm" and other works were widely read and cited to support arguments about the pleasures of lesbian sex. Countless sexual encounters, seductions, and relationships began in the context of lesbian feminist consciousness-raising groups, collective households, and political meetings. Some radical lesbians enjoyed the erotic charge of baring their breasts at women's dances and public marches. Lesbian feminist art and music celebrated the sensuality and sexuality of women's bodies, as did lesbian feminist books, poems, and periodicals.

At the same time, many radical lesbian feminists believed that male-defined sexual liberation had worked against women's interests by promoting rape, pornography, and the commodification, objectification, and exploitation of women's bodies. Some added that gay-defined sexual liberation, insofar as it emphasized anonymous, promiscuous, public, and sadomasochistic sex, seemed more like an extension than a rejection of dominant male values. In one 1972 incident, two Radicalesbians-NY members attached a statement of protest over a photograph of a nude woman that a gay man had included in a gay community center collage. Criticisms of sexual liberation led some lesbian feminists to argue that women needed liberation *from* sex. More commonly, radical lesbian feminists in this period wrestled with the question of how to empower women sexually while challenging the sexual subjugation of women.

As for gender dissent, radical lesbian feminists developed a complex set of positions. At the core of their political vision was the notion that women were oppressed by conservative gender values and traditional feminine stereotypes, which kept women dependent on men and wedded to compulsory heterosexuality. But they also called on feminists to be "women-identified" and reject male and masculine values. In practice, many lesbian feminists favored countercultural styles, which could be both feminine and androgynous, but were critical of butch–fem relationships, which they saw as replicating oppressive gender roles. In part, this reflected and contributed to the failure of lesbian feminists, most of whom were middle class and white, to bridge the divides that separated them from other lesbians, many of whom were working class, nonwhite, and butch or fem. At the same time, while some lesbian feminists saw drag queens, transvestites, and transsexual women as fellow gender dissidents and some supported gay effeminism, many were critical of what they regarded as the sexism of drag, the male privileges of transvestites, and the masculine presumptions of transsexual women. In general, lesbian feminists did not see trans women as women. Conflicts between lesbian feminists and trans women exploded in 1973, as is discussed below, but throughout this period lesbian feminism's politics of gender and sexual liberation were in flux.

Meanwhile, radical lesbian feminism joined gay liberation in trying to locate itself in relation to the movement of movements. Some lesbian feminists endorsed lesbian separatism in this era and more did so later in the 1970s. The Furies, which greatly influenced the politics of lesbian separatism, declared in its 1971 founding statement, "Revolutionary lesbians are not only fighting against the institutions of male heterosexual power and privilege but are attacking the very foundations of the male world view—a view which is based on competition, aggression, and acquisitiveness. Lesbians choose to reject that world view and to live apart from men who have perpetuated those values for thousands of years."[8] In the early 1970s, some radical lesbian feminists established rural communes and participated in building what *Village Voice* journalist Jill Johnston referred to as a "lesbian nation."[9] Throughout the country, lesbian feminists debated the politics of lesbian separatism.

In general, however, radical lesbian feminists continued to work toward alliances with other oppressed groups and other radical movements. They were particularly interested in building relationships with the women's movement and were remarkably successful in doing so, but they also worked with gay liberation, anti-war, black power, countercultural, anti-imperialist, and other activists. Some radical lesbians continued to participate in gay liberation groups. Most radical lesbians who became separatists did so after they encountered sexism and homophobia in other movements and after their coalition-building efforts failed. When this occurred, they paradoxically used separatist templates that originated in other movements, including black nationalism. They generally embraced separatism as a short-term strategy rather than a long-term goal. Most did not envision complete separation from all men; what they wanted was to expand the times and territories in which lesbians could live autonomously.

Radical lesbian feminists developed these ideas as they engaged in political activism. As was the case with gay liberationists, many believed that consciousness-raising was a necessary first step and a vital ongoing process in promoting revolutionary change. Lesbian feminist consciousness-raising groups provided opportunities for discussion, reflection, and critique. Many lesbian feminists lived in collective households in which they tried to put their ideas into practice in everyday life. They also sponsored classes, seminars, and workshops for women on various subjects, including art, film, health, literature, mechanical skills, music, poetry, and self-defense. Reaching beyond their local communities, they published influential periodicals, including *Ain't I A Woman* in Iowa City, *Amazon Quarterly* in Oakland, California (and later in Somerville, Massachusetts), *The Furies* in Washington, D.C., *Killer Dyke* and *Lavender Woman* in Chicago, the *Ladder* in Reno, *Lesbian Tide* in Los Angeles, and *Spectre* in Ann Arbor. Together, these periodicals reached tens of thousands of readers in the early 1970s.

Radical lesbian feminists regarded the development of autonomous institutions and territories for women as key political activities. Across the country, they started, sponsored, supported, and sustained women's arts and crafts businesses, bookstores, coffeehouses, community centers, health centers, inns, publishing companies, and sports teams. They promoted women's art, film, literature, music, poetry, and theater, along with women's studies courses in colleges and universities. They also led and participated in projects that addressed sexual health, reproductive freedom, and violence against women. Much of this work addressed women in general, but some of it focused on lesbians. In 1971, for example, lesbian feminists established the Gay Women's Services Center in Los Angeles, the Lesbian Center in New York, and the Gay Women's Resource Center (later renamed the Lesbian Resource Center) in Seattle. In 1972 the Lesbian Resource Center opened in Minneapolis. In 1973 the Women's Center in Chicago began to be referred to as the Lesbian Feminist Center. Lesbian feminists also claimed public space by selecting particular bars, clubs, coffeehouses, and restaurants to frequent and by sponsoring dances, which attracted thousands of women.

Some lesbian feminists declined to work with men, but most participated in both single-sex and mixed-sex activities. In 1970, Gay Women's Liberation participated in the APA convention protests in San Francisco while Radicalesbians worked with GLF-NY on the march that turned into a riot and the NYU protests. In 1971, Radicalesbians-Buffalo participated in the Albany law reform demonstrations. In Philadelphia, GLF men publicized the first local Radicalesbians meeting and cosponsored the new group's first dance; Radicalesbians then picketed with other gay and lesbian groups at local mayoral campaign headquarters and joined with GLF to offer a gay liberation workshop for the local free university. In 1972, the Radicalesbians-Philadelphia newsletter listed activities for women only (including bicycle trips, dances, and film screenings) and activities for lesbians and gay men (including baseball games, picnics, and religious services). Radicalesbians-Philadelphia offered a women's-only free university course on lesbianism and feminism, but after each class the students joined their counterparts from a gay liberation course for a mixed-sex gay coffee hour. Later in 1972, Radicalesbians-Philadelphia cosponsored a statewide gay and lesbian conference in Pittsburgh and the Atlanta Lesbian Feminist Alliance assisted the organizers of a regional gay and lesbian conference in Athens, Georgia. In 1973, Lesbian Feminist Liberation participated in the campaign to convince the New York City Council to pass a sexual orientation antidiscrimination law. As is discussed below, many lesbian feminists participated in annual commemorations of the Stonewall riots. Paradoxically, many did so with separatist signs, banners, and t-shirts.

Radical lesbian feminist efforts to work with other activists did not always succeed. Conflicts with gay, trans, and feminist activists occurred throughout this period. Some radical lesbian feminists responded by adopting more separatist politics while others persisted in their efforts to build alliances. A particularly significant set of developments occurred before, during, and after the Black Panthers' 1970 Revolutionary People's Constitutional Convention in Philadelphia. Radicalesbians-NY activists participated in the convention planning process and approximately twenty-five women attended the convention's Lesbian Workshop. While the multiracial Male Homosexual Workshop was well-received, the predominantly white Lesbian Workshop traded accusations about racism and sexism with the convention's organizers. In the end, most of the radical lesbian feminists walked out.

Notwithstanding these conflicts, radical lesbian feminists participated in various types of demonstration and protest. As individuals and as members of gay liberation and lesbian feminist groups, they marched in countless antiwar demonstrations and they supported and spearheaded numerous feminist protests. They often did so as women's liberationists, but also began to do so openly as lesbian feminists. In 1970, for example, Radicalesbian Martha Shelley denounced anti-lesbian police harassment at a Women's Strike for Equality rally in New York. Later that year, after *Time* magazine identified literary critic Kate Millett as bisexual in an apparent attempt to discredit the women's movement, Radicalesbians-NY members organized a press conference where thirty prominent feminist and lesbian activists declared, "Women's liberation and homosexual liberation are both struggling towards a common goal: a society free from defining and categorizing people by virtue of gender and/or sexual preference."[10] In 1972, Radicalesbians-Philadelphia initiated the planning process for a Women's Strike Day march.

As the Lavender Menace action suggested, the women's movement itself was the target of radical lesbian feminist protests. Across the country, radical lesbians pressed women's liberationists to address the politics of lesbianism, sometimes using confrontational and disruptive tactics. In fact, Kate Millett's outing by *Time* followed an incident at a Columbia University lecture in which a Radicalesbian asked her repeatedly whether she was a lesbian. Also in 1970, Gay Women's Liberation-LA disrupted a meeting of the local NOW chapter, which then passed a resolution recognizing "the oppression of lesbians as a legitimate concern of feminism." This became the basis of a similar resolution adopted at NOW's 1971 national conference in Los Angeles.[11] This was probably the gay and lesbian movement's most significant endorsement since the ACLU adopted a new policy on homosexuality in the 1960s.

Radical lesbian feminists also targeted businesses and institutions that contributed to the oppression of lesbians. In 1970, Bay Area activists boycotted an Oakland lesbian bar that refused to allow them to post a flier about a gay women's liberation meeting. Gay Women's Liberation in San Francisco organized a demonstration to protest discrimination against women in a University of California-Berkeley karate class and another to protest KGO-TV's sexist coverage of the incident. In 1971 and 1972, lesbian feminists in Philadelphia and Chicago criticized gay bars that excluded women and lesbian bars that charged exorbitant prices, prohibited same-sex dancing, and mistreated women in other ways. In Los Angeles, lesbian activists held a kiss-in at a local restaurant that had told two women they would have to leave if they continued to hold hands. In Minneapolis, they staged a dance-in at a straight bar that had expelled two lesbians for dancing together. In 1973, Lesbian Feminists organized the First National Lesbian Kiss-In to protest the minimal inclusion of female and lesbian artists at the Los Angeles County Museum of Art. In New York, twenty-five members of Lesbian Feminist Liberation obtained tickets for the *Dick Cavett Show* and disrupted his interview with an antifeminist and antilesbian author. Lesbian Feminist Liberation also organized a demonstration with 200 human participants and a large lavender dinosaur to protest sexism at the American Museum of National History and picketed a Lincoln Center movie theater that was showing Rainer Fassbinder's *The Bitter Tears of Petra Von Kant*, which featured depictions of lesbian sadomasochism that some feminists found offensive.

In a short period of time, radical lesbian feminism changed the gay, lesbian, and women's movements, with ramifications that have lasted for decades. Nevertheless, many of the influential radical lesbian groups of the early 1970s, including Radicalesbians-NY and the Furies, lasted for only a few years; most were gone by 1973. Many of the developments that contributed to the collapse of gay liberation—political repression, internal divisions, personal burn-out, and conflicts with other movements—contributed to the collapse of radical lesbian feminist groups in the early 1970s. In addition, radical lesbian feminism had to compete with other movements, including gay liberation, women's liberation, and race-based movements, for the support of lesbians. After 1973, the character of radical lesbian feminism diversified and changed, though it continued to play an important role in the gay and lesbian movement.

Gay and Lesbian Liberalism, 1969–73

There was much more to the gay and lesbian movement in this period than radical gay liberation and radical lesbian feminism. Gay and lesbian social, cultural, and political groups proliferated, numbering more than 1000 by 1973. Many were for people interested in particular sports, hobbies, and other leisure activities. More than 200 youth and student groups were established. New professional, research, and scholarly organizations included the International Gay and Lesbian Archives in Los Angeles, the Gay Academic Union and Lesbian Herstory Archives in New York, and the American Library Association's Task Force on Gay Liberation. Gay and lesbian lawyers, psychiatrists, seminarians, social workers, and teachers began to organize. Lesbian mothers formed support and advocacy groups. Gay and lesbian deaf people founded the Silent Society in San Francisco. Gay Alcoholics Anonymous groups began meeting. Participants in leather, bondage, sadomasochism, and other sexual subcultures organized new groups. This was also an era of increased transgender and bisexual organizing.

Many groups embraced newly popular gay and lesbian colors and symbols. Lavender had long been linked with same-sex sexuality, in part because it is the result of combining red (associated with femininity) and blue (associated with masculinity). Many adopted the Greek letter lambda, which signifies changes in energy. Others reclaimed the pink triangle, which homosexuals had been forced to wear in Nazi concentration camps. Many lesbians adopted the labrys, a double-sided axe, which was associated with goddesses and Amazons. Some lesbians favored the use of intersecting symbols for the planet Venus (circles with crosses below), which signified female relationships, while some gay men promoted the use of intersecting symbols for Mars (circles with arrows pointing upward to the right), which signified male relationships.

One of the movement's notable organizational developments in this period was the formation of a significant number of groups for people of color and members of religious communities. Many were social and support groups, but some engaged in political activism. In the early 1970s, the short-lived Third World Gay Revolution groups in New York and Chicago were joined by the Black Lesbian Caucus and Third World Caucus of the Gay Activists Alliance in New York, the Native American Gay Rap Group in San Francisco, and several Latino/Latina groups in California and New York, including Comité Homosexual Latinoamericano, Gay Latinos, Gay Liberated Chicanos, Unidos, United Gay Chicanos, and a collective that published *Afuera*, a literary magazine. These groups criticized homophobia and sexism in communities of color, challenged gay and lesbian racism, and provided opportunities for social interaction and political engagement. In 1972, for example, the Comité Homosexual Latinoamericano criticized the organizers of New York's Puerto Rican Day Parade for not allowing the group to march. Jewish groups included Achvah Chutzpah in San Francisco, Beth Chayim Chadashim in Los Angeles, and Congregation Beth Simchat Torah in New York. Gay and lesbian Christian groups were also established, including more than thirty Metropolitan Community Church congregations, multiple chapters of Dignity (which served Catholics), and caucuses within the Society of Friends and the Unitarian-Universalist General Assembly.

Homophile groups did not disappear after the Stonewall riots. Mattachines in Chicago, New York, and Washington, D.C., remained active for several years and new Mattachines formed in several locations, including Buffalo and Pittsburgh. DOB dissolved its national structure in 1970, but DOBs in Los Angeles, New York, and San Francisco continued their work and were joined by approximately twenty new DOB groups, including a particularly active one in Boston. Philadelphia's Homophile Action League, San Francisco's Society for Individual Rights, Seattle's Dorian Society, and other autonomous groups founded in the pre-Stonewall era also contributed to the upsurge in gay and lesbian activism in the early 1970s, as did new groups such as the Homophile Union of Boston and the Texas Homophile

Educational Movement, whose names underscored the ongoing relevance of the pre-Stonewall movement.

One of the movement's more significant organizational developments was the formation of Gay Activists Alliances (GAA) and similarly named groups across the United States. In many locations, these became the most influential gay and lesbian groups in the early 1970s. The first GAA was established in New York in December 1969, when disaffected members of GLF-NY, including Jim Owles, Marty Robinson, Arthur Evans, and Arthur Bell, broke away to form a new group that would focus exclusively on gay and lesbian issues. GLF's decision to provide financial support to the Black Panthers was the immediate reason for their departure, but more generally GAA's founders were critical of GLF radicalism. Many GAA members continued to support radical movements, but did so as individuals because they believed that GAA could work most effectively and best promote gay and lesbian mobilization if it avoided entanglements with other movements, especially the radical ones that many gays and lesbians did not support.

There were three other significant differences between GLF-NY and GAA-NY. First, the founders of GAA believed that the anarchist and countercultural ethos of GLF had made it dysfunctional, so the new group operated in a more conventional fashion, with a written constitution, elected officers, and rules for membership, voting, and decision-making. Second, GAA joined GLF in emphasizing the value of coming out, but focused less attention on the idea that everyone should come out. GAA based more of its arguments and strategies on the notion that gays were a minority group and deserved rights on that basis. Third, GAA shared with GLF a long-term vision of liberation, but concentrated on securing legal rights and political reform, which it regarded as necessary components of liberation. For many GLF activists, this meant that GAA did not appreciate or understand the radical meanings of liberation.

Over the next few years, GAA-NY inspired the creation of dozens of similarly named groups in all parts of the country. It is difficult to generalize about the politics of these groups, but they tended to work toward reform rather than revolution. Many were founded by former homophiles and gay liberationists who supported gay liberation's emphasis on coming out and its use of militant tactics, but opposed radical coalitions and rejected "structureless structure." Less disdainful about working within "the system" but also willing to confront "the system" when it was not responsive, these activists integrated elements of homophile militancy and gay liberationism to develop a new politics of gay and lesbian liberalism.

Many of these groups described themselves as "alliances" and "coalitions," which reflected their goal of bringing together different groups of gays and lesbians. Nevertheless, they represented some constituencies better than others. In general, they were more age diverse than were gay liberation groups, but also were more white, middle class, male, and gender normative. In terms of race, there were exceptions, including the members of GAA-NY's Black Lesbian Caucus and the Chicago Gay Alliance's Women's Caucus, but gay and lesbian groups that rejected coalitions with radical movements and that did not see gay and lesbian racism as a major problem had less appeal to many people of color. In terms of class, these groups typically featured significant contributions by working-class people, but tended to be dominated by middle-class white gay men.

The gay alliances were founded at a time when more lesbians were becoming interested in feminism, which is one of the reasons the alliances were not successful in attracting large numbers of women. While some long-time lesbian activists such as Barbara Gittings and Kay Lahusen worked with gay reformers in the early 1970s, others were more influenced by the rise of women's liberation. In a widely circulated statement that echoed Robin Morgan's feminist denunciation of the male left, DOB founder Del Martin announced in 1970 that after fifteen years of dealing with gay movement sexism, she was saying "goodbye to all that" and turning her attention to feminism.[12] As for younger women, in many cases the gay liberation pattern repeated itself. In 1971, for instance, the Gay Women's Caucus declared its independence from the Chicago Gay Alliance. In 1973, the Lesbian Liberation Committee of GAA-NY broke away to form Lesbian Feminist Liberation. Among the reasons that the alliances did not attract more women was their apparent disinterest in confronting sexism, their rejection of coalitions with feminist groups, and their focus on issues that were of greater concern to gay men.

The gay alliances were also less successful in appealing to transgender activists. Again, there were exceptions. GAA-NY's Street Theatre Subcommittee included trans activists and others who supported trans self-expression. GAA-Philadelphia had a Queens Liberation Caucus, which renamed itself Radical Queens. GAA-San Francisco denounced police harassment of transsexuals and housing discrimination against drag queens. More generally, however, trans activists were suspicious about the politics of the new gay alliances. GAA-NY, for example, endorsed a proposal to repeal New York State's laws against cross-dressing, but its campaign to win passage of a city law banning sexual orientation discrimination was criticized by trans activists because the proposed law did not address antitrans discrimination. In some respects, the new groups revived the politics of homophile respectability, which in challenging stereotypes of gay femininity and lesbian masculinity often privileged normative gender expression. Trans activists continued to participate in gay and lesbian reform groups, but the politics of gay and lesbian reform helped convince many trans activists to organize autonomously.

Gay and lesbian reformers joined their homophile, gay liberation, and lesbian feminist counterparts in providing assistance to individuals in need; making referrals to doctors, lawyers, and other professionals; establishing support groups; organizing social activities; sponsoring dances and drag shows; founding community centers; hosting lectures and presentations; responding to requests for speakers; and developing education and outreach programs. They also helped create new agencies, centers, and programs that focused on gay and lesbian physical health, mental health, and sexually transmitted diseases. Activists saw these efforts as having intrinsic value, but also hoped that they would encourage political mobilization, which they did.

In their political work, gay and lesbian reformers focused on multiple issues, but police practices were among their main targets. Around the country, they challenged police raids on bars, police entrapment practices, and other forms of police mistreatment. They met with police officials, filed complaints, publicized negative incidents, asked politicians to intervene, supported litigation, and organized demonstrations. In 1970, for example, GAA-NY worked with GLF-NY on the 500-person march to protest about bar raids. GAA-NY also picketed City Hall to demand a meeting to discuss police practices with Mayor John Lindsay, confronted Lindsay about the issue at public events, convinced the Village Independent Democrats to write a letter of protest to the mayor, and persuaded U.S. representatives Ed Koch and Bella Abzug to denounce antihomosexual police practices. GAA-NY eventually secured a meeting with representatives of the mayor and police commissioner, though they did not obtain promises of reform. Later that year, after another period of increased police harassment, GAA-NY worked with GLF-NY on the large protest march that turned into a riot, though GAA withdrew after violence broke out. Toward the end of 1970, after a DOB-NY meeting was raided by the police and its president was given a court summons, GAA-NY and seven other gay and lesbian groups attended her hearing. In 1971, after police raided a DOB-NY dance, DOB and GAA staged a demonstration and met with mayoral aides; the charges against the organizers soon were dropped.

Gay and lesbian reformers elsewhere targeted police practices as well. In 1970, hundreds of Los Angeles gay and lesbian activists marched to protest police abuses. In 1971, litigation involving four Miami bartenders who had been arrested in a police raid succeeded in overturning the city's law against employing or serving homosexuals in bars. In 1972, after ten men were arrested for dancing at a Memphis club, they successfully contested the charges and forced the city to acknowledge that same-sex dancing was not illegal. In the same year, six GAA-DC activists were arrested while protesting police entrapment at the Iwo Jima Memorial in Virginia. In 1973, gay advocates won a California Supreme Court ruling that restricted the ability of the police to conduct surveillance in public bathrooms. Seattle Gay Alliance activists demonstrated at their city's police headquarters and the home of the city's police chief. GAA-DC held a sit-in at the offices of the D.C. police chief after he refused to meet with them. Hundreds of Denver Gay Coalition members attended Denver City Council meetings to protest increased police harassment after the state's sodomy law was repealed. The Houston Gay Political Coalition lobbied the Houston City Council to end police harassment. While it would be difficult to determine whether liberationists or liberals were more effective in challenging police mistreatment, their combined efforts led to reductions in bar raids, police entrapment practices, and other forms of police abuse, harassment, and violence.

Gay and lesbian reformers regarded state sodomy laws as a linchpin of sexual oppression, in part because these laws were cited to justify multiple forms of antihomosexual discrimination. In the early 1970s, they lobbied unsuccessfully for sex law reform in California, Massachusetts, Michigan, Minnesota, New York,

Pennsylvania, Washington, D.C., and other locations. There was greater support for sodomy law repeal in liberal cities, but most states included conservative regions and religious constituencies that were less sympathetic. Reform critics also linked sodomy to homosexuality and pedophilia, which greatly influenced public opinion. Meanwhile, there were failed efforts to end the criminalization of same-sex sex through litigation in Arkansas, Missouri, Oklahoma, Texas, Virginia, and Washington, D.C. Alaska and Florida courts invalidated their states' bans on crimes against nature, but not their sodomy laws.

Notwithstanding these setbacks, sodomy law repeal was achieved in Colorado, Delaware, Hawaii, North Dakota, Ohio, and Oregon. In these states, repeal occurred through the legislative process rather than through litigation. Gay and lesbian activists could not claim direct credit for all of these successes; in most cases, reform occurred in the context of general criminal code revision. Sex law reformers in the 1950s and 1960s, however, influenced the development of the penal code reform proposals that were adopted in the 1970s. In Delaware, one of the country's first paid gay rights lobbyists had begun working on sodomy law reform in the late 1960s. In all of these states, homophile activism had indirect effects by changing the national conversation about homosexuality. Illinois and Connecticut had repealed their laws earlier, so by the end of 1973, eight states had decriminalized private same-sex sex for consenting adults. After the American Bar Association endorsed sodomy law repeal in 1973, there were new reasons to be hopeful about sex law reform, though in some locations sodomy law repeal was followed by increased sexual policing through laws against indecency, lewdness, loitering, and solicitation.

While gay and lesbian reformers did not generally prioritize trans issues, many supported the repeal of laws that criminalized cross-dressing; in several cases they worked with trans groups and ACLU lawyers on this issue. In 1972, the National Coalition of Gay Organizations, an alliance of 450 groups that formed in advance of that year's presidential election, endorsed the repeal of laws against cross-dressing. Queens Liberation Front successfully used litigation to overturn New York City's law, as did GAA activists in Miami. Laws against cross-dressing were also overturned through litigation in Chicago, Fort Worth, and Toledo in the early 1970s.

Meanwhile, reformers promoted the passage of laws against sexual discrimination in housing, employment, and public accommodations. Many jurisdictions banned discrimination based on race and sex in these three areas; gay and lesbian activists wanted these laws extended to include sexual preference (the preferred legal term in this period). Beginning in 1970, GAA-NY waged a particularly intense campaign for a city law banning antihomosexual employment discrimination. Its efforts began with a petition drive and escalated in confrontations with a City Council member from Greenwich Village who initially refused to accept the petitions; after she was publicly badgered and embarrassed, she agreed to cosponsor the legislation. GAA-NY activists confronted Mayor Lindsay on the issue at the Metropolitan Museum of Art, the Metropolitan Opera, and Radio City Music Hall. They obtained one-third of the tickets for a taping of the mayor's weekly television program and then interrupted the show with questions about gay rights. A short time later, Eleanor Holmes Norton, chair of the New York City Commission on Human Rights, met with GAA activists and promised an investigation; GAA provided her with extensive documentation of discrimination. Additional protests, including City Hall demonstrations and a City Hall sit-in, yielded a mayoral endorsement in 1971 and an executive order prohibiting city agencies from making hiring decisions based on private sexual orientation in 1972. The City Council, however, did not pass the proposed legislation. Activists in the cities of Boulder, Chicago, Minneapolis, and Philadelphia and the states of Florida, Massachusetts, Minnesota, New York, and Pennsylvania also campaigned unsuccessfully for antidiscrimination laws, but there were successes in Ann Arbor, East Lansing, and San Francisco in 1972 and in Berkeley, Seattle, and Washington, D.C., in 1973.

Gay and lesbian reformers campaigned against employment discrimination in other ways as well. In 1969, they convinced the California Supreme Court to rule that the state board of education could not revoke a teaching license based solely on evidence of private homosexual conduct. In 1970, they persuaded the American Federation of Teachers to adopt a resolution that criticized personnel actions taken against teachers on the basis of private homosexual conduct. Also in 1970, GAA-NY and DOB-NY staged an attention-grabbing protest at Fidelifacts, a private investigation agency whose president had boasted to a reporter about the information his company supplied to clients about homosexual job applicants. After the president explained that "if one looks like a duck, walks like a duck, associates only with ducks, and quacks like a duck, he is probably a duck," GAA and DOB activists, armed with rubber duckies, demonstrated at the company's offices with one member dressed up as a duck.[13] Minneapolis activist Michael McConnell went to court in 1970 to challenge the University of Minnesota's decision to withdraw a job offer after his efforts to marry Jack Baker were publicized; he appealed the decision all the way to the U.S. Supreme Court, which declined to consider the case.

Challenges to employment discrimination continued in the next few years. In 1971, 1972, and 1973, San Francisco activists demonstrated at the offices of Pacific Telephone to protest its explicitly antihomosexual hiring policy and its refusal to accept a Yellow Pages advertisement that contained the word "homophile." Relying on the city's new antidiscrimination statute, they forced the company to revise its policies in 1973. In 1972, Joseph Acanfora, supported by the National Education Association, unsuccessfully sued his Maryland school district for removing him from his classroom teaching position after learning that he was gay. In the same year, GAA-DC convinced the D.C. school board to ban sexual orientation discrimination in the school system. Also in 1972, gay and lesbian reformers convinced the University of Minnesota to ban campus employment recruiters that discriminated on various bases; this was then used to convince the Minneapolis-based Honeywell Corporation to reverse its policy against hiring homosexuals. Similar policies were later adopted by many colleges and universities.

There was a significant breakthrough on federal employment discrimination in this period. With ACLU support, Frank Kameny and others continued to support litigation against the Civil Service Commission, Defense Department, and U.S. military; in several cases, the Supreme Court declined to consider their appeals. San Francisco activists publicized the problem in 1971, when they showed up at a federal office building and volunteered to work for various agencies. They were "fired" and two of their leaders were arrested after officials noticed that they were wearing signs that identified themselves as homosexuals who were working for the federal government. Finally, in 1973, after the Society for Individual Rights filed a class action lawsuit and a federal court enjoined the Civil Service Commission from rejecting or terminating employees based solely on homosexuality, the Commission announced a new policy: henceforth federal agencies could not exclude or dismiss employees based solely on homosexual identity or conduct. This was a major achievement, though it soon became clear that exceptions would be made for the CIA, FBI, National Security Agency, and jobs requiring security clearances. Reformers were less successful when trying to address discrimination by the military and the tax system. They had some victories in censorship cases, but the Supreme Court's obscenity rulings continued to condone sexual discrimination. There were a few victories in immigration and naturalization appeals, but in circumstances that limited their application; a federal court, for example, ruled that a Cuban immigrant could not be denied naturalization based on homosexuality since he had acknowledged his sexual orientation when he entered the country.

Same-sex marriage was not high on the agenda of most activists and it was criticized by many radicals, but it was important to some. In addition to the Minneapolis and Seattle examples cited above, there were unsuccessful efforts by same-sex couples to obtain marriage licenses in Los Angeles, Louisville, and Milwaukee in the early 1970s. In 1971, after the New York City Clerk made negative public comments about same-sex marriage, GAA-NY held an engagement party for two same-sex couples in the offices of the Marriage Bureau. In 1972, Metropolitan Community Church (MCC) leader Troy Perry conducted a same-sex marriage ceremony outside the Democratic Party Convention in Miami. In 1973, after a Methodist minister in Boston married a gay couple, he lost his job and was expelled from the ministry. Same-sex couples held marriage ceremonies in many places, though these were not recognized legally. Transsexuals faced distinct challenges in relation to restrictions on same-sex marriage. Most states did not permit transsexuals to change their legal sex/gender, which created difficulties for female-to-male transsexuals who wanted to marry legal women and male-to-female transsexuals who wanted to marry legal men. In the few states that allowed transsexuals to change their legal sex/gender (Arizona, Illinois, and Louisiana were early examples), female-to-male transsexuals who wanted to marry legal men and male-to-female transsexuals who wanted to marry legal women had to choose between changing their legal sex/gender and maintaining their access to marriage.

In the early 1970s, more gay and lesbian reformers began to focus on the rights of parents. This was a particularly significant issue for lesbians involved in custody disputes with their former husbands; courts in such cases typically awarded custody to the fathers. In noteworthy cases in California, Michigan, North Carolina, Oregon, and Washington in 1972 and 1973, gay and lesbian parents won custody of their children, though in several instances the courts stipulated that the parents could not live with their partners or socialize with other gays or lesbians. In a 1972 Seattle case, for example, the ex-husbands of two Christian fundamentalist women went to court to obtain custody of their children (four in one case, two in the other) after the two women became a couple. The judge rejected the argument that the women's lesbianism was necessarily harmful to their children and awarded custody to the mothers, but he stipulated that they could not live together if they wanted to keep their children. In most other cases, the outcomes were negative, which led to the formation of advocacy groups that provided advice, support, and assistance for lesbian (and less often gay) parents.

Gay and lesbian reformers, in contrast to their radical counterparts, devoted significant attention to electoral politics. In part, this reflected new confidence about the potential power of the gay and lesbian voting bloc, especially in cities where there were large concentrations of gay and lesbian voters. The turn to electoral politics also was related to changes in the major political parties and especially the increased power of civil rights, feminist, and liberal constituencies in the Democratic Party, which created new openings for gay and lesbian reformers. Some gays and lesbians supported the Republicans, endorsed third parties, or avoided political partisanship, but the majority favored the Democrats. In this period, gay and lesbian liberals took significant steps toward their goal of becoming a recognized component of the Democratic electoral coalition.

Gay and lesbian reformers participated in electoral politics in multiple ways. Some organized voter registration drives in locations favored by gays and lesbians. Activists in California, Delaware, Massachusetts, New Jersey, New York, North Carolina, Pennsylvania, Washington, and Washington, D.C., distributed questionnaires to candidates and publicized their responses. In these and other locations, they attended candidate forums and asked questions about gay and lesbian rights. More aggressively, they confronted candidates in various states, organized demonstrations at mayoral campaign headquarters in Philadelphia, and held a sit-in that resulted in five arrests at the offices of the Republican State Committee in New York City. Among the prominent politicians targeted were New York Governor Nelson Rockefeller, New York gubernatorial candidate Arthur Goldberg, Pennsylvania gubernatorial candidate Milton Shapp, and Philadelphia mayoral candidate Frank Rizzo. San Francisco activists continued to host candidate forums and in 1971 formed the Alice B. Toklas Memorial Democratic Club. Partly as a result of these and other efforts, dozens of political candidates endorsed gay and lesbian rights. Los Angeles, New York, and San Francisco politicians in particular recognized the potential significance of the gay and lesbian voting bloc.

Gay and lesbian activists took credit for contributing to the election of several political candidates in this period. In New York, U.S. Representatives Bella Abzug and Ed Koch were elected with significant gay and lesbian support, as was Mayor John Lindsay, State Assembly member Antonio Olivieri, and City Council member Arthur J. Katzman. In California, gay and lesbian voters helped elect Mayor Tom Bradley, City Attorney Burt Pines, and City Council member Robert Stevenson in Los Angeles, Board of Supervisors President Dianne Feinstein and Sheriff Richard Hongisto in San Francisco, and State Assembly member Willie Brown. In Houston, gay and lesbian activists contributed to the election of Mayor Fred Hofheinz. Several of these politicians proved to be reliable allies for their gay and lesbian constituents; others did not.

While gay and lesbian reformers contributed to the election of allies, they fared less well when they promoted the election of openly gay or lesbian candidates. In 1971, Frank Kameny failed in his bid to be elected as Washington, D.C.'s new nonvoting delegate to the U.S. House and Alan Rockway lost his campaign to be elected Dade County Commissioner. In 1972, however, Human Rights Party candidates Nancy Wechsler and Jerry DeGriek were elected to the Ann Arbor City Council. Both came out during their terms and are typically cited as the first openly lesbian and gay elected officials in the United States. Also in 1972, Cape Cod's Gerry Studds, Boston's Barney Frank, and Minneapolis's Allan Spear, not yet openly gay but supporters of gay and lesbian rights, were elected to the U.S. House, Massachusetts House, and Minnesota Senate. In 1973, openly gay and lesbian candidates ran unsuccessfully for the city councils of Detroit, Minneapolis, and New York and the San Francisco Board of Supervisors.

Gay and lesbian reformers viewed the 1972 national elections as a promising opportunity to politicize their community and promote gay and lesbian interests. In February, the National Coalition of Gay Organizations developed a platform for the upcoming elections. The platform called for the repeal of laws against private and consensual sex acts and laws against cross-dressing; the adoption of a federal law prohibiting antihomosexual discrimination in employment, housing, and public accommodations; an executive order prohibiting antihomosexual employment discrimination by the federal government; repeal of the ban on gay and lesbian immigrants; and (more controversially) an end to laws governing the age of sexual consent. GAA-NY asked each presidential candidate to commit to ending antihomosexual discrimination in employment, housing, and the military; Shirley Chisholm, Hubert Humphrey, John Lindsay, Eugene McCarthy, and George McGovern responded favorably. After McGovern backtracked, Minneapolis activists disrupted one of his campaign appearances and GAA-NY occupied his campaign headquarters until he reaffirmed his support. GAA-NY also zapped a fundraising event for Edmund Muskie, the only major Democratic candidate who refused to endorse gay and lesbian rights. GAA-Philadelphia activists zapped speeches by McGovern, Humphrey, and Muskie, along with vice presidential candidate Sargent Shriver. They also chained themselves for three hours to the doors at Richard Nixon's local campaign headquarters.

In several states, gay and lesbian activists participated in the Democratic primaries, caucuses, and conventions. In Minnesota, they attended the Democratic-Farmer-Labor Party caucuses, participated in the party's state convention as openly gay and lesbian delegates, and convinced the state party to endorse sodomy law repeal and the legalization of same-sex marriage. Jim Foster of San Francisco and Madeline Davis of Buffalo were selected as openly gay and lesbian delegates to the Democratic National Convention in Miami; there were also three openly gay or lesbian alternate delegates from New York and Minnesota. Foster and Davis delivered nationally televised gay rights speeches to the convention, though they were scheduled for the middle of the night. The convention defeated a proposal to adopt a gay rights plank, but the gay and lesbian presence at the convention was part of a larger effort to become a constituency that would be taken seriously by the Democrats. In one sign of success, McGovern advertised for support in the *Advocate*. Gay and lesbian activists also participated in protest demonstrations at both major party conventions in Miami. Most gay and lesbian liberals were disappointed by the re-election of Nixon, but heartened by the election of Democratic congressional majorities and their new visibility in the Democratic Party.

Beyond their efforts to influence government policies and practices, gay and lesbian reformers targeted four sectors of society, one of which was business. Among the corporations they criticized for discriminatory employment practices were AT&T, Honeywell, New York Telephone, Northwestern Bell, Pacific Telephone, and Pan American. In 1970, the Homophile Action League released the results of a study it had initiated in the pre-Stonewall era: the group had written to 500 major corporations to ask about employment discrimination against homosexuals; of the twenty replies received, only Bantam Books indicated that it did not discriminate based on sexual orientation. In 1970–71, San Francisco activists demonstrated and organized a boycott of a Macy's store after a large number of men were arrested for having sex in the store's bathrooms; Seattle Gay Alliance picketed a coffeeshop that prohibited public displays of same-sex affection; and GAA-NY demonstrated at the Household Finance Corporation, which denied loans to individuals identified as homosexual by private investigators. In 1972–73, GAA-NY's Lesbian Liberation Committee held dance-ins at three bars; Minneapolis activists demonstrated at the offices of Northwestern Bell and at a bar that refused admission to lesbians; and GAA-San Francisco picketed a Tenderloin hotel that had evicted more than thirty trans residents. Activists staged multiple protests at gay and lesbian bars that discriminated against people of color, women, and gender transgressors.

The second nongovernmental target was organized religion. In 1970, the Lutheran Church in America and Presbyterian Church (U.S.A.) endorsed the decriminalization of private same-sex sex by consenting adults, though both made it clear that they disapproved of homosexuality. The Unitarian Universalist Association called for the repeal of sodomy laws and an end to all forms of antihomosexual discrimination, but activists zapped the Unitarian General Assembly in Seattle after a gay man was rejected for ordination. In 1971, DOB-NY picketed outside

St. Patrick's Cathedral, the Homophile Action League demonstrated at Carl McIntire's Bible Presbyterian Church in New Jersey, and MCC held a protest service on the steps of St. Stephen's Episcopal Church in Washington, D.C. Eleven denominations were represented at the First National Conference on Religion and the Homosexual in New York in 1971. In 1972, the United Church of Christ became the first major U.S. denomination to ordain an openly gay man as a minister. That year, the United Methodist Church endorsed civil rights for homosexuals, though it indicated that it did not condone homosexuality. In 1973, the American Baptist Association, American Lutheran Association, Religious Society of Friends, United Methodists, and United Presbyterians launched the National Task Force on Gay People in the Church.

The third main nongovernmental target was the mass media and popular culture, which activists held responsible for promoting negative stereotypes about homosexuality and erasing, marginalizing, and pathologizing the voices, values, and viewpoints of gays and lesbians. In addition, they believed that media activism had the potential to reach, mobilize, and politicize the public in general and the gay and lesbian public in particular. Gay and lesbian activists wrote to countless periodicals to register their complaints; their targets included the *Atlanta Journal, Life, Los Angeles Times, New York Times*, and *San Francisco Examiner*. In 1970, after three *New York Post* columnists made hostile comments about homosexuality, GAA-NY activists went to the newspaper's offices, discussed their criticisms with one editor, and met several days later with another. The *Post*'s coverage of gay and lesbian news soon improved. Later in 1970, GAA-NY occupied the offices of *Harper's* after the magazine published a nasty article about homosexuality. In this case, GAA carefully planned its friendly invasion. Forty activists arrived early one morning (with a television news crew) and greeted each employee as they arrived by shaking their hands, identifying themselves as homosexuals, and offering them coffee, doughnuts, literature, and conversation. When they found the editor who had worked on the article, they forcefully challenged her bigotry and the article's contribution to the oppression of homosexuals. In 1972, GAA-NY staged major demonstrations at the *New York Daily News* and the Inner Circle Dinner, which was an annual event sponsored by New York political reporters.

Live television presented promising opportunities for activist interventions. In 1970, GAA-NY made plans to disrupt the *Dick Cavett Show* after his guests repeatedly made antigay jokes. After learning about the plans, Cavett agreed to interview several gay activists on his show. Similar developments led to the appearance of GAA members on the *Jack Paar Show*. The most successful practitioner of this form of media activism was Mark Segal and the Philadelphia-based Gay Raiders. They began by zapping local television stations in 1972, but in 1973 reached wider audiences by disrupting Walter Cronkite and the *CBS Evening News*, Johnny Carson and the *Tonight Show*, Mike Douglas and the *Mike Douglas Show*, and Frank Blair and the *Today Show*. In several instances, Segal and his allies chained or handcuffed themselves to television cameras or other fixed objects, making it difficult for security officers to remove them quickly. Also in 1973, GAA-NY learned (thanks to an ABC insider) about an upcoming episode of *Marcus Welby, M.D.*, in which Dr. Welby told a divorced father that his homosexual feelings were signs of a serious illness. After ABC refused to revise the script, GAA picketed and held a sit-in at ABC headquarters; six protesters were arrested. Meanwhile, activists demonstrated against negative depictions of homosexuality in film at the 1972 Academy Awards, met with representatives of the Association of Motion Picture and Television Producers in 1973, and followed that up by developing a set of guidelines for the treatment of homosexuality in film and television. While most mainstream television and film portrayals of homosexuality continued to be problematic, there were occasional exceptions and activists took credit for the improved quantity and quality of mainstream newspaper and magazine coverage.

The fourth main nongovernmental target was science and medicine. In this case, the combined efforts of gay liberationists, lesbian feminists, gay and lesbian reformers, and scientific allies led to one of the movement's greatest achievements. Activists zapped appearances by antihomosexual psychologists and psychiatrists in various locations in the early 1970s, but their main focus was the American Psychiatric Association (APA). Following up on the protests at the APA's annual conventions in 1970 and 1971 (described above), Barbara Gittings and Frank Kameny organized an exhibit titled "Gay, Proud, and Healthy: The Homosexual Community Speaks" for the APA's 1972 convention in Dallas. They also arranged for "Dr. Anonymous," a masked gay psychiatrist, to join them on a panel titled "Psychiatry, Friend or Foe to Homosexuals?" Working with well-placed psychiatric allies and building on the scholarship of Alfred Kinsey, Evelyn Hooker, Judd Marmor, and others, gay and lesbian activists then convinced the APA to schedule a session titled "Should Homosexuality Be in the APA Nomenclature?" at its 1973 convention in Hawaii; more than 1000 psychiatrists attended. In December 1973, the APA's board of trustees voted to declassify homosexuality as a mental disorder in its *Diagnostic and Statistical Manual*. Several months later, after a group of psychiatrists challenged the board's decision, the APA held an extraordinary referendum to determine whether the decision would stand. Approximately 58 percent of the APA members who participated affirmed the decision. While the APA simultaneously approved the creation of a new category, "sexual orientation disturbance," for homosexuals (but not heterosexuals) who were disturbed by or wished to change their orientation, the declassification of homosexuality as a mental disorder significantly weakened one of the main justifications for antihomosexual discrimination in the United States.

Throughout this period, gay and lesbian radicals criticized the reformers for accepting the basic principles and structures of U.S. society and abandoning the revolutionary politics of gay liberation and lesbian feminism. It was difficult for them to deny the effectiveness of the reformers in winning increased mainstream tolerance and acceptance, but from a variety of radical perspectives this was precisely the problem: gay liberationists and lesbian feminists were suspicious of mainstream tolerance and acceptance. Nevertheless, by the end of this period liberal reformers were ascendant within the movement.

Gay and Lesbian Commemorations of Stonewall

Commemorative marches, rallies, programs, and events to mark the anniversary of the Stonewall riots were first held in Boston, Chicago, Los Angeles, Minneapolis, New York, and San Francisco in 1970; in the next few years they spread to most large U.S. cities and many smaller ones. For gay, lesbian, and trans participants, the commemorations provided opportunities to celebrate the distinctive aspects of their cultures; promote the visibility, diversity, and unity of their communities; and highlight ongoing experiences of oppression and resistance. For friends, families, and allies, the commemorations created vehicles for signaling their support and enjoying the spectacle. For the general public, they were impressive demonstrations of the size, scale, character, and power of the gay, lesbian, and trans movements.

In many respects, the history of the first four years of Stonewall commemorations reflects the diverse and changing politics of the movement in this period. The decision to commemorate the riots was made initially at a regional homophile movement conference held in Philadelphia toward the end of 1969, when participants voted to replace the Annual Reminder pickets at Independence Hall with an annual demonstration marking the anniversary of the Stonewall rebellion. They agreed that the demonstration would be called Christopher Street Liberation Day and would first take place in New York in June 1970, but activists in other parts of the country were encouraged to organize parallel events. In the years to come, the history of the Annual Reminders and the larger history of the homophile movement would be forgotten as many people, thanks in part to the Stonewall commemorations, came to believe that the gay, lesbian, and trans movement began in the summer of 1969.

The early history of Stonewall commemorations also reflects the geography of gay, lesbian, and trans activism in this era. They began in the three largest U.S. cities (New York, Chicago, and Los Angeles), the two commonly regarded as the country's gay and lesbian capitals (New York and San Francisco), and two other cities with large and politicized gay and lesbian communities (Boston and Minneapolis). In 1970, more than 1000 people participated in Los Angeles and more than 5000 did so in New York. In 1972, approximately 50,000 participated in San Francisco. They typically took place, at least in part, in gay and lesbian neighborhoods. The commemorations soon spread to other large cities, though in some cases they initially had hundreds rather than thousands of participants. Smaller commemorations took place elsewhere, but people from around the country also began making special trips to attend big-city Stonewall anniversary events. While the large marches received more attention, the smaller ones arguably required more courage on the part of those who participated.

The politics of the early commemorations also reflect the diverse and changing nature of the movement in the early 1970s. Many of the earliest marches were organized by coalitions of gay liberationists, lesbian feminists, and gay and lesbian reformers, but over time gays and lesbians without strong political affiliations (but in some cases with strong business interests) began taking the lead. The earliest marches had more of the qualities of political demonstrations, but within a few years many of the organizers began to envision what they increasingly called "parades" as celebrations of "pride" and "unity"; in some instances, they deliberately downplayed confrontational politics and activist protest.

Gay and lesbian activists debated the politics of their annual commemorations with great intensity. Who should organize and lead the marches? Who should speak and perform at pre- and post-march rallies? How should organizers balance the competing demands of unity and diversity? Should the organizers encourage the participation of business interests, including bars? Should they present gays and lesbians as respectable citizens or sexual liberators? How should the organizers reconcile the representational demands of gay, lesbian, bisexual, and trans communities? What about controversial constituencies, including drag queens, nudists, sadomasochists, sex workers, transsexuals, and man-boy lovers? What should they do about gay effeminacy and lesbian masculinity? What should be the roles of straight politicians and allies? Should the marches orient themselves to the gay, lesbian, and trans community, the straight public, or social, cultural, and political elites? How "political" should the marches be? There were particularly heated debates about the politics of race, gender, and sexuality at the Stonewall commemorations. In many instances, the large percentage of white male participants, the lack of attention to sexism and racism, and the emphasis on political content and cultural entertainment that appealed primarily to white men left many lesbians and people of color feeling marginalized. Lesbian separatists wrestled with the question of whether to participate in commemorations that included men. In these contexts, lesbians and people of color in several cities began organizing autonomous events. In Chicago, African American lesbians took the lead in organizing an annual picnic on Lake Michigan (timed to coincide with the larger downtown march and rally); within a few years, thousands of African American gays and lesbians were participating. In New York, the first gay pride week in 1970 included events for women at the city's new Lesbian Center; in 1972, a Lesbian Pride Week was organized to coincide with Gay Pride Week. The Lesbian Resource Center in Minneapolis organized that city's first lesbian pride march in 1972. Some believed that these types of events violated the politics of unity that the Stonewall commemorations typically emphasized; others celebrated them for recognizing and affirming diversity.

At some of the early commemorations, there were major clashes between lesbian and trans participants who traded accusations about sexism and made competing claims about their contributions to the Stonewall riots and post-Stonewall political activism. These conflicts intersected with debates about the politics of respectability, with some gay and lesbian activists expressing concern about negative public responses to trans visibility and others arguing that trans liberation was an integral component of, and necessarily linked to, gay and lesbian liberation. In 1972, for example, some Philadelphia lesbians welcomed the participation of drag queens in the city's first major march to commemorate Stonewall, but others objected. In the same year, conflicts between gay defenders and lesbian critics of drag at the San Francisco march degenerated into violence. Partly as a result, in 1973 there were two competing events in San Francisco, one welcoming and one excluding trans participants. Also in 1973, New York's march included contingents representing STAR and Queens Liberation Front, but when STAR's Sylvia Rivera demanded to speak at the post-march rally, Jean O'Leary of Lesbian Feminist Liberation insisted on responding. She did so by denouncing drag as misogynist and criticizing the male-dominated nature of the march. This led Lee Brewster of Queens Liberation Front to denounce antitrans lesbian feminists. Peace was temporarily restored when singer Bette Midler, a gay favorite, performed the song "You've Got to Have Friends," but gay, lesbian, and trans activists did not feel particularly friendly toward one another during and after these episodes.

Lesbian and trans activists also clashed at another major event in 1973. At the West Coast Lesbian Conference, held in Los Angeles and attended by approximately 1500 women, conflict erupted when some lesbian feminists denounced the presence and performance of singer Beth Elliot. A lesbian feminist and former DOB-San Francisco vice president who had been invited to perform along with other lesbian musicians, Elliot was also a pre-operative male-to-female transsexual whom DOB-San Francisco had narrowly voted to expel a few months earlier. Some conference participants regarded her as a man who should not have been permitted to attend and perform at a conference for lesbians; they disrupted Elliot's performance and demanded that "he" leave the conference. Conference organizers then polled the 1300 women at the concert. A narrow majority voted to permit Elliot to perform, though a vocal minority strenuously objected. The next day, keynote speaker Robin Morgan's speech, widely reprinted in the lesbian feminist press, referred to transvestism as obscene, attacked drag queens, and called Elliot an opportunist, infiltrator, destroyer, and rapist. Having raised the question of who should be allowed to claim an authentic lesbian identity, Morgan in turn was criticized for denouncing Elliot when she was involved in a heterosexual and reproductive relationship with a gay effeminist. Meanwhile, the successful effort to declassify homosexuality as a mental disorder created further divisions. While some trans liberationists joined gay and lesbian activists in rejecting medical pathologization, many transsexuals depended on medical diagnoses in order to access hormones and surgery. Gay and lesbian denunciations of medical experts created new challenges for transsexuals, as it did for people with disabilities and people with sexually transmitted diseases.

While the gay and lesbian movement experienced internal conflicts and divisions in the late 1960s and early 1970s, it also continued to confront major external challenges. In fact, some activists began to raise concerns about conservative back-lash against the movement. In 1970, a homophile clubhouse in Phoenix went up in flames in a fire believed to have been started by arsonists. In 1972, several GAA-NY activists were brutally attacked at the Inner Circle Dinner protest, the San Francisco MCC was damaged by arson, and two Philadelphia gay bars burned down in mysterious circumstances. In 1973, there were suspicious fires that destroyed the MCCs in Los Angeles and San Francisco and damaged the MCC in Nashville; the Gay Services Center in Buffalo went up in flames; a bomb explosion destroyed a gay bar in Springfield, Massachusetts; and two gay bars were destroyed during Gay Pride Week in San Francisco. Brutal campaigns of police repression occurred in Lexington and Louisville, Kentucky, in San Antonio, Texas, and in countless other places. In a particularly horrible 1973 incident, a firebomb killed thirty-two people at a New Orleans gay bar.

While these were ominous signs of the hatred and hostility that gays and lesbians continued to confront in U.S. society, gay and lesbian activists at the end of 1973 faced the future knowing that they had achieved unprecedented political mobiliza-tion and significant political change over the previous four years. New organizations that formed in 1973 suggested some of the directions that the movement would take in the coming years. In 1970, GAA-NY had been founded by GLF activists who were troubled by GLF's radicalism; in 1973, a group of GAA veterans who now thought that GAA was too radical created the National Gay Task Force, which pursued liberal reform through political lobbying and professional advocacy. The Task Force took the lead in the final months of the campaign to convince the APA to declassify homosexuality as a mental disorder. Several other important organizations were also founded in 1973. Lambda Legal Defense and Education Fund was actually established in 1972, but its application for incorporation in New York was denied until 1973. Also in 1973, the ACLU Sexual Privacy Project began working with gay and lesbian activists in countless court cases, NOW established a Sexuality and Lesbianism Task Force, Parents of Gays was formed as a valuable movement ally, and Olivia Records, which was created by several former members of the Furies, helped chart a new direction for lesbian feminism. These were among the groups that played important roles in the next phase of the gay and lesbian movement.

4

GAY AND LESBIAN ACTIVISM IN THE ERA OF CONSERVATIVE BACKLASH, 1973–81

U.S. gay and lesbian activists faced many familiar challenges after 1973, but a new set of problems developed in this period. The rise of the New Right and Christian Right, their acquisition of significant government power, and the rightward shift in national politics meant that the gay and lesbian movement confronted formidable new obstacles. In this context, there were significant setbacks for gay and lesbian activism, but the movement's accomplishments in these years are notable in part because they occurred in such difficult circumstances.

The movement's dominant tendencies in this era were liberal and reformist, as they had been before the heyday of gay liberation and radical lesbian feminism. In general, the movement after 1973, when compared with its previous four years, was less revolutionary in its goals, less committed to radical coalitions, and less interested in liberating everyone's same-sex desires. In one sign of change, radical arguments that urged everyone to come out as gay or lesbian were largely eclipsed by liberal calls for everyone who was gay or lesbian to come out. Though there were many exceptions, movement activists increasingly presented themselves as minority rights advocates who practiced interest group politics rather than participants in a sexual liberation movement that wanted to change society as a whole. The mass mobilization and public visibility that had developed after the Stonewall riots, however, did not disappear after 1973; they became important components of gay and lesbian liberalism. Gay and lesbian radicalism also did not disappear. While gay and lesbian liberals achieved substantial reforms in this period, lesbian feminists, gays and lesbians of color, sexual liberationists, and gay and lesbian leftists promoted more radical visions of social transformation.

Changing Contexts

The gay and lesbian movement confronted a changing political context after 1973. At the national level, Republican Richard Nixon, facing imminent impeachment because of the Watergate scandal, became the first U.S. president to resign in 1974. He was replaced by Republican Gerald Ford, who was defeated by Democrat Jimmy Carter in 1976, who in turn was defeated by Republican Ronald Reagan in 1980. While Congress continued to have Democratic majorities and many local and state governments were controlled by the Democrats, both major parties were affected by the rise of conservatism. As for the Supreme Court, five appointments by Nixon and Ford shifted the balance of power; from 1975 until 2009 the nine-person Court never had more than two Democratic appointees. In short, while all three branches of the federal government had been controlled by Democrats through much of the 1960s, there was divided government for the next few decades, making liberal reforms more difficult to achieve. Energy crises in 1973 and 1979, economic recessions in 1973–75 and 1980–82, and the Iranian hostage crisis in 1979–81 made it even less likely that the country would focus on sexual equality.

The political context was also changing because of the rise of the New Right, which was a diverse coalition of economic, foreign policy, racial, religious, and social conservatives. Some New Right supporters were long-standing conservatives; others became conservative because of what they viewed as the liberal excesses of the 1960s. Alongside their complaints about affirmative action, communist subversion, high taxation, racial desegregation, social welfare, and urban crime, many New Right advocates had grave concerns about the changing nature of gender, sexuality, marriage, and the family. Conservatives had campaigned for decades against abortion, birth control, homosexuality, interracial sex, nonmarital reproduction, nonmarital sex, pornography, and sex education, but the Christian Right, which was a key component of the New Right, became more organized, more powerful, and more politically engaged during the 1970s. Although their support for legal restrictions on abortion, homosexuality, and pornography contradicted rightwing criticisms of "big government," Christian conservatives were valued coalition partners in the New Right.

During the 1970s, New Right and Christian Right leaders mobilized millions of U.S. Americans in campaigns against gender and sexual liberalism, which in turn helped constitute the New Right and Christian Right as powerful movements. In 1970, conservatives rallied public support by denouncing the Presidential Commission on Obscenity and Pornography, which had recommended the liberalization of obscenity laws. Beginning in 1972, when Congress passed the Equal Rights Amendment, conservatives worked successfully to prevent the required number of states from ratifying the measure, which would have added to the U.S. Constitution a ban on sex discrimination by the United States and the states. They also attacked the Supreme Court's recognition of limited abortion rights in 1973. While conservative activists failed to overturn the *Roe v. Wade* decision, they succeeded in restricting access to and denying public funding for abortions. As is discussed below, the New Right and Christian Right aggressively opposed gay and lesbian rights as well. In the late 1970s, they began to have great influence on the Republican Party and in 1980 they helped elect Reagan. In this period, gay and lesbian activists confronted a powerful new conservative coalition that had access to far more resources than the gay and lesbian movement could hope to secure. At the same time, there were conflicts and contradictions within the New Right and Christian Right, which weakened their potential power, and conservative initiatives stimulated strong counter-mobilizations.

Gay and lesbian activists confronted additional problems as liberals and leftists reoriented themselves after the end of the Vietnam War. Some movements commonly associated with the 1960s, including black power, sexual liberation, women's liberation, and movements representing Asian Americans and Pacific Islanders, Latinos and Latinas, and Native Americans and Native Alaskans, were arguably more powerful in the 1970s than they had been in the 1960s. They also intersected in new ways, as was evident in the growth of multicultural, third world, and anti-racist feminisms. After the trials, tribulations, and traumas of the 1960s, however, many activists disengaged from politics, focused on alternative cultures, and turned inward during the "me decade." While support for civil rights and opposition to the Vietnam War had brought together many activists in the 1960s, they had less success in uniting around a shared set of goals in the 1970s. One reason is that straight, white, and male activists did not always respond favorably to the emergence of strong movements representing other social groups. Many reacted with complaints about divisiveness and disunity, which helped make both a reality. State repression also undermined the power of liberals and leftists. All of this threatened their ability to respond effectively to the New Right and Christian Right.

Another changing context for gay and lesbian activism was the larger gay and lesbian culture. As was the case in earlier eras, only a minority of people who engaged in same-sex sex were activists, but there now seemed to be more people who regarded themselves as gay or lesbian and more who participated in the movement. New developments in gay and lesbian cultures also influenced the movement. For various reasons, including the changes associated with the sexual revolution and women's liberation, the transformations of U.S. cities and suburbs, and the reductions in some forms of sexual and gender policing, there was a gay and lesbian cultural renaissance in the 1970s. Urban gay and lesbian neighborhoods grew in number, size, and complexity, as did gay and lesbian communities in smaller towns and rural enclaves. The Castro in San Francisco, Greenwich Village in New York, and West Hollywood in Los Angeles were among the best-known gay neighborhoods, but every large city featured at least one area with a large concentration of gay men and gay-oriented businesses. The Mission in San Francisco, Park Slope in New York, and Jamaica Plain in Boston were among the best-known lesbian neighborhoods, while Northampton, Massachusetts, was one of several smaller cities with a distinctly visible lesbian community. The number of businesses that catered to gays and lesbians grew and more of these were owned by gays and lesbians. By the mid-1970s, there were more than 2500 gay and lesbian bars and more than 150 gay bathhouses in the United States. Gay and lesbian vacation destinations also became more popular. On the East Coast, these stretched from Ogunquit and Provincetown in New England, through Fire Island, Atlantic City, and Rehoboth Beach in the mid-Atlantic, to Key West in Florida. Many people did not have access to these locations, which remained vulnerable to police crackdowns and social violence, but growing distinct neighborhoods, towns, businesses, and resorts were just four aspects of a multifaceted transformation in gay and lesbian culture.

In many respects, gay cultures and lesbian cultures converged in this era, but they also diverged. For gay men, there was an expanding world of sexual cruising, public sex, and male sociability on city streets and in bars, bathhouses, bookstores, clubs, discos, gyms, parks, and theaters. The masculine "clone" look—featuring muscular bodies, facial hair, jeans, and t-shirts—became more popular, as did a set of overlapping cultural preferences for leather and sadomasochism, sports and exercise, and drugs and alcohol. Favored music and dance genres included disco and salsa, rock and punk, Broadway and Motown, and classical and opera. Divas and drags entertained large gay audiences. Gay pornography became more accessible. The enlarged gay economy promoted gay consumption and the gay "lifestyle." Linked to all of these changes, there was a multicultural renaissance in gay-themed art, film, literature, and theater.

For lesbians, there was an expanding network of bars, clubs, and coffeehouses, a growing number of community centers and support groups, and a larger range of sports activities, with softball the most popular. Lesbians staffed and sustained a large set of bookstores and publishers, along with an array of other types of businesses, including craft retailers, credit unions, and food cooperatives. Some of these activities and enterprises were oriented to women in general, some to lesbians and gay men, some to lesbians specifically. Women's music became exceptionally popular among lesbians, with Olivia Records leading the way. The annual Michigan Womyn's Music Festival, founded in 1976, attracted large numbers of lesbians, as did other women's music events. Lesbians were typically less consumption-oriented than were gay men, in part because their average incomes were lower, but the lesbian economy expanded greatly and there was also a multicultural renaissance in lesbian-themed art, film, literature, and theater.

The renaissance sustained and was sustained by the growth of gay and lesbian media. In the 1950s and 1960s, most gay and lesbian periodicals had been published by homophile groups and attracted limited advertising. Many of their successors in the 1970s were published independently and some featured substantial advertising. By 1980, there were more than 600 gay and lesbian periodicals with a combined circulation of more than 500,000. The decade's most popular gay periodical, *The Advocate*, was based in California, celebrated gay consumerism, and promoted gay lifestyles. Most radicals and most women preferred Boston's *Gay Community News* and Toronto's *The Body Politic*. Local papers included *Bay Area Reporter*, *Philadelphia Gay News*, *Seattle Gay News*, and *Washington Blade*. *Country Women* and *RFD* served rural readers. *Amazon Quarterly, Big Apple Dyke News, Dyke, Lavender Woman,*

Lesbian Connection, Lesbian News, Lesbian Tide, and *Sinister Wisdom* were widely read lesbian periodicals. *Azalea*'s primary audience was third world lesbians; *Blacklight* and *Moja* were for black gays. *Drag* and *Radical Queen* were popular trans periodicals.

The transformed gay and lesbian culture of the 1970s simultaneously supported and undermined class, race, gender, and regional hierarchies. The expanded gay and lesbian economy challenged the heterosexism of capitalism but strengthened bourgeois consumerism. Gay and lesbian gentrification deconstructed and reconstructed social divisions in urban environments; in one common pattern, middle-class white gay men moved into economically depressed neighborhoods, raised property values, and displaced poorer and darker residents. Some aspects of gay and lesbian culture were more racially integrated than their straight counterparts; others were more segregated. Racist hierarchies were reproduced and subverted in sexual encounters, pornographic representations, print publications, commercial establishments, and everyday life. Relationships between gays and lesbians replicated and resisted the sexist dynamics that existed in relationships between men and women more generally. Masculine lesbians, feminine gay men, and transsexuals were celebrated in some gay and lesbian quarters and criticized in others. Gay and lesbian culture privileged cities, but also stimulated straight, gay, and lesbian anti-urbanism.

Changes in gay and lesbian culture had complex effects on the movement. On the one hand, the growth of gay and lesbian territories, the expansion of gay and lesbian businesses, and the renaissance in gay and lesbian culture strengthened the movement. Some of those who were responsible for these developments thought of themselves as activists and many were inspired to become activists by their experiences (positive and negative) in gay and lesbian culture. On the other hand, some of the cultural changes that occurred in the 1970s made it seem less necessary and desirable to participate in the movement. Activists remained concerned about how to politicize their communities; now they sometimes had to compete with the sexual, social, and cultural activities that were increasingly available to gays and lesbians. Gay and lesbian wealth supported the movement financially, but also influenced political priorities and strategies. While some business owners and cultural leaders participated in the movement and saw themselves as agents of change, others distanced themselves from movement activism and criticized political radicalism. Gay and lesbian activists typically claimed to represent their community, but they did not always do so with the support of the people they claimed to represent.

Mass Mobilization

In these multiple contexts, the gay and lesbian movement promoted social change. As had been the case in the 1960s, most movement groups in this period were organized on local or state levels, but several regional and national organizations became influential. Three of the most significant were the National Gay Task Force (founded 1973), Gay Rights National Lobby (founded 1976), and Human Rights Campaign Fund (founded 1980). Major legal advocacy groups included Lambda

Legal Defense and Education Fund (founded 1973), Gay Rights Advocates (founded 1977 and later renamed National Gay Rights Advocates), Lesbian Rights Project (founded 1977), and Gay and Lesbian Advocates and Defenders (founded 1978).

The new regional and national groups changed the movement. Most did not emphasize grassroots organizing, community mobilization, or participatory democracy; they relied on paid staff, professional fundraising, and centralized decision-making. These groups generally favored lobbying and litigation over direct action. They also tended to utilize arguments about minority and privacy rights rather than sexual liberation and social revolution. These were effective strategies for winning public support and influencing political elites, but not for promoting mass mobilization or radical transformation. In addition, the regional and national groups tended to be led by middle-class, urban, and gender-normative whites in their thirties, forties, and fifties, who were sometimes criticized for their class, race, gender, and regional politics. Attacked by radicals for their agenda-setting practices, insider tactics, and reformist objectives, they nonetheless were effective in promoting liberal social change.

At the local level, many gay and lesbian groups were similarly liberal, but others—especially those made up of lesbian feminists, gays and lesbians of color, sexual liberationists, and gay and lesbian leftists—were more radical. Examples include Bay Area Gay Liberation and Wages Due Lesbians in San Francisco, Combahee River Collective and *Gay Community News* Prisoner Project in Boston, Dyketactics in Philadelphia, and Lavender & Red Union in Los Angeles. Many of these groups linked gay and lesbian liberation to struggles against capitalism, imperialism, racism, and sexism. In some contexts, liberal strategies and goals were compatible with their radical counterparts; in other contexts, they conflicted. Some liberals and radicals worked together, for example, in supporting sodomy law reform and antidiscrimination legislation, but they often disagreed about military matters, same-sex marriage, and electoral politics. Many liberals complained about the damage caused by radicals in campaigns to influence public opinion and change public policy, but they profited when they could present themselves as reasonable reformers in contrast to their revolutionary rivals. Liberals also benefited, despite their resistance, when they were pressed by radicals to take more seriously the ideas and interests of people of color, trans people, and women.

One sign of the combined success of liberal and radical mobilization was the 1979 National March on Washington for Lesbian and Gay Rights, which brought more than 100,000 people to the nation's capital. Another was the growth of pride marches in many cities; by the end of the 1970s, hundreds of thousands of people participated in the annual marches and in autonomous activities organized by and for lesbians and people of color. The rainbow flag, which became an international symbol of gay and lesbian pride, debuted at San Francisco's Gay Freedom Day Parade in 1978. A third sign of success was the development and expansion of gay and lesbian community centers, health centers, and antiviolence projects. A fourth was the formation of new alliances. The ACLU continued to be the movement's most valuable ally, but gay and lesbian activists also developed productive relationships with various feminist, labor, left, professional, and religious groups. There were resolutions and initiatives supporting gay and lesbian rights, for example, by the AFL-CIO, American Federation of Teachers, American Jewish Congress, American Medical Association, American Nurses Association, American Psychiatric Association, Americans for Democratic Action, National Council of Churches, National Education Association, National Lawyers Guild, and NOW. The movement was sometimes recognized as part of broader liberal, left, and civil rights coalitions.

Some sectors of U.S. society experienced major upsurges in gay and lesbian organizing. Hundreds of groups for gay and lesbian students and allies were established at colleges and universities; dozens of high school and youth groups formed; and older gays and lesbians began to organize. In the late 1970s, for example, Senior Action in a Gay Environment and the Institute for the Protection of Lesbian and Gay Youth (later renamed the Hetrick-Martin Institute) were established in New York. For those with strong religious affinities, there were gay and lesbian groups for Catholics, Episcopalians, Jews, Lutherans, Methodists, Mormons, Presbyterians, Quakers, Unitarians, and United Church members, along with more than 100 Metropolitan Community Churches and various independent churches and congregations. Lesbians participated in feminist religious and spiritual projects. Radical Faeries celebrated sexuality, spirituality, and nature. Gay and lesbian atheists organized. There were also more groups focused on family issues, including Custody Action for Lesbian Mothers in Pennsylvania; Dykes and Tykes and Gay Fathers in New York; Fag Dads by the Bay, Gay and Lesbian Parents of Los Angeles, and Lesbian Mothers Union in California; Lesbian Mothers National Defense Fund in Washington; and Momazons in Ohio. National groups included the Gay Fathers Coalition and Parents and Friends of Lesbians and Gays, which soon had more than twenty chapters.

Scholars, researchers, professionals, and workers contributed to gay and lesbian mobilization in this era. Caucuses in the American Anthropological Association, American Historical Association, American Psychological Association, American Sociological Association, and Modern Language Association advocated for gays and lesbians who worked in these fields, criticized homophobia and heterosexism in higher education, and promoted gay and lesbian studies. Lesbians were central in the growth of women's studies. Specialized archives, libraries, and history projects were established in various cities. Gay and lesbian doctors, lawyers, psychiatrists, public health workers, social workers, and teachers formed professional groups. Healthcare specialists created the National Gay Health Coalition. Employee networks began to form in corporate workplaces. Gay and lesbian caucuses and initiatives also emerged in labor unions, including the American Federation of State, County, and Municipal Employees in Chicago; the Hotel and Restaurant Employees and Teamsters Newspaper Drivers Union in San Francisco; the

American Federation of Teachers, United Federation of Teachers, and United Auto Workers in New York; and, on the national level, AFSCME, AFT, and AFL-CIO.

Various gay, lesbian, and bisexual subcultures established new groups. Bi Forum formed in New York, the San Francisco Bisexual Center opened, and bisexual groups were established in many other places; by 1974, the National Bisexual Liberation Group had 1600 members in five cities. Larry Townsend's 1972 book *The Leatherman's Handbook* and *Drummer* magazine, first published in 1975, contributed to the growth of leather, bondage, and sadomasochism groups, including Gay Male S/M Activists and Lesbian Sex Mafia in New York, Hellfire Club in Chicago, and Society of Janus and Samois in San Francisco. Gays and lesbians with disabilities also mobilized. The National Rainbow Society of the Deaf was founded in 1977. In 1981, Connie Panzarino organized the first Disabled Lesbian Conference in Michigan. More gay and lesbian Alcoholics Anonymous groups were established. While gays and lesbians continued to distance themselves from the notion that homosexuality was a disability, gays and lesbians with disabilities encouraged disability and gay/lesbian activists to reconsider their attitudes.

As was the case earlier, some trans groups saw themselves as part of the gay and lesbian movement; some saw themselves as allies in a larger movement of gender and sexual dissidents; some did not see themselves as connected to gay and lesbian activism at all. Radical Queens, for example, began as a caucus of GAA-Philadelphia and viewed itself as part of the gay and lesbian movement, as did the Imperial Court System, which developed out of the charitable drag groups initiated by Jose Sarria in the 1960s, Fantasia Fair, which was an annual Provincetown event that began in 1975, and the Sisters of Perpetual Indulgence, which was a group of genderfuck performance artists that formed in San Francisco in 1979. In contrast, Virginia Prince's Foundation for Personality Expression, which became the Society for the Second Self in 1976, saw itself as a group for cross-dressing straight men. In 1979, the March on Washington's Transpeople Caucus fought successfully to have a trans speaker at the march rally and include references to trans issues in march literature, but did not win agreement to include "gay transpeople" in the march's name or address trans issues in the march's list of demands. The fact that the Caucus's preferred term was "gay transpeople," which recognized that some trans people identified as gay and others did not, is one example of the ways in which the trans movement was and was not part of the gay and lesbian movement.

Most transsexual groups did not see themselves as part of the gay and lesbian movement. And while some transsexual groups (such as the Transsexual Action Organization, which had ten chapters and a thousand members in the 1970s) joined the gay and lesbian movement in rejecting medical models, many transsexuals depended on medical diagnoses in order to access hormones and surgeries. For this reason, while the vast majority of gays and lesbians celebrated the APA's declassification of homosexuality as a mental disorder in 1973, transsexuals had more divided opinions about the APA's classification of transsexualism as a gender identity disorder in 1980. Some hoped that this would help improve access to health and medical services, but others were troubled by the pathologizing implications. Meanwhile, the gap between the trans and gay/lesbian movements widened as more gay activists celebrated gay masculinities and more lesbian feminists attacked transsexuals.

For gays and lesbians of color, this was a period of transformational mobilization. Working inside and outside white-dominated gay and lesbian groups, they criticized racism, white privilege, and white assumptions in gay and lesbian contexts. For example, they campaigned against discriminatory practices in gay and lesbian bars, racist representations in gay and lesbian media, and police practices and immigration restrictions that targeted gays and lesbians of color. Working inside and outside straight-dominated groups of people of color, they criticized homophobia, straight privilege, and heteronormative assumptions in nonwhite contexts. For instance, they urged civil rights groups to address religious intolerance, gender conservatism, and representations of homosexuality as white. In relation to feminist groups, they pursued similar initiatives that encouraged the women's movement to address class, gender, race, and sexuality. They produced influential essays, novels, plays, poems, and stories that explored interlocking oppressions, intersectional identities, and racialized desires. While building links between class-, gender-, race-, and sexuality-based movements, they established dozens of autonomous groups for gays and lesbians of color.

For Native Americans and Native Alaskans, Barbara Cameron and Randy Burns established Gay American Indians in San Francisco in 1975. The Intertribal Berdache Society was active on the West Coast. Mohawk poet Maurice Kenny published a groundbreaking essay on Native American homosexuality in *Gay Sunshine* in 1975–76. In the second half of the 1970s, there was a revival of interest in two-spirit traditions as well as an increase in concern about the status of gays, lesbians, and two-spirits in Native American communities and the status of Native Americans in predominantly white gay and lesbian communities.

African American gay and lesbian organizing increased significantly in this era. In 1974, a group of black feminists in Boston, led by Barbara and Beverly Smith, formed a chapter of the National Black Feminist Organization, which soon became the autonomous and mostly lesbian Combahee River Collective. In 1977, Combahee published a widely distributed statement that addressed the interlocking nature of class, gender, racial, and sexual oppression. In 1978, African American activists in Baltimore and Washington, D.C., led by Billy Jones, formed the National Coalition of Black Gays; soon there were affiliated groups in many cities. Other active groups included the Black Gay Caucus in San Francisco, Black Men's Caucus in Boston, Salsa Soul Sisters in New York, and Sapphire Sapphos in D.C. In 1979, after threatening to file a lawsuit, Lambda Student Alliance was recognized by Howard University, a historically black institution in D.C. African Americans also played key roles in planning the National Third World Gay and Lesbian Conference, which was organized to coincide with the 1979 March on Washington.

Latino/Latina gay and lesbian organizing also increased after 1973. In part, this reflected the growth in migration from Latin America, but it also was influenced by changes within established U.S. communities. Active groups included Alianza de Mujeres, Comunidad de Orgullo Gay, and Mujer Intégrate Ahora in Puerto Rico; Comité Homosexuales Latinoamericanos and Buenas Amigas in New York; Comité Latino de Lesbianas y Homosexuales in Massachusetts; Latinos Por Derechos Humanos in Florida; and Gay Chicano/a Caucus in Texas. Californians formed the Gay Alliance of Latin Americans, Gay Latino Alliance, Gay Latinos Unidos (later renamed Gay y Lesbian Latinos Unidos), Latina Lesbian Alliance, Latin American Lesbians, and Lesbianas Latina Americanas. In 1979, twelve lesbians and gays marched openly in the Puerto Rican Day Parade in New York and activist Juanita Díaz-Cotto spoke at the March on Washington. In 1980, movement groups assisted thousands of Cuban gays and lesbians who arrived in the United States as part of the Mariel boatlift.

Asian American and Pacific Islander organizing also was influenced by changing immigration patterns and political dynamics within established U.S. communities. Active groups included the Association of Lesbian and Gay Asians, Gay Asian Association, and Gay Asian Information Network in the Bay Area; Boston Asian Gay Men and Lesbians; and Asian Pacific Lesbians and Gays in Los Angeles. Some groups included whites; some did not. Unbound Feet, a collective of Asian American women writers that formed in California in 1979, included several lesbians. Activist and writer Michiyo Fukuya spoke at the 1979 March on Washington.

Gay and lesbian activists also formed multiracial coalitions, including GAA-NY's Third World Caucus; Gay Atlanta Minority Association; Gay Racially Equal and Together (GREAT) Men of the Rockies and Your Own Understanding (YOU) in Denver; Third World Lesbian Caucus in Los Angeles; Gente, Third World Gay Caucus, and Black and Third World Lesbians in San Francisco; and Lesbians of Color in Los Angeles, Newark, Palo Alto, San Diego, San Francisco, and Seattle. Salsa Soul Sisters was mostly African American, but included other women of color. More than 600 people participated in the National Third World Gay and Lesbian Conference, where Audre Lorde delivered the keynote speech. The March on Washington organizing committee called for 20 percent third world representation on all march planning committees; one of the two march coordinators was Joyce Hunter, who was biracial; and Salsa Soul Sisters was given the honor of carrying the main march banner. In 1980, Black and White Men Together was established in San Francisco; soon there were dozens of chapters. Also in 1980, Barbara Smith and Audre Lorde established Kitchen Table: Women of Color Press. One year later, Gloria Anzaldúa and Cherríe Moraga published *This Bridge Called My Back: Writings by Radical Women of Color*, which included many contributions by lesbians. Influenced by multiple movements, gays and lesbians of color mobilized to an unprecedented extent; in so doing, they changed and democratized the gay and lesbian movement.

As the examples above suggest, lesbian organizing also increased after 1973. In numerous contexts, including many of the groups referenced above, gay and lesbian activists worked side by side. The organizers of pride marches, the March on Washington, and the National Third World Gay and Lesbian Conference prided themselves on bringing men and women together, as did the leaders of many community centers and health centers. Some women organized separate lesbian pride events, but many participants also attended gay pride marches. The organizers of the March on Washington called for 50 percent female representation on all of its planning committees. *Gay Community News* was one of many periodicals that were produced and read by gays and lesbians. In countless locations, lesbians challenged gay sexism but worked with gay men.

Many lesbians, either in addition to or instead of working with gay men, focused on lesbian, feminist, and lesbian feminist projects. Hundreds of local lesbian and lesbian feminist groups were established in this period. Many were liberal and reformist, but a large number were leftist and radical. In 1977, lesbian activists convinced the National Women's Conference in Houston, which was sponsored by the U.S. federal government and attended by more than 20,000 women, to support a gay and lesbian rights plank in its National Plan of Action. In 1978, there was an attempt to establish a National Lesbian Feminist Organization and chapters formed in ten cities, but the project did not proceed. At the local level, lesbians contributed to the growth of women's businesses and organizations, bookstores and publishers, newspapers and magazines, libraries and archives, community centers and health centers, athletics and sports, and educational and research projects. They participated in virtually every type of feminist activism and played particularly strong roles in initiatives that addressed sexual health, reproductive freedom, and violence against women. Lesbians were also central in feminist cultural activism and in the development of women's art, literature, music, and theater.

Lesbian feminism was diverse and changing in this period. Many liberal lesbian feminists worked in electoral politics and in local, state, regional, and national groups that lobbied and litigated. Radical lesbian feminism existed in many inter-secting configurations, but there were several strong tendencies. One was lesbian cultural feminism, which celebrated female values, encouraged women's autonomy, and explored lesbian separatism. While some cultural feminists emphasized the positive in women rather than the negative in men, others campaigned against pornography, prostitution, rape, and violence, which they viewed as signs, symbols, symptoms, and sources of patriarchal oppression. Lesbian feminist sex radicals, in contrast, emphasized the pleasures as well as the dangers of sex for women. To support female sexual empowerment, they built alliances with sex workers, explored sadomasochism, revived butch/fem, and promoted lesbian pornography. Samois, for example, was founded in 1978 as a San Francisco-based lesbian sadomasochism group and became a strong defender of female sexual exploration. In the second half of the 1970s, cultural feminists and sex radicals engaged in fierce debates about sexual politics; lesbians were involved on both sides of these conflicts. Other radical lesbian feminists concentrated on socialist and/or anti-imperialist politics. Women of color participated in all of these configurations of lesbian feminism, critiqued them for failing to address class and race, and took the lead in promoting multicultural, third world, and antiracist lesbian feminisms.

The diversity of lesbian feminism was evident in wide-ranging debates about political radicalism, lesbian separatism, sexual liberation, and white racism, but another contentious subject was transsexualism. As was apparent in the narrow vote in favor of permitting Beth Elliot to perform at the West Coast Lesbian Conference in 1973, lesbian feminists were deeply conflicted about transsexualism. A few years later, major conflicts erupted again when women's music fans learned that Sandy Stone, who had been hired by Olivia Records in 1976 as a recording engineer, was a male-to-female transsexual. Olivia resisted the calls to fire Stone, but the Michigan Womyn's Music Festival adopted a policy of admitting only "women-born women." In 1979, feminist opposition to transsexuals culminated with the publication of Janice Raymond's book *The Transsexual Empire*, which depicted transsexuals as male rapists who colonized women's bodies, invaded their territories, and appropriated their identities. Some of Raymond's strongest critics were lesbian feminists, but many trans activists came to view lesbian feminism as promoting the liberation of some women at the expense of others. More generally, as the gay and lesbian movement organized and mobilized in the 1970s, its diversity proved to be one of its greatest strengths and one of its greatest challenges.

Gay and Lesbian Reform

The achievements of the gay and lesbian movement in the period from 1973 to 1981 were substantial but are difficult to capture. The movement contributed to the growth and development of gay and lesbian culture, but also maintained a critical distance from some aspects of that culture. Activists successfully promoted increased popular tolerance for and acceptance of homosexuality, though their efforts inspired conservative counter-mobilizations. In many cases, the movement was most effective when it presented gays and lesbians as a minority group made up of individuals with fixed and innate sexual orientations; thanks to the civil rights movement, many U.S. Americans were prepared to grant limited rights and freedoms to recognizable minority groups with a documented history of oppression. Sexual equality, however, was another matter; activists were not particularly successful in challenging the notion that heterosexuals and heterosexuality deserved special rights and privileges. Nor was the movement particularly effective when it presented homosexuality as a universal human potential; in some contexts, this was an inspirational and influential argument, but it led critics to attack the movement for encouraging people to "choose" homosexuality. Overall, the movement succeeded in reducing antihomosexual persecution, but sexual equality and sexual liberation remained more elusive.

One way to measure the movement's successes and failures in this period is to examine changes in law, politics, and policy. In general, this reveals great local variation, a general shift toward increased respect for gay and lesbian rights in the private sphere, and ongoing difficulties in achieving sexual equality in the public sphere. One of the movement's highest priorities was the decriminalization of private same-sex sex for consenting adults. Laws against consensual sex in the private sphere were rarely enforced, but many activists believed that it would be easier to argue for gay and lesbian rights more generally if these laws were repealed or overturned. They also hoped that straight people would support arguments about personal privacy, even if they did not believe in sexual equality. Eight states had repealed their sodomy laws earlier; in this period, sodomy laws were invalidated by state courts in two states (New York and Pennsylvania) and repealed by state legislatures in fourteen (Alaska, California, Indiana, Iowa, Maine, Nebraska, New Hampshire, New Jersey, New Mexico, South Dakota, Vermont, Washington, West Virginia, and Wyoming). Most of the states acted in the context of general criminal code revision, but several did so after debates that addressed homosexuality. By 1981, twenty-four states no longer criminalized private same-sex sex for consenting adults. In some jurisdictions, other laws commonly used against gays and lesbians were also invalidated, repealed, or restricted; this was the case for laws against lewd vagrancy in California, loitering and solicitation in Colorado, crimes against nature in Florida, unnatural and lascivious acts in Massachusetts, sexual importuning in Ohio, lewd solicitation in Pennsylvania, lewd and indecent acts in Washington, D.C., and cross-dressing in Chicago, Cincinnati, Columbus, Denver, Detroit, and Houston.

In part because of sex law reform but also because of police reform coalitions, gay and lesbian antiviolence campaigns, and gay and lesbian activism more generally, antihomosexual police practices declined in many cities and towns. Police mistreatment certainly did not disappear. Local authorities continued to target bars, bathhouses, bathrooms, bookstores, neighborhoods, parks, streets, and theaters favored by gays, lesbians, and other people interested in same-sex sex. In some contexts, the police did not interfere with more respectable gay and lesbian activities, but acted forcefully against public sex, sadomasochism, sex work, and sex businesses. In many contexts, people of color, prisoners, sex workers, trans people, and young people remained distinctly vulnerable. In several cases, police attacked nonviolent gay and lesbian protesters. Movement activists responded to all of this by lobbying, litigating, and demonstrating, which contributed to further declines in repressive police practices.

Notwithstanding these successes, in 1976, when gay and lesbian rights advocates appealed to the U.S. Supreme Court to overturn North Carolina's and Virginia's sodomy laws, which could have had national implications, the justices declined to do so. As the Court had made clear in earlier rulings, it was prepared to recognize rights of marital and reproductive privacy, but not rights of sexual privacy or sexual equality. Same-sex sex remained illegal in twenty-six states; in Washington, D.C., Puerto Rico, and various U.S. territories; and in the U.S. military and U.S. prisons. By 1981, several of these states had decriminalized cross-sex adultery, cohabitation, fornication, and sodomy, but retained or created newly specific prohibitions on same-sex sex. In many locations, laws against cross-dressing, disorderly conduct, indecency, lewdness, loitering, sex with minors, solicitation, and other crimes continued to be enforced in ways that discriminated against gays, lesbians, and others who engaged in same-sex sex.

On the issue of obscenity, gay and lesbian activists had a wide range of views and some lesbian feminists campaigned against pornography, but most movement participants were critical of sexual censorship, especially when it was based on standards that discriminated against same-sex sexual expression. Gay pornography businesses expanded greatly in the 1970s, but the Supreme Court still viewed sexual censorship as constitutionally permissible and it continued to use discriminatory standards when deciding obscenity cases. After the Court authorized the use of local standards in defining and judging obscenity in 1973, anticensorship advocates faced the difficult task of defending sexual expression in thousands of jurisdictions with different standards. In 1974, anticensorship advocates were unsuccessful when the Court upheld an obscenity conviction based on the mailing of a homoerotic advertisement for *The Illustrated Presidential Report of the Commission on Obscenity and Pornography*. In 1976, the Court signaled its acceptance of local zoning regulations that imposed special rules and restrictions on sex-oriented businesses. In 1980, after years of litigation, the Federal Bureau of Prisons agreed to stop restricting prisoner access to gay and lesbian publications, but this did not apply to materials classified as sexually explicit. Gay pornography proliferated in the 1970s, but it remained vulnerable to discriminatory policing.

Another major item on the movement's agenda was the passage of laws to restrict discrimination based on sexual preference and sexual orientation. In some respects, this was more difficult to achieve than was the decriminalization of same-sex sex since it was seen as a more significant step toward equality. It was also more difficult because some of the libertarian arguments that gay and lesbian advocates used in sodomy law reform campaigns, which criticized state interference with individual rights, could be deployed by conservatives to argue against state restrictions on the individual's right to discriminate. In other respects, the prospects of passing antidiscrimination laws were more favorable. These laws could be passed in local jurisdictions, whereas sodomy law repeal typically required state action. In addition, many U.S. Americans were more comfortable with the idea of outlawing discrimination than they were with the notion of condoning same-sex sex.

Using various tactics, activists convinced more than forty cities and counties to revise their civil rights statutes, which typically restricted discrimination based on race and sex, to cover discrimination based on sexual preference or orientation. Many of the measures, including New York's and Philadelphia's, applied only to public sector employment, but by 1981 more expansive laws that applied to employment, housing, and/or public accommodations had been enacted in a collection of big cities, college and university towns, and miscellaneous municipalities, the largest of which were Detroit, Los Angeles, Minneapolis, San Francisco, Seattle, and Washington, D.C. Most of the laws did not cover discrimination based on gender identity or expression, which was especially important for trans people, but the ones passed in Champaign, Los Angeles, Minneapolis, and Urbana did. In 1975, Pennsylvania became the first state to prohibit sexual discrimination in state government jobs; California was the second in 1979. These measures did not end sexual inequality, even in the areas specified, and religious organizations typically were exempted, but the laws discouraged overt discrimination and were useful tools for challenging antihomosexual policies and practices. In the context of decentralized governance in the United States, there were now places such as Chicago where both same-sex sex and sexual discrimination were legal and places such as Detroit where both were illegal. In the relatively small number of locations where same-sex sex was legal and there were laws against sexual discrimination, the legal status of homosexuality was arguably better than it was in Canada and England, two of the country's closest allies, but in most jurisdictions it was worse.

Activists had some success in using litigation to challenge sexual discrimination. New York and Florida courts ruled that applicants for licenses to practice law could not be denied based on sexual orientation. The Nevada Supreme Court decided that liquor control authorities could not revoke or suspend bar licenses based on homosexual patronage. The California Supreme Court overturned the firing of a teacher who had been arrested for sexual solicitation and ruled against Pacific Telephone in a class action lawsuit concerning antihomosexual hiring practices. Antidiscrimination litigation and legislation convinced Northwestern Bell to revise its antihomosexual hiring policies. A federal court overturned the University of Delaware's decision not to renew the contract of a faculty member because he had made public statements about gay rights. Another federal court overturned the firing of a Texas county employee because he planned to make public statements in favor of gay rights. Gay and lesbian student groups won official university recognition through litigation in Alabama, Missouri, New Hampshire, Oklahoma, Tennessee, and Virginia. Shortly after a South Dakota male student brought a male date to his high school prom, a federal court upheld the right of a Rhode Island male student to do the same.

In other cases, the courts were less sympathetic to gay and lesbian rights claims. A California court upheld a state medical board's decision to discipline a doctor for unprofessional conduct after he was convicted of lewd solicitation in a public bathroom. A federal court ruled that a Maryland school district could remove a gay man from his classroom teaching position because he had not mentioned his past membership in a gay student group on his job application. Another federal court ruled against a man who had challenged the Dallas Police Department's decision to not hire him because he was a gay activist. California, New Jersey, and Washington courts upheld the firing of public school teachers based on homosexuality, while an Oregon court decided in favor of a fired lesbian teacher but did not order her reinstated. The Wisconsin Supreme Court ruled that a state home for boys could fire an employee based on his homosexuality and his use of makeup. The U.S. Supreme Court declined to consider the Mississippi Gay Alliance's appeal of a decision permitting Mississippi State University's student newspaper to refuse to publish an advertisement for the group. Most forms of antihomosexual discrimination remained perfectly legal in the United States.

While the decriminalization of same-sex sex and the passage of antidiscrimination laws enjoyed overwhelming movement support, the legalization of same-sex marriage continued to be controversial among gays and lesbians. Some viewed marriage reform as a crucial step toward freedom and equality or believed that same-sex marriage could change marriage for the better. Others were motivated by practical matters, including the special rights and privileges reserved for the married in areas such as healthcare, immigration, and inheritance. Some opposed the legalization of same-sex marriage precisely because of those special rights and privileges, which discriminated against the unmarried. There was also opposition based on the notion that the institution of marriage was oppressive, restrictive, sexist, and straight.

Many same-sex couples had wedding celebrations and commitment rituals in this period, but the movement to legalize same-sex marriage did not achieve its goals. The Arizona Supreme Court voided and revoked the marriage license that two men had obtained in Phoenix. A Washington court rejected two men's claim that refusal to grant them a marriage license violated the state's ban on sex discrimination. A New York court nullified the marriage of two people it classified as women, one of whom had presented himself as a man. An Ohio court refused to grant a divorce to two women who claimed to have had a common-law marriage. Two gay men—one a naturalized U.S. citizen born in the Philippines and the other an Australian citizen—had a wedding ceremony at the Metropolitan Community Church (MCC) in Los Angeles and then flew to Colorado after learning that a Boulder County clerk was issuing marriage licenses to same-sex couples. Several days later, Colorado invalidated Boulder's six same-sex marriages, but the gay couple tried to use their marriage to prevent the Australian man's deportation. The Immigration and Naturalization Service (INS) refused to acknowledge the marriage and the U.S. Supreme Court later declined to consider their appeal. There were other unsuccessful efforts to legalize same-sex marriage through litigation in other states. In response to these efforts, twenty-five states passed legislation recognizing only marriages between one man and one woman. Meanwhile, by the end of the 1970s, legal restrictions on same-sex marriage meant that gay and lesbian transsexuals had more access to marriage in the thirty-eight states that did not allow them to change their legal sex/gender than they did in the twelve states that did.

Some of the movement's ambivalence about marriage carried over to its views on parenting, but while same-sex marriage was commonly viewed as something new, gay and lesbian parenting was an existing social reality. Lesbian and gay advocates began to devote substantial attention to parental custody litigation in this period. Most of the cases involved lesbian mothers whose parental rights were challenged by their ex-husbands, though there were other types of challenges as well. In most of these cases, the courts ruled against the lesbian and gay parents, basing their decisions at least in part on antihomosexual arguments. In this context, many lawyers advised their clients to make concessions in custody, visitation, and child support negotiations. In some instances, however, there were partial victories. In at least six states, gay and lesbian parents won custody and visitation rights, but with stipulations that required the parent to terminate their same-sex relationships, not live with their partners, and not expose their children to gay or lesbian partners or friends. Even when gay and lesbian parents won custody and visitation, the courts often made it clear that in general they privileged straight parenthood. There were more positive outcomes when California and Washington courts lifted earlier stipulations that had granted custody to lesbian mothers as long as they did not live with their partners. Other positive outcomes occurred when Massachusetts and New York courts ruled that there had to be specific demonstrations of harm to the child to justify depriving gay and lesbian parents of their custody and visitation rights. As for foster care, social workers in New York, Maryland, and Washington began to place gay and lesbian teenagers with gay and lesbian foster parents, though in at least one case a Washington judge rejected this type of arrangement. Additional victories in parenting cases occurred in various states, though most courts continued to have strong biases against gay and lesbian parents.

In the context of the uneven progress of local and state reform, gay and lesbian activists pursued antidiscrimination initiatives at the federal level. In 1975, after years of lobbying and litigation, the U.S. Civil Service Commission (CSC) removed "immoral conduct" as a disqualification for federal government employment and announced that individuals would not be found unsuitable based solely on homosexual identity or conduct. In 1979, a federal court ruled that the FBI, which was not covered by CSC regulations, could not fire an employee based solely on his admission of homosexuality. In 1980, a new CSC policy affirmed the privacy rights of federal government job applicants and employees and prohibited inquiries into and actions based on conduct that was not job related. The CSC and the courts continued to permit sexual discrimination in jobs requiring security clearances, but gay and lesbian litigants were occasionally successful in challenging security-based discrimination. Meanwhile, in 1974 U.S. Representative Bella Abzug from New York proposed an amendment to the Civil Rights Act of 1964 that would restrict discrimination based on sexual or affectional preference in employment, housing, and public accommodations. Abzug initially found few supporters in Congress; by 1981, just fifty-nine U.S. representatives and a few U.S. senators (mostly Democratic, but some Republican) had endorsed federal legislation against sexual orientation discrimination.

Nor did the movement succeed in its efforts to end sexual discrimination in the military. This was another area of activist ambivalence, as the United States was just concluding a destructive war in Vietnam and many questioned the actions of the U.S. military in other parts of the world. Most gay and lesbian activists, however, favored fair and equal treatment for those who served in the armed forces. While movement advocates lobbied for policy changes and supported many legal appeals, their successes were limited. In 1973, a federal court upheld the Navy's decision to deny an honorable discharge to a man who admitted to having a sexual relationship with a shipmate. In 1977, a federal court ruled in favor of a woman who had been dismissed from the Navy after she admitted to engaging in homosexual acts, but this was reversed on appeal. In 1980, two gay men who had been discharged from the Air Force and Navy—Leonard Matlovich and Vernon Berg—won a federal court ruling stipulating that the military had to explain why the two men had not been eligible for the exceptions that were sometimes made in cases concerning homosexuality. The case concerning Technical Sergeant Matlovich, a Republican Mormon who had served three tours of duty in Vietnam, won a Bronze Star and Purple Heart, and disclosed his homosexuality to the Air Force as part of an effort to challenge military policies, received unprecedented national publicity. When the Air Force and Navy refused to offer explanations, a court ordered the men reinstated, but after the military offered financial settlements and their lawyers expressed pessimism about their chances of winning, they agreed to resign. Another notable case concerned Army Reserve Sergeant Miriam Ben-Shalom, who had been discharged in 1976 after acknowledging that she was a lesbian but not admitting to homosexual conduct. Ben-Shalom won a 1980 federal court ruling that overturned her discharge on First Amendment grounds, but the Army delayed her reinstatement until 1987 and then used new regulations to deny her request for reenlistment. Annual military discharges based on homosexuality in this period ranged from 900 to 1800. Most of those affected were men, but women were disproportionately discharged for homosexuality.

A partial breakthrough in immigration law began in 1974, when the American Psychiatric Association and American Bar Association urged the INS to revise its antihomosexual policies, which had been rendered obsolete by the APA's declassification of homosexuality as a mental disorder. In 1977, National Gay Task Force and ACLU representatives met with INS officials to advocate for change and the Public Health Service (PHS) informed the INS that it planned to stop administering the policies. Two years later, U.S. Surgeon General Julius Richmond announced that the PHS would no longer conduct medical examinations to certify that homosexual aliens were psychopathic personalities or sexual deviates. The INS, however, continued to enforce the ban; immigration officials questioned male aliens about their sexual orientation, for example, if they were wearing earrings and female aliens if they were entering the country to attend the Michigan Womyn's Music Festival. In 1980, gay and lesbian activists convinced their congressional allies to introduce legislation to repeal the ban, but it did not pass. That year, Dutch gay activists highlighted their opposition to U.S. immigration policies by borrowing police uniforms and questioning U.S. tourists at Amsterdam's airport about their sexual orientations.

The U.S. government faced a quandary when Cuba's communist government announced in 1980 that it would temporarily permit "undesirables," including homosexuals, to migrate to the United States. Of the more than 124,000 people who left Cuba as part of the Mariel boatlift that year, a sizable number were gay or lesbian or claimed they were to facilitate their departure. Faced with a choice between enforcing their antihomosexual immigration policies or presenting their country as a haven for Cuban exiles, U.S. officials accepted the Cubans. In this context, the INS announced in late 1980 that aliens would no longer be questioned about their sexual preferences but would be excluded or deported if they indicated that they were homosexual. While INS and State Department officials violated the new policy on a regular basis, it became more difficult to exclude and deport gay and lesbian aliens.

In addition to lobbying, litigating, and demonstrating, gay and lesbian activists participated in electoral politics. In this period, gay and lesbian activists established Democratic Party clubs in more cities, founded Republican Party clubs in several locations, and engaged with electoral politics in other ways. It remained difficult for openly gay or lesbian candidates to win elections, but there were a few successes. In 1974, Kathy Kozachenko was elected to the Ann Arbor City Council, Elaine Noble was elected to the Massachusetts House, and Allan Spear, a member of the Minnesota Senate, came out as gay. In 1977, Harvey Milk was elected to the San Francisco Board of Supervisors; Harry Britt was appointed to replace him in 1978 and was elected to the Board in 1979. In Wisconsin, Jim Yeadon was elected to the Madison City Council in 1978 and Dick Wagner to the Dane County Board of Supervisors in 1980. Also in 1980, Karen Clark was elected to the Minnesota House and Gerald Ulrich was elected the mayor of Bunceton, Missouri. All of these politicians were Democrats except for Kozachenko, who was a member of the Human Rights Party. No openly gay or lesbian candidates were elected to the U.S. Congress, though two Republican and two Democratic House members (Robert Bauman of Maryland, Jon Hinson of Mississippi, Frederick Richmond of New York, and Joseph Wyatt of Texas) were caught up in same-sex sex scandals; Bauman and Hinson later came out as gay.

Most movement activists believed that it was more important to elect supporters of gay and lesbian rights than to elect gay or lesbian candidates. To accomplish this, they promoted voter registration, educated voters about candidate records and positions, sponsored and attended election forums, criticized and confronted politicians, and participated in election campaigns. Over the course of the 1970s, gay and lesbian voters contributed significantly to the election of several dozen city council members, local mayors, county supervisors, state legislators, and members of Congress. This tended to happen in jurisdictions with large concentrations of gay and lesbian voters, as was the case in Boston, Houston, Los Angeles, Minneapolis, New York, San Francisco, Seattle, and Washington, D.C. Gays and lesbians also helped elect several of the country's first African American big-city mayors, including Tom Bradley of Los Angeles and Richard Arrington of Birmingham.

Most gay and lesbian activists who were oriented to electoral politics supported the Democratic Party. At the Party's 1976 convention in New York, there were four openly gay or lesbian delegates. As was the case in 1972, there was a failed effort to persuade the Democrats to adopt a gay and lesbian rights plank, but presidential candidate Jimmy Carter campaigned for gay and lesbian votes, advertised in the *Advocate*, and endorsed federal legislation to restrict sexual orientation discrimination. After he was elected, he appointed Margaret Costanza, who was a lesbian but not publicly known as such, as a special assistant to the president and director of the Office of Public Liaison. In 1977, Costanza invited fourteen activists selected by the National Gay Task Force (NGFT) to an unprecedented meeting at the White House, where they discussed various issues. She then arranged for NGTF representatives to meet with officials at the Justice Department, INS, PHS, Civil Rights Commission, Federal Communications Commission, and Federal Bureau of Prisons. In some cases, these discussions led to policy changes, including the immigration reforms mentioned above. The National Coalition of Black Gays, which was excluded from the 1977 meeting, subsequently arranged for a group of gay and lesbian activists of color to meet with White House officials in 1979. Many gays and lesbians, however, were disappointed with Carter and especially with his failure to challenge New Right initiatives and support gay and lesbian equality more forcefully. In 1977, they staged protests at public appearances by Carter in New York and Vice President Walter Mondale in San Francisco.

For gay and lesbian activists, the 1980 presidential campaign illustrated the promise and perils of electoral politics. Democratic candidates Jimmy Carter, Jerry Brown, and Edward Kennedy campaigned for gay and lesbian votes. At the Party's convention in San Francisco, where Carter won the nomination, there were seventy-seven openly gay and lesbian delegates and alternates. In a symbolic gesture, Melvin Boozer, an African American gay man from Washington, D.C., was nominated to run as the party's vice presidential candidate and delivered an inspirational convention speech before Mondale was acclaimed as the Party's choice. For the first time, the Party platform included a gay and lesbian rights plank, which criticized discrimination based on sexual orientation.

Gay and lesbian activists thus succeeded in making inroads with the Democrats, but the Republicans tried to turn this to their advantage by criticizing Carter for supporting gay and lesbian rights. While the 1980 Republican convention in Detroit, which selected Reagan as the Party's presidential candidate, included several gay and lesbian delegates, the Party's platform supported the Family Protection Act, which proposed to deny federal funding to individuals or groups that presented homosexuality as an acceptable lifestyle, prohibit the government-funded Legal Services Corporation from participating in gay and lesbian rights litigation, and amend the Civil Rights Act to make clear that the law did not apply to sexual orientation discrimination. Several Republican, New Right, and Christian Right leaders were gay or engaged in same-sex sex, but the Party strongly opposed gay and lesbian rights initiatives. Some gay and lesbian activists supported the Republicans, in part because they believed that its small-government and libertarian tendencies might reduce the scope of antihomosexual persecution, but they underestimated the extent to which social conservatives would not permit this to happen. Just before the election, New Right and Christian Right supporters paid for advertisements and mailings that criticized Carter for supporting gay and lesbian rights. When Reagan defeated Carter, gay and lesbian activists lost much of the access to the White House that they had gained during the Carter years, while their conservative opponents gained new power.

Beyond their efforts to promote change in law, politics, and policy, gay and lesbian activists targeted business, religion, and popular culture. In terms of business, while there were radicals who believed that capitalism was fundamentally opposed to gay and lesbian liberation, most activists promoted reform within the existing economic system. In lobbying for laws and pursuing litigation to restrict discrimination in employment, housing, and public accommodations, they hoped that the state could be used to make businesses change their ways, but the movement also worked more directly to reform business practices. Activists persuaded more than fifty major corporations, including ABC, AT&T, Bank of America, CBS, Citibank, General Electric, IBM, J.C. Penney, NBC, and Sears, to adopt policies against employment discrimination based on sexual orientation. In some instances, labor unions made this a priority. In two early successes, Seattle Public Library workers represented by AFSCME and Ann Arbor Transportation Authority workers represented by the Transportation Employees Union secured the adoption of such policies in 1974. In many cases, arguments about good business practices, appeals to fairness, and threats of boycotts, litigation, and protests were persuasive, though most businesses continued to discriminate against gay and lesbian employees and consumers.

Gay and lesbian activists also targeted businesses that engaged in particularly egregious forms of discrimination. In 1974, two straight Teamsters joined forces with Harvey Milk and other San Francisco activists to promote a successful national boycott of Coors beer to protest the company's antihomosexual and anti-union practices. This was an important episode in the formation of stronger alliances between the labor and gay/lesbian movements. As is discussed below, gay and lesbian activists also criticized media companies that disseminated particularly offensive content. Meanwhile, the movement continued to organize protests and pursue litigation against mainstream businesses that excluded and ejected gays and lesbians, while also targeting discriminatory gay and lesbian businesses. Protests against racism, sexism, and transphobia at gay and lesbian bars occurred, for example, in Philadelphia in 1973, St. Paul and Chicago in 1974, San Francisco in 1975, Los Angeles in 1975–76, and Memphis in 1981.

The movement also challenged religious intolerance. While some radicals believed that organized religion was fundamentally antihomosexual, most activists supported religious reform. Building on earlier initiatives, they promoted dialogue with religious believers, organized caucuses within mainstream denominations, supported the ordination of gay and lesbian religious leaders, requested access to space in churches and synagogues, and campaigned for the adoption of supportive resolutions and policies. They formed autonomous Christian churches, Jewish congregations, and religious groups, including Dignity for Catholics and Integrity for

Episcopalians. They also criticized conservative doctrines and organized protests against religious groups, leaders, and institutions. Many religious reform projects were based in large cities, but gay and lesbian religious groups in small towns and cities were distinctively important when they were the primary local vehicles for gay and lesbian activism.

Most major U.S. religions continued to condemn homosexuality, but reformers convinced some to reconsider their positions. The Unitarian Church, United Church, and Society of Friends (Quakers) were generally regarded as the most gay- and lesbian-affirmative mainstream churches. The United Church continued to ordain ministers who were openly gay or lesbian and the Unitarians began to do so. The Episcopalian Church ordained a lesbian priest in 1977, but shortly thereafter adopted a policy against ordaining practicing homosexuals, as did the Presbyterian Church in 1978. The Disciples of Christ and the Reformed Church joined the Lutherans and Presbyterians in opposing the criminalization of private same-sex sex by consenting adults. The Episcopalian Church endorsed civil rights for gays and lesbians. In 1975, the National Council of Churches endorsed legislation against antihomosexual discrimination, though it refused to accept the MCC for membership. In 1974, the Union of American Hebrew Congregations, which represented Reform Jews, approved the membership of a Los Angeles gay and lesbian congregation. Three years later, the Union and the Central Conference of American Rabbis, which also represented Reform Jews, affirmed their opposition to the criminalization of private same-sex sex by consenting adults.

Gay and lesbian activists were less successful in convincing other religions to modify their views. In fact, Roman Catholics and Southern Baptists, two of the largest U.S. denominations, became increasingly strident in opposing gay and lesbian rights, as did African American Baptists, Methodists, and Pentecostals, other Protestant evangelicals and fundamentalists, and Orthodox Jews. Even in these denominations, however, there were exceptions. Many African American churches were pulled in one direction by their commitments to civil rights and in another by their religious conservatism. While the Roman Catholic Church adopted a strong statement that condemned homosexuality in 1975, the Church had pockets of gay and lesbian support. In 1974, the National Federation of Roman Catholic Priests' Councils adopted a resolution opposing the criminalization of private same-sex sex by consenting adults and criticizing antihomosexual discrimination. In the same year, Brother Grant-Michael Fitzgerald, an openly gay African American member of a Catholic religious order, testified in favor of a proposed gay and lesbian rights law in Philadelphia. In 1977, the archbishops of Seattle and Minneapolis/St. Paul endorsed sexual orientation antidiscrimination legislation. In the same year, Sister Jeannine Gramick and Father Robert Nugent founded New Ways Ministry, which served gay and lesbian Catholics in Washington, D.C. Several independent Catholic churches (not recognized by the Vatican) had primarily gay and lesbian congregations.

Gay and lesbian activists also targeted popular culture. Major campaigns against invisibility and negative visibility were led by the NGTF in New York, Gay Media

Task Force in Los Angeles, Gay Media Action in Boston, Gay Media Project in Philadelphia, and, after the 1979 March on Washington, Lesbian and Gay Media Advocates. In many cases, their efforts began with critical letters and requests for meetings, escalated with public denunciations, and culminated with demonstrations, sit-ins, and boycotts. Media targets included the *Boston Globe*, *Chicago Daily News*, *Los Angeles Times*, *Ms.*, *New York Times*, *Science*, and *Village Voice*. Gay and lesbian activists also criticized episodes on popular television programs, including *Barney Miller*, *The Carol Burnett Show*, *The Dick Cavett Show*, *Kojak*, *M*A*S*H*, *Soap*, and *The Streets of San Francisco*. There were especially strong protests against a 1974 episode of *Police Woman* that featured three lesbians who were murdering the residents of their nursing home. Activists also targeted particularly offensive Hollywood films and television movies, including *Born Innocent*, *The Laughing Policeman*, and *Windows*. After the script for *Cruising*, a film that starred Al Pacino as a policeman who goes undercover to investigate a series of gay murders, was leaked to a gay activist in 1980, hundreds of protesters disrupted the filming of the movie in New York; hundreds more demonstrated at theaters that screened the film.

As was the case with their business and religion campaigns, gay and lesbian efforts to reform popular culture had successes and failures. In general, the mass media continued to privilege and promote heterosexuality. Many mainstream newspapers and magazines refused to cover significant gay and lesbian news, publish gay and lesbian features, or use the words "gay" or "lesbian." Many television and radio news shows did likewise. For the most part, television programs and mainstream films did not feature major gay or lesbian characters. When gays, lesbians, and people who engaged in same-sex sex were represented in most mainstream newspapers, magazines, television programs, and Hollywood films, they were usually depicted as narcissistic, pathetic, pedophilic, psychotic, ridiculous, tragic, or violent.

All of that said, there were breakthroughs in this era. In response to gay and lesbian protests, some sponsors and advertisers withdrew their support for particular shows, some local television stations refused to broadcast offensive programs, some movie theaters declined to show specific films, and some national television networks revised their syndication and re-run plans. In 1974, for example, activists convinced seven major sponsors to withdraw their advertising for an episode of *Marcus Welby, M.D.*, that featured a junior high school boy who had been raped by his male teacher; seventeen ABC affiliates decided to not air the episode. In 1980, the National News Council ruled that a *CBS Reports* documentary on homosexuality violated journalistic ethics and standards; CBS News issued a partial apology. Various media executives agreed to meet with their gay and lesbian critics. Many directors, producers, editors, and writers began to consult with gay and lesbian activists about their articles, scripts, and programs. The quantity of mainstream media coverage of homosexuality increased. Though many activists continued to be disappointed by the quality, some thought that this was improving as well. There were also more gay and lesbian characters and more appealing ones on more than a dozen television programs and in various independent films. Most media activists believed that Hollywood was lagging behind, though there were occasional television and big-screen films that featured attractive, complex, and sympathetic gay and lesbian characters. In mainstream popular culture, gay men received more attention than lesbians, whites more than nonwhites, and middle-class more than working-class people, but this, too, began to change.

The gay and lesbian movement cannot take all of the credit for the positive changes that occurred in the treatment of same-sex sexuality in the period from 1973 to 1981. Nor can it take all of the blame for the lack of change in some areas and negative developments in others. Many factors contributed to the dynamics of sexual continuity and change. The gay and lesbian movement, however, played a key role in the process of social transformation, which helps explain why opponents of gay and lesbian rights began to conclude that they, too, needed to organize and mobilize a strong and powerful movement.

New Right and Christian Right Backlash

As the gay and lesbian movement began to achieve greater success in the post-Stonewall era, New Right and Christian Right activists responded by organizing major campaigns against homosexuality. In fact, these campaigns helped establish the New Right and Christian Right as powerful political forces. Religious and other types of conservatives had attacked homosexuality in the 1940s, 1950s, and 1960s, but in the 1970s they began to focus more intensively on the subject. Utilizing church-based networks, direct mail fundraising, and radio and television programs, they supplemented traditional arguments against homosexuality with new assertions about the recent successes of a powerful gay and lesbian movement that was determined to win special rights, recruit followers, corrupt children, destroy families, and revolutionize American culture. As gay and lesbian reformers increasingly based their campaigns on claims about the fixed and innate nature of sexual orientation, critics of gay and lesbian rights increasingly argued that homosexuality was a choice that should be resisted and rejected.

A diverse set of groups campaigned against gay and lesbian rights, but several of the most influential were the American Family Association, Christian Voice, Concerned Women for America, Focus on the Family, the Moral Majority, Save Our Children, and the Traditional Values Coalition. In many cases, the same groups responsible for massive campaigns against abortion rights, pornography, and women's right also mobilized against gay and lesbian rights. Roman Catholics, Southern Baptists, and other types of evangelical and fundamentalist Protestants led many of these efforts; Mormons and Orthodox Jews played key roles as well. In some contexts, businessmen, firemen, and policemen were active in these campaigns. The opposition to gay and lesbian rights was predominantly white, but some African American and Latino leaders supported these efforts, partly for religious reasons and partly because they objected to the gay and lesbian movement's use of race-based arguments and analogies.

Beginning in the early 1970s, conservative activists fought actively against sodomy law reform and campaigned for the recriminalization of same-sex sex. Two of their notable successes occurred in 1972, when Idaho reversed its 1971 decision to decriminalize sodomy, and 1977, when Arkansas approved a new ban on same-sex sex after decriminalizing sodomy in 1975. In 1981, New Right activists persuaded the U.S. House to overturn a recent decision by Washington, D.C., over which it exercised legislative veto powers, to decriminalize sodomy and solicitation. Conservatives succeeded in blocking sex law reform in other jurisdictions as well.

New Right and Christian Right activists also campaigned against antidiscrimination laws. In many locations, conservatives who opposed all antidiscrimination measures formed alliances with supporters of laws against racial and religious discrimination who opposed their extension to cover sexual discrimination. Together, they capitalized on radical gay and lesbian arguments that presented homosexuality as a universal human potential, which conservatives depicted as a recruitment strategy, while also criticizing gays and lesbians for claiming that they were a minority group, which conservatives believed was inappropriate for individuals who chose to sin. In addition, conservatives accused homosexuals of transgressing gender norms, which placed gay and lesbian activists in the difficult position of having to reject, embrace, or complicate the links that were being made between same-sex sexuality and transgenderism.

Believing that gay and lesbian rights measures lacked popular support and confident that they could mobilize opposition by criticizing homosexuality, conservative advocates convinced elected officials in many locations, including New York City and Philadelphia, to defeat proposals to restrict antihomosexual discrimination in employment, housing, and public accommodations. They also used popular referenda to overturn laws against sexual preference and sexual orientation discrimination in Boulder in 1974; Dade County (Florida) in 1977; Eugene, St. Paul, and Wichita in 1978; and Santa Clara County (California) and San Jose in 1980. The victorious Dade County campaign, led by Anita Bryant, received extensive national publicity and contributed to antihomosexual mobilization around the country. New Right activists also convinced Florida to become the first state to ban adoptions by gays and lesbians in 1977 and Oklahoma to pass a law permitting local school districts to fire public school teachers who publicly advocated, encouraged, or promoted homosexuality in 1978.

While New Right and Christian Right activists were victorious in many of their antihomosexual campaigns, they lost in others. In 1978, their efforts to overturn Seattle's law against sexual orientation discrimination failed when it only gained 37 percent support. In the same year, 58 percent of California's voters voted against the Briggs Initiative, which proposed to disqualify for public school employment anyone, regardless of sexual orientation, who advocated, encouraged, or promoted homosexuality (inside or outside the classroom). At the federal level, New Right and Christian Right activists failed to win passage of the Family Protection Act.

As these defeats suggest, conservative campaigns against homosexuality inspired counter-mobilizations. Many gay and lesbian groups were founded, many grew substantially, and many achieved success after New Right and Christian Right initiatives contributed to increases and changes in gay and lesbian organizing. Across the United States, gay and lesbian businesses and groups held fundraisers to support the campaigns in Florida, California, and elsewhere. After the Dade County results were announced, thousands participated in protest marches in Boston, Chicago, Denver, Houston, Indianapolis, Los Angeles, New Orleans, New York, and San Francisco. In California, Harvey Milk effectively responded to conservative arguments about gay and lesbian recruitment by declaring, "I want to recruit you. I want to recruit you for the fight to preserve democracy."[1] When Anita Bryant toured the country after her victory, she was greeted by protesters not only in large urban centers, but also in a dozen smaller cities and towns. Gay and lesbian activists organized a boycott of Florida orange juice until the state citrus commission terminated Bryant's work as a spokesperson. Thanks in part to the conservative campaigns, gay and lesbian pride parades increased in number and size, financial contributions to gay and lesbian groups grew, new gay and lesbian groups formed, and national networks strengthened.

In the context of these campaigns, gay and lesbian activists forged new alliances and coalitions. The campaign against the Briggs Initiative, for example, secured a wide range of endorsements from civil rights organizations, professional associations, religious groups, and labor unions. Gay and lesbian activists in California and Seattle, in contrast to some of their less successful counterparts elsewhere, gained the support of influential leaders from communities of color. In California, they convinced prominent Democratic and Republican politicians, including Gerald Ford, Jimmy Carter, and Ronald Reagan, to release statements opposing the Briggs Initiative. In many locations and at the 1979 March on Washington, gay and lesbian activists worked to overcome conflicts within their movement between liberals and radicals, men and women, and whites and people of color, along with divisions based on class, region, and religion. More white gay activists recognized the value of having lesbians and people of color in movement leadership positions; more lesbians and people of color reconsidered the politics of gender and racial separatism; and more activists from different classes, regions, and religions recognized their mutual interdependence. Many liberals and radicals continued to criticize one another and racism, sexism, and transphobia continued to interfere with movement unity, but gay and lesbian activists learned to work together in new ways. In 1979, New Right and Christian Right campaigns helped motivate many people to attend the March on Washington. While there were significant conflicts at the march and trans activists in particular criticized march planners for failing to address their concerns, movement activists successfully highlighted their community's extraordinary diversity and its strength in numbers.

Notwithstanding the successes of gay and lesbian counter-mobilization, New Right and Christian Right campaigns contributed to an environment of hate and hostility that had tragic and fatal consequences. There were reports of major increases in antihomosexual violence in many cities and towns after the Dade County referendum and other conservative campaigns against gay and lesbian rights. In many instances, the violence was committed or condoned by the police and not treated seriously by the courts. Fires, many caused by arson, damaged and destroyed gay and lesbian businesses, centers, churches, and offices in various parts of the country. Abuse, harassment, and violence had long plagued gay and lesbian communities and most conservatives did not endorse antihomosexual violence, but New Right and Christian Right rhetoric supported the attitudes and beliefs that promoted and perpetuated these attacks.

A particularly horrific incident took place in San Francisco in 1978, just weeks after the defeat of the Briggs Initiative. Dan White, an ex-policeman and ex-fireman who was a vocal opponent of gay and lesbian rights, had just resigned from the San Francisco Board of Supervisors. When he tried to retract his resignation, Mayor George Moscone, who was an ally of City Supervisor Harvey Milk, declined to accept the retraction. White then entered San Francisco City Hall through a window with a loaded gun and assassinated Moscone and Milk. That night, tens of thousands of mourners held a candlelight march in honor of the two victims. Several months later, a jury declined to convict White for first-degree murder, found him guilty of manslaughter, and sentenced him to less than eight years in prison, in part because of the "Twinkie defense," which attributed the attacks to excessive sugar consumption. In response, thousands of protesters participated in the "White Night Riots" in the streets of San Francisco. Several months later, many activists attributed the success of the March on Washington to Milk's leadership role in supporting the march and their determination to honor his memory.

By the early 1980s, there appeared to be a political stalemate in the United States on matters related to gay and lesbian rights. One component of the stalemate was local variability. At one extreme, there were state and local jurisdictions where same-sex sex was legal and there were laws that restricted sexual orientation discrimination; at the other extreme, there were jurisdictions where same-sex sex was illegal and there were no laws restricting sexual orientation discrimination. While there was every reason to believe that state and local conflicts about gay and lesbian rights would continue to occur, there was little likelihood that supporters or opponents of gay and lesbian rights would be able to claim total victory at the national level. A second component of the stalemate was increased respect for gay and lesbian rights in the private sphere, as was evident in the decriminalization of sodomy in almost half the states, the reduction in some forms of sexual policing, and the increase in support for gay and lesbian privacy rights among liberals and libertarians. A third component was ongoing resistance to sexual equality in the public sphere, which was pervasive in diverse social, cultural, and political contexts. More U.S. Americans seemed willing to grant gays and lesbians some degree of freedom and liberty in the private sphere, but the vast majority did not think that homosexuality and heterosexuality should be treated equally in the public sphere.

For most gay and lesbian activists, the stalemate represented an improvement over the situation that had prevailed in the 1950s and 1960s, but even the most favorable state and local jurisdictions were limited in what they could do to promote sexual equality in the absence of fundamental changes in law and policy at the federal level and major changes in U.S. society and culture more generally. At the same time, sexual freedom in the private sphere would never be secure without sexual equality in the public sphere. For these and many other reasons, the gay and lesbian movement regarded the stalemate achieved in the 1970s as unstable and unsatisfactory. With the election of New Right icon Ronald Reagan as U.S. president in November 1980, many gay and lesbian activists wondered whether the situation was about to get worse. It did get worse, but not primarily in the ways they expected.

5

GAY AND LESBIAN ACTIVISM IN THE AGE OF AIDS, 1981–90

In the 1980s, the U.S. gay and lesbian movement confronted two huge problems: (1) the increased power of sexual conservatives in the Christian Right, the New Right, the Republican Party, and national politics more generally, and (2) the AIDS epidemic, which had devastating consequences around the world, destructive effects on multicultural gay and lesbian communities, and dire implications for men who had sex with men. Much of the movement's attention focused on the health crisis in this period; gay and lesbian activists in coalitions of people with AIDS, AIDS service organizations, AIDS activist groups, and gay and lesbian movement groups contributed significantly to the fight against AIDS. In turn, AIDS contributed to the mobilization of the gay and lesbian movement in the first half of the decade, its radicalization in the second half, and its changing fortunes throughout this period. In the context of the epidemic, the movement renegotiated its external relationships with friends and foes and its internal configurations of ability, age, class, gender, health, race, region, and religion. From 1981, when AIDS was first recognized, to 1990, when the emergence of queer activism signaled a reorientation and rejection of gay and lesbian politics, AIDS greatly influenced the movement and the movement greatly influenced the process of social change in the United States.

Changing Contexts

In January 1981, the gay and lesbian movement immediately understood that it confronted a new political situation when Ronald Reagan, the first U.S. president elected with substantial support from the New Right and Christian Right, took office. In contrast, several months later, most movement activists did not recognize the significance of early gay press reports about "an exotic new disease" that was affecting gay men or Centers for Disease Control articles on clusters of Los Angeles,

New York, and San Francisco patients with weakened immune systems and rare cancers, pneumonias, and viruses. Given the long history of scientific conceptions of homosexuality as a disease, there were good reasons to be distrustful of public health reports that linked the medical mystery to the "homosexual lifestyle."[1]

Over the next few months, gay and lesbian concerns grew as the number of reported cases increased and experts began referring to Gay-Related Immune Deficiency (GRID). Epidemiologists soon identified Haitians, hemophiliacs, and heroin users as other "risk groups" and noted that heterosexuals and children were affected, but many government officials, scientific experts, media commentators, and conservative leaders promoted the notion that this was a gay disease. At the same time, there were fears that it was contagious and that contact with gay people or people who had the disease was dangerous. Especially in the early years of the epidemic, there was widespread anxiety, confusion, hysteria, and panic. Even after gay and lesbian activists convinced public health authorities to replace GRID with AIDS (Acquired Immune Deficiency Syndrome) in 1982, even after the virus that causes AIDS was isolated in 1983 and named HIV (Human Immunodeficiency Virus) in 1986, and even after it was established that unprotected sexual intercourse and exposure to contaminated blood were the primary routes of transmission, most U.S. Americans continued to associate the epidemic with homosexuality. This contributed to the negative treatment of people with HIV and AIDS, who were persecuted in diverse social contexts, and the negative treatment of gays, lesbians, and bisexuals, who were blamed for the health crisis. In the context of AIDS, there was an epidemic of prejudice, discrimination, and violence in the United States.

AIDS began to spread decades before it was recognized as an epidemic, but the numbers and locations affected grew exponentially in the 1980s. By the end of the decade, there were hundreds of thousands of U.S. Americans living with HIV, tens of thousands living with AIDS, and tens of thousands who had died of AIDS-related illnesses. While everyone in the United States was at risk and transmission was based on acts rather than identities, African Americans, gay men, hemophiliacs, intravenous drug users, Latinos, poor people, prisoners, sex workers, and trans people were disproportionately affected, as were men who had sex with men, blood transfusion recipients, and children whose mothers were HIV-positive while pregnant. Those who belonged to more than one of these groups were especially vulnerable. Medical developments in the second half of the 1980s made it possible to test for HIV, slow the progression of HIV and AIDS, and improve treatment for AIDS-related illnesses, but the number of people living with and dying of HIV/AIDS continued to grow. In response, the gay and lesbian movement reoriented, revived, and radicalized.

Timing played a critical role in this process. By the early 1980s, gays and lesbians had enjoyed more than a decade of sexual liberalization, territorial expansion, economic development, institutional growth, and political mobilization. These now served as the bases for gay and lesbian responses to AIDS, even as some people blamed the epidemic on these developments. Just a few years earlier, gay and lesbian activists had campaigned successfully against the classification of homosexuality as a mental illness; now they needed assistance from the medical system they had criticized. In the 1970s, many activists had condemned federal, state, and local governments for persecuting gays and lesbians and interfering with private sexual matters; now the movement called on the state for assistance, funding, and support. Various civil rights, feminist, labor, left, and professional groups had begun to support gay and lesbian rights in the 1970s, but in many cases their sexual politics were still in flux when they learned about the epidemic in the 1980s. This was also a moment of transition in the sexual politics of U.S. business, religion, and popular culture. The specific historical moment in which AIDS was recognized as an epidemic mattered greatly for the gay and lesbian movement.

A second changing context for gay and lesbian activism was the increased power of the Republican Party and the strengthened position of the New Right and Christian Right. With substantial support from social conservatives, Republicans won all three U.S. presidential elections in the 1980s, putting Reagan in office from 1981 to 1989 and George Bush for the next four years. The Reagan and Bush administrations were critical of most gay and lesbian rights initiatives and generally did not support strong and effective AIDS policy responses. Nor did their civil rights, economic, education, health, or welfare policies create favorable environments for gay and lesbian reform or HIV/AIDS prevention and treatment. Reagan did not make substantive public comments about AIDS until 1987, by which time more than 4000 U.S. Americans had died of AIDS-related illnesses. More often than not, Republican leaders expressed far more concern about the spread of AIDS into the "general population" than they did about its impact on the communities most severely affected. Reagan and Bush also appointed five Supreme Court justices, who strengthened the Court's conservative majority, and the Republicans had a majority in the U.S. Senate from 1981 to 1987. In institutional terms, Republicans and conservatives had not been in such a strong position since the 1920s.

U.S. voters however, did not permit the Republicans to govern alone. They maintained Democratic control of the House, gave Democrats control of the Senate in 1987, and elected Democratic governors and legislatures in many states. Moreover, the Reagan and Bush administrations experienced internal conflicts between different types of conservative. Some Republicans did not regard sexual politics as a priority, preferred antihomosexual symbolic gestures to substantive sexual policymaking, or did not favor a strong role for the federal government in legislating sexual morality. Some administration officials, including Surgeon General C. Everett Koop and Presidential Commission on the HIV Epidemic Chair James Watkins, supported more effective HIV/AIDS policies. The conservative political context was not favorable to the gay and lesbian movement, but there were openings that activists could pursue and new possibilities for counter-mobilization.

Gay and lesbian activists also faced an empowered New Right and a strengthened Christian Right. By the 1980s, the Christian Right had become more than a movement seeking to influence government from the outside; it was a powerful party faction that often was a necessary component of Republican electoral success. The New Right and Christian Right had wide-ranging agendas, but many of their supporters campaigned against abortion rights, gay and lesbian rights, pornography, sex education, and women's rights. Some prominent New Right and Christian Right leaders depicted AIDS as divine retribution for the sins of homosexuality; some called for quarantining, segregating, and tattooing people with HIV/AIDS. Leading the charge were many conservative groups founded in the 1970s along with new ones such as the Christian Coalition, Family Research Council, and Family Research Institute.

New Right and Christian Right activists were successful during the 1980s, but also were disappointed. They were frustrated when Republicans did not pass various pieces of conservative legislation and did not govern in accordance with New Right and Christian Right principles. They were unhappy with the compromises forged by the Supreme Court in abortion rights, affirmative action, civil rights, obscenity, and women's rights cases. They also did not always agree with one another; in some cases, religious and social conservatives began to question the sexual politics of other types of conservative, whom they suspected of forming purely strategic coalitions without intending to support sexually conservative legislation. Moreover, many New Right and Christian Right policies did not have majority public support and antagonized moderate voters. The general situation was not favorable for gay and lesbian activism, but some of these conflicts and divisions created new possibilities for liberal reform.

In this respect, too, timing was critical. The epidemic was recognized at a specific moment in the history of gay and lesbian relationships to the major political parties, the New Right, and the Christian Right. By the early 1980s, the Democrats increasingly regarded gays and lesbians as important constituents, but this was new, ambivalent, and contested. In any case, the Republicans were ascendant and they tended to oppose gay and lesbian rights. AIDS was first recognized four years after the Dade County referendum, three years after the Briggs Initiative and the assassination of Harvey Milk, and two years after the March on Washington. By the early 1980s, the political stalemate described in the last chapter, which featured significant local variability, more respect for gay and lesbian rights in the private sphere, and ongoing opposition to sexual equality in the public sphere, was unstable. This was also a moment when voters were electing more candidates who supported reductions in government support for social programs, many of which would be important in addressing sexual equality and AIDS.

A third context for gay and lesbian activism was the changing nature of liberal and leftist movements. Building on developments in the 1970s and motivated by conservative successes, liberals and leftists forged new coalitions in the 1980s. Gay and lesbian activists developed mutually beneficial relationships with various civil rights, feminist, labor, and leftist groups and established closer ties with movements that focused on censorship, disability, healthcare, homelessness, prisoners, and reproduction. In 1982, for example, the Leadership Conference on Civil Rights reversed its earlier rejection of the National Gay Task Force for membership. One year later, the organizers of a demonstration to mark the twentieth anniversary of the 1963 March on Washington invited Audre Lorde to speak after rebuffing earlier efforts to include a gay or lesbian speaker. Meanwhile, in response to U.S. actions in the Caribbean, Central America, the Middle East, and elsewhere, gays and lesbians helped revive movements that challenged colonialism, imperialism, militarism, and war. Many also supported the Rainbow Coalition, which in 1984 and 1988 promoted the Democratic presidential candidacy of African American civil rights leader Jesse Jackson, who attempted to unite gays and lesbians, poor people, racial minorities, unemployed people, union members, women, working-class people, and others. While gay and lesbian activists continued to encounter homophobia and heterosexism in liberal and leftist contexts, they received unprecedented support from allies in the 1980s.

One final important context for gay and lesbian activism in this era was the multicultural gay and lesbian community and the larger world of people who engaged in same-sex sex, both of which were affected by AIDS. Over the course of the decade, gay, lesbian, and AIDS activists increasingly recognized that most people who engaged in same-sex sex, including many immigrants, people of color, and working-class people, did not consider themselves gay or lesbian and were not reached by AIDS and other initiatives that targeted gay and lesbian communities. AIDS encouraged many people to come out as gay or lesbian, but it had the opposite effect on others. In multiple ways, AIDS helped expose the limitations of political strategies that were based on the assumption that everyone who engaged in same-sex sex was gay or lesbian and that all such people could, should, and would come out if encouraged to do so.

More generally, U.S. gay and lesbian communities changed in the 1980s, and this had implications for political activism. Initially in large cities but eventually in every gay and lesbian community, AIDS had enormous effects on everyone, but especially on people living with and dying of HIV/AIDS; on their employers, employees, and coworkers; on their families, friends, partners, and lovers; and on those who participated in caregiving, education, healthcare, prevention, research, and treatment. In the context of the country's primarily private healthcare system, the absence of strong public policy responses, and the discrimination that gays, lesbians, and people with HIV/AIDS experienced in mainstream health, education, and welfare programs, gays and lesbians organized to care for their own and for others affected by the epidemic. They also were inspired by AIDS and other developments in the 1980s to continue the cultural renaissance that had begun in the 1970s, with notable contributions in art, dance, film, literature, photography, theater, and video.

Influenced by the epidemic but also by economic dislocation and urban decline, gay and lesbian businesses, neighborhoods, and resorts faced new challenges in this era. Many gay and lesbian bars, bookstores, clubs, gyms, restaurants, and other businesses survived and thrived, but others did not. Gay pornography and telephone sex businesses expanded, in part because they offered opportunities for sexual expression with minimal health risks. In contrast, many bathhouses were criticized by gay leaders, condemned by politicians, harassed by the police, and closed by public health officials. Other popular locations for public sex and sexual cruising, including pornographic bookstores, movie theaters, and public parks, also were targeted for police repression. Some popular neighborhoods and resorts experienced economic hard times because of AIDS, though in some cases lesbian residents and visitors replaced gay ones.

Gay sexual cultures changed in the context of AIDS, with distinct effects related to age, class, generation, health, race, region, and other factors. Many gay men continued to enjoy public sex, sexual cruising, and sexual promiscuity, but others adopted new values and practices. For many men, the adaptability and flexibility of gay sexual cultures meant that safer sex (including sex with condoms and non-penetrative sex) could be embraced and eroticized and that there was no necessary conflict between sexual freedom and healthy sex. In fact, many believed that the healthiest responses to AIDS recognized the value most people placed on physical intimacy, sexual satisfaction, and erotic pleasure. Other gay men became vocal proponents of domesticity and monogamy and strong critics of promiscuity. Some advocated abstinence and celibacy. To protect themselves and others, millions of gay men modified their sexual practices.

Lesbian cultures also changed in the 1980s. In the aftermath of the New Right's antihomosexual campaigns and the assassination of Harvey Milk in the late 1970s, many lesbians became less separatist. Autonomous lesbian activities and institutions, including bars, bookstores, clubs, coffeehouses, community centers, music events, and sports teams, remained important, but defenses of lesbian separatism became less intense. This shift was strengthened as lesbians responded to AIDS with great compassion and energy, despite the fact that far more gay men than lesbians were affected. In some respects, there was a convergence between gay and lesbian sexual cultures in the 1980s, as more gay men embraced domesticity and monogamy and more lesbians became interested in pornography, promiscuity, and sadomasochism.

The class and race dynamics of gay and lesbian cultures also changed in the 1980s. AIDS exposed the vulnerability of poor, working-class, and middle-class gays and lesbians to health crises, widened the gap between those who could afford healthcare and those who could not, and exacerbated the problems of anti-homosexual economic discrimination. Poverty, unemployment, and homelessness were increasingly recognized as gay and lesbian problems, even as gay and lesbian wealth supported various community initiatives. AIDS also exposed the economic difficulties faced by many gays and lesbians of color; made gay, lesbian, and straight racism more visible; and highlighted racial differences in sexual cultures. Demographic changes also influenced gay and lesbian communities. U.S. Census figures suggest that between 1970 and 1990, the black population grew from 11 percent to 12 percent of the total U.S. population; Hispanics grew from 5 percent to 9 percent; Asians and Pacific Islanders grew from 1 percent to 3 percent; and

American Indians/Alaska Natives grew from 0.4 percent to 0.8 percent. Beyond demographics, the visibility of gays and lesbians of color increased in diverse social contexts.

As gay and lesbian cultures changed in the 1980s, so did their periodicals. *The Advocate* continued to have the largest circulation. *Gay Community News* and *The Body Politic* had more radical politics, as did *Out/Look*, a new San Francisco-based magazine. New local periodicals included *Bay Windows* in Boston, *Montrose Voice* in Houston, *New York Native* and *Outweek* in New York, *Frontiers* and *The News* in Los Angeles, and *Windy City Times* in Chicago. Influenced by the decline in separatist politics and ongoing economic difficulties, many older lesbian publications did not survive into the 1980s, but those that did, including *Azalea, Lesbian Connection, Lesbian News*, and *Sinister Women*, were joined by new ones, including *Bad Attitude* and *On Our Backs*, which were sex magazines, and *Onyx*, which was oriented to African Americans. *Blacklight, Blackheart*, and *BLK* also focused on African Americans. Some of these periodicals were more liberal; others were more radical. Some emphasized consumption and leisure; others focused on arts and culture; many concentrated on news and politics. Some were oriented primarily to white gay men, others to lesbians and/or people of color, some to multicultural communities. Most devoted substantial space to AIDS, in many cases long before mainstream periodicals did, but they responded to it in diverse ways, especially in addressing its relationship to the politics of sexual freedom. By 1990, there were more than 700 U.S. gay and lesbian periodicals with a combined circulation of one million.

The changes that occurred in gay and lesbian communities had complex effects on the movement. Many activists were living with and dying of HIV/AIDS, many were caring for friends and partners, and many were experiencing tremendous personal losses, which intensified feelings of anger, anxiety, depression, fear, sadness, and shame. AIDS inspired many people to become gay and lesbian activists; it also led to the formation of groups for people with HIV/AIDS (PWAs), AIDS service organizations (ASOs), and AIDS activist groups, many of which addressed gay and lesbian issues. Some gay and lesbian activists had focused on sexually transmitted diseases in the 1950s, 1960s, and 1970s (the National Coalition of Gay Sexually Transmitted Disease Services, founded in 1979, was a network of more than fifty groups and individuals), but the movement made AIDS one of its central issues in the 1980s. Meanwhile, the epidemic increased the prejudice, discrimination, and violence that gays and lesbians encountered, but also created new possibilities for compassion, tolerance, and acceptance.

AIDS also changed the movement's internal dynamics. For example, while some lesbians criticized the lack of attention paid to their health issues, many lesbians became AIDS activists, caregivers, and educators. Gay sexism remained pervasive and some men did not acknowledge that AIDS affected women, but many gay activists were profoundly moved by strong lesbian responses to the epidemic. For example, Blood Sisters, formed initially in San Diego and later established in other locations, encouraged lesbians to donate blood for gay PWAs after federal officials banned donations from gay men. Gay activists also benefited from lesbian feminists' expertise in the politics of health and medicine, their critiques of science and the state, and their experiences with anticensorship and abortion rights activism. Meanwhile, trans activists played important roles in early safer sex campaigns, ASOs, and AIDS activist groups. The San Francisco-based Sisters of Perpetual Indulgence, for example, began promoting safer sex in 1982. While gay and lesbian transphobia continued to exist, alliances between gay/lesbian and trans activists strengthened as they developed overlapping criticisms of U.S. politics, economics, and healthcare. As it became obvious that trans people were living with and dying of HIV/AIDS in large numbers, many gay and lesbian activists re-evaluated their trans politics.

As for race, AIDS was devastating to racial minorities in general and African American, Latino, and other men of color who engaged in same-sex sex in particular. The mobilization of gays and lesbians of color had increased in the late 1970s, which meant they were well-positioned to criticize white-dominated AIDS groups that failed to address the needs of people of color and straight-dominated groups of people of color that failed to address the needs of gays, lesbians, and people with HIV/AIDS. Over time, AIDS contributed to significant changes in race relations within the gay and lesbian movement, while also reshaping relationships between the gay and lesbian movement and people of color movements. The process of change was slow, but many activists began paying more attention to the intersecting politics of class, gender, race, and sexuality in the 1980s.

Relationships between movement liberals and radicals also changed. For many, this was not the time to debate the merits of liberalism and radicalism, but setting aside their differences was easier said than done. In the context of AIDS, gay and lesbian liberals tended to present themselves as defenders of sexual minorities; gay and lesbian radicals did so as well, but were more likely to emphasize that homosexuality was a universal human potential. For many liberals, AIDS bolstered the case for domesticity, monogamy, privacy, and respectability; for many radicals, it had never been more important to emphasize sexual liberation. Many liberal ASOs worked within the constraints of the existing health, education, and welfare systems; many radical AIDS activists demanded fundamental change. Liberals tended to favor social service programs, memorial vigils, respectful lobbying, and peaceful protests. Radicals supported much of this, but also expressed their anger and grief in demonstrations, die-ins, marches, and zaps, many of which featured civil disobedience. In general, liberals were dominant in the early 1980s, when ASOs, lobbyists, and litigators led the way in responding to AIDS, but from the earliest days of the epidemic, gay liberationists and lesbian feminists insisted on the relevance of their perspectives and positions. In the late 1980s, gay, lesbian, and AIDS movements radicalized as activists strongly criticized capitalism, homophobia, racism, and sexism and forcefully challenged corporate greed, government inaction, media complicity, and religious intolerance.

Mass Mobilization

In these changing contexts, the gay and lesbian movement organized and mobilized. Several national groups founded before 1981 grew substantially in this period. The National Gay Task Force, renamed the National Gay and Lesbian Task Force in 1985, continued to engage in lobbying and other political activities, but in the late 1980s began to place more emphasis on grassroots community mobilization. In 1989, the Task Force appointed Urvashi Vaid, a former *Gay Community News* staffer and a lesbian of South Asian descent, as its executive director; many saw this as a step toward diversifying the movement's leadership. The Human Rights Campaign Fund (HRCF), which absorbed the Gay Rights National Lobby in 1985, focused on lobbying federal officials and supporting electoral politics. With its large fundraising events for wealthy donors, which were praised and criticized for their class politics, HRCF eventually surpassed the Task Force in terms of the size of its staff and budget.

Other regional and national organizations also were influential in the 1980s. Several legal advocacy groups founded in the 1970s, including Gay and Lesbian Advocates and Defenders, Lambda Legal Defense, Lesbian Rights Project (renamed the National Center for Lesbian Rights in 1989), and National Gay Rights Advocates (NGRA), expanded their activities, though NGRA became inactive at the end of the decade. Parents and Friends of Gays was renamed Parents and Friends of Lesbians and Gays in 1981. The Gay Fathers Coalition became Gay and Lesbian Parents Coalition International in 1986. Major new groups included the Gay and Lesbian Alliance Against Defamation (GLAAD, founded 1985), the ACLU Lesbian and Gay Rights Project (founded 1986), and the Gay, Lesbian, and Straight Education Network (founded 1990). More than 500,000 people participated in the 1987 National March on Washington for Lesbian and Gay Rights. Beginning in 1988, National Coming Out Day was celebrated on October 11, which was the anniversary of the 1987 march.

Notwithstanding the effects of AIDS, the proliferation of gay and lesbian social, cultural, and political groups continued in the 1980s. The number of Christian, Jewish, and atheist groups increased and Buddhist groups also were established. There were more organizations and programs for seniors, students, and youth, including the first school-based gay–straight alliances and the first schools for gay and lesbian youth. Organizing in corporate workplaces, professional occupations, and trade unions increased. New antiviolence projects were created. Additional caucuses formed in academic disciplines and the field of gay and lesbian studies began to be institutionalized. More sports clubs, leagues, and teams were established. In 1982, approximately 1300 people participated in the first Gay Games in San Francisco. The event was originally called the Gay Olympics, but the U.S. Olympic Committee successfully sued the organizers for using the term "olympics" without permission. The next Gay Games took place in San Francisco in 1986 and Vancouver in 1990.

The number of groups representing various gay, lesbian, and bisexual subcultures also continued to grow. More bondage, leather and sadomasochism groups formed. New bisexual organizations were established. Many were primarily social, but BiPOL, founded in San Francisco in 1983, and the North American Bisexual Network, founded in 1990, were more political. Bisexual activists failed to convince the organizers of the 1987 March on Washington to refer to bisexual rights in the march's title and demands; in part, this reflected ongoing debates about whether the terms "gay" and "lesbian" were capacious enough to include bisexuals. For people with disabilities, the National Rainbow Society of the Deaf became the Rainbow Alliance of the Deaf; *Dykes, Disability & Stuff* began publication in Wisconsin; and *Ring of Fire: A Zine of Lesbian Sexuality* was established in Seattle. Thousands participated in campaigns to support Sharon Kowalski, a Minnesota lesbian with disabilities who was at the center of a guardianship dispute involving her partner and parents. AIDS contributed to new alliances between the gay/lesbian and disability movements and new recognition of gays and lesbians with disabilities.

Many trans groups from the 1970s did not survive into the 1980s, but new ones included the ACLU Transsexual Rights Committee, American Educational Gender Information Service, Educational TV Channel (later renamed TransGender San Francisco), FTM (later renamed FTM International), International Foundation for Gender Education, and J2PC. Active genderfuck performance groups included the Sisters of Perpetual Indulgence in San Francisco and United Fruit Company in Boston. *Metamorphosis*, based in Toronto, and *Tapestry*, based in Boston, were significant new trans periodicals. As was the case in the 1970s, some trans groups saw themselves as connected to the gay and lesbian movement; some did not. Many trans activists hoped that the APA's classification of transsexualism as a gender identity disorder in 1980 would result in improved access to health and medical services, but this did not occur. The 1987 March on Washington Steering Committee reserved seats for trans activists, but did not reference trans rights in the march's title or demands. In general, this was a difficult period for trans activism, as AIDS inflicted huge losses on trans communities, health and welfare programs were cut, and there were ongoing conflicts with some components of the gay and lesbian movement. At the same time, new alliances between the gay/lesbian and trans movements were forged, a process that culminated with the consolidation of LGBT coalitions in the 1990s.

For Native Americans and Native Alaskans, Gay American Indians (GAI) remained active; by the late 1980s it had more than 1000 members. In 1988, GAI compiled *Living the Spirit: A Gay American Indian Anthology*. Another significant group, American Indian Gays and Lesbians (AIGL), based in Minneapolis, formed in 1987. In 1988, AIGL organized a transnational conference, "The Basket and the Bow," which initiated a series of annual conferences that were held in different locations. The 1990 conference in Winnipeg adopted "two-spirit" as the preferred term for gender-crossing in Native American, Native Alaskan, and Canadian First Nations cultures. WeWah and BarCheeAmpe, later renamed Gay and Lesbian

Indigenous People, was established in New York in 1989, as were similar groups in several other locations.

By the end of the 1980s, there were more than 200 groups and more than twenty periodicals for African American gays and lesbians. The National Association of Black and White Men Together was established in 1981; by 1990 it had dozens of local affiliates, including some that called themselves Men of All Colors Together or People of All Colors Together. In 1984, the National Coalition of Black Gays was renamed the Black Coalition of Black Lesbians and Gays. The Unity Fellowship Church Movement, founded in Los Angeles in 1985 for African American gays and lesbians, soon spread to other cities. In 1987, the National Black Lesbian and Gay Leadership Forum formed in Los Angeles. Barbara Smith's *Home Girls* (1983), Joseph Beam's *In the Life* (1986), Marlon Riggs's *Tongues Untied* (1989), and Isaac Julian's *Looking for Langston* (1989) were groundbreaking anthologies and films that addressed African American gay and lesbian issues.

Influenced by changing immigration patterns, developments in diasporic and immigrant communities, and increased political organizing by gays and lesbians of color in the late 1970s, there was substantial growth in the number of Latino/Latina and Asian/Pacific gay and lesbian groups in the 1980s. Most of these were local, but the National Latina/o Lesbian and Gay Organization (LLEGÓ) and the Asian Pacific Lesbian Network, which was national in scope, were established in 1987. In the same year, the groundbreaking anthology *Compañeras: Latina Lesbians*, edited by Juanita Diaz-Cotto, was published. During the 1980s, South Asian gays and lesbians began to form autonomous newsletters and groups, including Anamika and Trikone, and Arab American gays and lesbians also began to organize.

New multicultural gay and lesbian coalitions formed as well. There was a second national third world lesbian and gay conference in Chicago in 1981 and a third one in Berkeley in 1984. More than 200 people attended the National Lesbians of Color Conference in Los Angeles in 1983. Three years later there was an International Lesbian and Gay People of Color Conference in Los Angeles. The organizers of the 1987 March on Washington agreed that at least 25 percent of the members of its steering committee would be people of color and at least one of the three march co-chairs would be a person of color (African American lesbian Pat Norman was selected). The organizers also adopted a statement that linked gay and lesbian liberation to struggles against racism, sexism, and anti-Semitism, denounced South African apartheid, and invited prominent straight civil rights leaders, including Cesar Chavez and Jesse Jackson, to speak at the march rally.

Gays and lesbians of color pursued seven overlapping political projects in the 1980s. First, they organized groups for gays and lesbians from distinct communities and formed coalitions of gays and lesbians of color. Second, they criticized racism in gay, lesbian, and feminist communities. In 1983, for example, Black and White Men Together picketed a New York gay club with a racist admissions policy and, after bringing evidence of discrimination to the New York Division of Human Rights, won punitive damages. Third, they criticized homophobia, sexism, and transphobia in communities of color. For instance, they challenged community leaders for demonizing homosexuality and distancing themselves from struggles against AIDS. Fourth, they participated alongside whites in gay and lesbian campaigns. In Philadelphia, for example, they worked with white allies to pass a sexual orientation antidiscrimination law in 1982. Fifth, they participated alongside other people of color in campaigns that challenged racism. For instance, they worked against the Reagan and Bush administrations' efforts to undermine affirmative action and civil rights initiatives. Sixth, they forged coalitions that brought together class-, gender-, race-, and sexuality-based groups. For example, they helped build the multicultural alliances that elected several African American big-city mayors. Seventh, from their unique positions as gays and lesbians of color, they addressed AIDS, homelessness, imperialism, nativism, poverty, sexism, and war.

Lesbian feminism continued to exist in diverse forms, but it, too, changed in the 1980s. With the decline of lesbian separatism and the spread of AIDS, alliances between gays and lesbians strengthened, though many women continued to support autonomous organizing by and for lesbians. Liberal lesbian feminism continued to be a strong component of the movement, though it often received less recognition than its more radical counterparts. In 1984, for example, more than 400 women participated in a NOW-sponsored lesbian rights conference in Milwaukee; more than 1000 attended a similar NOW-sponsored conference in San Diego in 1988. Multicultural lesbian feminism, which had become increasingly influential in the late 1970s, expanded and diversified in the 1980s, with lasting consequences for the gay and lesbian movement. Many lesbian feminists participated in leftist organizing, the peace movement, Central American solidarity work, anti-apartheid activism, antiviolence campaigns, and struggles for reproductive rights and freedoms. They also played important roles in AIDS activism and made distinct contributions to debates about women and AIDS.

Conflicts between cultural feminists and sex radicals exploded in the early 1980s in what came to be known as the sex wars. While tensions had begun to increase in the late 1970s, when some cultural feminists joined forces with the New Right and Christian Right in attacks on pornography and sadomasochism, they escalated in 1982 at a Barnard College feminist conference on sexuality, which was picketed and condemned by a group of cultural feminists. Lesbians were prominent on both sides of these conflicts. While lesbian cultural feminists attacked pornography, sadomasochism, prostitution, and butch/fem cultures, lesbian sex radicals supported lesbian sex magazines, sadomasochism groups, sex workers, and butch/fem erotics. Cultural feminists and their conservative allies worked in various locations to pass local antipornography ordinances, but lesbian sex radicals participated in counter-mobilizations. They were active, for example, in the Feminist Anti-Censorship Task Force (founded in 1984) and the founders of the lesbian sex magazine *On Our Backs* selected its name as a playful rejoinder to the politics of the feminist periodical *Off Our Backs*. By the second half of the 1980s, there seemed to be growing support for the notion that lesbian activism could and should address the dangers and pleasures of sex, which many sex radicals noted had been their position all along.

AIDS Activism

The most significant development in gay and lesbian activism during the 1980s was mobilization in response to AIDS. Many gay and lesbian movement groups, health projects, and popular periodicals turned their attention to the epidemic in this period and gays and lesbians also played central roles in PWA coalitions, AIDS service organizations, and AIDS activist groups, many of which were substantially or predominantly gay and lesbian. The first PWA groups formed in California and New York; soon they were established in other locations as well. In 1983, at the National Lesbian and Gay Health Conference in Denver, a group of PWAs developed an influential statement on self-empowerment and formed the National Association of People with AIDS. The Denver Principles criticized references to PWAs as victims and emphasized the rights of PWAs to have access to medical care and social services without discrimination, make informed decisions about research and treatment, enjoy full and satisfying sexual and emotional lives, have privacy and respect, and live and die with dignity.

ASOs were established in the context of the failures of the healthcare system to address the epidemic's causes and consequences. Two of the earliest, both founded in 1982, were Gay Men's Health Crisis (GMHC) in New York and the Kaposi's Sarcoma Research and Education Foundation, which became the San Francisco AIDS Foundation in 1983. Playwright and novelist Larry Kramer, a GMHC founder, issued an influential call for gay mobilization in a 1983 *New York Native* article titled "1,112 and Counting." "If this article doesn't scare the shit out of you," he warned, "we're in real trouble. If this article doesn't rouse you to anger, fury, rage, and action, gay men may have no future on this Earth. ... Unless we fight for our lives, we shall die."[2] Other early ASOs were established in Atlanta, Boston, Chicago, Houston, Los Angeles, and Seattle. The National AIDS Network, the American Foundation for AIDS Research, and Project Inform were established in 1985; *AIDS Treatment News* began publication in 1986. In 1986–87, Cleve Jones founded the NAMES Project AIDS Memorial Quilt, which had its first major public display on the National Mall during the 1987 March on Washington; it eventually included more than 40,000 individual panels.

In the epidemic's early years, gay and lesbian activists, working primarily through PWA coalitions, ASOs, and gay and lesbian movement groups, health projects, and popular periodicals, criticized business, government, media, religious, and scientific responses to AIDS, challenged AIDS-related discrimination, developed educational programs, and provided services to people with HIV/AIDS. ASOs established caregiving networks, counselling programs, hospice systems, telephone hotlines, and testing centers; provided financial, food, housing, and legal assistance; and facilitated access to health, education, and welfare programs. Gay, lesbian, and AIDS activists promoted safer sex, created needle exchange programs, developed underground drug networks, disseminated information about disease transmission, promoted confidential testing, and provided updates about prevention and treatment. They criticized scientific researchers, public health officials, and drug companies for impeding the development of safe, effective, and affordable treatments and launched community-based research projects. They attacked health insurance companies for denying coverage to gays, lesbians, and people with HIV/AIDS. They critiqued the mass media and popular culture. They challenged government officials for remaining silent about the epidemic, providing inadequate funding for AIDS programs, supporting mandatory testing and reporting, and proposing to segregate and quarantine people with HIV/AIDS. Together, they saved and extended millions of lives.

In their early responses to the epidemic, gay, lesbian, and AIDS activists worked together in countless contexts, but also had strong disagreements. Kramer, for example, raged against gay political apathy, but others believed that this was a form of victim-blaming. Most activists supported community-based AIDS initiatives, but some argued that this enabled federal, state, and local governments to shirk their responsibilities. Some called on gay men to reject sexual promiscuity (this, for example, was the position taken by influential AIDS journalist Randy Shilts and Kramer, both of whom were gay); others saw this as an attack on gay culture and argued that openly promiscuous safe sex was less risky than theoretically mono-gamous unsafe sex. Some were critical of public sex and supported crackdowns on bathhouses; others responded that public sex venues could serve as educational sites, especially since many men who used them did not identify as gay and were not reached by AIDS campaigns that targeted gay men. Activists engaged in intense debates about whether people with and without HIV/AIDS should have sex with one another, how to negotiate sexual encounters in the context of so much fear and uncertainty, and whether people should be tested for HIV before there were effective treatments.

Running through many of these discussions were disagreements about the meaning and relevance of gay liberation. Some activists had never supported the radical aspects of gay liberation; others turned from supporters to critics in the context of the epidemic. Those who emphasized gay liberation's ongoing relevance did not necessarily agree on what gay liberation was. For some, it was a reform movement concerned with basic rights and freedoms, which had special relevance in the age of AIDS. For others, it was a countercultural movement that rejected sexual exploitation and objectification and celebrated same-sex love and affection, which could be useful in the struggle against AIDS. For still others, it was a sexual liberation movement that could promote healthy gay sex and challenge sexually repressive responses to AIDS.

Strong disagreements emerged about the gender and race politics of ASOs. Many were founded and led by white gay men, who also were the majority of ASO staff and clients. Most of their early initiatives focused on the gay community, which was predominantly white. Many assumed that men who had sex with men would be reached through projects that targeted predominantly white gay institutions and territories and relied on concepts, terms, and images that resonated with white gay men. Some ASO campaigns were regarded as culturally insensitive or socially inappropriate by some people of color. As it became obvious that many ASOs were not serving the needs of people of color, straights, women, and men who had sex with men but did not identify as gay, conflicts developed between gay-oriented ASOs and other ASOs, between gay-oriented ASOs and community organizations that served people of color and women, and within gay-oriented ASOs as people of color and women voiced their concerns. Over time, many gay-oriented ASOs broadened their services to address diverse communities, but others did not or failed when they tried. Meanwhile, African American, Asian/Pacific, Latina/Latino, and Native American gay and lesbian groups developed AIDS projects, while new AIDS initiatives targeted women and people of color. Early examples include the Minority AIDS Project in Los Angeles; the Minority Task Force on AIDS and Hispanic AIDS Forum in New York; and the Third World AIDS Advisory Task Force and Women's AIDS Network in San Francisco. The National Minority AIDS Council and National Task Force on AIDS Prevention were established in 1987 and 1988.

A series of developments in the mid-1980s led to the radicalization of AIDS activism. As the number of people living and dying with HIV/AIDS grew, government silence and inaction began to seem more intolerable. The U.S. Supreme Court's 1986 decision in *Bowers v. Hardwick*, which upheld state sodomy laws and ridiculed the claims of gay and lesbian rights advocates, literally added insult to injury. For many gays, lesbians, and people with HIV/AIDS, the Court's rejection of gay and lesbian privacy rights broke the stalemate that had been achieved in the late 1970s, damaged the confidence they had placed in liberal reform, and demonstrated that the political system had little respect for their lives, loves, lusts, and losses. Around the same time, Reagan proposed reductions in government spending on AIDS, many Republican and Democratic governors did the same, and the Justice Department announced that federal law did not prohibit employment discrimination based on HIV/AIDS. Later that year, California voters defeated a proposal to authorize quarantines for people with HIV and AIDS, but the fact that the measure was on the ballot infuriated many people touched by the epidemic.

The troubles continued in 1987. After the U.S. Food and Drug Administration (FDA) approved the country's first HIV/AIDS drug (AZT), its manufacturer began selling it at extraordinarily high prices. When Reagan finally delivered a substantive speech on AIDS, his major recommendations focused on expanded testing rather than prevention or treatment. The federal government soon imposed mandatory testing on federal prisoners and aliens seeking to enter the country; aliens with HIV or AIDS were not allowed to enter or establish permanent residency in the United States without special permission. Around the same time, Reagan appointed a Presidential Commission on the HIV Epidemic, but included no PWAs, no AIDS activists, one gay man, and several antigay conservatives. Toward the end of 1987, after U.S. Senator Jesse Helms brought sexually explicit GMHC educational materials to Reagan's attention, Republicans and Democrats in the U.S. Congress passed what came to be known as the Helms Amendment, which prohibited the use of federal funds for AIDS education or prevention materials that promoted, encouraged, or condoned homosexual sex or illegal drug use.

In these contexts, many gay, lesbian, and AIDS activists continued to support ASO initiatives, somber vigils, peaceful protests, and the ongoing work of lobbying and litigation, but others decided that this was insufficient. In 1985, John Lorenzini, a gay PWA, chained himself to the Federal Office Building in San Francisco to protest inadequate government responses to AIDS. Soon thereafter, 200 San Franciscans participated in a Mobilization Against AIDS demonstration and nine began what became a ten-year AIDS vigil on United Nations Plaza. In New York, 600 people attended a Gay and Lesbian Alliance Against Defamation meeting to discuss AIDS hysteria, 100 demonstrated at City Hall against proposals to close gay bathhouses, and 800 joined a GLAAD protest against the *New York Post*'s antigay AIDS coverage. In 1986, eight members of Citizens for Medical Justice were arrested during a sit-in at the offices of California's governor to protest his AIDS policies. In Los Angeles, 4000 people marched to the headquarters of a conservative group that supported quarantining people with HIV/AIDS. In New York, the Lavender Hill Mob occupied the offices of a U.S. senator and served him with mock arrest warrants for contributing to the deaths of PWAs. Toward the end of 1986, a group of New York gay artists began plastering their city with posters that featured a black background, a pink triangle, and the words "SILENCE = DEATH." In February 1987, the Lavender Hill Mob, with several members dressed in concentration camp uniforms with pink triangles, disrupted a Centers for Disease Control conference in Atlanta on mandatory HIV testing.

In March 1987, two days after an angry speech by Larry Kramer at the New York Lesbian and Gay Community Services Center, 300 New Yorkers formed ACT UP, the AIDS Coalition to Unleash Power, which described itself as a "diverse, non-partisan group of individuals united in anger and committed to direct action to end the AIDS crisis."[3] Similar impulses soon led to the formation of ACT Ups in Houston, Los Angeles, New Orleans, Philadelphia, and Seattle and MASS ACT OUT in Boston. AIDS Action Pledge, established in San Francisco in 1987, renamed itself ACT UP-SF. In Chicago, Dykes and Gay Men Against Repression/ Racism/Reagan/the Right Wing (DAGMAR) began focusing on AIDS in 1987; it joined forces with other activists to form Chicago for AIDS Rights, which became ACT UP-Chicago. Within a few years, there were more than fifty local ACT Ups and similar groups inside and outside the United States. In New York, ACT UP worked closely with a set of activist arts groups, including the Silence = Death Project, Gran Fury, Little Elvis, Testing the Limits, and DIVA TV. ACT NOW (the AIDS Coalition to Network, Organize, and Win) was established as a national association of AIDS activist groups at the 1987 March on Washington. Over the next few years, thousands participated in ACT UP movement protests, which changed public consciousness about and political responses to AIDS. Together, they saved and extended millions of lives.

While the ACT UP movement featured significant local variations, a good starting place for considering its politics is to concentrate on ACT UP-NY and similar groups in other large cities.[4] The movement brought together people with diverse economic and political backgrounds, including many who had worked with PWA groups and ASOs, many who had participated in gay/lesbian, trans, feminist, and other social movements, and many who were new to political activism. AIDS activist groups included people who were living with HIV/AIDS, people who were not, and people who did not know their HIV status. Most were white gay men in their twenties, thirties, and forties, but white lesbians, trans people, people of color, and straights also participated. ACT UP-NY's Majority Action Committee was predominantly nonwhite and its Women's Caucus included many lesbians. ACT UP-Chicago also had a Women's Caucus and ACT UP-LA had a People of Color Coalition. MASS ACT OUT had more lesbians than gay men, but when ACT UP Boston formed a short time later, it was mostly gay. ACT UP-NY featured strong participation by Jews, but this was not necessarily the case in other locations.

In general, ACT UP movement groups valued participatory democracy rather than centralized leadership and hierarchical decision-making. In New York especially but also in other large cities, movement meetings were fast-paced, high-energy, and emotionally intense. They also were erotically charged, inspiring countless liaisons involving gays, lesbians, and straights in expected and unexpected combinations. ACT UP men tended to embody, embrace, and encourage gay masculinities, but gender dissidents were active in the movement as well. The movement also was distinctive in the ways in which it drew on and developed the expertise of its participants. Many AIDS activists, for example, educated themselves about scientific matters so they could challenge medical experts, public health officials, and drug company representatives in private meetings and public demonstrations. The movement also included a large number of artists who produced powerful banners, buttons, fliers, photographs, posters, stickers, t-shirts, videos, and other visual materials that were key components of AIDS activism. ACT UP movement actions, many of which were designed to capture public attention, were defiant, disruptive, and dramatic. The movement was radical not only in the ways it organized itself and the strategies it embraced, but also in its leftist political vision, which placed the epidemic within frameworks that criticized capitalism, homophobia, racism, and sexism, challenged conservative and liberal politics, and demanded universal healthcare, sexual freedom, and human rights.

In its first three years, the ACT UP movement organized hundreds of protests. ACT UP-NY's first demonstration took place on Wall Street in March 1987, when more than 250 activists disrupted traffic and seventeen were arrested in a protest that attacked "business as usual," criticized drug prices, and challenged the FDA's drug approval system.[5] ACT UP then targeted New York's General Post

Office on April 15. Knowing that many people would be rushing to meet the federal tax deadline and that this would be covered by the media, the group staged a demonstration that criticized the federal government's failure to devote significant tax dollars to AIDS programs. In July, 300 AIDS activists demonstrated at St. Patrick's Cathedral to protest the appointment of Cardinal John O'Connor to the Presidential HIV Commission. In December, they met with New York City's Health Commissioner, who had proposed to begin mandatory HIV testing for sex workers and sex and drug offenders. When he refused to renounce the proposal, eight ACT UP members refused to leave his office and were arrested.

AIDS activists elsewhere also "acted up." In June 1987, ACT UP-NY, Mobilization Against AIDS and the Human Rights Campaign Fund sponsored demonstrations in Washington, D.C., at the Third International Conference on AIDS and the White House, where sixty-four people were arrested. This was one of many instances in which the police assigned to an ACT UP protest wore yellow rubber gloves, which infuriated AIDS activists and led to the campy chant: "Your Gloves Don't Match your Shoes! You'll See it on the News!"[6] In various gay and lesbian pride parades in the summer of 1987 and at the March on Washington in October, AIDS activist contingents were among the largest, liveliest, and loudest. In August, DAGMAR sponsored an AIDS vigil with hundreds of participants at the home of the Illinois governor. One month later, AIDS activists interrupted the Presidential HIV Commission's first meeting in Washington, D.C., where they demanded to be heard. In October, ACT UP activists in Virginia disrupted Christian Right leader Pat Robertson's announcement of his presidential candidacy.

ACT UP-NY remained focused on treatment issues in 1988, but also continued to link AIDS to other issues. In January, the group's Women's Caucus organized a 150-person protest at the offices of *Cosmopolitan* magazine to criticize a racist and sexist article that downplayed HIV/AIDS risks for straight women in the United States. In February, ACT UP again targeted the Presidential Commission, this time using "AIDSGATE" and "He Kills Me" posters featuring images of Reagan.[7] In April and May, fifty groups affiliated with the ACT UP movement staged nine days of protests around the country to highlight a set of AIDS-related issues. On the day devoted to homophobia, ACT UP-NY staged a gay and lesbian kiss-in at Sheridan Square, produced "Read My Lips" posters featuring same-sex kissing couples, and distributed fliers that denounced the Helms Amendment and other antigay responses to AIDS.[8] The group also reached out to African American and Latino churches to promote AIDS awareness, held a joint rally with the Association for Drug Abuse Prevention and Treatment at City Hall to demand drug treatment and needle exchange programs, organized a protest at the State Office of Corrections to condemn the treatment of prisoners with HIV/AIDS, staged an action at FAO Schwarz's flagship toy store to criticize unethical drug trials for pediatric AIDS, and distributed safer sex information at high schools. At a Mets baseball game at Shea Stadium, 300 activists distributed condoms and fliers that called on straight men to take more responsibility for AIDS prevention. In November, ACT UP occupied the lobby of the Trump Tower to protest city policies on housing and homelessness.

Outside New York, AIDS activists continued to organize protests in 1988. In January, hundreds of San Francisco activists marched to the regional headquarters of Burroughs-Wellcome, the manufacturer of AZT, to demand reduced drug prices; nineteen were arrested. In May, Chicago for AIDS Rights demonstrated for reduced drug prices at the headquarters of Lyphomed; ten protesters were arrested. That month, AIDS activists occupied the California governor's office to demand increased AIDS funding. In June, ten ACT UP members were arrested after they blocked a Philadelphia highway to protest cuts in state funding for AIDS programs. In July, ACT UP-LA set up a mock AIDS ward outside a county hospital and staged a week-long series of protests to criticize the lack of services for PWAs. In October, more than 1000 activists demonstrated at the Department of Health and Human Services in D.C. and more than 1500 went to the FDA headquarters in Maryland, where they demanded fundamental changes in drug research protocols. Civil disobedience at the FDA led to 176 arrests. Around the same time, hundreds of San Francisco AIDS activists disrupted the filming of an episode of the NBC television program *Midnight Caller*, which featured a bisexual and promiscuous PWA who knowingly transmitted HIV to his partners.

In 1989 and early 1990, many AIDS activists continued to focus on treatment issues. In January 1989, ACT UP held a sit-in at San Francisco General Hospital to criticize lack of access to AIDS drugs. In April, four ACT UP members disguised themselves as businessmen, entered the Burroughs Wellcome headquarters in North Carolina, and locked themselves inside an office to demand lower AZT prices. In June, AIDS activists converged on the Fifth International Conference on AIDS in Montreal to demand changes in drug testing protocols, access to AIDS treatments, attention to the needs of women, drug users, and prisoners, and increased support for global AIDS initiatives. In September, seven ACT UP members used fake identifications to gain access to the New York Stock Exchange, where they chained themselves to a banister, displayed a banner that said, "Sell Wellcome," and disrupted trading with a foghorn.[9] After they were arrested, 1500 activists followed up with a demonstration and foghorns outside the Exchange.

In 1989 and early 1990, ACT UP movement activists criticized the federal government for its handling of AIDS treatment issues, its underfunding of AIDS initiatives, its restrictions on AIDS education programs, and its policies on a wide range of AIDS-related subjects. In October 1989, they highlighted the problems of homeless PWAs in a mass demonstration in Washington, D.C., against government policies on housing and homelessness. In the first several months of 1990, they helped organize an international boycott of the Sixth International Conference on AIDS, scheduled to take place in San Francisco in June, to protest restrictive U.S. immigration policies that targeted people with HIV/AIDS.

AIDS activists also criticized local and state governments. In 1989, ACT UP-LA staged a series of demonstrations at meetings of the Los Angeles County Board of Supervisors to demand the creation of an AIDS ward at a county hospital; dozens were arrested. In March 1989, more than 5000 people demonstrated at New York City Hall to criticize Mayor Ed Koch's inadequate support for effective AIDS programs; more than 200 were arrested. In June, 200 ACT UP-NY members disrupted traffic on the Brooklyn Bridge and demonstrated against the Health Commissioner's support for mandatory reporting and contact tracing for people who tested positive for HIV. Later that month, ACT UP disrupted a speech by Koch, who was participating in the dedication of Stonewall Place on Christopher Street to mark the twentieth anniversary of the Stonewall riots. In October, ACT UP-NY's Youth Brigade began distributing condoms and safer sex/clean needle information at high schools. In January 1990, ACT UP-NY zapped Governor Mario Cuomo at his State of the State Address and demonstrated outside the State Capitol. In March, 2500 AIDS activists demonstrated at the New York State Capitol and wrapped the Governor's Mansion in red tape. Around the same time, ACT UP-NY's Needle Exchange Committee, without authorization from local authorities, began a needle exchange program for intravenous drug users.

In 1989 and early 1990, the ACT UP movement strengthened its connections to abortion rights and women's rights activism. In April 1989, hundreds of AIDS activists participated in a massive abortion rights demonstration in Washington, D.C. In October, ACT UP-Chicago worked with abortion rights advocates to set up a Freedom Bed in Chicago, where passersby watched skits about sex and reproduction that were interrupted by activist-performers dressed up as Supreme Court justices, U.S. Senator Jesse Helms, and other conservative politicians. In January 1990, hundreds of AIDS activists demonstrated at the Georgia state capitol against the state's sodomy law and then rallied at the Atlanta-based Centers for Disease Control (CDC), which continued to define AIDS in ways that excluded symptoms that were more common in women, children, and people of color; forty-nine activists were arrested. In April 1990, after targeting the headquarters of the American Medical Association for its opposition to universal health insurance and the offices of Chicago-based health insurance companies for their discriminatory policies and high prices, AIDS activists rallied at Cook County Hospital, which was refusing to treat women with HIV/AIDS; more than 130 activists were arrested during this series of actions.

The ACT UP movement also maintained its focus on media and religion. In the second half of 1989, ACT UP-NY targeted the coverage of AIDS in the *New York Times*. "Buy your lies here" stickers were applied to newsstands, "out of order" stickers were used for newspaper vending machines, and countless protest faxes were sent to the *Times*.[10] In July, 200 ACT UP members demonstrated outside the headquarters of the newspaper and the home of its publisher. In December, 4500 ACT UP and Women's Health Action Mobilization (WHAM!) activists participated in a demonstration at St. Patrick's Cathedral to criticize the Catholic Church's opposition to sex education, its rejection of condoms, its hostility to homosexuality, and its opposition to abortion rights; 112 people were arrested as protesters chanted, "They Say Don't Fuck, We Say Fuck You!"[11] Around the same time, ACT UP-LA defaced four Catholic churches with red paint and posters that labeled the local archbishop a murderer.

As many of these actions suggest, AIDS activists were determined to capture public attention and they often succeeded in doing so. In January 1989, eighty AIDS activists blocked traffic on the Golden Gate Bridge in San Francisco. In October, hundreds demonstrated at a federal government office building in Los Angeles; eighty were arrested. Also in 1989, the Gran Fury collective in New York produced eye-catching posters that featured three kissing couples—one straight, one gay, one lesbian, and all interracial—and the words: "Kissing Doesn't Kill: Greed and Indifference Do." Commissioned as part of a public art project, the posters were mounted on buses and subways in Chicago, New York, San Francisco, and Washington, D.C., though they were attacked for promoting homosexuality, there were efforts to censor them, and a caption that declared, "corporate greed, government inaction, and public indifference make AIDS a political crisis" was removed.[12] In January 1990, AIDS activists in San Francisco again blocked traffic on the Golden Gate Bridge and ACT UP-LA interrupted the Rose Parade with a sign that read: "Emergency. Stop the parade. 70,000 dead of AIDS."[13]

In the second half of the 1980s, AIDS activists changed public policy and political consciousness. In response to forceful movement protests and compelling scientific arguments, the FDA sped up its drug approval process and changed its research protocols. AIDS activists contributed to improvements in drug regimens in the late 1980s and early 1990s, which in turn led to treatment breakthroughs in the mid-1990s. They also convinced the CDC to change its clinical definition of AIDS to include more women, children, and people of color. AIDS activists successfully fought for increased government funding for AIDS programs, helped defeat most proposals for mandatory HIV testing, supported the expansion of anonymous and confidential HIV testing, and played leading roles in the development of safer sex and clean needle programs. They persuaded drug companies to reduce prices for some treatments, discouraged health insurance companies from denying coverage to people with HIV/AIDS, and convinced many businesses to reduce the scope of discrimination against people with HIV/AIDS. They supported the work of ASOs, improved access to healthcare for people with HIV/AIDS, and highlighted the AIDS-related needs of children, drug users, gay men, homeless people, lesbians, men who have sex with men, people of color, prisoners, women, and youth. Challenged by AIDS activists, the mass media improved its coverage of the epidemic and diversified its portrayal of people with HIV/AIDS. While doing all of this, AIDS activists in general and the ACT UP movement in particular strengthened social movement coalitions, supported struggles for universal healthcare, empowered medical patients, challenged the politics of science and art, and provided models for future forms of political activism.

Gay and Lesbian Reform, 1981–90

AIDS and AIDS activism had deep and lasting effects on the gay and lesbian movement. Much of the movement's attention focused on AIDS in the 1980s, but gay and lesbian activists worked on other issues as well. In the context of conservative political ascendancy and the devastating health crisis, the pace of gay and lesbian legal reform slowed. Activists continued to lobby, litigate, and demonstrate for sex law reform, for example, but only one state—Wisconsin—repealed its sodomy law in this period, meaning that by 1990 twenty-five states still criminalized private same-sex sex by consenting adults. Conservative political power and social responses to AIDS made sodomy law reform more difficult to achieve, but so did the fact that most of the country's more liberal states had already decriminalized sodomy by the 1980s. Four more states decriminalized cross-sex but not same-sex sodomy, bringing ten the number of states that had done so by the early 1990s. Meanwhile, state courts in California, Massachusetts, New York, and Ohio limited the use of laws against loitering, lewdness, and solicitation and a federal court invalidated St. Louis's law against cross-dressing. In many jurisdictions, however, the police continued to target gays, lesbians, and others who engaged in same-sex sex in their enforcement of laws against disorderly conduct, indecency, lewdness, loitering, solicitation, and other vaguely worded crimes. In some contexts, the police used AIDS to justify increased sexual repression. In response, there were major protests against antihomosexual police practices.

In the movement's most significant legal setback in the post-Stonewall era, the U.S. Supreme Court's 1986 ruling in *Bowers v. Hardwick* upheld the constitutionality of Georgia's sodomy law. In many ways, this was not an auspicious time to bring a sodomy case to the Supreme Court, but the justices had recognized constitutional rights of marital and reproductive privacy in earlier decisions, which convinced many legal advocates that the Court would also recognize constitutional rights of sexual privacy. When the Court finally addressed the issue directly, five of the nine justices ruled against Michael Hardwick, who had been arrested for engaging in consensual same-sex sex in his home, which the police discovered when attempting to contact him about an earlier public drinking episode. Although the Georgia law, which criminalized oral and anal sex, applied to same-sex and cross-sex liaisons, the Court's ruling focused on "homosexual sodomy." According to the majority, the Court's precedents in family, marriage, and procreation cases did not apply since homosexuality had nothing to do with family, marriage, and procreation. After ridiculing a set of arguments about the relevance of the country's traditional respect for liberty, the Court concluded that immorality was a legitimate basis for Georgia's criminalization of same-sex sex.[14]

As suggested above, the *Bowers* decision broke the political stalemate that had existed since the late 1970s. Most gay and lesbian activists had known that achieving equality in the public sphere would be difficult, but they had been more confident about winning the battle for sexual privacy. While *Bowers* did not mean that same-sex sex would be re-criminalized in the states that no longer had sodomy laws, it sent a clear message about the social, cultural, legal, and political status of homosexuality in the United States. When that message was received, the movement responded. In the hours and days following the Court's decision, tens of thousands of gays, lesbians, and allies participated in angry demonstrations around the country. The protests continued when thousands disrupted the July Fourth centennial celebration of the Statue of Liberty and thousands more disrupted appearances by the Supreme Court justices in various locations. One year later, more than 500,000 people, motivated in part by anger about *Bowers* and AIDS, participated in the March on Washington. Two days later, approximately 600 people were arrested for committing civil disobedience at the Supreme Court.

While gay and lesbian activists continued to oppose the criminalization of same-sex sex after *Bowers*, they grew more pessimistic about the likelihood of achieving this through the courts, especially as the federal judiciary came to be dominated by Republican appointees. In 1990, a Michigan county court ruled that the state's sodomy law was unconstitutional, but this decision did not necessarily apply elsewhere in the state. A Kentucky court overturned that state's sodomy law in 1986, but it took years of litigation before the state supreme court upheld the lower court's decision in 1992. Notwithstanding the negative implications of *Bowers* for achieving sodomy law reform through the courts, national publicity about the case contributed to gay and lesbian political mobilization, raised public consciousness about the legal status of homosexuality, and increased public support for sex law reform.

A second major goal of gay and lesbian reformers was to reduce the scope of antihomosexual censorship. Here, too, the movement experienced setbacks in the 1980s. In 1986, the U.S. Attorney General's Commission on Pornography recommended increased sexual censorship. The Supreme Court continued to deny First Amendment protection to materials classified as obscene, used antihomosexual standards in defining and judging obscenity, and accepted discriminatory zoning regulations for sex-oriented businesses. In 1985, the Court made its sexual preferences clear when it declared that its definition of obscenity did not include materials that aroused only "normal" and "'good, old fashioned, healthy' interest in sex."[15] Four years later, the Court ruled that federal prison officials could not deny inmates the right to receive sexually explicit materials in general, but could do so for homosexual materials because of security concerns. As for other types of censorship, in 1986 a federal court ruled that the New York City police could not deny Dignity (the gay and lesbian Catholic group) the right to demonstrate in front of St. Patrick's Cathedral during a gay pride parade. The ruling stipulated, however, that only twenty-five activists could participate, they could demonstrate for only thirty minutes, they would have to do so behind police barricades, and antihomosexual protesters would have to be granted equal time and space.

Activists had greater success in challenging new types of restriction on sexual expression. In 1984, they helped convince Minneapolis's mayor to veto an anti-pornography ordinance that had been drafted by cultural feminists and passed by the city council. The legislation targeted materials that depicted the sexually explicit subordination of women, but also applied to materials that depicted the sexually explicit subordination of men, children, and transsexuals. Gay and lesbian critics joined other activists in raising multiple objections to the proposed ordinance, but also emphasized that gay and lesbian pornography would likely be targeted. Shortly thereafter, Indianapolis passed a modified version of the Minneapolis law, which was subsequently struck down as unconstitutional, as was a similar law passed in Bellingham, Washington, a few years later. Several other cities and counties came close to passing related legislation, but activist campaigns helped defeat these initiatives.

Gay and lesbian activists devoted considerable time and energy to legal disputes concerning government funding for education and the arts. Following their successes in denying public funding for abortions in the 1970s, conservatives began targeting public funding for AIDS education in the 1980s. In 1986, the Centers for Disease Control (CDC) issued guidelines that denied CDC funding for "offensive" AIDS education materials; the guidelines noted that materials designed for gay men would be classified as offensive if most educated adults other than gay men would regard them as such. The rules were modified in 1990 to prohibit funding for materials if the majority of the intended audience or a majority outside the intended audience would find them offensive, though exceptions could be made if their potential benefits in preventing HIV transmission outweighed their potential offensiveness. Meanwhile, in 1987 the U.S. Congress prohibited the use of federal funds for AIDS education materials that promoted or encouraged homosexual sex; this was modified in 1988 to prohibit funding for obscene materials and materials that promoted or encouraged homosexual or heterosexual activity. In 1992, after years of lobbying and litigation, a federal court invalidated the CDC restrictions and Congress dropped some of its content restrictions on AIDS education materials. Gay, lesbian, AIDS, and anticensorship advocates thus won victories in the long term, but before and after this occurred there were major restrictions on federally funded AIDS education materials.

Federal funding for the arts also became contentious. In 1989, New Right, Christian Right, and Republican Party leaders began attacking the National Endowment for the Arts (NEA) for providing financial support to art museums that had exhibited or were planning to exhibit homoerotic and sadomasochistic art, including the photography of Robert Mapplethorpe. Shortly thereafter, Congress banned NEA funding for projects with obscene contents; this was defined to include materials that depicted sadomasochism, homoeroticism, the exploitation of children, or sex acts. Around the same time, the NEA attempted (unsuccessfully) to rescind a grant for a New York exhibition on AIDS that included the gay-themed work of David Wojnarowicz. In 1990, the federal legislation was modified to direct the NEA chair to take general standards of decency into consideration when making funding decisions. That year, after an NEA peer-review panel voted in favor of awarding grants to four performance artists whose work addressed gay, lesbian, and sexual themes, the NEA's director vetoed the grants.

While conservatives organized campaigns to promote sexual censorship, gay, lesbian, and anticensorship activists fought back with lobbying, litigation, demonstrations, and art. In 1989, there was a major protest at the Corcoran Gallery in Washington, D.C., which had cancelled a Mapplethorpe exhibit. In 1990, the director of a Cincinnati museum that had exhibited Mapplethorpe's works was found not guilty on obscenity charges. The four performance artists whose grants were vetoed also fought back. They won two lower court rulings and the NEA agreed to make financial restitution, though in 1998 the Supreme Court ruled against the artists and upheld the NEA's indecent standard. Throughout this period, gay, lesbian, and allied artists addressed censorship in their art and supported efforts to bring controversial work to greater public attention. In general, the gay and lesbian movement experienced setbacks in its struggles against censorship, though restrictions on sexual expression also contributed to gay and lesbian counter-mobilizations.

Gay and lesbian activists were more successful in fighting for local and state antidiscrimination laws. Wisconsin in 1982 and Massachusetts in 1989 became the first states to prohibit sexual orientation discrimination in employment, housing, and public accommodations, while Colorado, Minnesota, New Mexico, New York, Ohio, Oregon, Rhode Island, and Washington joined California and Pennsylvania in prohibiting sexual orientation discrimination in state employment. More than forty additional cities and counties passed laws against sexual orientation discrimination in public employment, bringing the total to more than eighty by 1990. Baltimore, Boston, Chicago, New York, Philadelphia, San Diego, and several smaller cities enacted more expansive laws that covered employment, housing, and public accommodations; by 1990, most of the largest U.S. cities had passed these types of law. Harrisburg, Seattle, and St. Paul joined the small number of cities that also prohibited discrimination based on gender identity or expression. Twelve states and several cities passed hate crimes laws that recognized and in many cases increased penalties for crimes motivated by antihomosexual prejudice.

Building on their earlier successes in blocking, limiting, and overturning laws against sexual orientation discrimination, conservative activists continued their efforts in this period. They blocked the passage of these laws in many places and limited them to public employment in others. Using popular referenda, they over-turned the laws passed in Athens (Ohio), Concord (California), Duluth, Houston, Irvine, Tacoma, and Wooster (Ohio); they failed in Austin, Davis, and Seattle. A popular referendum in Oregon repealed that state's law in 1988, but a state court later ruled that this violated the state constitution. Conservatives tried to repeal the Massachusetts law through a popular referendum, but this was blocked by a state court. Gay and lesbian activists thus expanded the territories covered by these types of law, but antihomosexual discrimination remained legal at the federal level and restrictions on sexual orientation discrimination continued to vary at the state and local levels. Conservatives also blocked the passage of sexual orientation hate crimes legislation in various states.

Gay and lesbian advocates continued to use litigation to challenge sexual discrimination. They won several cases in California and Texas that addressed employment discrimination by police departments. Gay and lesbian student groups successfully challenged public universities in Arkansas and Texas that refused to recognize or fund them. Merle Woo won a two-year contract as a visiting lecturer at the University of California as part of a settlement in a case that addressed racial and sexual discrimination. The Florida Supreme Court struck down a state law that denied funding to public universities that provided meeting places for groups that advocated sex outside of marriage, including gay and lesbian groups. In 1985, the U.S. Supreme Court invalidated the Oklahoma law that authorized the firing of public school teachers who publicly advocated, encouraged, or promoted homosexuality. A Wisconsin chef who had been fired from his job after he discussed gay issues on television used his state's new antidiscrimination law to win back pay. A short time later, a federal court ruled against a Kentucky bank that had forced one of its managers to resign after he announced his plans to serve as the president of a local group for gay, lesbian, and allied Episcopalians.

Other antidiscrimination litigation was not successful. An Ohio court ruled in favor of a high school guidance counsellor whose contract had not been renewed because of her bisexuality, but this was later overturned by a federal court. A lesbian editor did not win her job back after she sued the *Christian Science Monitor*, which had fired her for refusing to seek treatment for her homosexuality, though she later received a financial settlement. A federal court upheld Louisiana State University's decision to deny a graduate student a teaching assistantship because of her relationship with a female undergraduate who was not her student. Around the same time, an Arizona court upheld the firing of a police officer because he was gay and a San Diego County grand jury endorsed the county sheriff's policy of not hiring gay or lesbian deputies. In 1981, an openly gay California Eagle Scout who had been rejected for a leadership position in the Boy Scouts because of his homosexuality sued the organization; after seventeen years of litigation the Supreme Court of California ruled against him in 1998. Gay and lesbian advocates won hundreds of discrimination cases in the 1980s, but they also lost hundreds. The legal remedies available to gays and lesbians who experienced discrimination continued to vary greatly in different jurisdictions and in different aspects of social, cultural, and political life.

Gay and lesbian activists in the 1980s expressed concern about two types of marriage-based discrimination: discrimination against same-sex couples who wanted to marry and discrimination against the unmarried. Many activists continued to support the legalization of same-sex marriage; others did not see this as attainable, important, or desirable. There were few major court cases concerning same-sex marriage in this era. One occurred in 1984, when a Pennsylvania court refused to grant a divorce to two men who claimed to have a common-law marriage. Another occurred in 1988, when an Indiana judge denied two gay prisoners a marriage license and fined them $2800 for requesting one. By 1990, forty states had passed legislation that restricted marriage to relationships involving one man and one woman. Meanwhile, the number of states that permitted transsexuals to change their legal sex increased from twelve in 1980 to twenty in 1990, which altered the legal situation for transsexuals who wanted to marry.

Marriage did not become a major movement priority until the 1990s, but in this period the ACLU, the San Francisco and California Bar Associations, the California Democratic Party, and the San Francisco Board of Supervisors endorsed the legalization of same-sex marriage. The 1987 March on Washington's first demand, which was approved after extensive national consultations, called for the legal recognition of lesbian and gay relationships. Significantly, the demand did not refer to same-sex marriage; it stated instead that lesbian and gay domestic partners were entitled to the same rights as married straight couples and called on society to recognize and celebrate diversity in family relationships. Same-sex marriage proponents, however, showcased the issue at a mass wedding on the day before the March. More than 3000 witnesses and nearly 2000 couples participated in the ceremony, which was held in front of the Internal Revenue Service building to highlight the marital tax benefits that were denied to same-sex couples. In 1988, 100 same-sex couples in San Francisco participated in a mass wedding ceremony to call attention to the need for marriage reform.

For many gays and lesbians, the discriminatory treatment of same-sex relationships came into stark relief after Sharon Kowalski was severely disabled in a 1983 car accident. The following year, a Minnesota judge selected Kowalski's father as her guardian, though he granted hospital visitation and medical consultation rights to her partner Karen Thompson. Conflicts over how best to care for Kowalski—fueled by antihomosexual prejudice—escalated after her father moved her to a nursing home. In 1985, the judge terminated Thompson's rights and Kowalski's father cut off all contact between Thompson and her partner, despite Kowalski's repeated requests to go home with her. In 1986, the U.S. Supreme Court declined to consider an appeal that focused on whether Kowalski had the capacity to select her own lawyers. Thompson then turned to the court of public opinion, where her supporters mobilized an international campaign to "free Sharon Kowalski." In 1989, after medical experts confirmed that Kowalski wanted to see her partner and that she would benefit from the care recommended by Thompson, a judge ordered her transferred to a rehabilitation center. He also permitted Thompson to visit Kowalski for the first time in more than three years. A few years later, the courts awarded guardianship to Thompson; shortly thereafter, Kowalski returned home to live with Thompson and her new partner. It had taken almost a decade for Kowalski's wishes to be respected, but publicity about her case helped educate the public about sexual discrimination and promoted new alliances between lesbian, disability, gay, and feminist activists.

More generally, family law litigation yielded mixed results. Many courts and judges, especially in more conservative regions, continued to make biased rulings against lesbian and gay parents in custody and visitation cases. Some were intensely and vocally hostile to lesbian and gay parenthood; others were less strongly biased, but held lesbian and gay parents to a higher standard. Many courts continued to impose discriminatory stipulations when granting custody and visitation rights to lesbian and gay parents; common restrictions required that the lesbian or gay parent not expose their children to or cohabit with their partners. Over time, more courts and judges in more states began awarding custody and visitation rights to lesbian and gay parents without discriminatory comments or stipulations, but this varied greatly.

There were also mixed developments for lesbians and gays who wanted to adopt children or serve as foster parents. In 1985, after the publication of sensational media stories about two gay foster parents in Boston, Massachusetts officials removed two young children from their home. A short time later, Governor Michael Dukakis's administration announced new guidelines that privileged married couples in foster care placements and all but banned gays and lesbians from serving as foster parents. One year later, an Arizona court ruled that a bisexual man could be denied the right to adopt children based on his sexual orientation. In 1987, New Hampshire prohibited gays and lesbians from adopting or fostering children. There were more positive developments in other states. In 1982, New York prohibited sexual discrimination in adoption. One year later, an openly gay California man was allowed to adopt his foster son. By the mid-1980s, at least six states permitted gays and lesbians to serve as foster parents for gay and lesbian youth. In 1990, after years of lobbying, litigation, and protests, Massachusetts adopted new foster care guidelines that emphasized parenting experience rather than marital status.

Meanwhile, gay and lesbian activists persuaded a few local governments to adopt domestic partnership plans that provided coupled gay and lesbian employees with some of the benefits enjoyed by married straights. This was particularly important in the context of the U.S. healthcare system, which depended heavily on employer-based family health insurance plans. Some gay and lesbian radicals criticized domestic partnership plans for condoning discrimination against the non-coupled and encouraging partnered domesticity, but most gay and lesbian activists supported fair and equal treatment for same-sex couples. In 1982, the San Francisco Board of Supervisors approved a domestic partnership plan that covered health insurance and bereavement leave for city employees, but Mayor Dianne Feinstein vetoed it. In 1984 and 1985, Berkeley and West Hollywood became the first U.S. municipalities to provide benefits for the domestic partners of city employees. In the next few years, domestic partnership plans were adopted in Los Angeles, Minneapolis, New York, San Francisco, Seattle, and several smaller cities and counties. San Francisco voters repealed that city's domestic partner benefits plan in 1989, but approved a more limited plan in 1990 and then a more expansive one in 1991. Seattle voters rejected an effort to repeal its family leave benefits policy for domestic partners in

1990. None of these laws provided same-sex couples with the same benefits available to married couples; they did not address state and federal benefits and they tended to offer only limited local benefits. In many respects the significance of these measures had more to do with the symbolism of relationship recognition than the material benefits gained or the substantive equality achieved.

Litigation to support the rights of gay and lesbian domestic partners had mixed success. In 1983, a gay man whose partner had died as a result of a work-related injury successfully used litigation to obtain the death benefits that the California Worker's Compensation Board provided to married dependents. In 1985, however, a California court ruled that the state could deny spousal dental benefits to the same-sex partners of state employees. This was after the state had prohibited employment discrimination based on sexual orientation, but the court ruled that the denial was based on marital status. In 1987, another California court ruled that Southern Pacific Transportation could deny bereavement leave to a gay man whose partner had died; the court ruled that the relevant provisions of the company's collective bargaining agreement did not apply because the men were not married. Gay rights litigators had more success in 1989 when a state court ruled that New York City's rent control law, which granted cohabiting family members the right to remain in rent-controlled apartments after the primary renter died, applied to a gay PWA whose partner had died. Notwithstanding this precedent, by 1990 discrimination against same-sex couples and discrimination against the non-coupled remained entrenched.

Gay and lesbian activists were pessimistic about many antidiscrimination initiatives at the federal level during the Reagan/Bush years, but they continued to fight for change in federal civil rights, military, and immigration policies. Every year, gay and lesbian activists lobbied Congress to pass an amendment to the U.S. Civil Rights Act that would address sexual orientation discrimination. Beginning in 1979, the proposed legislation in the House covered employment, housing, and public accommodations, while the proposed measure in the Senate covered just employment. By 1990, only seventy-nine U.S. representatives and twelve U.S. senators (mostly Democrats, but some Republicans) had promised to support the legislation. Gay and lesbian activists also did not succeed in extending the U.S. Civil Service Commission's antidiscrimination policies to cover government agencies with special exemptions. In 1987, for example, a federal judge ruled in favor of High Tech Gays in a case that challenged the Defense Department's policy of denying security clearances to homosexuals, but this was reversed by a higher court in 1990. Also in 1987, a federal appellate court upheld the FBI's decision not to hire a woman based on her lesbianism. In 1988, the Supreme Court upheld the firing of a National Security Agency employee based on his homosexual relationships with foreign nationals. In the same year, the Court ruled that the Central Intelligence Agency's firing of an employee based on homosexuality was subject to judicial review, but the firing was subsequently upheld. While a few individuals successfully challenged antihomosexual employment discrimination by these types of government agency, the decisions made it clear that the Civil Service Commission's rules did not apply. The courts increasingly required these agencies to explain why they discriminated against gays and lesbians, but they accepted most of the answers provided.

Efforts to change antihomosexual military policies and practices, which some activists opposed in the context of U.S. interventions in Central America, the Caribbean, and the Middle East, were equally unsuccessful. Responding to earlier court decisions that had challenged the military's inconsistent policies and practices, in 1982 the Defense Department announced a new policy under which no exceptions would be made in excluding homosexuals from the military. The policy applied to those who stated that they were homosexual and those who engaged in homosexual acts, though it permitted service members to defend themselves by proving that their homosexual conduct was consensual, a departure from their regular behavior, and unlikely to recur. This policy was used to deny Army Reserve Sergeant Miriam Ben-Shalom's request for reenlistment, which was upheld by a federal court in 1989. In 1990, the Supreme Court declined to consider Ben-Shalom's appeal and a related appeal by a naval officer.

Gay and lesbian advocates supported dozens of appeals by men and women who had served or were serving in the U.S. military, but they had limited success. One rare victory occurred in 1990, when the Supreme Court declined to review a federal court ruling in favor of Perry Watkins, who had been denied reenlistment by the Army. Watkins had informed the Army about his homosexuality at various points in his career and the Army had not discharged him; nor had it denied him reenlistment on three previous occasions. The court ruled that in these unique circumstances the Army could not deny Watkins's reenlistment. The military's antihomosexual policies, however, remained in place. Annual military discharges based on homosexuality were 1600–2000 from 1980 through 1986 and then dropped to 900–1400 from 1987 through 1990. As had been the case earlier, more men were affected but the percentage of women discharged based on homosexuality was far greater than the percentage of men.

In 1990, the gay and lesbian movement achieved three major legislative victories at the federal level: (1) passage of the Americans with Disabilities Act, which applied to people with HIV/AIDS, (2) inclusion in hate crimes legislation, and (3) repeal of the ban on gay and lesbian immigrants. The Americans with Disabilities Act, which was a major achievement for civil rights advocates during the Reagan/Bush era, became an important tool for challenging AIDS-based discrimination and other types of discrimination experienced by gays and lesbians with disabilities. The Hate Crimes Statistics Act required the Justice Department to collect and publish annual data on crimes committed at least in part because of prejudice based on ethnicity, race, religion, or sexual orientation. While the law did not mandate further action, it raised public and police consciousness about sexually motivated hate crimes.

As for immigration reform, toward the end of 1980 the new INS policy of excluding homosexual aliens without Public Health Service certificates was tested by British reporter Carl Hill, who told an immigration inspector in San Francisco that he was gay. The INS attempted to exclude Hill, who won an initial federal court ruling that permitted him to enter the country while the INS developed new exclusion procedures. In 1981, gay and lesbian activists in Amsterdam, Dublin, London, Oslo, Ottawa, Stockholm, and Toronto staged simultaneous protests against the U.S. policy of excluding gay and lesbian immigrants. Two years later, a federal court ruled that the INS could not exclude gay and lesbian immigrants without a PHS certificate. In the same year, however, a different federal court ruled that the INS, even without PHS certification, could deny a long-time U.S. resident's application for citizenship after he admitted that he was a homosexual and had engaged in homosexual acts before entering the country. Despite the conflict between the lower courts, in 1984 the Supreme Court declined to review the decision in the latter case. Six years later, after lobbying by gay and lesbian activists and legislative maneuvering by U.S. Representative Barney Frank, Congress repealed the law that had made homosexual aliens excludable and deportable as psychopathic personalities since 1952 and sexual deviates since 1965. They were still not eligible for the immigration preferences granted to the spouses and family members of U.S. citizens and residents, but most gay and lesbian activists regarded this as an important victory.

In this same period, however, in a striking illustration of the theory that new forms of freedom are often accompanied by new forms of regulation, the United States adopted new immigration restrictions for people with HIV and AIDS. In 1987, the U.S. government added AIDS and then HIV to the list of "dangerous contagious diseases" for which aliens could be excluded from the United States. Two years later, after the INS was criticized for detaining a Dutch AIDS educator who was attempting to attend a gay and lesbian health conference in San Francisco, the INS agreed to permit waivers under special circumstances. Under pressure from national and international activists and experts, many of whom boycotted an international AIDS conference in San Francisco in 1990 and promised to do the same for an upcoming conference in Boston, Congress dropped the automatic HIV exclusion in 1990. Under the new policy, the Centers for Disease Control (CDC) would determine whether HIV should be listed as an excludable condition. After the CDC recommended that HIV should not be listed, conservatives campaigned successfully to reinstate the HIV exclusion in 1991, though waivers were again permitted under special circumstances. This remained official U.S. policy until 2010.

Many gay and lesbian activists promoted political reform by lobbying, litigating, and demonstrating, but many also believed that progress depended on participation in electoral politics. This was often frustrating in a period of conservative ascendancy, but at the very least it helped build alliances and educate voters. One significant problem was that the more success gays and lesbians had in winning acceptance as part of the Democratic electoral coalition, the more problems they had with the Republicans. Yet there seemed to be little that sexual liberals could do to counter the influence of conservatives on the Republican Party. Gay and lesbian reformers thus tended to promote the election of Democratic candidates, worked with Democratic allies, and cultivated the small number of Republican politicians who supported gay and lesbian rights. Gay and lesbian participation in electoral politics contributed to some liberal victories and blocked some conservative initiatives, though all of this occurred within the narrow spectrum of mainstream U.S. politics.

The number of openly gay or lesbian elected officials in the United States increased during the 1980s. Two Democratic members of the U.S. House acknowledged publicly that they were gay: Gerry Studds of Massachusetts in 1983 and Barney Frank of Massachusetts in 1987. Two Republicans who served in the House in the 1980s—Steve Gunderson of Wisconsin and Jim Kolbe of Arizona—publicly acknowledged their homosexuality in the 1990s. Republican U.S. Representative Stuart McKinney of Connecticut did not similarly acknowledge his homosexuality, but after he died of AIDS-related complications in 1987 there were media reports about his gay life. Meanwhile, openly gay and lesbian politicians were elected to state legislatures in Connecticut, Maine, Minnesota, New York, and Washington and to local government positions in Boston, Dane County (Wisconsin), and San Francisco. Laguna Beach elected an openly gay mayor in 1982, Key West and Santa Cruz did so in 1983, and Santa Monica elected an openly lesbian mayor in 1990. When West Hollywood was incorporated as a city in 1984, it elected two gay men and a lesbian to its five-person city council, which then elected the lesbian (Valerie Terrigno) as the city's first mayor. Democrat William Allain was elected governor of Mississippi in 1983 in the midst of sensational allegations about his homosexuality, which he denied. By 1990, there were approximately fifty openly gay or lesbian elected officials in the United States.

For advancing gay and lesbian agendas, the election of political allies was critical. As had been the case in the 1970s, gay and lesbian voters made the difference in the election of dozens of U.S. House members, state legislators, county supervisors, local mayors, and city council members. One notable development was the support gay and lesbian voters provided in the election of African American big city mayors in Birmingham, Chicago, Detroit, Los Angeles, New York, Philadelphia, and Washington, D.C. Another major development was the work of the Human Rights Campaign Fund (HRCF), which contributed millions of dollars to hundreds of candidates who supported gay and lesbian rights. This did not come close to the amounts raised and used by sexually conservative political action committees, but it provided an important counterweight.

For gay and lesbian activists who were oriented to electoral politics, the Democratic Party was the party of choice. Former Vice President Walter Mondale, the leading contender for the 1984 Democratic nomination for U.S. president, spoke at an HRCF fundraising dinner in New York in 1982. Jesse Jackson and Senator Gary Hart, Mondale's main rivals, spoke at gay and lesbian events in New York and Los Angeles in 1983. During the 1984 campaign, Mondale, Jackson, and Hart endorsed gay and lesbian rights legislation, but Jackson was most active in courting gay and lesbian votes. Just before the 1984 party convention in San Francisco, approximately 100,000 people marched in the streets to encourage the Democrats to strengthen their support for gay and lesbian rights. There were sixty-five openly gay or lesbian delegates and alternates at the convention and the party platform again included a gay and lesbian rights plank. After the Democrats selected Mondale as their candidate, many gays and lesbians worked on his campaign, but President Reagan was reelected in a landslide.

Gay and lesbian Democrats approached the 1988 national elections with increased confidence, in part because no political party had retained presidential power for more than eight years since the Roosevelt/Truman era. This time there were ninety-eight openly gay or lesbian delegates or alternates at the party convention and the platform endorsed equal access to government services, employment, housing, business, and education regardless of sexual orientation. In a wide field of candidates, many gays and lesbians supported Jackson, but Governor Michael Dukakis was selected as the Party's nominee. This was an awkward situation for gay and lesbian voters, most of whom regarded Dukakis as more favorable than Republican nominee George Bush but many of whom knew that Dukakis had implemented antihomosexual foster care policies in Massachusetts. It did not help that Dukakis seemed ambivalent about campaigning for gay and lesbian votes. When Dukakis lost to Bush, gays and lesbians faced another four years of Republican rule, though they helped limit Republican power by contributing to the election of Democratic majorities in the House and Senate.

With the Republican Party, the situation seemed to go from bad to worse. Gay and lesbian lobbyists occasionally met with members of President Reagan's Office of Public Liaison, but antihomosexual activists had far greater access to the White House during the 1980s. In 1984, there was a reception for gay and lesbian delegates and alternates at the Republican Party convention, but only three alternates identified themselves openly as gay. During the 1984 election campaign, New Right, Christian Right, and Republican Party activists stepped up their attacks on the Democrats as the party of gay rights, which they underscored by high-lighting the fact that the Democratic convention had taken place in San Francisco. They also presented themselves as having a monopoly on what they increasingly referred to as "family values."

In 1988, internal divisions within the New Right and the Republican Party began to grow when Pat Robertson challenged Vice President Bush and U.S. Senator Robert Dole for the Republican presidential nomination. Bush was nominated, but the strength of Robertson's campaign was a sign of the Christian Right's growing power within the Republican Party, which was increasingly hostile to gay and lesbian rights. The party platform that year emphasized traditional family values and promoted AIDS education programs that focused on sexual abstinence outside of marriage, which meant no same-sex sex. Approximately eighty people attended a Republican convention reception for gay and lesbian delegates and alternates, though few identified themselves publicly as gay or lesbian. Two years later, a collection of local gay and lesbian Republican clubs established the Log Cabin Federation, but they did not convince many gays or lesbians to join the Party. In March 1990, gay and lesbian criticisms of Republican Party officials culminated when NGLTF executive director Urvashi Vaid interrupted President Bush's first major speech about AIDS. As she heckled Bush, Vaid held up signs that read "Remember Gay People With AIDS" and "Talk is Cheap, AIDS Funding is Not." By the end of this period, Republican Party opposition to gay and lesbian rights was firmly entrenched.

As was the case in the 1970s, the gay and lesbian movement's four main nongovernmental targets in the 1980s were science, business, religion, and popular culture. Gay and lesbian activists had continued to challenge scientific bias, prejudice, and discrimination after the APA's declassification of homosexuality as a mental illness in 1973. In the context of AIDS, science again became a central movement concern, but activists also developed new criticisms of the APA, which in 1980 revised its *Diagnostic and Statistical Manual* to add "gender identity disorder" and replace "sexual orientation disturbance" with "ego dystonic homosexuality." In 1987, the APA removed "ego dystonic homosexuality" from the *DSM*, but gay and lesbian activists continued to criticize the APA's handling of gender and sexual matters. There were also criticisms of the antihomosexual motivations, methods, and effects of scientific studies that addressed the causes of homosexuality.

Business policies and practices were another major concern; in fact, much of the gay, lesbian, and AIDS activism highlighted above focused on business-based discrimination, which was pervasive. In countless contexts, gays and lesbians who experienced discrimination as employees or consumers fought back by speaking up about their mistreatment, sharing their stories in gay and lesbian periodicals, working with movement groups to lodge complaints, seeking assistance from labor unions, and organizing demonstrations and boycotts.

Over the course of the 1980s, gay and lesbian activists persuaded more businesses, colleges, and universities to adopt policies banning employment discrimination based on sexual orientation; a smaller number also prohibited discrimination based on gender identity or expression. Some of this occurred because of significant growth in the number and size of gay and lesbian union caucuses, labor organizations, employee networks, and student groups. In 1983, gay and lesbian labor activists convinced the AFL-CIO to endorse legislation against sexual orientation discrimination. There were also supportive resolutions by the American Federation of State, County, and Municipal Employees, the American Federation of Teachers, the International Ladies' Garment Workers' Union, the Service Employees International Union (SEIU), and other unions. Meanwhile, gay and lesbian labor activists persuaded many unions to fight for the adoption of antidiscrimination policies in collective bargaining; in some cases, this resulted in contractual language that banned sexual orientation discrimination.

Another goal of gay and lesbian business reformers was the adoption of domestic partner benefits plans. Many U.S. employers provided a variety of benefits—including spousal pensions, spousal health insurance, medical leaves, and bereavement leaves—to their married employees. Since same-sex marriage was not legally recognized in the United States, same-sex couples did not have access to these benefits. In 1982, a gay and lesbian union caucus convinced the *Village Voice* to become the country's first business known to offer same-sex partner benefits for its employees, though it is likely that some gay and lesbian businesses quietly did so earlier. Over the next few years, the ACLU, the American Friends Service Committee, the American Psychological Association, Ben and Jerry's, and Planned Parenthood adopted domestic partner benefits plans. By 1990, more than twenty private and public employers had done so. These plans did not offer same-sex couples the same benefits that were available to married couples and some critics argued that they further institutionalized discrimination against the uncoupled. For same-sex partners, however, they were an improvement over the benefits previously available to them.

Gay and lesbian activists also continued to target individual businesses that engaged in particularly egregious forms of discrimination. Much of their work focused on businesses that discriminated against people with HIV/AIDS, but they also addressed other forms of discrimination. In 1984, for example, two men won a discrimination suit against Disneyland, which had denied them the right to dance together, and a lesbian couple won a discrimination suit against a Los Angeles restaurant that refused to seat them in a section reserved for romantic dates. Until 1987, when the AFL-CIO ended its boycott of Coors, many gay and lesbian activists supported the boycott; in fact, many maintained it after 1987. Media, drug, and insurance companies were common targets of gay and lesbian protests. Partly as a result, several insurance companies began to offer same-sex couples the same policies that were available to married couples, though most declined to do so. Gay and lesbian activists also continued to target mainstream bars and restaurants that mistreated gay and lesbian customers and gay and lesbian businesses that mistreated female, nonwhite, and trans patrons.

Building on their successes in the 1970s, gay and lesbian religious reformers pursued two general projects during the 1980s: developing autonomous religious groups and encouraging social change in mainstream religions. For those who focused on the latter, there were three large groupings of denominations. At the beginning of this period, the most responsive to gay and lesbian concerns were the Society of Friends, the Unitarian Church, and the United Church. All three welcomed gay and lesbian members, the Unitarian and United Churches continued to ordain gay and lesbian ministers, and in 1984 the Unitarians endorsed religious ceremonies for same-sex unions. Reform and Reconstructionist Judaism also became increasingly responsive to gay and lesbian concerns; both began to ordain gay and lesbian rabbis in the 1980s. A second large grouping consisted of denominations that were partially respon- sive to gay and lesbian concerns. These included the Episcopalians, Lutherans, Methodists, and Presbyterians. Most of these criticized sodomy laws and endorsed legislation against sexual orientation discrimination. In various contexts, gay and lesbian activists sought to counter the political power of the Christian Right by asking for assistance from the influential denominations within this grouping, most of which supported some gay and lesbian rights initiatives as matters of basic civil rights. At the same time, these denominations condemned homosexuality as antithetical to Christianity, opposed the ordination of practicing homosexuals, and declined to endorse same-sex religious unions. In 1983, the National Council of Churches again denied the Metropolitan Community Church's request for membership. In 1983 and 1984, the Presbyterian Church and United Methodist Church confirmed their rejection of homosexuality and their opposition to the ordination of practicing homosexuals.

Dissidents within these denominations, however, pressed for change. In 1982, a Methodist bishop ordained an openly gay man as a minister in Denver. He was absolved of heresy charges, but the Methodists' antihomosexual policy remained in place. In 1987, a New Hampshire Methodist minister who had come out as a lesbian was defrocked. In 1989, an Episcopalian bishop violated church policy by ordaining an openly gay man as a priest. The bishop was accused of heresy, though the charges were later dropped. In 1990, two lesbians and a gay man were ordained by two Lutheran churches in San Francisco. The ordinations were not recognized by the Evangelical Lutheran Church, which suspended and later expelled the two churches. Meanwhile, dissident Methodists and Presbyterians in Washington, D.C., and dissident Episcopalians in Massachusetts and New Jersey endorsed religious ceremonies for same-sex couples. Conservative Judaism also began to consider changing its policies and practices.

The third large grouping consisted of Roman Catholics, Mormons, Orthodox Jews, Southern Baptists, and a variety of other fundamentalist and evangelical Protestants. Many African American Baptist, Methodist, and Pentecostal churches fell within this grouping, though others were more responsive to gay and lesbian concerns. Many of these denominations became more strongly antihomosexual in the 1980s than they had been in the 1970s. In 1985, for example, the Southern Baptist Convention adopted a statement that condemned homosexuality and rejected the notion that homosexuals were a minority group. Many of these denominations strongly opposed sex law reform, aggressively supported sexual censorship, forcefully campaigned against sexual orientation antidiscrimination legislation, and actively opposed AIDS initiatives that condoned homosexuality.

In the early 1980s, some Roman Catholic dissidents continued to challenge the Church's antihomosexual positions, but this became less possible in the late 1980s. In 1982, a San Francisco archdiocese task force on homosexuality issued a report with dozens of gay- and lesbian-affirmative recommendations. In the same year, Milwaukee's Roman Catholic archbishop joined prominent Episcopalian, Lutheran, and Methodist leaders in Wisconsin in endorsing that state's sexual orientation antidiscrimination legislation. Also in 1982, Baltimore's archbishop celebrated a mass for more than 300 Dignity members. In 1984, however, Sister Jeannine Gramick and Father Robert Nugent were forced to resign from New Ways Ministry because of their work with gay and lesbian Catholics. In 1986, the Vatican adopted a new statement that referred to homosexuality as evil and immoral, condemned the gay and lesbian movement, and rejected the use of church property by gay and lesbian groups. In response, nine members of New York City's Lavender Hill Mob stood up silently during a sermon by an archbishop, unfurled their banner, and marched out. Over the next few years, Dignity chapters were denied permission to continue meeting in various Catholic churches around the country, including in New York, where a regular mass for Dignity members had been held since 1979. In 1987, eleven gay activists were arrested at St. Patrick's Cathedral after they stood silently during the archbishop's sermon and refused to leave. Also in 1987, Dignity Twin Cities unsuccessfully challenged, as a violation of Minneapolis's antidiscrimination ordinance, its expulsion from the University of Minnesota's Catholic Newman Center. That same year, gay and lesbian activists participated in a large demonstration against the Pope during his visit to San Francisco. In 1988, ten gay and lesbian activists were arrested after they blocked traffic in front of St. Patrick's Cathedral to protest the Catholic Church's antihomosexual policies and practices. By 1990, gay and lesbian activists had succeeded in winning support from a variety of liberal religious denominations, but their efforts had inspired a strongly conservative religious backlash.

Popular culture was a fourth major nongovernmental target of gay and lesbian activism. Many of the most influential gay and lesbian media activist groups of the 1970s did not survive into the 1980s, but in 1982 Lesbian and Gay Media Advocates published *Talk Back! The Gay Person's Guide to Media Action*. After 1985, GLAAD became the country's leading gay and lesbian media activist group. GLAAD and other groups focused a great deal of critical attention on media coverage of the AIDS epidemic, representations of people with HIV and AIDS on television and in film, and gay and lesbian invisibility and negative visibility in popular culture. In 1983, for example, gay and lesbian activists met with several *New York Times* editors to challenge the paper's coverage of gay, lesbian, and AIDS issues. They won an expression of regret and shortly thereafter the *Times* published several significant articles on AIDS.

Protests continued in the next several years. GLAAD organized major demonstrations at the *New York Post* in 1985 and 1986, after which the quality and quantity of its gay, lesbian, and AIDS coverage improved. In 1986, gay and lesbian activists picketed the *Chicago Sun-Times* after it published a series of columns that referred to homosexuality as unhealthy and endorsed mandatory tattooing to identify PWAs. In this case, the paper's publisher and editors agreed to meet with their critics and later that year assigned a reporter to cover AIDS and the gay/lesbian community. In 1986 and 1987, the *Wall Street Journal* and *New York Times* dropped their long-standing bans (not consistently enforced) on the use of the word "gay" to refer to homosexuality and homosexuals (except in direct quotations and organizational names, where it had been permitted earlier). In 1987, GLAAD demonstrated at the *National Review* to protest a column by William F. Buckley that called for tattooing PWAs; Buckley subsequently met with GLAAD activists and publicly disavowed his proposal. That same year, gay and lesbian activists criticized many media outlets for offering minimal or no coverage of the March on Washington. In 1989, after the *New York Times* published a homophobic article on the new lesbian baby boom, criticisms by NGLTF, GLAAD, and the ACLU led the *Times* to print a partial retraction. By 1990, U.S. newspaper and magazine coverage of gay, lesbian, and AIDS issues was better than it had been just a few years earlier, though gays and lesbians remained invisible in many media contexts and were represented in predominantly negative ways in many others.

Gay and lesbian activists grew increasingly concerned about the power and influence of Christian Right radio programs in the 1980s, but focused more attention on television. While social conservatives launched a set of initiatives aimed at challenging what they regarded as sexual immorality on television, gay and lesbian activists worked to counteract their influence and improve the depiction of gays and lesbians. In 1981, for example, after NBC executives took steps to minimize the homosexuality of the main character on the *Love Sidney* program, gay and lesbian activists criticized the network for caving in to conservative pressure. The Alliance for Gay Artists, which was founded in Los Angeles in 1981 and renamed the Alliance for Gay and Lesbian Artists in 1984, began to consult with television executives, producers, and writers to improve the representation of gays and lesbians on television. In the early 1980s, the Alliance began presenting annual awards for major gay and lesbian achievements in television and film.

Gay and lesbian media activists found much to celebrate about television representations in the 1980s, but they found more to criticize. In 1983, they denounced an HBO comedy special featuring Eddie Murphy for its offensive comments about homosexuality and AIDS. In 1986, gay, lesbian, and AIDS activists attacked the Public Broadcasting Service for its hostile and unethical portrayal of a promiscuous African American hustler with AIDS on *Frontline*. As noted previously, hundreds of San Francisco AIDS activists disrupted the filming of a 1988 episode of the NBC program *Midnight Caller*; activists in several cities then demonstrated at NBC affiliates on the day the episode was broadcast. In 1988 and 1989, gay and lesbian activists criticized the limitations placed on the first regular lesbian character featured on a prime time television show (a nurse practitioner on the medical drama *Hearbeat)* and then attacked ABC for cancelling the show, in part because of pressure from social conservatives. In 1989, GLAAD convinced comedian Bob Hope, whom they had criticized for telling fag jokes on *The Tonight Show*, to make a televised public service announcement that denounced antigay bigotry, prejudice, and violence. Later that year, GLAAD criticized CBS news commentator Andy Rooney for stating that homosexuality often led to premature death. The network's news president promised that Rooney's work would be edited more carefully in the future, but a short time later Rooney made a set of offensive comments about gay people and African Americans, which led CBS to suspend him for one month. Around the same time, GLAAD asked for and received an apology from Wendy's Restaurants for stating, in response to conservative threats of a boycott, that its sponsorship of a gay-themed *L.A. Law* episode was inappropriate.

By 1990, many gay and lesbian activists believed that representations of homosexuality on television and in film had never been better, and yet they remained profoundly dissatisfied. In general, mainstream television and film continued to privilege and promote heterosexuality and they continued to present homosexuality and heterosexuality as mutually exclusive orientations. Gay and lesbian issues received minimal attention on television news broadcasts. Most television comedies and dramas and most Hollywood films did not include gay or lesbian characters. Those that did confined those characters to minor roles or one-time appearances. Most gay and lesbian characters were young, middle-class, and single white men. Most were villains or victims. Representations of same-sex sexual affection and intimacy were rare. Few enjoyed the romantic relationships, career successes, or happy endings that were commonly featured in mainstream television and film. There were exceptions that gay and lesbian audiences appreciated and enjoyed, especially in independent film and video, but popular culture continued to support and sustain sexual inequality in the United States.

More generally, the gay and lesbian movement's accomplishments during the 1980s were extraordinary, especially given the devastating effects of AIDS, yet by 1990 sexual inequality remained firmly entrenched in the United States. This was one of the main paradoxes of the movement during this period. Gay and lesbian activists played leading roles in the fight against AIDS and in so doing saved and extended millions of gay, lesbian, and straight lives. At the same time, at the end of the decade the number of people living with and dying of HIV/AIDS was increasing and the epidemic continued to inspire antihomosexual prejudice, discrimination, and violence. Over the course of the decade, the gay and lesbian movement successfully challenged many discriminatory policies and practices, but in 1990 sexual equality remained a distant and elusive goal. During the 1980s, increasingly gays and lesbians were recognized as part of the Democratic Party's electoral coalition, but they were increasingly attacked by the Republican Party. By 1990, the movement arguably had more friends and more foes than ever before. The movement had successfully promoted social change in science, business, religion, and popular culture, yet in each of these realms gays and lesbians continued to encounter resistance, reaction, repression, and retrenchment.

Building on its successes and failures in the 1980s and influenced by the transformations wrought by AIDS, the gay and lesbian movement achieved unprecedented social and sexual change in the last decade of the twentieth century and the first years of the twenty-first. At the same time, the movement changed so significantly that it becomes much more difficult to talk about a gay and lesbian movement after the 1980s. As the final chapter discusses, in many respects it makes more sense, when considering movement politics after 1990, to refer to the LGBT movement and the queer movement rather than the gay and lesbian movement. This is the second major paradox of the movement in the 1980s: it had never been more consequential, and yet many activists and academics were about to consign it to the dustbins of history.

6

LGBT AND QUEER ACTIVISM
BEYOND 1990

The U.S. gay and lesbian movement of the 1950s, 1960s, 1970s, and 1980s laid the foundation for transformative social, cultural, and political developments in the last decade of the twentieth century and the first part of the twenty-first. In many respects, the work of gay and lesbian activism continued after 1990 and it continues today. In other respects, however, the gay and lesbian movement was replaced or superseded by the LGBT (lesbian, gay, bisexual, and transgender) and queer movements in the 1990s and early 2000s. This distinction is more than semantic. Words matter and movements change. We should not assume that just because there was a gay and lesbian movement in the past there necessarily is one in the present.

Historians typically shy away from studying the last twenty years, partly because it often seems impossible to assess the long-term significance of very recent developments. In the 1990s, my doctoral research, which addressed the 1940s through the 1970s, was derisively labeled "current events" by several historians in my graduate program. More recently, one of my colleagues referred to a course I teach as "contemporary history," an oxymoronic phrase whose usage often reflects the disciplinary anxieties associated with historians who research and teach about the recent past, though in this case the course actually began in the eighteenth century. I often tell students that the weakest parts of many books by historians are the final "bring the story up to the present" chapters that many publishers encourage them to produce. (This perspective has haunted the writing of this chapter.) Part of the problem is that the present is a moving target; many claims about "today" quickly become obsolete, as will inevitably be the case with much of what this chapter says about the current moment. We have to wait for the dust to settle, many historians say, and we benefit from the critical distance that the passage of time allows. Other disciplines study the present, they emphasize; the distinctive mission of historians is to study change and continuity in the past, by which they do not mean the very recent past.

This book concentrates on the period from 1950 to 1990; it does not offer as much coverage of the post-1990 era, which is explored in greater depth by other scholars. As is the case with all works of history, *Rethinking the Gay and Lesbian Movement* is very much situated in and informed by the moment in which it was written (2010–12), but I will leave it for others to consider how this book is immersed in and engaged with the world of the early twenty-first century. None of us can know today whether future historians will say that the U.S. gay and lesbian movement ended in the 1990s or continued to exist in the early twenty-first century. Perhaps they will find it more useful to adopt a genealogical approach, which might involve starting with the gender and sexual movements of the twenty-first century and exploring their historical antecedents in earlier periods. Nor can we know whether future historians will explore the gay and lesbian, LGBT, or queer movements in national as opposed to local, regional, or transnational terms. The frameworks that future historians use will be influenced by developments that have not yet occurred; we cannot predict them in advance.

This book is based on the notion that the U.S. gay and lesbian movement of 1950–90 was a significantly important and reasonably coherent historical phenomenon, but the existence and character of that movement was not inevitable. Most forms of sex have not become the bases of strong sexual identities, communities, or movements. In most cultural contexts, same-sex sex has not been a major focus of political activism. Alternative historical developments could have led gay activism and lesbian activism to be far less conjoined than they were. There could have been a broader coalition of gender and sexual freedom fighters. There could have been more of an issue-based movement that addressed sexual liberation rather than an identity-based movement for gays and lesbians. There could have been a stronger alliance of oppressed groups. If any of this had occurred, there would have been compelling reasons for this volume to be framed in different ways. But the fact that this book is based on the conviction that there was a U.S. gay and lesbian movement from 1950 to 1990 does not mean that it is also based on the conviction that there was one after 1990. Was there? Is there a U.S. gay and lesbian movement today?

The New Queer Activism

A series of developments in the late 1980s and early 1990s suggested that something significant was happening to and within the gay and lesbian movement. One sign of change was the increased use of the term "queer" by activists and academics. Some movement participants in the 1950s, 1960s, 1970s, and 1980s had described themselves as queer, but this became much more common in the 1990s. In October 1989, Bad Object-Choices, a New York-based study group, sponsored a conference entitled "How Do I Look? Queer Film and Video"; this was then used as the name of a 1991 book based on the conference presentations. In February 1990, film studies scholar Teresa de Lauretis began referring to "queer theory" at a conference held at the University of California, Santa Cruz. In her formulation, "queer" could be positioned as a radical alternative to "gay and lesbian," which many activists and academics now regarded as too assimilationist, conservative, and normative and too bound up with fixed gender and sexual identities. When the scholarly journal *differences* published a special issue based on the conference papers in 1991, it used "Queer Theory: Lesbian and Gay Sexualities" for the title.[1]

Meanwhile, in April 1990 a group of New York activists, many of whom had participated in the ACT UP movement, formed Queer Nation, which they envisioned as a radical direct action group to promote LGBT visibility, sexual liberation, and gender transformation. Two months later, a collection of activists who referred to themselves as Queers distributed a confrontational leaflet at New York City's gay and lesbian pride march; headlined "Queers Read This," it attacked heterosexist privilege, declared "I Hate Straights," and called on queers to reject assimilation, demand freedom, and fight for equality.[2] Within a year there were dozens of Queer Nation and other queer activist groups inside and outside the United States. Similar and related impulses led to the formation of Transgender Nation in San Francisco and Lesbian Avengers in New York in 1992.

Early queer activists used many of the strategies and tactics that had worked for the ACT UP movement, but concentrated on sex, gender, and sexuality rather than AIDS. Queer activism varied across time and place, but many of its early projects focused on defending queer people and places, criticizing LGBT conservatism and liberalism, and celebrating gender and sexual transgression. Politicized queers organized antiviolence marches, sponsored self-defense workshops, patrolled LGBT neighborhoods, and warned that queers "bash back."[3] Because publicity rather than privacy was their goal, they held kiss-ins and other visibility actions in public space, including shopping malls and public parks, bars and restaurants, schools and churches, and sports and leisure venues. Determined to protect and defend queer space, they also wanted to queer everyone and everything. Influenced by the ACT UP movement, queer activists staged lively and raucous protests to challenge antiqueer bias, discrimination, and prejudice in business, education, media, politics, popular culture, religion, and science.

"Queer" was a multivalent term that meant different things to different people. Commonly regarded as a negative epithet that had been used against gender and sexual dissidents, it was reclaimed by activists to proclaim their defiant pride in rejecting gender and sexual norms. But there were significant differences in how the term was deployed. While many used "queer" as a synonym for "lesbian, gay, bisexual, and transgender" and supported its coalitional effectiveness, others positioned queer activism as a radical challenge to the LGBT movement, which queers criticized for aspiring to inclusion within normative institutions such as marriage and the military. Along similar lines, while some activists thought that all LGBT people were queer and all non-LGBT people were nonqueer, others argued that non-LGBT people who defied gender and sexual norms were queerer than LGBT assimilationists.

Many queers claimed that they were critical of all fixed gender and sexual identities and all forms of identity politics. One of the reasons they liked the term "queer," for example, was that it did not reference sex differences in the same ways that "gay and lesbian" did. The term also was embraced by people whose sexes, genders, and sexualities did not align in conventional ways: by gays and lesbians who had straight sex, straights who had gay and lesbian sex, gays and lesbians who had sex with each other, people whose gender and sexual preferences changed over time, individuals who rejected binary gender and sexual categories, and trans people and their partners. Many queers, however, acted in ways that suggested that "queer" was a new identity with its own set of norms about how to act, look, talk, and think. In addition, while queers prided themselves on their antinormative politics, they did not necessarily agree on what was normative and what was not. Were straight sex workers queer? Were their clients? What about asexuals? And transsexuals who accepted binary gender norms? What about straight people who engaged in intergenerational, interracial, public, polyamorous, polygamous, promiscuous, or sadomasochistic sex? If queers were antinormative, were pedophiles and rapists queer, or did queers think that pedophilia and rape were normative? Did it matter that many of these people would not call themselves queer? Queer ambivalence about policing boundaries helps explain why "nationalism" soon disappeared from the queer lexicon (as early as 1990, Philadelphians formed Queer Action rather than Queer Nation). In contrast, the term "queer" became increasingly popular, but its meanings continued to change and diversify.

Use of the term "queer" quickly became controversial among LGBT activists. Some were reluctant to reclaim a word that was linked to a long history of hate and hostility. Some rejected the militancy and radicalism associated with the term or did not think that "queer" was the best way to describe their ongoing struggles for the legalization of same-sex marriage, the right to serve in the military, the right to parent, and the right to privacy, none of which seemed very queer. Some were anxious about antagonizing potential allies. There also were concerns about losing the political specificity of terms such as "lesbian," "gay," "bisexual," and "transgender." Meanwhile, some people of color, poor people, women, and working-class people identified as queer, but others thought the term was bourgeois, white, and male, perhaps even more so than "gay and lesbian." Some trans people and some bisexuals identified as "queer"; others did not.

Meanwhile, there were gender and sexual radicals who thought that queer generalizations about the gay and lesbian movement erased the history of radical tendencies within the movement, which at times had promoted queer positions and projects. Were queer criticisms of mainstream gay and lesbian politics just updated versions of earlier radical critiques of mainstream gay and lesbian activism? Many queer attacks on gay and lesbian identity politics, for example, missed the fact that there always had been components of the gay and lesbian movement that rejected the notion of innate sexual identities. Some gay and lesbian radicals resented the arrogance of queers who acted as though gays and lesbians had never understood the limitations of identity politics, minority models, and essentialist concepts. Some also resented the "queerer than thou" attitudes of the new generation of activists, who in attacking the gay and lesbian movement exaggerated their own radicalism, ignored their own normative investments, and failed to acknowledge the foundational role of gay and lesbian activism in making queer politics possible. Notwithstanding these criticisms, in the 1990s and early 2000s more and more activists described themselves as "queer," sometimes as a signifier of radical gender and sexual dissidence and sometimes as a synonym for LGBT. In some ways, this was reminiscent of the transformations in the meanings of "gay liberation," which initially had referenced radical gender and sexual dissidence but later came to be used as a synonym for gay and lesbian activism more generally.

The emergence of queer activism was not the only sign that gender and sexual movements were changing in potentially fundamental ways in the late 1980s and early 1990s. Trans activism was also transforming, as was signaled by the redefinition and popularization of the term "transgender." Initially used in the 1980s for gender transgressors who did not identify as transsexual, "transgender" came to be understood in the 1990s as a coalitional term that referenced a broad range of people with nonnormative gender identities and nonnormative ways of expressing their genders, including transsexuals. The publication of Sandy Stone's essay "The Empire Strikes Back: A Posttranssexual Manifesto" in 1991, the release of Leslie Feinberg's pamphlet "Transgender Liberation" in 1992, and the formation of Transgender Nation as an affinity group within Queer Nation-San Francisco in 1992 were important milestones in the transformation of trans politics.[4] Significantly, all three rejected trans assimilationism, just as many queer activists rejected LGBT assimilationism. And just as some LGBT activists rejected the queer turn, some transsexual and transgender activists rejected the new trans politics. Nevertheless, the intersections, parallels, and relationships between the gay, lesbian, trans, and queer movements (and the fact that many people identified with more than one) suggested to many activists that the movements should work more closely together in the future.

There were also significant developments in bisexual activism in this period. In 1990, more than 400 people attended the First National Bisexual Conference in San Francisco, which led to the founding of the North American Bisexual Network (later renamed BiNet U.S.A.). These events, along with the publication in 1991 of *Bi Any Other Name: Bisexual People Speak Out*, edited by Loraine Hutchins and Lani Ka'ahumanu, helped spark a significant upsurge in bisexual activism, some of which overlapped with queer and trans activism.[5]

All of this helps explain why it became increasingly common in the 1990s and 2000s to refer to the LGBT movement and the queer movement, both of which can be seen as the culmination of long coalition-building processes. For complex reasons, the intersex movement, which expanded with the formation of the Intersex

Society of North America in 1993, remained somewhat more independent, though some intersex activists identified as queer. While many people resisted the strengthening of these coalitions and each of the coalition partners retained significant autonomy, in many ways the LGBT and queer movements of the 1990s and early 2000s replaced and superseded the gay and lesbian movement of the pre-1990 era.

Race relations within the gay and lesbian movement also were changing in the late 1980s and early 1990s, with important ramifications for the future of gender and sexual politics. This was the period when Native American, Native Alaskan, and Canadian First Nations activists adopted "two-spirit" as the preferred term for people in their cultures who crossed, mixed, or expressed genders in distinctive ways. Meanwhile, African American, Asian American and Pacific Islander, Latina and Latino, and Native American and Native Alaskan critiques of racism in the gay, lesbian, and AIDS movements were increasing. One significant set of episodes occurred in 1990–91, when gays and lesbians of color, led by Asian Lesbians of the East Coast and Gay Asian and Pacific Islander Men of New York, criticized Lambda Legal Defense and the Lesbian and Gay Community Services Center in New York for planning fundraising events that would feature performances of the Broadway musical *Miss Saigon*, which they considered Orientalist, racist, and sexist. As they voiced their concerns, the U.S. government responded to Iraq's invasion of Kuwait with an invasion of Iraq, which critics of colonialism, imperialism, and militarism linked to U.S. Orientalism, racism, and sexism. In this context, the Lesbian and Gay Community Services Center decided to cancel its event, but Lambda did not. In April 1991, 500 LGBT people of color and their allies demonstrated outside the Lambda fundraising event, while two activists disrupted the performance inside. Five days later, a smaller group demonstrated at the show's opening night performance. In the aftermath of the controversy, Lambda's executive director resigned, criticisms of movement racism increased, and more LGBT people of color began to support queer challenges to mainstream gay and lesbian activism.

Yet another sign that the movement was changing was the eruption of controversies about "outing." For decades, journalists, politicians, and others had publicly identified various individuals as gay or lesbian. Sometimes this involved media reports about ordinary people accused of sex or gender crimes; sometimes the targets were athletes, celebrities, entertainers, and politicians who did not wish to be known publicly as gay or lesbian. There also was a long history of outing prominent people from the past. Before the late 1980s, however, the gay and lesbian movement had rarely used the outing of contemporary public figures as a major political strategy. This changed in 1989–91, when some AIDS, LGBT, and queer activists, many affiliated with the New York-based newspaper *Outweek*, outed dozens of well-known individuals. In many cases, the goal was to criticize them for opposing gender and sexual liberation, not supporting the LGBT movement, and not joining the fight against AIDS. Outing was also used to challenge conservative sexual presumptions, attack political hypocrisy, strengthen LGBT visibility, and criticize the mainstream LGBT movement for privileging privacy over publicity. Among the people outed by AIDS, LGBT, and queer activists were prominent public figures from the worlds of business, entertainment, fashion, film, journalism, literature, music, politics, religion, sports, and television.

Many activists supported outing, but others condemned it. Some endorsed outing in principle, but criticized its use in specific cases, especially when it targeted public figures who supported LGBT rights or when it was used against women and people of color, who faced unique challenges in the public sphere. Some questioned the class politics of outing, since job loss was one of its potential consequences. Outing was also attacked for violating sexual privacy, which seemed at odds with the goals of LGBT and queer activism, and for presuming that all people who engaged in same-sex sex were gay or lesbian, which conflicted with queer critiques of identity politics. Some critics of outing were uninterested in claiming as LGBT anyone who did not want to be known as such, since this did not promote LGBT pride. Nevertheless, the outing debates of the late 1980s and early 1990s, which challenged the movement's ideas about privacy, publicity, and politics, were another sign that LGBT activism was changing.

Fast forward twenty years and it is difficult to predict the future of queer activism. Queer criticisms of the mainstream LGBT movement continue, but it is now common to conflate the queer and LGBT movements. Some queer activists still dream of a broad-based movement of gender and sexual dissidence, yet there is little evidence that many non-LGBT people see themselves as queer. Queer theorists continue to critique gay and lesbian identity politics, but they often do so without seeming to recognize the salience of gender and sexual identities (including their own) in the past and present. Nor do they seem to acknowledge that identities do not have to be understood as fixed and innate; they can be viewed as flexible, fluid, performative, political, and strategic. Queers have offered powerful criticisms of mainstream gay and lesbian politics, but they have been less successful at developing alternative agendas for gender and sexual change. As some activists and academics declare that queer theory is dead and announce the arrival of post-queer politics, it is difficult to know how queer the future will be.

LGBT Movement Successes and Failures

While the rise of queer activism has been one of the most notable developments in gender and sexual politics in the 1990s and early 2000s, another has been the remarkable accomplishments of the LGBT movement. Most historians are critical of simplistic narratives that assume that progress over time is inevitable and linear, but it also can be misguided to deny the existence of progress when it is defined in specific ways and when it is evident in the historical record. Social conservatives and radical queers may question the desirability of many recent LGBT movement achievements, but the fact that the movement has made progress toward reaching many of its self-defined goals is more difficult to challenge. At the same time, it is difficult to deny that many of the movement's goals—and especially its more radical ones—have not been achieved.

Several explanations have been offered for why the movement has accomplished as much as it has in this period. Some point to shifts in the general political environment. Republicans, for example, won five of six U.S. presidential elections in the period from 1968 to 1988, but Democrats won three of five from 1992 to 2008. While most national elections since the 1950s have yielded divided government, in 1992 and 2008 the Democrats won control of the White House and Congress. Having become a recognized part of the Democratic electoral coalition, the LGBT movement was able to reap some rewards when its allies took power. The international political environment also has encouraged change in the United States. As various countries have decriminalized same-sex sex, legalized same-sex marriage, and adopted other gender and sexual reforms, many U.S. politicians and policymakers have realized that it is difficult to present the United States as a world leader in protecting and defending human rights when it lags behind other countries in promoting LGBT freedom and equality.

Other explanations for the movement's recent successes focus on social and cultural developments. Some highlight the effects of changing gender relations, family structures, and sexual cultures, which have created more supportive contexts for gender and sexual diversity. As more women have entered traditionally male spheres of work, leisure, and politics; as rates of divorce, nonmarital cohabitation, nonmarital reproduction, and interracial marriage have increased; as the number of childless, single-parent, and two-income households has grown; and as gender and sexual mores have changed, more people have adopted "live and let live" attitudes. Others emphasize the social and cultural effects of AIDS, which have increased compassion for, identification with, and understanding of LGBT Americans. Still others point to the influence of recent increases in LGBT visibility, which have contributed to more tolerance and acceptance, especially among younger people; recent public opinion polls suggest that personal connections with LGBT people are positively correlated with support for their rights and freedoms.

While these explanations focus on the effects of political, social, and cultural liberalization, others argue that the movement's successes are attributable to the fact that many of its recent demands have resonated with the country's conservative values. Struggles for privacy rights are arguably consistent with antigovernment sensibilities. Campaigns for the legalization of same-sex marriage, domestic partner benefits, and LGBT reproductive rights are in some respects based on traditional family values. Efforts to end the ban on LGBT service in the armed forces are in many ways an affirmation of U.S. militarism, nationalism, and patriotism. Attempts to promote LGBT business reform can be seen as a way to strengthen corporate capitalism. Trans struggles can affirm binary and conservative gender norms. As the movement has increasingly based its demands for rights on claims about the fixed and innate nature of LGBT identities, it has sacrificed its radical aspirations to liberate everyone's gender and sexual desires. Many who attribute the movement's recent successes to its conservative agendas and arguments see LGBT normalization as the price of and ticket to success.

All of these factors help explain the achievements of the LGBT movement in the 1990s and early 2000s. *Rethinking the Gay and Lesbian Movement*, however, underscores the significance of another important contribution: the work of the gay and lesbian movement from 1950 to 1990. For better and for worse, gay and lesbian activism in the 1950s, 1960s, 1970s, and 1980s shaped the character and content of LGBT social change after 1990. We can see this by reviewing the main spheres of LGBT activism in the past and present.

One major goal of the movement before 1990 was to end the AIDS epidemic. While this has not been achieved, gay and lesbian activists in the 1950s, 1960s, and 1970s laid the foundations for strong responses to the epidemic during and after the 1980s. Gay and lesbian political groups that were established in the 1960s and 1970s, for example, were critical first responders when AIDS was initially recognized. This was also the case for gay and lesbian media publications, community centers, health projects, and STD initiatives. Gay liberation, lesbian feminism, gay and lesbian liberalism, and multicultural gay and lesbian activism, which were powerful movement tendencies in the 1960s and 1970s, influenced the sexual, gender, racial, and class politics of AIDS activism. Gay and lesbian political strategies from the 1950s, 1960s, and 1970s, which included lobbying, litigation, media activism, and direct action protest, were adapted for use in the struggle against AIDS. Since 1981, AIDS has been at the center of gay and lesbian politics, and the influence of the gay and lesbian movement's first decade of AIDS activism, which saved and extended millions of lives, remains strong today.

In the 1990s and early 2000s, LGBT and AIDS activists have continued to play leading roles in AIDS education, prevention, and treatment, while also contributing to the fight against AIDS-related bias, discrimination, and prejudice. More AIDS activists have come to be recognized and valued for their expertise by politicians, policymakers, researchers, and scientists. Multicultural LGBT and AIDS activists have highlighted the devastating effects of AIDS on people of color in general and LGBT people of color in particular. LGBT and AIDS activists have contributed to treatment breakthroughs and have helped expand access to AIDS drugs inside and outside the United States. They have helped build the case for universal healthcare in the United States, inspired patient empowerment movements, and increased attention to the global dimensions of AIDS.

At the same time, LGBT and AIDS activists have not succeeded in ending the epidemic. They have helped slow its spread and reduce its rate of increase, but more people contract HIV and develop AIDS each year. In 2011, more than one million people in the United States are living with HIV/AIDS. Approximately half are said to be men who have sex with men; approximately half are said to be African American; many are African American men who have sex with men. Approximately 600,000 people have died of AIDS-related illnesses in the United States. Millions have died around the world. Discrimination against people with HIV and AIDS remains pervasive. Restrictions on sex education and AIDS education continue to undermine the struggle against the epidemic. Many people continue to associate HIV transmission with sexual identities rather than sex, drug, and other practices. Exorbitant healthcare costs and drug prices still leave treatment out of reach for many people inside and outside the United States.

For a variety of reasons, the strength and vitality of radical AIDS activism declined in the 1990s and early 2000s. In the early 1990s, the ACT UP movement began to weaken. After years of intense political activity, many ACT UP activists burned out, various movement groups lost their ability to overcome internal conflicts, and large numbers of AIDS activists shifted their attention to AIDS policy-making, AIDS service provision, and queer activism. The ACT UP movement also was affected by perceptions of increased government responsiveness to LGBT and AIDS issues, which led more activists to favor lobbying and litigation over direct action protest. While AIDS activism reinvented itself in the 1990s and early 2000s, with particularly important campaigns that have focused on people of color and the Global South, AIDS remains a major LGBT problem, a major U.S. problem, and a major global problem.

A second important goal of the pre-1990 movement was sex law reform and especially the elimination of oppressive police practices and the decriminalization of same-sex sex. Here, too, the first four decades of gay and lesbian activism laid the foundation for significant developments in more recent years. Directly and indirectly, the movement contributed greatly to sex law reform in the 1950s, 1960s, 1970s, and 1980s. Activist campaigns led to reductions in antihomosexual police conduct, including sexual entrapment and routine harassment of gay and lesbian people and places. Police raids on gay and lesbian bars, for example, were common at mid-century; by 1990 they were rare. The movement also helped convince many states and municipalities to repeal or overturn their laws against cross-dressing and other gender and sex crimes. Sodomy law reform began in the 1960s and picked up speed in the 1970s. There were fewer successes in the 1980s, but by 1990 twenty-five states had repealed or invalidated their sodomy laws.

Building on their earlier work, LGBT activists convinced twelve more states to decriminalize sodomy in the 1990s and early 2000s. In contrast to the pre-1990 era, this occurred primarily through court-based litigation rather than legislative action. By 2003, when the U.S. Supreme Court announced its decision in *Lawrence v. Texas*, thirteen states still banned sodomy. In four of these states, including Texas, the law only applied to same-sex sex. Sodomy laws were rarely enforced, but they were frequently invoked by opponents of gay and lesbian rights and they carried immense symbolic weight. *Lawrence* concerned a white man and a black man who had been arrested, jailed, and convicted for having consensual sex in a private apartment; the police had entered the white man's apartment based on a false report that there was an armed black man on the premises. In its decision, the Supreme Court (with seven Republican and two Democratic appointees) overturned its 1986 ruling in *Bowers*. According to the majority, state sodomy laws, when they criminalized private sex by consenting adults, violated constitutional privacy rights. Most gay and lesbian rights advocates regarded this as one of the movement's greatest successes ever.

Notwithstanding this achievement, the *Lawrence* decision did not mark the end of the struggle for the decriminalization of consensual sex or the elimination of anti-LGBT police practices. Future U.S. presidential elections and Supreme Court appointments could lead to the recriminalization of sodomy; some believe that the Court in 2012 is one vote shy of reversing *Lawrence*. In the meantime, state and local governments still ban what they classify as public sex and sexual solicitation. Some states continue to use different ages of consent for same-sex and cross-sex sex; some set the age of consent as high as eighteen; some ban sex between partners just above and just below the age of consent (so that, say, an eighteen-year-old can be charged with a sex crime for having sex with a seventeen-year-old). Several states and thousands of municipalities maintain restrictions on what they define as non-marital and nonfamilial cohabitation. Local police still target LGBT people, same-sex sex, and cross-gender conduct in their enforcement of laws against disorderly conduct, public sex, and sexual solicitation; people of color, sex workers, trans people, and young people remain distinctly vulnerable. They also continue to discriminate against LGBT crime victims, many of whom are revictimized by the criminal justice system, and they have not successfully addressed the pervasive nature of anti-LGBT violence. Federal courts have held that the *Lawrence* decision applies to the armed forces, but there continue to be rules against same-sex sex and transgender conduct in the U.S. military and in federal and state prisons. Even if consensual sex acts were decriminalized and antihomosexual police practices were eliminated in all U.S. jurisdictions, sexual freedom and equality would not be achieved until U.S. society stopped privileging heterosexuality.

A third major goal of gay and lesbian activism from 1950 through 1990 was obscenity law reform and the elimination of antihomosexual censorship. Over the course of the 1950s, 1960s, 1970s, and 1980s, the movement won many victories in obscenity cases and reduced the scope of censorship in the United States. Gay and lesbian activists helped limit the suppression of homophile periodicals and physique magazines in the 1950s and 1960s; then they successfully challenged the censorship of more sexually explicit materials in the 1970s and 1980s. By the early 1990s, LGBT representations in general and same-sex sexual representations in particular were commonly accessible in books, films, magazines, newspapers, and videos. In the 1990s and early 2000s, changing technologies and the growth of the internet have contributed to the proliferation of LGBT representations, but so has the work of LGBT activists.

In this area, too, the movement has not achieved all of its goals. Over the last two decades, the U.S. Supreme Court has continued to rule that obscenity is not protected by the U.S. Constitution and it still defines obscenity in ways that discriminate against LGBT sexual expression. The courts continue to treat sexual speech as a special case; they permit far more restrictions on sexual representations than they do on violent ones. The courts still maintain that prison officials cannot prevent inmates from receiving sexual publications in general, but can block homosexual contents. Many municipalities use zoning laws to restrict the locations of sex businesses, including those that specialize in LGBT books, films, periodicals, videos, and DVDs. In the 1990s, the Supreme Court ruled that the National Endowment for the Arts could take "decency" into consideration when making decisions about federally funded grants; in the early twenty-first century, the National Endowment for the Humanities has overruled its own expert panels to veto grants for projects that address gay and lesbian history. The U.S. federal government and many state and local governments still impose anti-LGBT content restrictions on publicly funded AIDS education and sex education programs. Many of these programs still focus primarily or exclusively on sexual abstinence outside of marriage. Even in the absence of legal restrictions on LGBT materials, popular culture tends to favor and foster heterosexual and gender-normative values.

A fourth important goal of the gay and lesbian movement from 1950 through 1990 was the enactment of antidiscrimination laws and the elimination of discriminatory policies and practices by all levels of government. In the 1950s and 1960s, homophile activists began to have success in challenging sexual orientation discrimination by the police, the Post Office, and the Civil Service Commission. Many more victories followed in the 1970s and 1980s. By the early 1990s, the Civil Service Commission banned sexual orientation discrimination in most federal government jobs, federal legislation mandated the collection of statistics on anti-homosexual hate crimes, and the United States no longer excluded and deported gay and lesbian aliens as psychopathic personalities or sexual deviates. Two states had laws that restricted sexual orientation discrimination in employment, housing, and public accommodations; ten more banned antihomosexual discrimination in public employment. More than eighty cities and counties restricted sexual orientation discrimination in public employment; some of these laws also covered gender identity, gender expression, housing, and/or public accommodations. By 1990, trans activists had convinced twenty states to permit transsexuals to change their legal sex.

In the 1990s and early 2000s, the LGBT movement has contributed to the adoption of more antidiscrimination laws and the elimination of more discriminatory government policies and practices. In 1996, gay and lesbian advocates won an important victory when they persuaded the U.S. Supreme Court, which was dominated by Republican appointees, to strike down a Colorado state constitutional amendment that invalidated all state and local laws against sexual orientation discrimination and prohibited all state and local government recognition of sexual orientation discrimination claims. According to the Court's ruling in *Romer v. Evans*, the amendment violated the U.S. Constitution's equal protection clause. As of 2012, the LGBT movement has convinced sixteen states and Washington, D.C., to enact relatively comprehensive laws against discrimination based on sexual orientation, gender identity, and gender expression in employment, housing, and public accommodations. Fifteen additional states have less comprehensive laws (covering, for example, sexual orientation discrimination in public employment). More than 175 cities and counties have adopted laws against employment discrimination based on sexual orientation; more than 135 restrict employment discrimination based on gender identity and/or gender expression. Many of these local laws also apply to housing and public accommodations. In the 1990s and early 2000s, most voter initiatives to repeal general laws against sexual orientation and gender identity discrimination have failed.

In the last two decades, the LGBT movement has convinced the federal government to adopt antidiscrimination initiatives as well. As of 2012, the U.S. federal government and most states permit transsexuals to change their legal sex. The United States and thirty-one states have passed hate crimes statutes that apply to crimes motivated by real or perceived sexual orientation; these laws provide for criminal penalties, enhanced penalties, and supplemental investigative and prosecutorial resources for specified types of federal and state hate crimes. The United States and thirteen states have enacted laws that apply to hate crimes motivated by antitrans prejudice. The U.S. federal government now accepts asylum claims based on sexual orientation, gender identity, and gender expression. In the early 1990s, the movement convinced President Bill Clinton to propose an end to the ban on homosexuals in the U.S. military. Strong opposition led to the adoption of the "don't ask, don't tell" policy, which permitted gays, lesbians, and bisexuals to serve as long as they did not disclose their homosexuality, directly or indirectly, to the military. This was presented as a liberal reform, since service members would no longer be questioned routinely about their sexual identities and practices, but more than 14,000 people were discharged under the policy. After years of lobbying and litigation, in 2010 Congress authorized the termination of "don't ask, don't tell," which President Barack Obama ordered in 2011. This was another major movement achievement.

Notwithstanding these successes, anti-LGBT discrimination remains pervasive and legal remedies are limited in the United States. In nineteen states and countless local jurisdictions, there are no specific laws that restrict discrimination based on sexual orientation, gender identity, or gender expression. In these locations, there is little legal recourse when people are fired from their jobs, denied housing, or excluded from public accommodations because of anti-LGBT prejudice. In fifteen other states and many municipalities, antidiscrimination laws do not apply to gender identity or gender expression or only apply to public sector jobs. Even in the sixteen states and more than 100 municipalities where there are relatively comprehensive antidiscrimination laws, there are exemptions for religious institutions, the laws do not apply to federal policies and practices, they mostly do not apply to marriage, and they do not prohibit most forms of private discrimination. In 2000, for example, the U.S. Supreme Court ruled that the Boy Scouts could expel a New Jersey assistant scoutmaster because the state's law against sexual orientation discrimination does not apply to private associations. Thirty-seven states do not have relatively comprehensive hate crimes laws (and most crimes fall under state rather than federal jurisdiction). Moreover, as valuable as antidiscrimination laws are, they do not and cannot address many forms of discrimination, especially when those who wish to discriminate find ways to do so without violating the letter of the law.

At the federal level, legislation to restrict employment discrimination on the basis of sexual orientation and gender identity has been endorsed by approximately 150 House and forty Senate members as of 2012, this is well shy of the numbers needed for passage. In any case, the legislation does not cover housing or public accommodations, it exempts military and religious employers, it does not apply to businesses with fewer than fifteen workers, and some versions of the legislation have deleted the gender identity provisions. Meanwhile, the federal courts have held that discrimination based on sexual orientation, in contrast to discrimination based on race, religion, and gender, is subject to only minimum judicial scrutiny, which in practice means almost no scrutiny at all. There are federal and state restrictions on who may change their legal sex; many jurisdictions, for example, require medical certifications and specific surgeries, while also limiting access to trans healthcare. The U.S. immigration and asylum systems discriminate on the basis of sexual orientation and gender identity by not recognizing many LGBT families, marriages, and relationships and not accepting many asylum claims related to anti-LGBT persecution. Victories in asylum cases are often accompanied by racist denunciations of gender and sexual practices in the Global South. Trans people are still barred from serving openly in the military. Trans veterans are still denied trans-related healthcare. Federal, state, and local governments continue to preserve and protect sexual discrimination.

A fifth major goal of the movement from 1950 through 1990 was legal equality, freedom, and recognition for gay and lesbian families, marriages, partnerships, and relationships. In the 1950s and 1960s, movement advocates began to promote the legalization of same-sex marriage, equal treatment for same-sex relationships, and gay and lesbian parenting rights. In the 1970s and 1980s, they began to win occasional victories in parental custody and visitation cases. Some states began to permit gays and lesbians to adopt children and serve as foster parents. Several municipalities began to provide limited same-sex partner benefits for public sector employees. Some courts began to recognize same-sex partners as family members.

In the 1990s and early 2000s, the movement has had much greater success in promoting family, marriage, partnership, and relationship rights and benefits. In 1997, Hawaii began allowing same-sex couples to register as reciprocal beneficiaries and thereby gain access to a limited set of benefits ordinarily reserved for married couples. In 1999, California created a domestic partnership registry, which allowed same-sex couples to have access to several benefits ordinarily available to married people only. In 2000, Vermont became the first state to legalize same-sex civil unions; this provided registered same-sex couples with all the rights and benefits granted by the state to married couples except the right to marry. In 2003, the Massachusetts Supreme Judicial Court ruled that the state's refusal to grant marriage licenses to same-sex couples violated state-based marriage and equality rights. The following year, Massachusetts began granting marriage licenses to same-sex couples.

As of 2012, eight states (Connecticut, Iowa, Maryland Massachusetts, New Hampshire, New York, and Vermont and Washington), Washington, D.C., and two Native American tribes have legalized same-sex marriage; ten other states have legalized same-sex civil unions or domestic partnerships. The legalization of same-sex marriage in several states and the increased ability of transsexuals to change their legal sex have expanded trans access to marriage. Meanwhile, the federal government, sixteen states, and more than 150 cities and counties provide limited same-sex partner benefits to public sector workers. As of 2012, the vast majority of states permit gays and lesbians to adopt children and serve as foster parents (in some cases as individuals, in some as couples). About half permit second-parent adoptions by the partners of gay and lesbian parents. Fifteen allow same-sex couples to adopt children jointly. Some do not permit discrimination based on sexual orientation and gender identity in parental custody and visitation decisions.

While the movement has won important victories in its efforts to improve the legal status of LGBT families, marriages, partnerships, and relationships, it has encountered significant obstacles and suffered major setbacks. Conservative activists continue to campaign aggressively against same-sex marriage, claiming that its legalization will demean and destroy heterosexual marriage. As of 2012, forty-two states do not allow same-sex couples to marry within their borders. More than forty states have enacted statutes or adopted constitutional amendments that explicitly deny legal recognition of same-sex marriages. Many prohibit government agencies and public institutions from extending domestic partnership benefits to same-sex couples. Of the states that have not legalized same-sex marriage, thirty-two do not recognize same-sex domestic partnerships or civil unions. Most state and local jurisdictions do not provide domestic partner benefits (including health insurance) for government workers. Those that offer some benefits do not provide the full range that are available to married employees. Meanwhile, transsexuals confront a complicated set of restrictions on marriage: depending on whom and where they want to marry, they are affected by laws against same-sex marriage, laws that limit their ability to change their legal sex, and policies and practices that apply to transsexual marriage specifically.

The LGBT marriage equality movement also has had limited success and suffered setbacks at the federal level. The Defense of Marriage Act (DOMA), passed by Congress and signed into law by President Clinton in 1996, defines marriage as the union of one man and one woman and denies federal recognition of same-sex marriages. DOMA is currently being challenged in the courts, but as of 2012 married same-sex couples are denied access to more than 1000 federal rights and benefits linked to marriage. These include immigration, inheritance, Medicaid, Social Security, tax, and veterans' benefits, along with a wide range of benefits (including healthcare and health insurance) that are provided to military service members and federal government workers who are married. The federal government has expanded the list of domestic partner benefits that are provided to its employees, but the list does not include most of the benefits that are provided to workers whose marriages are recognized by the federal government.

As for parenting, in 2012 several states still formally restrict the ability of LGBT people to adopt children individually or jointly, serve as foster parents, or arrange for second-parent adoptions. Several restrict the ability of LGBT people to adopt or serve as foster parents through policies that favor people whose marriages are recognized by the state. Many states have not resolved the question of whether same-sex couples may jointly adopt children or petition for second-parent adoptions. In many jurisdictions, government officials, family court judges, and social workers discriminate against LGBT people in adoption and foster care cases and in decisions about child custody and parental visitation.

For many radical queer activists, the struggle for same-sex marriage best illustrates what is wrong with the mainstream LGBT movement today. Marriage, some say, was never a major gay and lesbian goal; it was pushed by a limited number of movement leaders, who then disclaimed responsibility for placing it at the top of the LGBT agenda. Some argue that marriage has been an oppressive institution for women and has contributed to the mistreatment of children, people of color, and poor people. Why would LGBT people want to gain access to a heteronormative institution and further institutionalize discrimination against the unmarried, they ask? Why not campaign for universal healthcare, for example, rather than use arguments about spousal healthcare benefits to gain access to marriage? Some queers argue that marriage, insofar as it is based on domesticity and monogamy, is inconsistent with sexual freedom, which is a core queer value. Why should the state privilege couples rather than singles or trios or networks or other types of relationship, they wonder? If the state must have a role in offering special rights and benefits to people involved in certain types of relationships, why not offer a more flexible menu of options so that individuals could distribute these rights and benefits as they saw fit? Some queers ask why the state should have any role in recognizing or legitimizing personal relationships. Why not disestablish marriage, removing its connections to the state in much the same way that Christian churches were disestablished in past centuries? People could then marry religiously (or nonreligiously), but the disestablishment of marriage would sever the state's relationship to marriage. For many queer activists, the struggle for same-sex marriage offers inclusion on heteronormative terms and is inconsistent with the pursuit of freedom and equality. Whether or not one agrees with these criticisms, it is important to acknowledge that they are not new; the movement has been debating and discussing these issues since the 1950s.

While the LGBT movement of the 1990s and early 2000s has pursued reform in the five policy areas highlighted above, it also has participated in electoral politics. In this case, too, recent activists have followed up on earlier movement initiatives.

In the 1950s and 1960s, homophile activists began to focus on electoral politics and gay and lesbian voters began to play significant electoral roles in several local jurisdictions. In the 1970s and 1980s, gay and lesbian citizens influenced more election outcomes, several openly gay and lesbian candidates were elected to positions in local and state government, and two openly gay men were elected to the U.S. House. During this period, the gay and lesbian movement began to be recognized as part of the Democratic Party's electoral coalition, the Democrats began to support more gay and lesbian policy initiatives, and gay and lesbian Republicans began to organize.

In the 1990s and early 2000s, more openly LGBT candidates have been elected. Over the course of this period, there have been six openly gay or lesbian U.S. representatives (Democrats Barney Frank of Massachusetts, Tammy Baldwin of Wisconsin, Jared Polis of Colorado, and David Cicilline of Rhode Island and Republicans Jim Kolbe of Arizona and Steve Gunderson of Wisconsin). As of 2012, two openly lesbian women and one openly gay man have been appointed as federal district court judges. At the state level, one governor, Democrat James McGreevey of New Jersey, has publicly acknowledged his homosexuality. Approximately thirty states have had openly gay, lesbian, or bisexual state legislators. Massachusetts was reportedly the first to elect a trans state legislator (Althea Garrison). As of 2012, more than twenty U.S. cities have elected openly gay or lesbian mayors; some of the largest have been Houston, Portland (Oregon), Lexington (Kentucky), Providence, and Hartford. In 2008, Stu Rasmussen of Silverton, Oregon, reportedly became the country's first openly trans mayor. In 2010, Victoria Kolakowski of Alameda County (California) reportedly became the first openly trans elected judge. As of 2012, there have been more than 100 openly LGBT state and local judges and more than 500 openly LGBT state and local elected officials in the United States.

Notwithstanding the increased successes of openly LGBT candidates, it remains exceedingly difficult for them to win election or appointment to the highest positions in national politics. There has never been an openly LGBT U.S. president, vice president, cabinet member, Supreme Court justice, or senator. There have been openly gay and lesbian members of the U.S. House, but none who is openly trans. In 2012, less than one percent of U.S. senators and representatives are openly gay or lesbian and none of these is a Republican. Republican House member Mark Foley of Florida came out as gay after he resigned in the midst of a 2006 sex scandal. Republican Senator Larry Craig was arrested for lewd conduct in a men's bathroom in 2007, but denied that he was gay and did not run for re-election. As of 2012, no openly LGBT person has won appointment to the federal court of appeals (the level just below the Supreme Court); one was nominated in 2010, but his appointment was blocked by Republican Senators in 2011. Less than 1 percent of federal district court judges are openly gay or lesbian. As for state and local government, very few openly LGBT candidates have been elected to statewide office. Governor McGreevey announced his resignation in the same 2004 speech in which he came out as gay. Approximately twenty states have never elected an openly LGBT state legislator. Only one of the country's largest twenty-five cities has elected an openly LGBT mayor. The number of openly LGBT elected officials has increased, but it remains a tiny fraction of the total.

In the 1990s and early 2000s, the movement has had greater success in promoting the election of LGBT rights supporters. In recent national elections, approximately 35–60 percent of the voting age population has voted. If LGBT election participation rates are similar, many LGBT people have not voted. The reasons likely relate to political disengagement and disinterest, along with the sense that the political system is not responsive to their needs, the belief that their votes will not matter, and the conviction that the differences between the two major political parties are not that great. Many queers, like many other radicals, believe that electoral politics are not effective vehicles for promoting social change. All of that said, in the last few national elections, 3 to 4 percent of voters have reported that they are gay, lesbian, or bisexual. Of these, 70 to 80 percent have voted for the Democrats, 20 to 30 percent for the Republicans, and smaller numbers for other parties. We do not know whether trans people and people who engage in same-sex sex but do not identify as gay, lesbian, or bisexual (or do not tell pollsters that they do) similarly lean toward the Democrats.

The movement's success in promoting the election of LGBT rights supporters helps explain many of its legislative and litigation victories in the 1990s and early 2000s. Democratic presidents Clinton (1993–2001) and Obama (2009–present) campaigned for LGBT votes, accepted invitations to speak to LGBT groups, and supported significant LGBT reforms. Democratic majorities in the House (1990–95 and 2007–11) and Senate (1990–95, 2001–3 and 2007–12) have enacted some LGBT rights legislation and blocked some anti-LGBT measures. In 2008, there were more than 300 LGBT delegates and alternates at the Democratic Party convention; this was approximately 6 percent of the total. In the same year, there were two dozen LGBT delegates and alternates at the Republican convention. Though they have risked alienating conservatives in their party, a small number of Republican politicians and Republican-appointed judges have played critical roles in several major LGBT reforms, including the U.S. Supreme Court's invalidation of sodomy laws in *Lawrence*, New York's legalization of same-sex marriage, and Congress's repeal of "don't ask, don't tell."

In the last two decades, the movement also has experienced setbacks in its efforts to promote the election of LGBT rights supporters. U.S. Presidents George H. W. Bush (1989–93) and George W. Bush (2001–9) were not strong supporters of LGBT rights. Republican majorities in the House (1995–2007 and 2011–12) and Senate (1995–2001 and 2003–7) have blocked LGBT reforms. The Supreme Court has been dominated by Republican appointees and has become more conservative since the 1970s. Even when the Democrats have controlled the White House and Congress, weak party discipline and weak support for LGBT rights have meant that conservative Democrats and Republicans could reject reform initiatives. In some instances, Democrats have championed anti-LGBT legislation. "Don't ask, don't tell" was adopted in 1993, when the Democrats controlled the White House and Congress. In 1996, the Senate voted 85–14 and the House voted 342–67 to pass DOMA, which President Clinton then signed. President Obama has not endorsed the legalization of same-sex marriage. Meanwhile, conservative leaders and activists have campaigned against LGBT rights supporters in both major parties. Christian Right and Tea Party conservatives have punished Republican defenders of LGBT rights by supporting more conservative candidates. In the context of strong Republican opposition to and significant Democratic ambivalence about LGBT rights, there are good reasons to be pessimistic about the prospects of achieving full LGBT freedom and equality through electoral politics, though the movement will likely need the support of elected officials to achieve its goals.

The LGBT movement of the 1990s and early 2000s, like the gay and lesbian movement of 1950–90, has targeted more than just law, politics, and policy. Four major spheres of LGBT activism have been science, business, religion, and popular culture. In the case of science, recent activists have followed through on movement initiatives that began much earlier. Homophile activists in the 1950s and 1960s challenged medical, psychiatric, and scientific perspectives on sex, gender, and sexuality; their efforts culminated in 1973, when the American Psychiatric Association declassified homosexuality as a mental disorder. In the late 1970s and 1980s, the movement convinced the APA to remove "sexual orientation disturbance" and "ego dystonic homosexuality" from its list of disorders. Gay and lesbian activists contributed to significant improvements in gay and lesbian healthcare in the 1970s and played leading roles in challenging and supporting scientific responses to AIDS in the 1980s. Throughout this period, the movement criticized gender and sexual bias in various types of scientific research.

Since 1990, LGBT activists have continued to challenge anti-LGBT tendencies in psychiatry, psychology, and psychoanalysis. For example, some have criticized the pathologizing aspects of the APA's "gender identity disorder" diagnosis, denounced experts who testify against homosexuality and transgenderism in legislative hearings and court cases, and renounced specialists who mistreat LGBT clients and patients. The movement has fought successfully for improvements in LGBT healthcare, LGBT reproductive services, and AIDS education, prevention, and treatment. Activists have forcefully disputed the claims of scientists who promote "cures" for homosexuality and transgenderism. They also have raised compelling questions about the motivations, methods, and effects of scientific studies that try to explain why some people are LGBT (and, less often, why some people are not).

While the movement's efforts to challenge anti-LGBT science have succeeded in many respects, they also have failed. Small but influential groups of psychiatrists, psychologists, and psychoanalysts continue to promote the notion that homosexuality is a mental disorder; some emphasize the desirability and feasibility of "cures." Medical experts still force transsexuals and transgenders to be diagnosed with "gender identity disorders" before they will provide surgeries and hormones. Many healthcare providers do not treat LGBT people with care and consideration, do not educate themselves about LGBT healthcare needs, and do not provide appropriate health and reproductive services for LGBT patients. Gender and sexual bias continues to affect AIDS education, prevention, and treatment. Scientific education and research still promote conservative ideas about sex, gender, and sexuality. Many scientific projects that offer biological or familial explanations of why some people are LGBT rest on problematic assumptions about sex, gender, and sexuality. Many people who use science to support the notion that LGBT people are "born this way" assert that this must be true because no one would choose to be LGBT, which makes LGBT identities and practices seem profoundly undesirable. Many scientists continue to presume that homosexuality and heterosexuality are mutually exclusive; they do the same for male and female identities. Many activists continue to place their faith in "good" science, but science continues to promote gender and sexual inequality.

A second nongovernmental target of LGBT activism has been business. In this case, too, recent movement initiatives can be traced back to the work of earlier gay and lesbian activists. In the 1950s and 1960s, the homophile movement began to document and criticize business-based sexual orientation discrimination, which affected both workers and consumers. In the 1970s and 1980s, gay and lesbian activists persuaded many businesses to adopt sexual orientation antidiscrimination policies and restrict AIDS-related discrimination. A smaller number of businesses began to provide domestic partner benefits and a few adopted policies against gender identity discrimination. Gay and lesbian activists formed productive alliances with the labor movement, which strengthened their efforts to reduce discriminatory business practices. The movement used lobbying, litigation, boycotts, direct action, and union activism to challenge businesses that discriminated against gays and lesbians, while also targeting gay and lesbian businesses that discriminated against people of color, trans people, and women.

Building on these achievements, the LGBT movement of the 1990s and early 2000s has had remarkable success in promoting business reform. As of 2012, 86 percent of the Fortune 500 (the largest publicly traded U.S. corporations) have adopted sexual orientation nondiscrimination policies; 50 percent have policies against gender identity discrimination. Approximately 60 percent offer same-sex partner benefits; 41 percent offer trans health benefits. In 2012, ten of the country's twenty largest corporations received 100 percent LGBT workplace equality ratings by the Human Rights Campaign, which looks at nondiscrimination policies, partner benefits, and trans health benefits, along with diversity training, LGBT employee groups and diversity councils, positive contributions to the external LGBT community, and the absence of major contributions to anti-LGBT campaigns and initiatives.

U.S. businesses, however, continue to support and sustain anti-LGBT discrimination. Many LGBT employees report ongoing problems with workplace bias, prejudice, and mistreatment. National movement boycotts of Cracker Barrel restaurants (1991–2002), which had a history of firing LGBT employees, and United

Airlines (1997–99), which refused to comply with a San Francisco domestic partner benefits law covering city contractors, were necessary before these companies agreed to change their policies and practices. In 2012, there is an ongoing boycott of Exxon-Mobil, which is the largest U.S. corporation without a policy against sexual orientation discrimination. (The other top twenty Fortune-ranked companies that received very low Human Rights Campaign ratings in 2012 are Berkshire Hathaway and Verizon.) Many large U.S. corporations have not adopted the minimum policies recommended by the mainstream LGBT movement. Others have done little more than the minimum; for example, many provide only limited domestic partner and trans health benefits. Smaller businesses are less likely to have taken even these minimum steps. Few large corporations have openly LGBT high-level executives, while LGBT people are also excluded from various white-, blue-, and pink-collar work sites. Many workplaces have a token LGBT employee but do not provide equal opportunities for LGBT workers. Countless businesses do not respond effectively to anti-LGBT bias, discrimination, harassment, and prejudice in the workplace.

As for the consumption side of business politics, many corporations use marketing strategies that promote dominant gender and sexual norms. For example, LGBT images and representations are rarely featured in mainstream advertising, much of which promotes goods and services by selling conventional family life and hetero-sexual intimacy, love, pleasure, and romance. Large corporations and small busi-nesses, including some that advertise in LGBT venues and support LGBT pride events, provide large sums of money to anti-LGBT political candidates and cam-paigns. Many also mistreat LGBT clients, consumers, and customers. During the week that this paragraph was drafted in 2011, a lesbian was forced to leave a Southwest Airlines flight after a fellow passenger complained that she was kissing her partner. This is just one small illustration of the ongoing nature of business-based gender and sexual discrimination.

A third target of recent LGBT activism has been organized religion, which the gay and lesbian movement began challenging in the pre-Stonewall era. In the 1950s and 1960s, homophile activists criticized religious doctrines, policies, and practices, promoted dialogue and discussion with Christian and Jewish leaders, established gay and lesbian groups for Roman Catholics, and formed autonomous gay and lesbian churches. In the 1970s and 1980s, gay and lesbian activists convinced several Christian and Jewish denominations to reconsider their sexual values, provide space for gay and lesbian groups, establish gay and lesbian caucuses, ordain gay and lesbian religious leaders, endorse same-sex commitment ceremonies, and participate in gay and lesbian law reform campaigns. Hundreds of gay and lesbian Christian churches and Jewish congregations formed, as did associations of gay and lesbian atheists and groups for gay and lesbian members of various Christian, Jewish, Buddhist, and alternative religious traditions.

In the 1990s and early 2000s, the number of LGBT Christian churches, Jewish congregations, and Christian, Jewish, and Buddhist groups has grown, and LGBT

Bahais, Hindus, Muslims, and Sikhs have also established associations and organizations. As of 2012, several of the most liberal Christian and Jewish denominations—the Society of Friends, the Unitarian-Universalist Church, the United Church, Reconstructionist Judaism, and Reform Judaism—welcome LGBT members, allow for the ordination or recognition of LGBT religious leaders, and permit individual churches and congregations to offer religious ceremonies for same-sex unions and/ or marriages. The Evangelical Lutheran Church and Presbyterian Church (U.S.A.) have begun to ordain openly gay and lesbian ministers. The Episcopal Church has begun to ordain openly gay and lesbian priests. The United Methodist Church ordains openly gay and lesbian ministers if they agree to be celibate and permits trans pastors to retain their positions. The Episcopal Church and Presbyterian Church (U.S.A.) allow individual churches to bless same-sex unions; the Evangelical Lutheran Church plans to begin doing so. Conservative Judaism has approved the ordination of gay and lesbian rabbis and also permits individual congregations to offer same-sex commitment ceremonies. Some Orthodox Jewish, Conservative Jewish, and Muslim authorities have accepted the religious legitimacy of sex reassignment surgery. There is at least one openly gay Muslim imam in the United States and he has performed same-sex marriage ceremonies. Even in more conservative religious traditions, there are dissident movements that promote LGBT acceptance and inclusion.

Notwithstanding these signs of change, most of the largest religious denominations in the United States strongly reject homosexuality, which they regard as sinful. They arguably are more outspoken in their opposition to homosexuality today than they were before the founding of the gay and lesbian movement. Three of the four largest churches in the United States (the Roman Catholic Church, the Southern Baptist Convention, and the Church of Jesus Christ of Latter-Day Saints) are leading opponents of LGBT rights and freedoms. Eastern Orthodox Christianity, Orthodox Judaism, and Sunni and Shia Islam are strongly critical of homosexuality, as are most fundamentalist and evangelical Protestant churches. Many of these denominations actively campaign against gay and lesbian equality. Most reject transgenderism. The Episcopal Church, Evangelical Lutheran Church, Presbyterian Church (U.S.A.), and Conservative Judaism have taken significant liberalizing steps, but few openly LGBT ministers and rabbis have been ordained within these traditions; many of their member churches and congregations decline to perform same-sex commitment ceremonies; many continue to regard oral and/or anal sex as sinful; and disagreements about LGBT issues have led to major denominational schisms. Even within some of the most liberal denominations, there are many individual churches and congregations that reject homosexuality and transgenderism and many that disagree with the LGBT reforms that have been adopted by their regional, national, and transnational associations.

LGBT activists in the 1990s and early 2000s have also targeted popular culture and in so doing have followed up on the work of earlier gay and lesbian activists. In the 1950s and 1960s, homophile activists criticized book, film, magazine, newspaper, and television representations of homosexuality. They challenged the absence of representations in some contexts, attacked the predominance of negative representations in others, and promoted more respectful inclusion of gay and lesbian values, viewpoints, and voices in mainstream popular culture. In the 1970s and 1980s, the movement convinced many mainstream newspapers and magazines to improve their coverage of gay and lesbian issues. There were also significant breakthroughs in television and occasional breakthroughs in film. Throughout this period, the movement supported and sustained the development of gay and lesbian culture, which by 1990 featured an impressive array of gay and lesbian books, films, magazines, and newspapers and significant accomplishments in gay and lesbian art, dance, music, photography, poetry, and theater.

In the 1990s and early 2000s, the LGBT movement has built on the achievements of its gay and lesbian predecessors and achieved major changes in mainstream popular culture. Many major magazines, newspapers, and news-oriented radio shows, television programs, and internet websites have offered respectful coverage of LGBT stories, included LGBT people in other types of report, interviewed LGBT sources, hired LGBT staff, taken editorial positions in favor of LGBT rights, reviewed LGBT-themed books and films, and announced LGBT commitment ceremonies, marriages, and weddings. There have been dozens of major LGBT characters and storylines on popular television programs and in successful films and videos; many have been well received by LGBT audiences. Recent broadcast television examples include *Brothers and Sisters*, *Buffy*, *Dawson's Creek*, *Ellen*, *ER*, *Glee*, *Grey's Anatomy*, *L.A. Law*, *Melrose Place*, *Modern Family*, *My So-Called Life*, *Northern Exposure*, *Roseanne*, *Thirtysomething*, *Ugly Betty*, and *Will and Grace*; recent cable television examples include *The L Word*, *Nip/Tuck*, *Noah's Arc*, *Queer As Folk*, and *Six Feet Under*; recent film examples include *Boys Don't Cry*, *Brokeback Mountain*, *The Color Purple*, *The Hours*, and *Philadelphia*. There has been a significant number of openly LGBT reality show participants (on shows such as *Amazing Race*, *Dancing with the Stars*, *Real World*, and *Survivor*), talk show guests and hosts (including Ellen DeGeneres and RuPaul); and news program anchors, reporters, commentators, and hosts (including Don Lemon, Rachel Maddow, and Thomas Roberts). There also has been a large number of prominent actors, choreographers, dancers, and musicians who are openly LGBT and many others who are openly supportive of LGBT rights.

For many LGBT activists and especially for those who remember the pre-1990 era, the positive changes in recent popular culture have been astonishing, but there are also ongoing problems. Many newspapers, magazines, and news-oriented websites avoid covering LGBT news, only discuss LGBT people in LGBT-themed stories, decline to interview LGBT sources, do not hire openly LGBT staff, editorialize against LGBT rights, and promote the views of anti-LGBT conservatives. Many periodicals and websites that offer relatively balanced or sympathetic coverage of LGBT news also publish articles, columns, editorials, and letters that attack LGBT people in ways that would not be permitted if other groups were targeted. Many conservative and Christian periodicals, radio shows, and television programs promote anti-LGBT hate and hostility. While the number of major LGBT television characters and storylines has increased, it is still quite small; according to a 2011 report by the Gay and Lesbian Alliance Against Defamation, 1 to 4 percent of scripted television series regulars in the previous several years were LGBT; few were women or people of color. It is far more likely to see LGBT television characters in artistic, comedy, sidekick, or victim roles than in roles as romantic leads, political leaders, police officers, athletic stars, or experts in law, medicine, or science. Many actors, directors, and others who work in television and film are not openly LGBT because they believe their careers would suffer if they came out publicly. While many LGBT actors, directors, and plots thrive in the world of alternative and independent cinema, they do not in mainstream Hollywood film, which continues to lag behind television in the quantity and quality of LGBT representations. LGBT amateur and professional athletes have come out in many sports, but many avoid doing so because of potentially negative repercussions in their athletic competitions and their financial endorsements and sponsorships. While there are many exceptions, U.S. popular culture discourages LGBT desires, acts, and identities.

In short, the LGBT movement has made substantial progress toward achieving its self-defined goals in the 1990s and early 2000s, but there is much more to be done. From a variety of queer perspectives, some of the LGBT movement's achievements are worthy of praise; some deserve criticism. Whatever one thinks about the desirability of recent LGBT reforms, however, the gay and lesbian movement of 1950–90 greatly influenced the process of social change after 1990. The reforms that have taken place did not just happen, happen spontaneously, or happen suddenly; in many respects, they occurred because there were collective, organized, and sustained efforts to promote change over a long period of time.

Back to School

There has been another important sphere of gay and lesbian, LGBT, and queer activism and it may have special relevance for the students and teachers who read this book. Many U.S. educational institutions examine and explore the history of political movements, but they also have been sites of movement activism. Political activists, for example, have helped convince many educational institutions to abandon policies and practices that excluded and segregated racial minorities, religious minorities, poor people, people with disabilities, and women. They also have helped persuade many primary, secondary, and postsecondary schools to establish learning units, courses, and programs in African American Studies, Asian American Studies, Disability Studies, Jewish Studies, Latino Studies, Native American Studies, and Women's Studies. As places of work and study for millions of U.S. Americans, educational institutions should not be ignored when thinking about social change. Students and teachers have not just studied political activism; they have been the agents and targets of political activism.

In the 1950s and 1960s, the gay and lesbian movement began to criticize the ways in which educational institutions addressed sexual matters. For example, they challenged the firing of gay and lesbian faculty, librarians, and staff; the expulsion of gay and lesbian students; the handling of sexual topics in courses on anthropology, biology, history, law, literature, medicine, politics, psychology, religion, and sociology; and the production of biased and prejudiced research. Homophile activists were invited to speak to college and university classes and to address student and faculty groups. They sponsored lectures, organized conferences, published articles, and distributed books that offered new ways of thinking about homosexuality. They initiated, participated in, and promoted promising research projects. Toward the end of the 1960s, gay and lesbian student and faculty groups began to form on college and university campuses, where they developed campaigns to promote gay and lesbian rights and freedoms.

In the 1970s and 1980s, the number of gay and lesbian student groups on college and university campuses expanded, high school groups and programs were established, and students fought successfully to have their groups recognized officially by their institutions. Students and faculty organized protests against antihomosexual speakers, teachers, and researchers; criticized the coverage of gay and lesbian subjects in campus newspapers; challenged campus healthcare providers who did not address gay and lesbian needs; fought back when gay and lesbian groups were denied access to space and resources; and developed programs to increase student awareness of gay and lesbian issues. Activists convinced many colleges and universities to adopt policies against sexual orientation discrimination in hiring and admissions; ban campus recruiters (including the U.S. military and various large corporations) that discriminated on the basis of sexual orientation; offer courses, lectures, and programs in gay and lesbian studies; address gay and lesbian issues in a variety of educational classes and contexts; and hire faculty with expertise on gay and lesbian subjects. Gay and lesbian activists also staged protests at academic conventions to challenge antihomosexual research, formed caucuses within scholarly disciplines, and promoted the development of gay and lesbian studies.

LGBT and queer activists in the 1990s and early 2000s have continued to fight for social change in U.S. educational institutions. In 2012, there are hundreds of primary and secondary schools with LGBT student groups, classroom teachers, and library resources, along with programs to address anti-LGBT bullying, harassment, and violence. In some locations, there are special schools and school programs for LGBT students. More schools treat LGBT parents and children with respect. In 2011, California became the first state to require its public schools to include the contributions of LGBT people in their social studies curricula.

California, however, is the only state that has done so. Many primary and secondary schools do not have strong sex education and AIDS education programs. Many do not have programs to deal with anti-LGBT bullying, harassment, and violence. Many do not ensure the safety and security of LGBT students and students perceived to be LGBT. Most do little about the hostile use of terms such as "faggot", "dyke", and "queer" and the casual use of offensive insults such as "that's so gay." Most do not explore LGBT topics in the arts, literature, or history. Most use foreign language, science, and social studies textbooks that are written as though LGBT people do not exist. In countless ways, most U.S. primary and secondary schools are failing their LGBT students and most are failing to teach their students about gender and sexual diversity.

The situation in colleges and universities is better, but falls far short of what is necessary to achieve educational excellence. Many colleges and universities have LGBT student groups, but many do not. Many have taken steps to address anti-LGBT discrimination in athletics, dormitories, fraternities, health services, restrooms, and sororities, but many have not. Many have policies against hate speech and hate crimes, but many LGBT students experience bias, prejudice, harassment, and violence on campus. Many colleges and universities have policies against discrimination based on sexual orientation, gender identity, and gender expression in admissions, hiring, tenure, and promotion, but many do not. Many LGBT faculty and staff are denied domestic partner benefits, healthcare benefits, and parental leaves. Many institutions with strong antidiscrimination policies practice indirect forms of discrimination, as is the case when departments refuse to hire specialists in LGBT studies, when tenure committees do not take anti-LGBT bias into consideration when assessing teaching evaluations, and when spousal hiring policies do not apply to LGBT faculty. Many colleges and universities have courses and programs in LGBT studies and queer studies and many address LGBT topics in courses and programs in feminist, gender, sexuality, and women's studies, but it is much less common to find these topics addressed in courses and textbooks in a variety of fields, including U.S. history.

Rethinking the history of the U.S. gay and lesbian movement could and should lead to the rethinking of U.S. history more generally. This will likely only occur, however, if more students, teachers, and scholars engage in political activism to change the ways in which history is learned and taught as a subject in primary, secondary, and postsecondary educational institutions. This might mean developing campaigns to encourage history departments to hire more specialists in LGBT studies, offer more courses on the LGBT past, assign more readings on LGBT topics, and do more to address LGBT issues in a variety of survey and specialized courses. It might mean writing to authors, editors, and publishers to complain about the inadequate treatment of LGBT topics in history textbooks. It might mean trying to convince LGBT, queer, gender, and sexuality studies programs to make the history of political activism more central in their courses and curricula. And it might mean developing new ways to promote critical thinking about LGBT history outside the classroom: in libraries and museums, on television and the internet, in film and video, and in various other venues. In these ways and in countless others, rethinking the history of the U.S. gay and lesbian movement could make important contributions to future struggles for freedom and equality.

NOTES

Introduction

1 Jonathan Ned Katz, *Gay American History* (1976; New York: Avon, 1978); Toby Marotta, *The Politics of Homosexuality* (Boston: Houghton Mifflin, 1981); John D'Emilio, *Sexual Politics, Sexual Communities: The Making of a Homosexual Minority in the United States, 1940–1970* (Chicago: University of Chicago Press, 1983).
2 See Lisa Duggan, "The Discipline Problem: Queer Theory Meets Lesbian and Gay History," *GLQ* 2, no. 3 (1995): 179–91; Vicki L. Eaklor, "How Queer-Friendly Are U.S. History Textbooks?" History News Network, 26 Jan. 2004, http://historynewsnetwork.org/articles/3200.html; Marc Stein, "Post-Tenure Lavender Blues," History News Network, 7 Jan. 2006, http://hnn.us/articles/19941.html; Marc Stein, "Committee on Lesbian and Gay History Survey on LGBTQ History Careers," *Perspectives* 39, no. 5 (May 2001): 29–31; Leila J. Rupp, "What's Queer Got To Do With It," *Reviews in American History* 38, no. 2 (Jun. 2010): 189–98.
3 Susan Stryker, *Transgender History* (Berkeley: Seal, 2008), 1; Joanne Meyerowitz, *How Sex Changed: A History of Transsexuality in the United States* (Cambridge, MA: Harvard University Press, 2002), 5.
4 George Chauncey, *Gay New York: Gender, Urban Culture, and the Making of the Gay Male World, 1890–1940* (New York: Basic, 1994); Elizabeth Lapovsky Kennedy and Madeline D. Davis, *Boots of Leather, Slippers of Gold: The History of a Lesbian Community* (New York: Routledge, 1993); Esther Newton, *Cherry Grove, Fire Island: Sixty Years in America's First Gay and Lesbian Town* (Boston: Beacon, 1993).
5 Judith Butler, *Gender Trouble: Feminism and the Subversion of Identity* (New York: Routledge, 1990).

1 Before the Movement, 1500–1940

1 Richard Godbeer, "'The Cry of Sodom': Discourse, Intercourse, and Desire in Colonial New England," *William and Mary Quarterly* 52, no. 2 (Apr. 1995), 277.
2 *Whip*, 29 Jan. 1842, 2; 5 Feb. 1842, 2; 12 Feb. 1842, 2; 19 Feb. 1842, 2; 26 Feb. 1842, 3; 5 Mar. 1842, 2.

3 Walt Whitman, *Leaves of Grass* (1855), ed. Malcolm Cowley (New York: Viking, 1959), 44, cited in Jonathan Ned Katz, *Love Stories: Sex Between Men Before Homosexuality* (Chicago: University of Chicago Press, 2001), 97; Whitman, *Leaves of Grass* (1856), intr. Gay Wilson Allen (Norwood, PA: Norwood, 1976), 229, cited in Katz, *Love Stories*, 109.

4 George H. Napheys, *The Transmission of Life*, 9th ed. (Philadelphia: Fergus, 1871), 29, cited in Jonathan Ned Katz, *Gay/Lesbian Almanac* (New York: Harper, 1983), 157; G. Frank Lydston, "Clinical Lecture: Sexual Perversion, Satyriasis and Nymphomania," *Medical and Surgical Reporter* 61, no. 10 (7 Sep. 1889), cited in Katz, *Gay/Lesbian Almanac*, 213; Charles Torrence Nesbitt, "Sexual Perverts," Nesbitt Papers, Duke University Library, cited in Katz, *Gay/Lesbian Almanac*, 218–19; Charles H. Hughes, "Postscript to Paper on 'Erotopathia,'" *Alienist and Neurologist* 14, no. 4 (Oct. 1893), 731–32, cited in Jonathan Ned Katz, *Gay American History* (1976: New York Avon, 1978), 66; Francis W. Anthony, "The Question of Responsibility in Cases of Sexual Perversion," *Boston Medical and Surgical Journal* 139, no. 12 (22 Sep. 1898), 290–91, cited in Katz, *Gay/Lesbian Almanac*, 294.

5 Ralph Werther, *The Female-Impersonators* (New York: Medico-Legal Journal, 1922), 3, 6, 146–50; Ralph Werther, *The Riddle of the Underworld* (1921), www.outhistory.org/wiki/Earl_Lind_(Ralph_Werther-Jennie_June):_The_Riddle_of_the_Underworld,_Pro logue_I._How_I_Came_to_Write_This_Book Accessed 28 March 2012.

6 Mary Casal, *The Stone Wall: An Autobiography* (Chicago: Eyncourt, 1930), 180–85.

7 Havelock Ellis and John Addington Symonds, *Sexual Inversion* (London: Wilson and Macmillan, 1897), 288–92, cited by Katz, *Gay American History*, 561–63.

8 James Mills Peirce to John Addington Symonds, reprinted in Ellis and Symonds, *Sexual Inversion*, 273–75, cited by Katz, *Gay American History*, 565; Katz, *Love Stories*, 313–14.

9 Miss S., quoted in Havelock Ellis, *Studies in the Psychology of Sex: Sexual Inversion* (Philadelphia: Davis, 1901), 134, cited by Katz, *Gay American History*, 564; Margaret Anderson, "Ms. Ellis's Failure," *Little Review* 2, no. 1 (Mar. 1915), 16–19, cited by Katz, *Gay/Lesbian Almanac*, 364–65.

10 Anonymous, quoted in Richard von Krafft-Ebing, "Perversion of the Sexual Instinct: Report of Cases," trans. H. M. Jewett, *Alienist and Neurologist* 9, no. 4 (Oct. 1888), 567–70, cited by Katz, *Gay American History*, 59–60.

11 Edward Irenaeus Prime-Stevenson [Xavier Mayne], *The Intersexes: A History of Simili-sexualism as a Problem in Social Life* (Rome, 1908), ix, 120–22, 520.

12 Ralph Werther, *Autobiography of an Androgyne*, ed. Scott Herring (1918; New Brunswick, NJ: Rutgers University Press, 2008), 75; Werther, *The Female-Impersonators*, 1, 36, 48, 99.

13 Werther, *The Female-Impersonators*, 151–63.

14 Emma Goldman, *Living My Life* (Garden City: Garden City Publishing, 1931), 269; Emma Goldman to Magnus Hirschfeld, Mar. 1923, cited by Katz, *Gay American History*, 571–72; Emma Goldman, quoted in S. D., "Farewell," *Free Society*, 13 Aug. 1899, 2, cited by Terence Kissack, *Free Comrades: Anarchism and Homosexuality in the United States, 1895–1917* (Oakland: AK, 2008), 15; Abe Isaak Jr., "Report from Chicago: Emma Goldman," *Free Society*, 9 Jun. 1901, 3, cited by Kissack, *Free Comrades*, 139.

15 John William Lloyd, *The Free Comrade*, Aug. 1902, 6, and Oct. 1902, 6–7, cited by Kissack, *Free Comrades*, 77–80.

16 Goldman, *Living My Life*, 555; Goldman to F. Heiner, 1–8 Jun. 1934, cited by Kissack, *Free Comrades*, 27; Goldman, *Living My Life*, 555–56; Anna W., "Emma Goldman in Washington," *Mother Earth*, May 1916, 517, cited by Kissack, *Free Comrades*, 145.

17 Goldman to Hirschfeld, March 1923, cited by Katz, *Gay American History*, 572–73; Goldman, 1928, quoted in Richard and Anna Maria Drinnon, eds., *Nowhere at Home: Letters from Exile of Emma Goldman and Alexander Berkman* (New York: Schocken, 1975), 132–33, cited by Lillian Faderman, *Odd Girls and Twilight Lovers: A History of Lesbian Life in Twentieth-Century America* (New York: Columbia University Press,

1991), 34; Alexander Berkman, *Prison Memoirs of an Anarchist* (New York: Mother Earth, 1912).

18 George W. Henry, *Sex Variants: A Study of Homosexual Patterns* (New York: Hoeber, 1941).

19 Morris Ernst, Defense Brief for *New York v. Donald Friede and Covici-Friede* (1929), 2, cited by Leslie A. Taylor, "'I Made Up My Mind to Get It': The American Trial of *The Well of Loneliness*, New York City, 1928–29," *Journal of the History of Sexuality* 10, no. 2 (Apr. 2001), 275.

20 *Gloria Record on Review* (1940), cited by George Chauncey, *Gay New York: gender urban culture, and the making of the gay male world, 1890–1940* (New York: Basic, 1994), 338–39.

21 Henry Gerber, "The Society for Human Rights—1925," *ONE*, Sep. 1962, 5–6. See also G. S. [Henry Gerber], letter to the editor, *ONE*, Jul. 1953, 22.

22 Society for Human Rights Charter, 1924, reprinted in Katz, *Gay American History*, 583; Gerber, "The Society," 5.

23 Gerber, "The Society," 6.

24 Ibid., 7–8.

25 Ibid., 8–10.

26 Gerber, letter to the editor, 22; Gerber, "The Society," 10.

27 Henry Gerber, *Contacts*, no. 10 (1939), cited by Jim Kepner and Stephen Murray, "Henry Gerber (1895–1972): Grandfather of the American Gay Movement," in Vern L. Bullough, ed., *Before Stonewall: Activists for Gay and Lesbian Rights in Historical Context* (New York: Haworth, 2002), 29.

28 Gerber correspondence with Manual Boyfrank, cited by Katz, *Gay/Lesbian Almanac*, 556–59.

29 Karen C. Sendziak, "Henry Gerber," *Encyclopedia of LGBT History in America*, ed. Marc Stein (New York: Scribners, 2003), vol. 1, 451; Gerber correspondence with Boyfrank, cited by Katz, *Gay/Lesbian Almanac*, 562–63; Gerber letter to *Time*, 5 Apr. 1944, cited by Katz, *Gay/Lesbian Almanac*, 561; Gerber to Boyfrank, 18 Feb. 1946, cited by Katz, *Gay/Lesbian Almanac*, 564.

2 Homophile Activism, 1940–69

1 Edythe Eyde, cited in Eric Marcus, *Making History: The Struggle for Gay and Lesbian Equal Rights, 1945–1990* (New York: HarperCollins, 1992), 10–11.

2 Harry Hay, "Children and Fools Speak the Truth: Les Mattachines (The Society of Fools)," Nov. 1950, in Harry Hay, *Radically Gay: Gay Liberation in the Words of Its Founder*, ed. Will Roscoe (Boston: Beacon, 1996), 79.

3 "Mattachine Society Missions and Purposes,"Apr. 1951, in Hay, *Radically Gay*, 131–32.

4 Chuck Rowland, cited in Marcus, *Making History*, 33.

5 H. L. Small, "Socialism and Sex," *Young Socialist* 5 (Winter 1952): 21, reprinted as an appendix in Christopher Phelps, "A Neglected Document on Socialism and Sex," *Journal of the History of Sexuality* 16, no. 1 (Jan. 2007), 13.

6 Donald Webster Cory, *The Homosexual in America: A Subjective Approach* (New York: Greenberg, 1951), 13–14, 233.

7 Paul Coates, "Well, Medium and Rare," *Los Angeles Mirror*, 12 Mar. 1953, cited by John D'Emilio, *Sexual Politics, Sexual Communities: The Making of a Homosexual Minority in the United States, 1940–1970* (Chicago: University of Chicago Press, 1983), 76.

8 Daughters of Bilitis Statement of Purpose, 1956, cited by Marcia M. Gallo, *Different Daughters: A History of the Daughters of Bilitis and the Rise of the Lesbian Rights Movement* (New York: Carroll and Graf, 2006), 11; Del Martin, 1959, quoted in *The Ladder*, Oct. 1959, 19.

9 *The Ladder*, Sep. 1959, 25.
10 "Homosexuality and Civil Liberties," *Civil Liberties*, Mar. 1957, 3.
11 Russell Wolden, quoted in *San Francisco Progress,* 7 Oct. 1959, cited by D'Emilio, *Sexual Politics*, 121.
12 Vanguard, 1966, cited by Susan Stryker, *Transgender History* (Berkeley: Seal, 2008), 72.
13 *Drum*, no. 26 (1967), 7.
14 Mattachine Society of Washington policy statement, 4 Mar. 1965, cited by D'Emilio, *Sexual Politics*, 164.
15 *Drum* advertisement, 1964 East Coast Homophile Organizations Conference Program, cited by Marc Stein, *City of Sisterly and Brotherly Loves: Lesbian and Gay Philadelphia, 1945–1972* (Chicago: University of Chicago Press, 2000), 232; Frank Kameny, typescript of presentation to the Second National Planning Conference of Homophile Organizations, Aug. 1966, cited by Marc Stein, *Sexual Injustice: Supreme Court Decisions from Griswold to Roe* (Chapel Hill: University of North Carolina Press, 2010), 146; Clark Polak to *Time* and *New Republic*, 26 Dec. 1964, reprinted in *Janus Society Newsletter*, Jan. 1965, 2.
16 Keith St. Clare, *Vanguard* 1, no. 5 (1967), 4, cited by Justin David Suran, "Coming Out Against the War: Antimilitarism and the Politicization of Homosexuality in the Era of Vietnam," *American Quarterly* 53, no. 3 (Sep. 2001), 465.
17 *Janus Society Newsletter*, May 1965, 2.
18 Leo Laurence, "Gay Revolution," *Vector*, Apr. 1969, 1.

3 Gay Liberation, Lesbian Feminism, and Gay and Lesbian Liberalism, 1969–73

1 Note that in this and later chapters I use "gay liberation" to refer to the radical activism of the late 1960s and early 1970s, not as a synonym for the movement as a whole.
2 Third World Gay Revolution, "The Oppressed Shall Not Become the Oppressor," 1970, reprinted in Mark Blasius and Shane Phelan, eds., *We Are Everywhere: A Historical Sourcebook of Gay and Lesbian Politics* (New York: Routledge, 1997), 400.
3 Carl Wittman, "Refugees from Amerika: A Gay Manifesto," *San Francisco Free Press*, 22 Dec. 1969, reprinted in Blasivs and Phelan, eds., *We Are Everywhere*, 381.
4 Gay liberation flier, July 1969, cited in Donn Teal, *The Gay Militants* (New York: Stein and Day, 1971), 36.
5 Flyer, "No Vietnamese Ever Called Me a Queer!" 15 Oct. 1969, cited by Justin Suran, "Coming Out Against the War: Antimilitarism and the Politicization of Homosexuality in the Era of Vietnam," *American Quarterly* 53, no. 3 (Sep. 2001), 485.
6 Note that in my usage "radical lesbian feminism" refers to a broad range of radical lesbian feminisms, including components of what others call cultural feminism, feminist sex radicalism, and multicultural, third world, intersectional, and antiracist feminisms.
7 Pat Maxwell, "Lavender Menaces," *Gay Power*, no. 17 (1970), cited in Teal, *The Gay Militants*, 180.
8 "Statement of the Furies," May 1971, cited by Anne M. Valk, "Living a Feminist Lifestyle: The Intersection of Theory and Action in a Lesbian Feminist Collective," *Feminist Studies* 28, no. 2 (Summer 2002): 310–11.
9 Jill Johnston, *Lesbian Nation: The Feminist Solution* (New York: Simon & Schuster, 1973).
10 Statement of 17 Dec. 1970, cited by Teal, *The Gay Militants*, 194.
11 NOW-LA resolution, 1970, cited by Lillian Faderman and Stuart Timmons, *Gay L.A.* (Berkeley: University of California Press, 2006), 184.
12 Del Martin, "'If That's All There Is," *Advocate*, 28 Oct. 1970, 21.
13 "Fidelifacts Oppresses Homosexuals," cited by David Eisenbach, *Gay Power* (New York: Carroll and Graf, 2006), 164.

4 Gay and Lesbian Activism in the Era of Conservative Backlash, 1973–81

1 Harvey Milk, Jun. 1978, cited by Dudley Clendinen and Adam Nagourney, *Out for Good: The Struggle to Build a Gay Rights Movement in America* (New York: Simon & Schuster, 1999), 381.

5 Gay and Lesbian Activism in the Age of AIDS, 1981–90

1 Lawrence Mass, "Disease Rumors Largely Unfounded," *New York Native*, 18 May 1981, 7; Centers for Disease Control, "Pneumocystis Pneumonia—Los Angeles," *Morbidity and Mortality Weekly Report*, 5 Jun. 1981, 250–52.
2 Larry Kramer, "1,112 and Counting," *New York Native*, 14 Mar. 1983.
3 See Douglas Crimp with Adam Rolston, *AIDS Demographics* (Seattle: Bay Press, 1990), 13.
4 I refer to the ACT UP *movement* to incorporate groups such as MASS ACT OUT that did not use the ACT UP name. I do not refer to ACT UP *chapters* because it was not a national organization with local affiliates; it was a loose association of autonomous local groups.
5 See Crimp, *AIDS Demographics*, 28.
6 Ibid., 33.
7 Ibid., 36, 46.
8 Ibid., 56–57.
9 Ibid., 117.
10 Ibid., 112.
11 *Outweek*, 24 Dec. 1989, 12.
12 See Richard Meyer, *Outlaw Representation: Censorship and Homosexuality in Twentieth-Century American Art* (New York: Oxford University Press, 2002), 234–40.
13 See Lillian Faderman and Stuart Timmons, *Gay L.A.: A History of Sexual Outlaws, Power Politics, and Lipstick Lesbians* (Berkeley: University of California Press, 2006), 315.
14 *Bowers v. Hardwick*, 478 U.S. 186 (1986), 188, 190, 191, 196.
15 *Brockett v. Spokane Arcades*, 472 U.S. 491 (1985), 494, 498–99.

6 LGBT and Queer Activism Beyond 1990

1 Bad Object-Choices, ed., *How Do I Look? Queer Film and Video* (Seattle: Bay, 1991); Teresa de Lauretis, ed., "Queer Theory, Lesbian and Gay Sexualities," *differences* 3, no. 2 (Summer 1991).
2 Queers, "Queers Read This: I Hate Straights," 1990, reprinted in *We Are Everywhere: A Historical Sourcebook on Gay and Lesbian Politics*, eds. Mark Blasius and Shane Phelan (New York: Routledge, 1997), 773–80.
3 Ibid., 780.
4 Sandy Stone, "The Empire Strikes Back: A Posttranssexual Manifesto," in *Body Guards: The Cultural Politics of Gender Ambiguity*, eds. Julia Epstein and Kristina Straub (New York: Routledge, 1991), 280–304; Leslie Feinberg, "Transgender Liberation: A Movement Whose Time Has Come," in *The Transgender Studies Reader*, eds. Susan Stryker and Stephen Whittle (New York: Routledge, 2006), 205–20.
5 Loraine Hutchins and Lani Ka'ahumanu, eds., *Bi Any Other Name: Bisexual People Speak Out* (Boston: Alyson, 1991).

SUGGESTIONS FOR FURTHER READING

Please note that the categories used below intersect and overlap, but each publication is listed only once.

General Studies of U.S. Gay and Lesbian History

Henry Abelove, *Deep Gossip* (Minneapolis: University of Minnesota Press, 2003)

Allida Black, ed., *Modern American Queer History* (Philadelphia: Temple University Press, 2001)

Michael Bronski, *A Queer History of the United States* (Boston: Beacon, 2011)

John D'Emilio, *Making Trouble: Essays on Gay History, Politics, and the University* (New York: Routledge, 1992)

John D'Emilio, *The World Turned: Essays on Gay History, Politics, and Culture* (Durham: Duke University Press, 2002)

Martin Bauml Duberman, Martha Vicinus, and George Chauncey Jr., eds., *Hidden from History: Reclaiming the Gay and Lesbian Past* (New York: New American Library, 1989)

Lisa Duggan, *Sex Wars: Sexual Dissent and Political Culture* (New York: Routledge, 1995)

Vicki L. Eaklor, *Queer America: A GLBT History of the 20th Century* (Westport: Greenwood, 2008)

Lillian Faderman, *Odd Girls and Twilight Lovers: A History of Lesbian Life in Twentieth-Century America* (New York: Columbia University Press, 1991)

Estelle B. Freedman, *Feminism, Sexuality, and Politics* (Chapel Hill: University of North Carolina Press, 2006)

Larry Gross and James D. Woods, eds., *The Columbia Reader on Lesbians and Gay Men in Media, Society, and Politics* (New York: Columbia University Press, 1999)

Kevin Jennings, ed., *Becoming Visible: A Reader in Gay and Lesbian History for High School and College Students* (Boston: Alyson, 1994)

Jonathan Ned Katz, *Gay American History* (New York: Crowell, 1976)

Jonathan Ned Katz, *Gay/Lesbian Almanac* (New York: Harper, 1983)

Regina Kunzel, *Criminal Intimacy: Prison and the Uneven History of Modern American Sexuality* (Chicago: University of Chicago Press, 2008)

John Loughery, *The Other Side of Silence: Men's Lives and Gay Identities* (New York: Holt, 1998)

Molly McGarry and Fred Wasserman, *Becoming Visible: An Illustrated History of Lesbian and Gay Life in Twentieth-Century America* (New York: Penguin, 1998)

Neil Miller, *Out of the Past: Gay and Lesbian History from 1869 to the Present* (New York: Vintage, 1995)

Kathy Peiss and Christina Simmons, eds. *Passion and Power: Sexuality in History* (Philadelphia: Temple University Press, 1989)

Leila J. Rupp: *A Desired Past: A Short History of Same-Sex Love in America* (Chicago: University of Chicago Press, 1999)

Marc Stein, ed., *Encyclopedia of Lesbian, Gay, Bisexual, and Transgender History in America* (New York: Scribners, 2003)

General Studies of U.S. Trans History

Peter Boag, "Go West Young Man, Go East Young Woman: Searching for the Trans in Western Gender History," *Western Historical Quarterly* 36, no. 4 (Winter 2005): 477–97

Paisley Currah, Richard M. Juang, and Shannon Price Minter, eds., *Transgender Rights* (Minneapolis: University of Minnesota Press, 2006)

Dan Irving, "Normalizing Transgressions: Legitimizing the Transsexual Body as Productive," *Radical History Review* 100 (Winter 2008): 38–59

Joanne Meyerowitz, *How Sex Changed: A History of Transsexuality in the United States* (Cambridge: Harvard University Press, 2003)

David Serlin, *Replaceable You: Engineering the Body in Postwar America* (Chicago: University of Chicago Press, 2004)

Susan Stryker, *Transgender History* (Berkeley: Seal, 2008)

Susan Stryker and Stephen Whittle, eds., *The Transgender Studies Reader* (New York: Routledge, 2006)

General Studies of U.S. Bisexual History

Steven Angelides, *A History of Bisexuality* (Chicago: University of Chicago Press, 2001)

Marjorie Garber, *Bisexuality and the Eroticism of Everyday Life* (New York: Routledge, 2000)

Loraine Hutchins and Lani Ka'ahumanu, eds., *Bi Any Other Name: Bisexual People Speak Out* (Boston: Alyson, 1991)

Native Americans and Native Alaskans

Evelyn Blackwood, "Sexuality and Gender in Certain Native American Tribes: The Case of Cross-Gender Females," *Signs* 10, no. 2 (1984): 27–42

Ramón Gutiérrez, *When Jesus Came, the Corn Mothers Went Away: Marriage, Sexuality, and Power in New Mexico, 1500–1846* (Berkeley: University of California Press, 1991)

Sue-Ellen Jacobs, Wesley Thomas, and Sabine Lang, eds., *Two-Spirit People: Native American Gender Identity, Sexuality, and Spirituality* (Urbana: University of Illinois Press, 1997)

Will Roscoe, ed., *Living the Spirit: A Gay American Indian Anthology* (New York: St. Martin's, 1988)

Will Roscoe, *Changing Ones: Third and Fourth Genders in Native North America* (New York: St. Martin's, 1998)

Walter L. Williams, *The Spirit and the Flesh: Sexual Diversity in American Indian Culture* (Boston: Beacon, 1986)

African Americans, Asian Americans/Pacific Islanders, Jewish Americans, Latinos/Latinas, and Native Americans/Alaskans

Christie Balka and Andy Rose, eds., *Twice Blessed: On Being Lesbian or Gay and Jewish* (Boston: Beacon, 1991)

Joseph Beam, ed., *In the Life: A Black Gay Anthology* (Boston: Alyson, 1986)

Keith Boykin, *One More River to Cross: Black and Gay in America* (New York: Anchor, 1996)

Julio Capó, "Queering Mariel: Mediating Cold War Foreign Policy and U.S. Citizenship among Cuba's Homosexual Exile Community, 1978–94," *Journal of American Ethnic History* 29, no. 4 (Summer 2010): 78–106

Delroy Constantine-Simms, ed., *The Greatest Taboo: Homosexuality in Black Communities* (Los Angeles: Alyson, 2000)

Anita Cornwell, *Black Lesbian in White America* (Tallahassee: Naiad, 1983)

John D'Emilio, *Lost Prophet: The Life and Times of Bayard Rustin* (Chicago: University of Chicago Press, 2003)

David L. Eng and Alice Y. Hom, eds., *Q & A: Queer in Asian America* (Philadelphia: Temple University Press, 1998)

Essex Hemphill, ed., *Brother to Brother: New Writings by Black Gay Men* (Boston: Alyson, 1991)

E. Patrick Johnson and Mae G. Henderson, *Black Queer Studies: A Critical Anthology* (Durham: Duke University Press, 2005)

Audre Lorde, *Sister Outsider* (Freedom, CA: Cross Press, 1984)

Cherríe Moraga and Gloria Anzaldua, eds., *This Bridge Called My Back: Writings by Radical Women of Color* (Watertown: Persephone, 1981)

Trinity A. Ordona, "Asian Lesbians in San Francisco: Struggles to Create a Safe Space, 1970s–1980s," in *Asian/Pacific Islander American Women: A Historical Anthology*, eds. Shirley Hune and Gail M. Nomura (New York: New York University Press, 2003), 319–34

Susana Peña, "'Obvious Gays' and the State Gaze: Cuban Gay Visibility and U.S. Immigration Policy during the 1980 Mariel Boatlift," *Journal of the History of Sexuality* 16, no. 3 (Sep. 2007): 482–514

Juanita Ramos, *Compañeras: Latina Lesbians* (New York: Latina Lesbian History Project, 1987)

Thaddeus Russell, "The Color of Discipline: Civil Rights and Black Sexuality," *American Quarterly* 60, no. 1 (2008): 101–28

Barbara Smith, ed., *Home Girls: A Black Feminist Anthology* (New York: Kitchen Table, 1983)

Michael J. Smith, *Colorful People and Places: A Resource Guide for Third World Lesbians and Gay Men* (San Francisco: Quarterly Press of BWMT, 1983)

Colonial America, the Nineteenth Century, and the Early Twentieth Century

Aliyah Abdur-Rahman, "'The Strangest Freaks of Despotism': Queer Sexuality in Antebellum African Slave Narratives," *African American Review* 40, no. 2 (Summer 2006): 223–37

William E. Benemann, *Male-Male Intimacy in Early America: Beyond Romantic Friendships* (New York: Routledge, 2006)

Lisa Duggan, *Sapphic Slashers: Sex, Violence, and American Modernity* (Durham: Duke University Press, 2000)

Thomas A. Foster, *Long Before Stonewall: Histories of Same-Sex Sexuality in Early America* (New York: New York University Press, 2007)

Thomas A. Foster, "The Sexual Abuse of Black Men under American Slavery," *Journal of the History of Sexuality* 20, no. 3 (Sep. 2011): 445–64

Richard Godbeer, *Sexual Revolution in Early America* (Baltimore: Johns Hopkins University Press, 2002)

Richard Godbeer, *The Overflowing of Friendship: Love between Men and the Creation of the American Republic* (Baltimore: Johns Hopkins University Press, 2009)

John Donald Gustav-Wrathall, *Take the Young Stranger by the Hand: Same-Sex Relations and the YMCA* (Chicago: University of Chicago Press, 1998)

Karen V. Hansen, "'No Kisses Is Like Youres': An Erotic Friendship between Two African-American Women during the Mid-Nineteenth Century," *Gender and History* 7 (Aug. 1995): 153–82

Jay Hatheway, *The Gilded Age Construction of Modern American Homophobia* (New York: Palgrave, 2003)

Susan Lee Johnson, *Roaring Camp: The Social World of the California Gold Rush* (New York: Norton, 2000)

Jonathan Ned Katz, *Love Stories: Sex Between Men Before Homosexuality* (Chicago: University of Chicago Press, 2001)

Terence Kissack, *Free Comrades: Anarchism and Homosexuality in the United States, 1895–1917* (Oakland: AK, 2008)

Kevin P. Murphy, *Political Manhood: Red Bloods, Mollycoddles, and the Politics of Progressive Era Reform* (New York: Columbia University Press, 2008)

Eve Kosofsky Sedgwick, *Epistemology of the Closet* (Berkeley: University of California Press, 1990)

Carroll Smith-Rosenberg, *Disorderly Conduct: Visions of Gender in Victorian America* (New York: Oxford University Press, 1985)

Jennifer Ting, "Bachelor Society: Deviant Heterosexuality and Asian American Historiography," in *Privileging Positions: The Sites of Asian American Studies*, eds. Gary Y. Okihiro, et al. (Pullman: Washington State University Press, 1995), 271–79

Ralph Werther, *Autobiography of an Androgyne*, ed. Scott Herring (New Brunswick: Rutgers University Press, 2008)

William Wright, *Harvard's Secret Court: The Savage 1920 Purge of Campus Homosexuals* (New York: St. Martin's, 2006)

World War Two and the U.S. Military

Allan Bérubé, *Coming Out Under Fire: The History of Gay Men and Women in World War II* (New York: Free Press, 1990)

Steve Estes, *Ask and Tell: Gay and Lesbian Veterans Speak Out* (Chapel Hill: University of North Carolina Press, 2009)

Elizabeth Lutes Hillman, *Defending America: Military Culture and the Cold War Court-Martial* (Princeton: Princeton University Press, 2005)

Leisa D. Meyer, *Creating GI Jane: Sexuality and Power in the Women's Army Corps during World War II* (New York: Columbia University Press, 1996)

Local and Regional Studies that Focus on the pre-World War Two Era

Peter G. Boag, *Redressing America's Frontier Past* (Berkeley: University of California Press, 2011)

Peter G. Boag, *Same-Sex Affairs: Constructing and Controlling Homosexuality in the Pacific Northwest* (Berkeley: University of California Press, 2003)

George Chauncey, *Gay New York: Gender, Urban Culture, and the Making of the Gay Male World, 1890–1940* (New York: Basic, 1994)

Chad Heap, *Slumming: Sexual and Racial Encounters in American Nightlife, 1885–1940* (Chicago: University of Chicago Press, 2009)

Kevin Mumford, *Interzones: Black/White Sex Districts in Chicago and New York in the Early Twentieth Century* (New York: Columbia University Press, 1997)

Nayan Shah, *Stranger Intimacy: Contesting Race, Sexuality and the Law in the North American West* (Berkeley: University of California Press, 2011)

Sharon R. Ullman, "'The Twentieth Century Way': Female Impersonation and Sexual Practice in Turn-of-the-Century America," *Journal of the History of Sexuality* 5, no. 4 (1995): 573–600

Local and Regional Studies that Focus on the pre-World War Two, World War Two, and post-World War Two Eras

Gary Atkins, *Gay Seattle: Stories of Exile and Belonging* (Seattle: University of Washington Press, 2003)

Brett Beemyn, ed., *Creating a Place for Ourselves* (New York: Routledge, 1997)

Nan Alamilla Boyd, *Wide Open Town: A History of Queer San Francisco to 1965* (Berkeley: University of California Press, 2003)

Lillian Faderman and Stuart Timmons, *Gay L.A.: A History of Sexual Outlaws, Power Politics, and Lipstick Lesbians* (Berkeley: University of California Press, 2006)

The History Project, *Improper Bostonians: Lesbian and Gay History from the Puritans to Playland* (Boston: Beacon, 1998)

John Howard, *Carryin' On in the Lesbian and Gay South* (New York: New York University Press, 1997)

John Howard, *Men Like That: A Southern Queer History* (Chicago: University of Chicago Press, 1999)

Daniel Hurewitz, *Bohemian Los Angeles and the Making of Modern Politics* (Berkeley: University of California Press, 2007)

Karen Christel Krahulik, *Provincetown: From Pilgrim Landing to Gay Resort* (New York: New York University Press, 2005)

Elizabeth Lapovsky Kennedy and Madeline D. Davis, *Boots of Leather, Slippers of Gold: The History of a Lesbian Community* (New York: Routledge, 1993)

Esther Newton, *Cherry Grove, Fire Island: Sixty Years in America's First Gay and Lesbian Town* (Boston: Beacon, 1993)

Bryant Simon, "New York Avenue: The Life and Death of Gay Spaces in Atlantic City, New Jersey, 1920–90," *Journal of Urban History* 28, no. 3 (Mar. 2002): 300–27

Susan Stryker and Jim Van Buskirk, *Gay by the Bay: A History of Queer Culture in the San Francisco Bay Area* (San Francisco: Chronicle, 1996)

Brock Thompson, *The Un-Natural State: Arkansas and the Queer South* (Fayetteville: University of Arkansas Press, 2010)

Local and Regional Studies that Focus on the World War Two and post-World War Two Eras

Christopher Agee, "Gayola: Police Professionalization and the Politics of San Francisco's Gay Bars, 1950–68," *Journal of the History of Sexuality* 15, no. 3 (Sep. 2006): 462–89

Elizabeth A. Armstrong, *Forging Gay Identities: Organizing Sexuality in San Francisco, 1950–1994* (Chicago: University of Chicago Press, 2002)

Beth Bailey, *Sex in the Heartland* (Cambridge: Harvard University Press, 1999)

Daneel Buring, *Lesbian and Gay Memphis: Building Communities Behind the Magnolia Curtain* (New York: Garland, 1997)

Manuel Castells, *The City and the Grassroots: A Cross-Cultural Theory of Urban Social Movements* (Berkeley: University of California Press, 1983)

David Eisenbach, *Gay Power: An American Revolution* (New York: Carroll and Graf, 2006)

Katie Gilmartin, "'We Weren't Bar People': Middle-Class Lesbian Identities and Cultural Spaces," *GLQ* 3, no. 1 (1996): 1–51

Karen L. Graves, *And They Were Wonderful Teachers: Florida's Purge of Gay and Lesbian Teachers* (Urbana: University of Illinois Press, 2009)

Charles Kaiser, *The Gay Metropolis, 1940–1996* (Boston: Houghton, 1997)

Moira Rachel Kenney, *Mapping Gay L.A.: The Intersection of Place and Politics* (Philadelphia: Temple University Press, 2001)

Kevin Allen Leonard, "Containing 'Perversion': African Americans and Same-Sex Desire in Cold War Los Angeles," *Journal of the History of Sexuality* 20, no. 3 (Sep. 2011): 545–67

Kevin J. Mumford, "The Trouble with Gay Rights: Race and the Politics of Sexual Orientation in Philadelphia, 1969–82," *Journal of American History* 98, no. 1 (Jun. 2011): 49–72

J. Todd Ormsbee, *The Meaning of Gay: Interaction, Publicity, and Community among Homosexual Men in 1960s San Francisco* (Lanham: Rowman, 2010)

Horacio Roque Ramírez, "'That's My Place!': Negotiating Racial, Sexual, and Gender Politics in San Francisco's Gay Latino Alliance, 1975–83," *Journal of the History of Sexuality* 12, no. 2 (Apr. 2003): 224–58

David A. Reichard, "'We Can't Hide and They Are Wrong': The Society for Homosexual Freedom and the Struggle for Recognition at Sacramento State College, 1969–71," *Law and History Review* 28, no. 3 (August 2010): 629–74

Tim Retzloff, "Seer or Queer?: Postwar Fascination with Detroit's Prophet Jones," *GLQ* 8, no. 3 (2002): 271–96

Gayle S. Rubin, "The Miracle Mile: South of Market and Gay Male Leather, 1962–97," in *Reclaiming San Francisco: History, Politics, Culture*, eds. James Brook, Chris Carlsson, and Nancy Joyce Peters (San Francisco: City Lights Books, 1998), 247–72

James T. Sears, *Lonely Hunters: An Oral History of Lesbian and Gay Southern Life, 1948–1968* (Boulder: Westview, 1997)

Marc Stein, *City of Sisterly and Brotherly Loves: Lesbian and Gay Philadelphia, 1945–1972* (Chicago: University of Chicago Press, 2000)

Rochella Thorpe, "'A House Where Queers Go': African-American Lesbian Nightlife in Detroit, 1940–75, in *Inventing Lesbian Cultures in America*, ed. Ellen Lewin (Boston: Beacon, 1996), 40–61

Twin Cities GLBT Oral History Project, *Queer Twin Cities* (Minneapolis: University of Minnesota Press, 2010)

Eric C. Wat, *The Making of a Gay Asian Community: An Oral History of Pre-AIDS Los Angeles* (Lanham: Rowman, 2002)

Studies that Focus on Gay and Lesbian Geographies

David Bell and Gill Valentine, eds., *Mapping Desire: Geographies of Sexualities* (New York: Routledge, 1995)

Gordon Brent Ingram, Anne-Marie Bouthillette, and Yolanda Retter, eds., *Queers in Space: Communities, Public Places, Sites of Resistance* (Seattle: Bay Press, 1997)

Politics, Law, and Governance

Ellen Ann Andersen, *Out of the Closets and Into the Courts: Legal Opportunity Structure and Gay Rights Litigation* (Ann Arbor: University of Michigan Press, 2005)

Robert W. Bailey, *Gay Politics, Urban Politics: Identity and Economics in the Urban Setting* (New York: Columbia University Press, 1999)

Carlos A. Ball, *From the Closet to the Courtroom: Five LGBT Rights Lawsuits That Have Changed Our Nation* (Boston: Beacon, 2010)

Patricia A. Cain, *Rainbow Rights: The Role of Lawyers and Courts in the Lesbian and Gay Civil Rights Movement* (Boulder: Westview, 2000)

Margot Canaday, *The Straight State: Sexuality and Citizenship in Twentieth-Century America* (Princeton: Princeton University Press, 2009)

William N. Eskridge Jr., *Dishonorable Passions: Sodomy Laws in America, 1861–2003* (New York: Viking, 2008)

William N. Eskridge Jr., *Gaylaw: Challenging the Apartheid of the Closet* (Cambridge: Harvard University Press, 1999)

David K. Johnson, *Lavender Scare: The Cold War Persecution of Gays and Lesbians in the Federal Government* (Chicago: University of Chicago Press, 2004)

Eithne Luibhéid, "'Looking Like a Lesbian': The Organization of Sexual Monitoring at the United States-Mexican Border," *Journal of the History of Sexuality* 8, no. 3 (Jan. 1998): 477–506

Joyce Murdoch and Deb Price, *Courting Justice: Gay Men and Lesbians v. the Supreme Court* (New York: Basic, 2001)

Craig A. Rimmerman, Kenneth D. Wale, and Clyde Wilcox, eds., *The Politics of Gay Rights* (Chicago: University of Chicago Press, 2000)

Rhonda R. Rivera, "Our Straight-Laced Judges: The Legal Position of Homosexual Persons in the United States," *Hastings Law Journal* 30 (1978–79): 799–955

Rhonda R. Rivera, "Recent Developments in Sexual Preference Law," *Drake Law Review* 30 (1980–81): 311–46

Rhonda R. Rivera, "Queer Law: Sexual Orientation Law in the Mid-Eighties, Part I," *University of Dayton Law Review* 11 (1985–86): 459–540

Rhonda R. Rivera, "Queer Law: Sexual Orientation Law in the Mid-Eighties, Part II," *University of Dayton Law Review* 12 (1986): 275–398

Daniel Rivers, "'In the Best Interests of the Child': Lesbian and Gay Parenting Custody Cases, 1967–85," *Journal of Social History* 43, no. 4 (Summer 2010): 917–43

Marc Stein, *Sexual Injustice: Supreme Court Decisions from Griswold to Roe* (Chapel Hill: University of North Carolina Press, 2010)

William B. Turner, "The Gay Rights State: Wisconsin's Pioneering Legislation to Prohibit Discrimination Based on Sexual Orientation," *Wisconsin Women's Law Journal* 22 (Spring 2007): 91–131

Comparative Studies of Politics, Law, and Governance

David Rayside, *On the Fringe: Gays and Lesbians in Politics* (Ithaca: Cornell University Press, 1998)

David Rayside, *Queer Inclusions, Continental Divisions: Public Recognition of Sexual Diversity in Canada and the United States* (Toronto: University of Toronto Press, 2008)

Miriam Smith, *Political Institutions and Lesbian and Gay Rights in the United States and Canada* (New York: Routledge, 2008)

Science, Medicine, and Psychiatry

Ronald Bayer, *Homosexuality and American Psychiatry: The Politics of Diagnosis* (New York: Basic, 1981)

Henry Minton, *Departing from Deviance: A History of Homosexual Rights and Emancipatory Science in America* (Chicago: University of Chicago Press, 2002)

Siobhan Somerville, "Scientific Racism and the Emergence of the Homosexual Body," *Journal of the History of Sexuality* 5, no. 2 (Oct. 1994): 243–66

Jennifer Terry, *An American Obsession: Science, Medicine, and Homosexuality in Modern Society* (Chicago: University of Chicago Press, 1999)

Studies of Art, Media, and Popular Culture

Edward Alwood, *Straight News: Gays, Lesbians, and the News Media* (New York: Columbia University Press, 1996)

Michael Bronski, *Culture Clash: The Making of Gay Sensibility* (Boston: South End, 1984)

Michael Bronski, *Pleasure Principle: Sex, Backlash, and the Struggle for Gay Freedom* (New York: St. Martin's, 1998)

Michael Bronski, ed., *Pulp Friction* (New York: St. Martin's, 2003)

Steven Capsuto, *Alternate Channels: The Uncensored Story of Gay and Lesbian Images on Radio and Television* (New York: Ballantine, 2000)

Robert J. Corber, *Homosexuality in Cold War America: Resistance and the Crisis of Masculinity* (Durham: Duke University Press, 1997)

Katherine V. Forrest, ed., *Lesbian Pulp Fiction: The Sexually Intrepid World of Lesbian Paperback Novels, 1950–1965* (Berkeley: Cleis, 2005)

Larry Gross, *Up from Invisibility: Lesbians, Gay Men, and the Media in America* (New York: Columbia University Press, 2001)

David K. Johnson, "Physique Pioneers: The Politics of 1960s Consumer Culture," *Journal of Social History* 43, no. 4 (Summer 2010): 867–92

Martin Meeker, *Contacts Desired: Gay and Lesbian Communications and Community, 1940s–1970s* (Chicago: University of Chicago Press, 2006)

Richard Meyer, *Outlaw Representation: Censorship and Homosexuality in Twentieth-Century American Art* (New York: Oxford University Press, 2002)

Vito Russo, *The Celluloid Closet: Homosexuality in the Movies* (New York: Harper, 1981)

Michael S. Sherry, *Gay Artists in Modern American Culture: An Imagined Conspiracy* (Chapel Hill: University of North Carolina Press, 2007)

Roger Streitmatter, *Unspeakable: The Rise of the Gay and Lesbian Press in America* (Boston: Faber, 1995)

Susan Stryker, *Queer Pulp: Perverted Passions from the Golden Age of the Paperback* (San Francisco: Chronicle, 2001)

Studies that Address Economics, Labor, and Work

M. V. Lee Badgett, *Money, Myths, and Change: The Economic Lives of Lesbians and Gay Men* (Chicago: University of Chicago Press, 2001)

Allan Bérubé, *My Desire for History: Essays in Gay, Community, and Labor History* (Chapel Hill: University of North Carolina Press, 2011)

Amy Gluckman and Betsy Reed, eds., *Homo Economics: Capitalism, Community, and Lesbian and Gay Life* (New York: Routledge, 1997)

Gerald Hunt, ed., *Laboring for Rights: Unions and Sexual Diversity Across Nations* (Philadelphia: Temple University Press, 1999)

Nicole C. Raeburn, *Changing Corporate America from Inside Out: Lesbian and Gay Workplace Rights* (Minneapolis: University of Minnesota Press, 2004)

James D. Woods, *The Corporate Closet: The Professional Lives of Gay Men in America* (New York: Free Press, 1993)

General Studies of the U.S. Gay and Lesbian Movement

Barry D. Adam, *The Rise of a Gay and Lesbian Movement* (New York: Twayne, 1987)

Mark Blasius and Shane Phelan, eds., *We are Everywhere: A Historical Sourcebook on Gay and Lesbian Politics* (New York: Routledge, 1997)

Paul D. Cain, *Leading the Parade: Conversations with America's Most Influential Lesbians and Gay Men* (Lanham: Scarecrow, 2002)

Margaret Cruikshank, *The Gay and Lesbian Liberation Movement* (New York: Routledge, 1992)

Steven Epstein, "Gay Politics, Ethnic Identity: The Limits of Social Constructionism," *Socialist Review*, nos. 93–94 (Jul. 1987): 9–54

Steven Epstein, "Gay and Lesbian Movements in the United States: Dilemmas of Identity, Diversity, and Political Strategy," in *The Global Emergence of Gay and Lesbian Politics*, eds. Barry D. Adam, Jan Willem Duyvendak, and André Krouwel (Philadelphia: Temple University Press, 1999), 30–90

Eric Marcus, *Making History: The Struggle for Gay and Lesbian Equal Rights* (New York: HarperCollins, 1992)

Studies of Homophile Activism

Peter Boag, "'Does Portland Need a Homophile Society?': Gay Culture and Activism in the Rose City between World War II and Stonewall," *Oregon Historical Quarterly* 105, no. 1 (Spring 2004): 6–39

Vern L. Bullough, ed., *Before Stonewall: Activists for Gay and Lesbian Rights in Historical Context* (New York: Haworth, 2002)

Douglas M. Charles, "From Subversion to Obscenity: The FBI's Investigations of the Early Homophile Movement in the United States, 1953–58," *Journal of the History of Sexuality* 19, no. 2 (May 2010): 262–87

David S. Churchill, "Transnationalism and Homophile Political Culture in the Postwar Decades," *GLQ* 15, no. 1 (2009): 31–66

John D'Emilio, *Sexual Politics, Sexual Communities: The Making of a Homosexual Minority in the United States, 1940–1970* (Chicago: University of Chicago Press, 1983)

Marcia M. Gallo, *Different Daughters: A History of the Daughters of Bilitis and the Rise of the Lesbian Rights Movement* (New York: Carroll and Graf, 2006)

Michael R. Gorman, *The Empress is a Man: Stories from the Life of José Sarria* (New York: Haworth, 1998)

Harry Hay, *Radically Gay: Gay Liberation in the Worlds of Its Founder*, ed. Will Roscoe (Boston: Beacon, 1996)

Jim Kepner, *Rough News—Daring Views: 1950s' Pioneer Gay Press Journalism* (New York: Haworth, 1998)

W. Dorr Legg, ed., *Homophile Studies in Theory and Practice* (Los Angeles: One Institute, 1994)

Craig M. Loftin, "Unacceptable Mannerisms: Gender Anxieties, Homosexual Activism, and Swish in the United States, 1945–65," *Journal of Social History* 40, no. 3 (Spring 2007): 577–96

Del Martin and Phyllis Lyon, *Lesbian/Woman* (San Francisco: Glide, 1972)

Martin Meeker, "Behind the Mask of Respectability: Reconsidering the Mattachine Society and Male Homophile Practice, 1950s and 1960s," *Journal of the History of Sexuality* 10, no. 1 (Jan. 2001): 78–116

Christopher Phelps, "A Neglected Document on Socialism and Sex," *Journal of the History of Sexuality* 16, no. 1 (Jan. 2007), 1–13

Christopher Phelps, "On Socialism and Sex: An Introduction," *New Politics* 12, no. 1 (Summer 2008): 12–21

John D. Poling, "Standing Up for Gay Rights," *Chicago History* 33 (Spring 2005): 4–17

Leila J. Rupp, "The Persistence of Transnational Organizing: The Case of the Homophile Movement," *American Historical Review* 116, no. 4 (Oct. 2011): 1014–39

James T. Sears, *Behind the Mask of Mattachine: The Hal Call Chronicles and the Early Movement for Homosexual Emancipation* (New York: Haworth, 2006)

Stuart Timmons, *The Trouble with Harry Hay: Founder of the Modern Gay Movement* (Boston: Alyson, 1990)

C. Todd White, *Pre-Gay L.A.: A Social History of the Movement for Homosexual Rights* (Urbana: University of Illinois Press, 2009)

Studies of pre-Stonewall Trans Activism

Aaron H. Devor and Nicholas Matte, "ONE Inc. and Reed Erickson: The Uneasy Collaboration of Gay and Trans Activism, 1964–2003," *GLQ* 10, no. 2 (2004): 179–209

Members of the Gay and Lesbian Historical Society of Northern California, "MTF Transgender Activism in the Tenderloin and Beyond, 1966–75," *GLQ* 4, no. 2 (1998): 349–72

Studies of Homophile Activism, the Stonewall Riots, Gay Liberation, and Lesbian Feminism

Brett Beemyn, "The Silence Is Broken: A History of the First Lesbian, Gay, and Bisexual College Student Groups," *Journal of the History of Sexuality* 12, no. 2 (April 2003): 205–23

Scott Bravmann, *Queer Fictions of the Past: History, Culture, and Difference* (New York: Cambridge University Press, 1997)

J. Louis Campbell, *Jack Nichols, Gay Pioneer: "Have You Heard My Message?"* (New York: Haworth, 2007)

David Carter, *Stonewall: The Riots That Sparked the Gay Revolution* (New York: St. Martin's, 2004)

Martin Duberman, *Stonewall* (New York: Dutton, 1993)

Simon Hall, "The American Gay Rights Movement and Patriotic Protest," *Journal of the History of Sexuality* 19, no. 3 (Sep. 2010): 536–62

Betty Luther Hillman, "'The Most Profoundly Revolutionary Act A Homosexual Can Engage In': Drag and the Politics of Gender Presentation in the San Francisco Gay Liberation Movement, 1964–72," *Journal of the History of Sexuality* 20, no. 1 (Jan. 2011): 153–81

Toby Marotta, *The Politics of Homosexuality* (Boston: Houghton Mifflin, 1981)

Tim Retzloff, "Eliding Trans Latino/a Queer Experience in U.S. LGBT History: José Sarria and Sylvia Rivera Reexamined," *Centro Journal* 19, no. 1 (2007): 140–61

James T. Sears, *Rebels, Rubyfruit, and Rhinestones: Queering Space in the Stonewall South* (New Brunswick: Rutgers University Press, 2001)

Justin David Suran, "Coming Out Against the War: Antimilitarism and the Politicization of Homosexuality in the Era of Vietnam," *American Quarterly* 53, no. 3 (Sep. 2001): 452–88

Kay Tobin and Randy Wicker, *The Gay Crusaders* (New York: Paperback Library, 1972)

Heather Rachelle White, "Proclaiming Liberation: The Historical Roots of LGBT Religious Organizing, 1946–76," *Nova Religio* 11, no. 4 (2008): 102–19

Gale Chester Whittington, *Beyond Normal: The Birth of Gay Pride* (Bangor: Booklocker. com, 2010)

Studies of post-Stonewall Gay Liberation and Lesbian Feminism

Dennis Altman, *Homosexual: Oppression and Liberation* (New York: Outerbridge and Dienstfrey, 1971)

Arthur Bell, *Dancing the Gay Lib Blues: A Year in the Homosexual Liberation Movement* (New York: Simon & Schuster, 1971)

Stephan L. Cohen, *The Gay Liberation Youth Movement in New York: "An Army of Lovers Cannot Fail"* (New York: Routledge, 2008)

Laud Humphreys, *Out of the Closets* (Englewood Cliffs: Prentice-Hall, 1972)

Karla Jay and Allen Young, *Out of the Closets: Voices of Gay Liberation* (New York: Douglas, 1972)

Terence Kissack, "Freaking Fag Revolutionaries: New York's Gay Liberation Front, 1969–71," *Radical History Review* 62 (Spring 1995): 104–34

Ian Lekus, "Queer Harvests: Homosexuality, the U.S. New Left, and the Venceremos Brigades to Cuba," *Radical History Review* 89 (Spring 2004): 57–91

Tommi Avicolli Mecca, ed., *Smash the Church, Smash the State!: The Early Years of Gay Liberation* (San Francisco: City Lights, 2009)

Richard Meyer, "*Gay Power* Circa 1970: Visual Strategies for Sexual Revolution," *GLQ* 12, no. 3 (2006): 441–64

Studies of Lesbian Feminism

Sidney Abbott and Barbara Love, *Sappho Was a Right-On Woman* (New York: Stein and Day, 1972)

Michal Brody, ed., *Are We There Yet? A Continuing History of Lavender Woman* (Iowa City: Aunt Lute, 1985)

Alice Echols, *Daring to Be Bad: Radical Feminism in America, 1967–1976* (Minneapolis: University of Minnesota Press, 1989)

Anne Enke, *Finding the Movement: Sexuality, Contested Space, and Feminist Activism* (Durham: Duke University Press, 2007)

Trisha Franzen, "Differences and Identities: Feminism and the Albuquerque Lesbian Community," *Signs* 18, no. 4 (1993): 891–906

Jane Gerhard, *Desiring Revolution: Second-Wave Feminism and the Rewriting of American Sexual Thought, 1920 to 1982* (New York: Columbia University Press, 2001)

Stephanie Gilmore and Elizabeth Kaminsky, "A Part and Apart: Lesbian and Straight Activists Negotiate Identity in a Second-Wave Organization," *Journal of the History of Sexuality* 16, no. 2 (Jan. 2007): 95–113

Karla Jay, *Tales of the Lavender Menace: A Memoir of Liberation* (New York: Basic, 1999)

Heather Murray, "Free for All Lesbians: Lesbian Cultural Production and Consumption in the United States during the 1970s," *Journal of the History of Sexuality* 16, no. 2 (May 2007): 251–75

Arlene Stein, *Sex and Sensibility: Stories of a Lesbian Generation* (Berkeley: University of California Press, 1997)

Verta Taylor and Leila J. Rupp, "Women's Culture and Lesbian Feminist Activism: A Reconsideration of Cultural Feminism," *Signs* 19, no. 1 (Autumn 1993): 32–61

Anne M. Valk, "Living a Feminist Lifestyle: The Intersection of Theory and Action in a Lesbian Feminist Collective," *Feminist Studies* 28, no. 2 (Summer 2002): 303–32

Deborah Goleman Wolf, *The Lesbian Community* (Berkeley: University of California Press, 1980)

Studies of the post-Stonewall Movement

Dudley Clendinen and Adam Nagourney, *Out for Good: The Struggle to Build a Gay Rights Movement in America* (New York: Simon & Schuster, 1999)

John D'Emilio, William B. Turner, and Urvashi Vaid, eds., *Creating Change: Sexuality, Public Policy, and Civil Rights* (New York: St. Martin's, 2000)

Amin Ghaziani, *The Dividends of Dissent: How Conflict and Culture Work in Lesbian and Gay Marches on Washington* (Chicago: University of Chicago Press, 2008)

Larry Gross, *Contested Closets: The Politics and Ethics of Outing* (Minneapolis: University of Minnesota Press, 1993)

Christina B. Hanhardt, "Butterflies, Whistles, and Fists: Gay Safe Street Patrols and the New Gay Ghetto, 1976–81," *Radical History Review* 100 (Winter 2008): 61–85

Emily Hobson, "'Si Nicaragua Venció': Lesbian and Gay Solidarity with the Revolution," *Journal of Transnational American Studies* (Fall 2012)

Randy Shilts, *The Mayor of Castro Street: The Life and Times of Harvey Milk* (New York: St. Martin's, 1982)

Studies of Sexuality and the New Right

Chris Bull and John Gallagher, *Perfect Enemies: The Religious Right, the Gay Movement, and the Politics of the 1990s* (New York: Crown, 1996)

Fred Fejes, *Gay Rights and Moral Panic: The Origins of America's Debate on Homosexuality* (New York: Palgrave, 2008)

Tina Fetner, *How the Religious Right Shaped Lesbian and Gay Activism* (Minneapolis: University of Minnesota Press, 2008)

Gillian Frank, "Discophobia: Antigay Prejudice and the Backlash against Disco," *Journal of the History of Sexuality* 15, no. 2 (May 2007): 276–306

Didi Herman, *The Antigay Agenda: Orthodox Visions and the Christian Right* (Chicago: University of Chicago Press, 1997)

Janice M. Irvine, *Talk about Sex: The Battles over Sex Education in the United States* (Berkeley: University of California Press, 2002)

Gayle Rubin, "Thinking Sex: Notes for a Radical Theory of the Politics of Sexuality," in *Pleasure and Danger: Exploring Female Sexuality*, ed. Carole S. Vance (London: Routledge, 1984), 267–319

Whitney Strub, *Perversion for Profit: The Politics of Pornography and the Rise of the New Right* (New York: Columbia University Press, 2011)

Studies of AIDS Activism

John-Manuel Andriote, *Victory Deferred: How AIDS Changed Gay Life in America* (Chicago: University of Chicago Press, 1999)

Jennifer Brier, *Infectious Ideas: U.S. Political Responses to the AIDS Crisis* (Chapel Hill: University of North Carolina Press, 2009)

Cathy J. Cohen, *The Boundaries of Blackness: AIDS and the Breakdown of Black Politics* (Chicago: University of Chicago Press, 1999)

Douglas Crimp, ed., *AIDS: Cultural Analysis/Cultural Activism* (Cambridge: MIT Press, 1988)

Douglas Crimp, *Melancholia and Moralism: Essays on AIDS and Queer Politics* (Cambridge: MIT Press, 2002)

Douglas Crimp with Adam Rolston, *AIDS Demographics* (Seattle: Bay Press, 1990)

Ann Cvetkovich, *An Archive of Feelings: Trauma, Sexuality, and Lesbian Public Cultures* (Durham: Duke University Press, 2003)

Steven Epstein, *Impure Science: AIDS, Activism, and the Politics of Knowledge* (Berkeley: University of California Press, 1996)

Ty Geltmaker, "The Queer Nation Acts Up: Health Care, Politics, and Sexual Diversity in the County of Angels," *Society and Space* 10, no. 6 (1992): 609–50

Deborah B. Gould, *Moving Politics: Emotion and ACT UP's Fight Against AIDS* (Chicago: University of Chicago Press, 2009)

Cindy Patton, *Inventing AIDS* (New York: Routledge, 1990)

Randy Shilts, *And the Band Played On: Politics, People, and the AIDS Epidemic* (New York: St. Martin's, 1987)

Studies of Queer Activism

Henry Abelove, "The Queering of Lesbian/Gay History," *Radical History Review*, no. 62 (Spring 1995): 44–57

Dangerous Bedfellows, ed., *Policing Public Sex: Queer Politics and the Future of AIDS Activism* (Boston: South End, 1996)

Lisa Duggan, "Making It Perfectly Queer," *Socialist Review* 22, no. 1 (Jan. 1992): 11–31

Michael Warner, ed., *Fear of a Queer Planet: Queer Politics and Social Theory* (Minneapolis: University of Minnesota Press, 1993)

Michael Warner, *The Trouble with Normal: Sex, Politics, and the Ethics of Queer Life* (Cambridge: Harvard University Press, 1999)

INDEX